HISTORICAL EVENTS IN THE DEVELOPMENT OF COLOR PHOTOGRAPHY

1882 First orthochromatic plates are manufactured.

1886 Frederick Ives unveils halftone process enabling photographs to be reproduced in the same operation as printing text.

1887 Baseball cards with photographs of players come with Old Judge cigarettes.

1888 The Kodak camera is marketed by George Eastman.

1890 *The Illustrated American,* the first U.S. photojournalism magazine, begins publication.

1891 Gabriel Lippmann invents an interference process that achieves natural colors without the use of dyes or pigments. Frederick Ives invents first practical one-shot color camera and designs the Kromskop for viewing color pictures.

1893 Auguste and Louis Lumiére invent a motion-picture camera.

1894 John Joly patents the first line-screen process for additive color images.

1895 Frederick Ives invents and produces the Kromscop camera and viewer.

1896 Joly Color process is commercially introduced. James McDonough patents a color line-screen process.

1897 McDonough process is marketed briefly.

1900 The $1 Brownie, designed by Frank Brownell, is marketed by Kodak.

1904 Lumiére brothers obtain patent for an additive-color plate with an integral mosaic screen. Dr. J. H. Smith's bleach-out process (dye-destruction), Uto paper is introduced.

1905 Thomas Manly patents his Ozobrome process (carbo process).

1906 First fully panchromatic plates are sold by Wratten and Wainwright. Clare L. Finlay patents improved additive line screen called Finlay Colour.

1907 Lumiére Autochrome plates marketed.

1908 Thames Colour screen, based on Finlay Colour, is introduced.

1909 Thames Colour Plate released.

1910 Louis Dufay's Dioptichrome Plate is unveiled.

1912 Rudolph Fisher and H. Siegrist patent tripack process with color couplers in three-layered emulsion.

1914 Kodachrome two-color process for portraiture introduced. *National Geographic* begins regular publication of color halftones from Autochrome plates.

1916 Agfa Colour plates introduced.

1923 Keller-Dorian, Berthon lenticular color movie process demonstrated.

1924 Leopold Mannes and Leopold Godowsky Jr. patent two-layer color process.

HISTORICAL EVENTS

1888 "Jack the Ripper" murders six women in London. First beauty contest held in Spa, Belgium. Eiffel Tower completed.

1891 W. L. Judson invents the clothing zipper.

1892 Rudolph Diesel patents internal combustion engine. Ellis Island opened as an immigrant receiving center.

1893 Karl Benz and Henry Ford make their first cars.

1896 A. H. Becquerel discovers radioactivity.

1898 United States declares war on Spain. Spain cedes Cuba, Puerto Rico, Guam, and the Philippines. Pierre and Marie Curie discover radium and polonium.

1899 Sigmund Freud's *The Interpretation of Dreams.*

1900 Max Planck formulates quantum theory. R. A. Fessenden transmits human voice via radio waves. First trial flight of Count Ferdinand von Zeppelin's airship.

1901 Guglielmo Marconi transmits first transatlantic telegraphic radio messages. Oil drilling begins in Persia. Instant coffee debuts.

1903 Orville and Wilbur Wright fly a self-propelled airplane.

1905 Albert Einstein formulates Special Theory of Relativity. Revolution in Russia, sailors mutiny on the battleship Potemkin.

1906 San Francisco earthquake. First radio program with music broadcast in the United States by R. A. Fessenden.

1907 First exhibition of cubist painters in Paris.

1908 Ford Motor Company produces first Model T cars. Jack Johnson becomes first black world heavyweight boxing champion.

1909 Vassily Kandinsky's first abstract paintings. Age of Plastic begins with the manufacture of L. H. Baekeland's Bakelite.

1911 Ernest Rutherford formulates his theory of atomic structure. Roald Amundsen reaches the South Pole.

1912 S. S. *Titanic* sinks.

1913 Armory Exhibition in New York introduces postimpressionism and cubism to America.

1914 World War 1 begins.

1915 Ernest Shackleton's ship *Endurance* is crushed in the Antarctic ice, touching off an epic self-rescue mission. Einstein formulates his General Theory of Relativity. Aspirin available.

1917 Lenin heads Bolshevik Revolution in Russia, czar abdicates. United States enters World War I.

1918 Armistice ends World War I (at least 8.5 million dead). Influenza epidemic starts (22 million die).

EXPLORING
COLOR PHOTOGRAPHY

© Marion Faller.
Halloween Skeletons, Marcellus, NY, 1989.

16 × 20 inches. Chromogenic color prints.

EXPLORING COLOR PHOTOGRAPHY

THIRD EDITION

Robert Hirsch

State University of New York at Buffalo

Boston, Massachusetts   Burr Ridge, Illinios   Dubuque, Iowa
Madison, Wisconsin   New York, New York   San Francisco, California   St. Louis, Missouri

McGraw·Hill

A Division of The **McGraw·Hill** *Companies*

Book Team

Publisher *Rosemary Bradley*
Developmental Editor *Joey Retzler*
Editorial Assistant *Karen D. Howery*
Production Editor *Marilyn Rothenberger*
Proofreading Coordinator *Carrie Barker*
Designer *K. Wayne Harms*
Art Editor *Miriam Hoffman*
Photo Editor *Leslie Dague*
Production Manager *Beth Kundert*
Production/Costing Manager *Sherry Padden*
Visuals/Design Freelance Specialist *Mary L. Christianson*
Marketing Manager *Kirk Moen*
Copywriter *Sandy Hyde*
Proofreader *Mary Svetlik Anderson*

Basal Text *10/12 Times Roman*
Display Type *Helvetica*
Typesetting System *Macintosh ™ QuarkXpress™*
Paper Stock *70# Sterling Matte*

Executive Vice President and General Manager *Bob McLaughlin*
Vice President of Business Development *Russ Domeyer*
Vice President of Production and New Media Development *Victoria Putman*
National Sales Manager *Phil Rudder*
National Telesales Director *John Finn*

Cover design by Fulton Design

Front cover photograph "Knows No Scents" © Jo Whaley 1991, courtesy of the Robert Koch Gallery, San Francisco

Back cover photograph "New World" © Bob Hirsch 1991

Proofread by Wendy Christofel

Copyedited by Laura Beaudoin

Library of Congress Catalog Card Number: 95–83397

ISBN 0–697–29230–4

Printed in the United States of America

10 9 8 7 6 5 4 3

To my mom, Muriel Hirsch, for teaching me to read; and my dad, Edwin Hirsch, for introducing me to photography; and my wife, Adele Henderson, for inspiration and support.

And to the memory of Ernest Shackleton and the crew of the *Endurance,* who have all provided me with insight into what true exploration is all about. "The qualities necessary to be an explorer are, in order of importance: optimism, patience, physical endurance, idealism, and courage. Optimism nullifies disappointment. Impatience means disaster. Physical endurance will not compensate for the first two moral or temperamental qualities."

—Ernest Shackleton
(1874–1922)
Explorer of the South Pole.

"We travel into or away from our photographs."

—Don Delillo, *MAO II*
New York: Viking, 1991
P. 141.

Contents

Preface

This book was written to provide a stimulating introduction to the techniques, images, and history of color photography at the college level. It assumes you have a basic working knowledge and understanding of black-and-white photography. For digital imaging it is presumed you have working experience in a basic word processing program and have access to imaging hardware and software.

Technological changes in the field of color photography continue at a rapid rate. Equipment and products considered state of the art one month are discontinued and replaced the next month. For this reason, the text is designed to provide you with a strong conceptual base from which aesthetic and technical explorations can be conducted.

The text is comprehensive and is ordered to provide the foreknowledge necessary to understand and think about photo-based color work. The approach is pragmatic, explaining how theory relates directly to the practice of the making of color photo-based images. The text presents tools that are necessary for the elaboration of ideas with the use of photography. The coverage is based on my everyday involvement as a teacher working with students and interns and as a curator who has an ongoing dialogue with artists. The opening chapters provide the groundwork of information needed to make intelligent work. The middle chapters furnish the process information. The latter chapters offer numerous working approaches. Each chapter is broken down into discrete units that should help you easily find major topics of interest. This arrangement also encourages you to skip around and discover your own ordering structure of the material. A new chapter on digital imaging has been created to reflect its growing influence in photographic practice. It is discussed in the context of being another one of the basic processes that is available for the thinking imagemaker. Another improvement is the expanded index. This is superior to a glossary since it covers ideas, images, people, processes, and terminology. It takes you directly to sources in the text that supply context for the discovery of meaning. This system of amplification facilitates a clearer definition and a broader understanding that is only possible through personal interaction with the materials being questioned.

The underlying premise of the book stresses visual thinking and encourages imagemakers to select materials and processes that express their internal ideas. To be an explorer is to investigate the unknown for the purpose of discovering truth. Once truth is uncovered it is possible to gain understanding. Understanding can lead to creation. From creation the uncovering of meaning is made possible. This book presents a structured starting place for ideas and techniques of known exploration. The text offers guided paths to get you involved with the spirit of discovery and to provide the means necessary to begin to express your visual voice. Since this book is not designed to be the final authority, additional sources of information are provided throughout the text to encourage you to make your own discoveries. Ultimately, you should be able to discard this guidebook and make your own way.

The illustration program in this third edition has been curated to represent an overview of the diversity of approaches currently employed by artists, professionals, teachers, and students. It is valuable for people entering color work to be exposed to the many diverse aspects the medium has to offer in terms of practice and content. The images reflect a contemporary trend by photographers to experiment and push the definitions and limits of what most of us tend to think a color photograph is about. I believe this is a vital concern that will expand the boundaries of color photography.

The captions are based on the extensive materials I have collected from statements, personal correspondence, and conversations, in which the photographers explain key aesthetic and technical choices made in the creation of the work. The captions provide a concise forum for letting the photographers speak about their work. Due to space limitations, I have condensed, edited, and clarified statements to show how the work relates to the text and to give insight into the photographer's working methods. They are not intended to be taken as the final closure of meaning. They should help to spur your thinking and encourage you to provide your own explanation and evaluation.

Critic Northrop Frye commented, "Poetry can only be made out of other poems; novels out of other novels [photographs from other photographs]." As this book is about the spirit of transmitting knowledge, I would like to thank the teachers who have made a difference to me: Mr. Rice, my high school art teacher, for giving me the hope to pursue my dream amidst the sea of boring conformist expectations; Stan McKenzie, for encouraging me to think; Judy Harold-Steinhauser, for supporting experimentation and group interaction; Art Terry, for not being a hypocrite; and the numerous imagemakers and writers who have shaped my thinking.

For this third edition I want to thank the contributors, expert consultants, and readers of the previous editions for their feedback and encourage future readers to send me specific ideas for improvement.

Thanks to all the people at Brown & Benchmark Publishers who have offered their cooperation, time, and knowledge in getting this manuscript together; to all the artists who have contributed their work for consideration; and to all my students at the University of Buffalo and my co-workers at the Center for Exploratory and Perceptual Art (CEPA Gallery) for their encouragement and participation in the process of creating this book.

Special thanks are in order for the following people who have made important contributions to this third edition:

Volkmar Wentzel, former photographer and writer on the foreign editorial staff at *National Geographic,* for the use of his amazing collection of early twentieth-century color images and his extensive personal knowledge about the subject;

David Wooters, Print Archivist at George Eastman House Photo Collection, for proofreading, image recommendations, and suggestions on organizing the historical processes and images;

Monona Rossol, of Arts, Crafts, and Theater Safety (ACTS) and co-author of the second edition of *Overexposure: Health Hazards in Photography,* for reading and making suggestions for the chapter on safety;

Wendy Erickson, Technical Training Specialist at Ilford, for her extremely thorough reading and detailed comments concerning Ilford's processes and products;

Henry Wilhelm, of Preservation Publishing Company in Grinnell, Iowa, for reading the section on the preservation of color materials;

Tom Weber, Kodak representative, for information on all of Kodak's processes and products;

Mike Doukas and Barbara Hitchcock of Polaroid, for information and images involving Polaroid products;

Bill Nordstrom and David Krause of Ever-Color, for information and assistance on the EverColor process;

John Valentino, with whom I co-created the digital chapter, with assistance from Tony Rozak, Tyrone Georgiou, and Gary Stanton of SUNY/Buffalo's art department. I asked John Valentino because of his varied expertise in photography and digital imaging. After we jointly created a working outline, John wrote the drafts while I acted as editor and rewriter;

Rosemary Bradley, Deborah Daniel, and Joey Retzler, my editors at Brown & Benchmark, for their support, understanding, and ideas;

Marilyn Rothenberger, my production editor; Laura Beaudoin, my copy editor; and Alexandra Nickerson, my indexer; for their thoughtful efforts in making improvements to this third edition; and to all my reviewers.

A word of caution: in many aspects of color photography you will be working with materials that can be hazardous to your health if they are not handled properly. To prevent problems from occurring with any process that you may encounter, read all directions, precautions, and safety measures (especially those outlined in the expanded chapter on safety) thoroughly before you begin to work. Preventative common sense will go a long way to ensure a safe, healthy involvement with color photography. Have fun in your explorations.

Bob Hirsch
Buffalo, New York

Reviewers

David R. Allison
Nothern Virginia Community College

James Gray Babcock
California State University

Thomas Barrow
University of New Mexico

Laurie J. Blakeslee
Boise State University

David L. DeVries
California State University, Fullerton

Susi Dugaw
Westchester Art Workshop

Wendy Erickson
Montclair State College

Peggy A. Feerick
Georgetown University

Gary Huibregtse
Colorado State University

Robert Kangas
Oakland Community College

Robert J. Kunst
California State University, Long Beach

David J. Levinson
Thomas Nelson Community College

William J. Martin
Scottsdale Community College

Steven P. Mosch
Savannah College of Art and Design

Kurt Nolin
Linn-Benton Community College

Daniel Overturf
Southern Illinois University

Gary B. Pearson
Ricks College

Michael Peven
University of Arkansas

Dr. Tom Seifert
Sam Houston State University

Wendel A. White
Stockton State College

Mark D. Wolfe
Northern Valley Community College

ONE

The Quest for Color in Photography

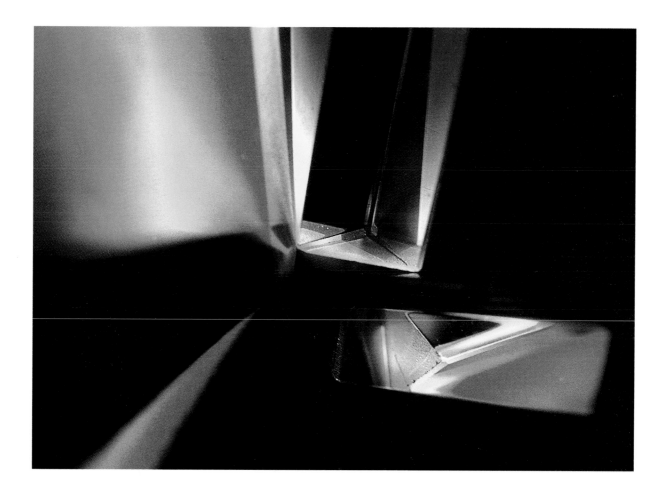

© Roger Camp.
Light Music #19, 1992.
16 × 20 inches. Dye-destruction print.

Newton's Light Experiment

In 1666 Sir Isaac Newton of England demonstrated that light is the source of color. Newton passed a beam of sunlight through a glass prism, making the rainbow of colors that form the visible spectrum. He then passed the rainbow back through a second prism, which converted all the hues back into white light (figure 1.1). From this experiment Newton determined that color is in the light, not in the glass prism as had been previously thought, and that the light humans see as white light is actually a mixture of all the visible wavelengths of the spectrum.

A prism, such as the one Newton used, separates the colors of light through the process of refraction. When light is refracted, each wavelength of light is bent to a different degree. This separates light into individual bands that make up the spectrum. It is the wavelength of the light that determines its visible color.

Separating Light

The colors of light are also separated by the surfaces of objects. We perceive the color of an object by responding to the particular wavelengths of light reflected back to our eyes from the surface of the object. For example, a red car looks red because it absorbs most of the light waves reaching it but reflects back those of the red part of the spectrum (figure 1.2). An eggshell appears white because it reflects all the wavelengths of light that reach it (figure 1.3).

If the light is filtered, it changes the color of any object that it illuminates. If the white eggshell is seen only by a red filtered light source, it appears to be red. This occurs because red is the only wavelength that strikes the eggshell, and in turn, red is the only color reflected back from the eggshell (figure 1.4). Objects that transmit light, such as

Figure 1.1
Isaac Newton's experiment proved that colors exist in white light and that white light is made up of the entire visible spectrum of colors.

color slides, also absorb some of the colors of light. They contain dyes that absorb specific wavelengths of light while allowing others to pass through. We perceive only the colors that are transmitted, that is, that are allowed to pass through the slide.

Young's Theory/RGB

By 1802 Thomas Young, an English physician and early researcher in physics, proved that light travels in waves of specific frequency and length. In 1807 Young advanced a theory of color vision, which states that the human eye is sensitive to only three wavelengths of light: red, green, and blue (RGB). These three primary colors are blended by the brain to form all the other colors. Young's ideas later formed the basis of the additive theory of light: white light is made up of R, G, and B light. All the remaining colors visible to the eye can be created by mixing two or more of these colors (see chapter 2). Young's theory has yet to be disproved, even though it does not seem to fully explain all the various phenomena concerning color vision (see chapter 5). It does continue to provide the most useful

Figure 1.2
A red object appears to be red because it reflects red wavelengths of light while absorbing most of the other wavelengths of light.

Figure 1.3
A white object looks white because it reflects all wavelengths of light that strike it.

model to date to explain all the principal photographic processes in which color images have been produced.

How We See Color

It is rare for us to see pure color, that is, light composed solely of one wavelength. Almost all the hues we see are a mixture of many wavelengths. Color vision combines both the sensory response of the eye and the interpretive response of the brain to the different wavelengths of the spectrum. Light enters the eye and travels

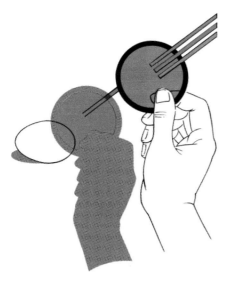

Figure 1.4
If a white object is illuminated by only a single-filtered source of light (e.g., red), it will appear to be only that single color. If only one color strikes an object, that color is the only color that can be reflected back.

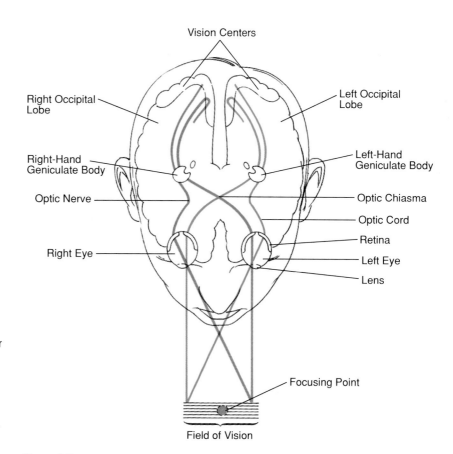

Figure 1.5
This top cutaway view of the human skull reveals how color images are believed to be formed in the brain.

through the cornea, passing through the iris, which acts as a variable aperture controlling the amount of light entering the eye. The image that has been formed at this point is now focused by the lens onto a thin membrane at the back of the eye called the retina. The retina contains light-sensitive cells called rods and cones, named after how they appear when viewed with a microscope. The cones function in daylight conditions and give us color vision. The rods function under low illumination and give vision only in shades of gray. The rods and cones create an image-receiving screen in the back of the eye. The physical information received by the rods and cones is sorted in the retina and translated into signals that are sent through the optic nerves to the nerve cells in the back of the brain. The optic nerves meet at the chiasma. Visual images from the right side of the brain go to the left and images from the left side of the brain go to the right (figure 1.5).

Humans can see a spectrum of about one thousand colors that ranges from red light, which travels in long wavelengths, through the midrange of orange, yellow, and greens, to the blues and violets, which have shorter wavelengths. The length of the light waves is determined by the distance from wave crest to wave crest. The difference between the longest and the shortest wavelengths is only about .00012 of an inch.

How the Brain Sees Color

In the brain this information is analyzed and interpreted. Scientists have not yet discovered the chemical and neurological reactions that actually let us perceive light or color. It is currently believed that the effects of light and color on an individual are dependent on our emotional, physical, and psychological states and our past experiences, memories, and preferences. It appears the brain is an active system where all data is constantly revised and recorrelated. There is nothing mechanical or cameralike, as every perception is a conception and every memory a reconception. There are no fixed memories, no "authentic" views of the past unaffected by the present.

Seeing color is a dynamic process, and remembering it is always a reconstruction as opposed to a reproduction. It has been proven that when a group views a single specific color, the responses of the individuals to it vary considerably (see chapter 4). Although color can be defined objectively with scientific instruments, we lack this ability and see color subjectively rather than quantifiably. The act of experiencing color and light involves a participatory consciousness in which we feel identified with what we are perceiving.

Color Blindness

Irregular color vision commonly manifests itself as the inability to distinguish red from green, followed by the inability to tell blue from yellow, but rarely is there the inability to perceive any color. Color blindness affects approximately 8 percent of males and 0.5 percent of females. The genes affecting color vision are transmitted by the mother. The reason for this anomaly is not certain because there appear to be many causes. It is possible to learn how to color print with mild color blindness, but it is not advisable for people with severe anomalous color vision to take on situations where precise evaluation is of critical importance.[1]

Young's Theory Applied to Color Film

Current techniques for creating color photographs make use of Thomas Young's theory that almost any color we can see may be reproduced optically by combining only three basic colors of light: red, green, and blue. For example, all color films are generally made up of three emulsion layers supported by an acetate base (figure 1.6). Each emulsion layer is primarily sensitive to only one of the three additive primary colors. The top layer is sensitive to blue light, the middle to green light, and the bottom to red light. Blue light is only recorded on the layer of film that is sensitive to blue, green light on the green-sensitive layer, and red light on the red-sensitive layer. All other colors are recorded on a combination of two or more of the layers.

[1]For detailed information about the effects of losing the sensation of color see Oliver Sacks, "The Case of the Colorblind Painter," *An Anthropologist on Mars: Seven Paradoxical Tales* (New York: Knopf, 1995), 3–41.

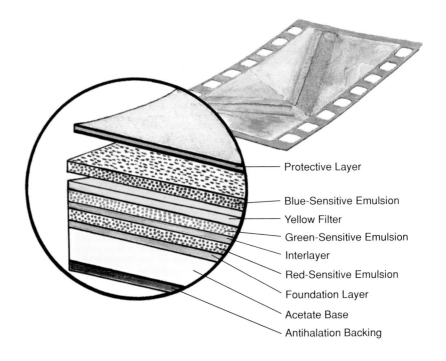

Protective Layer
Blue-Sensitive Emulsion
Yellow Filter
Green-Sensitive Emulsion
Interlayer
Red-Sensitive Emulsion
Foundation Layer
Acetate Base
Antihalation Backing

Figure 1.6
This enlarged cutaway view shows the general construction of three-layered color film.

How the Film Produces Color

During development each layer makes a different black-and-white image that corresponds to the amount of colored light that was recorded in each individual layer during the exposure (figure 1.7). The developer oxidizes and combines with the color chemical couplers in the emulsion to create the dyes. The green-sensitive layer forms the magenta dye, the blue-sensitive layer the yellow dye, and the red-sensitive layer the cyan dye. During the remaining stages of the process, the silver is removed from each of the three layers. This leaves an image created solely from the dyes in each of the three layers (figure 1.8). The film is then fixed, washed, and dried to produce a complete color image (see chapter 8 for a description of how a subject is recorded on film and translated into a print).

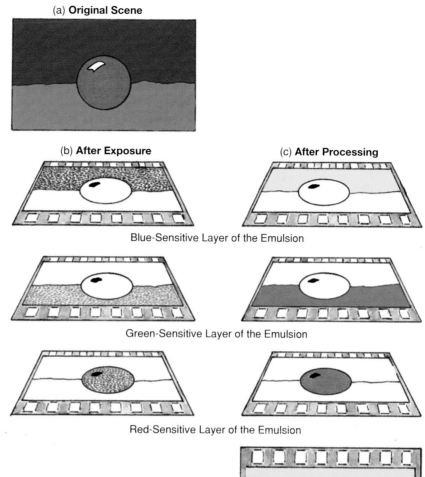

(a) **Original Scene**

(b) **After Exposure**   (c) **After Processing**

Blue-Sensitive Layer of the Emulsion

Green-Sensitive Layer of the Emulsion

Red-Sensitive Layer of the Emulsion

(d) **Final Negative**

Figure 1.7

This is a representation of how color negative film produces an image from a scene. (a) The original scene. (b) How each layer of the film records the colors. (c) How each layer responds to processing. (d) The final makeup of the color negative that is used to produce a color print.

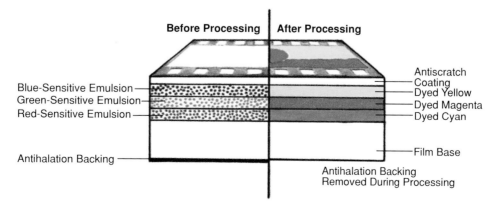

Before Processing | **After Processing**

Blue-Sensitive Emulsion
Green-Sensitive Emulsion
Red-Sensitive Emulsion

Antihalation Backing

Antiscratch Coating
Dyed Yellow
Dyed Magenta
Dyed Cyan

Film Base

Antihalation Backing Removed During Processing

Figure 1.8

A cross section of a typical contemporary color film before and after processing.

A Concise and Select History of Color Photography

© László Moholy-Nagy.
Study with Pins and Ribbons, 1937–1938.
34.9 x 26.5 cm. Assembly (Vivex Print).
Courtesy of George Eastman House.

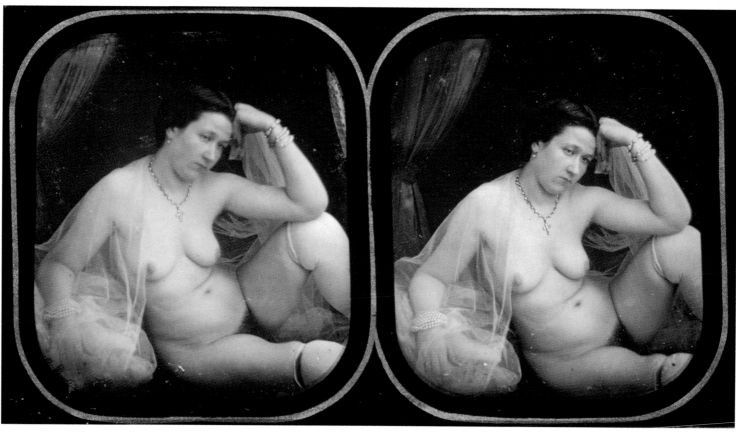

Figure 2.1

The first color photographs were black-and-white images that had the color applied by hand. This image is an outstanding example of what could be accomplished. Most were more crudely done, lacking the attention to detail that the colorist lavished upon this daguerreotype.

Unidentified photographer, French. *Female Nude*, circa 1858. Daguerreotype with applied color.
Courtesy of George Eastman House.

First Photographs: Applied Color Process

In 1839 Louis-Jacques-Mandé Daguerre made public the practical photographic process called the daguerreotype. It was a finely detailed, one-of-a-kind, direct-positive image, produced through the action of light on a silver-coated copperplate. These photographs astonished and delighted, but people nevertheless complained that the images lacked color. Immediately, other interested parties began to seek a way to overcome this deficiency. Not surprisingly, the first colored photographs made their appearance that same year. The color was applied directly on the daguerreotype's surface by hand (figure 2.1).

In the United States, four major methods were employed in the coloring of daguerreotypes: (1) applying paint directly to a gilded (gold-toned for appearance and stability) daguerreotype; (2) applying a transparent protective varnish over the plate, then hand coloring with paints; (3) applying transparent colors to specific areas of the image and fixing them by passing an electrical current through the plate with the aid of a galvanic battery; and (4) heating the back of the plate with a spirit lamp, instead of a battery, to fix colors that were selectively applied to the front of the plate.

By 1843 John Plumbe Jr. of Boston was advertising the ability to make colored daguerreotypes at his chain of six galleries in the Northeast. It would take nearly a hundred years of research and development to perfect the rendition of color through purely photographic means.

First Experiments: Direct Color Process

In 1840 Sir John Herschel, renowned British astronomer and also the originator of many seminal ideas in photography, reported being able to record blue, green, and red on silver-chloride-coated paper. These three colors corresponded to the rays of light cast on the paper by a prismed solar spectrum. Herschel's work suggested that color photographs could be made directly from the action of light on a chemically sensitive surface. Herschel was unable, however, to fix the colors on the coated paper. They could only be looked at very briefly under lamplight before they darkened into blackness. Other experimenters, including Edmond Becquerel in the late 1840s and early 1850s and Niépce de Saint-Victor in the 1850s and 1860s,

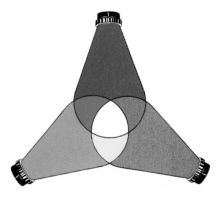

Figure 2.3
In the additive process separate colored beams of red, green, and blue light are mixed to form any color in the visible spectrum. When the three additive primaries are mixed in equal proportions, they appear as white light to the human eye.

Figure 2.2
Levi Hill stirred up a sensation in the 1850s by announcing he had discovered a way to make color photographs directly from nature. The photographic community waited in vain for Hill to publish repeatable results of his process. At the time, his claim was dismissed as a hoax.

© Rev. Levi L. Hill. *Landscape with Farmhouse*, 1851. Hillotype.
Courtesy of Division of Photographic History. Natural Museum of American History.

attempted to record colors directly on daguerreotypes. This was done through a process called Heliochromy, which did not make use of any filters or dyes. Although they did not fade by themselves, Niépce de Saint-Victor never found a method to permanently fix them. When exposed to direct light, without a protective coating, they quickly turned gray.

A Secret Direct Color Process

In early 1851 Levi Hill, a Baptist minister from Westkill, New York, announced a direct color process by which he was able to produce permanent color photographs (figure 2.2). Hill's announcement created quite a stir and temporarily brought the daguerreotype portrait business to a halt, since the public decided to wait for the arrival of the new color process. Everyone was clamoring to know how Hill had achieved this miracle. The public waited but nothing was forthcoming from Hill, and he was roundly denounced as a fake.

Five years later, Hill finally published, by advance subscription, his method in *A Treatise on Heliochromy* (1856). It was a rambling tale of his life and experiments that did not contain any workable instructions for his secret process of making color photographs. He did say the method was based on the use of a new developing agent (never stated) in place of mercury. At the time, the process was dismissed as a hoax that Hill had carried out by cleverly hand coloring his daguerreotypes. Just before his death in 1865, Hill still claimed to have made color photographs but said it had occurred by accident. He revealed that he had spent the last 15 years of his life attempting to repeat this accidental combination without success. Recently there has been new scientific evidence suggesting the possibility that Hill may have stumbled onto a direct color process.[1]

[1] See Herbert Keppler, "The Horrible Fate of Levi Hill: Inventor of Color Photography," *Popular Photography* 58, no. 7, July 1994, 42–43, 140.

First Color Photograph: The Additive Theory

The first true color photograph was made in 1861 by James Clerk Maxwell, a Scottish scientist. Maxwell used the additive theory developed by Thomas Young and refined by the German scientist Hermann Helmholtz. The additive theory was based on the principle that all colors of light can be mixed optically by combining in different proportions the three primary colors of the spectrum: red, green, and blue. Just two primary colors can be mixed in varying proportions to produce many colors. For example, a mixture of the right proportion of green and red light produces yellow. When all three of these primary colors are combined in equal amounts the result is white light (figure 2.3). When white light is passed through a primary-colored filter of red, green, or blue, the filter transmits only that particular color of light and absorbs the other colors. A red filter transmits red light, while absorbing all the other colors, which are combinations of green and blue light.

Maxwell's Triple Projection Process

Making use of this theory, Maxwell made three separate black-and-white negatives of a tartan plaid ribbon through three separate blue-violet, green, and red filters. Black-and-white positives were made from the three negatives. These positives were projected in register (the three images perfectly coinciding) onto a white screen, each from a different projector. Each slide was projected through the same colored filter that was used to make the original negative. For example, the positive originally photographed through the green filter was projected through the green filter. When all three positives were simultaneously projected, the result was a projected color image (not a photograph) of the multicolored ribbon (figure 2.4). Maxwell's demonstration not only proved the additive color theory, but it also provided a method, known as the triple projection process, for producing photographic color images.

A Mystery Solved

Later scientific investigation revealed that Maxwell's photographic emulsions were not capable of recording the full visible spectrum (neither orthochromatic or panchromatic emulsions had been invented), and the experiment should have failed. The emulsion was not sensitive to red and only slightly sensitive to green. It took scientists a century to figure out why Maxwell's experiment worked with an emulsion that was not sensitive to all the primary colors. It turned out that Maxwell's experiment succeeded because of two other deficiencies in the materials that canceled out the effect of the nonsensitive emulsion: (1) the red dye of the ribbon reflected ultraviolet light that was recorded on the red negative, and (2) his green filter was faulty and let some blue light strike the plate. Both of these defects corrected for the lack of sensitivity of the emulsion to red and green light. When done with today's panchromatic emulsions, sensitive to all the colors of the spectrum, Maxwell's

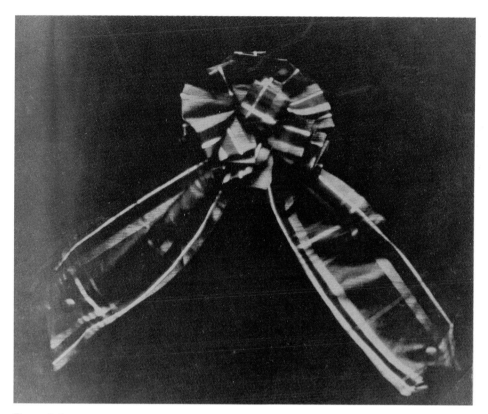

Figure 2.4
James Clerk Maxwell made the first true color photograph in 1861. Maxwell's success proved the additive color theory and provided the first path for the creation of a true color photographic process.

method works perfectly. This proves his experiment was theoretically sound. However, the first true panchromatic emulsions, which had their sensitivity extended through the use of dyes, were not commercially available until the twentieth century.

Additive Screen Processes

In 1869 Louis Ducos du Hauron, a French scientist, published *Photography in Color.* Among the methods he proposed was one in which the additive theory could be used to make color photographs in an easier manner than the one Maxwell devised. He speculated that a screen ruled with fine lines in the primary colors (red, green, and blue) would act as a filter to produce a color photograph with a single exposure instead of three, as were needed in Maxwell's experiment (figure 2.8).

Joly Color

In 1894 John Joly, a Dublin physicist, patented the first line-screen process for additive color photographs, based on Ducos du Hauron's idea. In this process, a glass screen with transparent ruled lines of blue, green, and red, about two hundred lines per inch, was placed against the emulsion of an orthochromatic plate (not sensitive to red light). The exposure was made and the screen was removed. The plate was processed and contact-printed on another plate to make a positive black-and-white transparency. This was placed in exact register with the same screen used to make the exposure. The final result was a limited-color photographic transparency that was viewed by transmitted light. This method was introduced in 1896 as the Joly Color process (figure 2.5). It enjoyed only a brief success, because it was expensive and the emulsions that were available

Figure 2.5
Joly Color, the first commercial line-screen process for additive color photographs, was introduced to the public in 1896. Although it had only limited success, it indicated the additive method could become a commercially viable way for making color photographs.

Unidentified photographer, Irish (?). *Stuffed Birds*, circa 1895. 4 x 5 inches. Joly Color.
Courtesy of George Eastman House.

Figure 2.6
Autochrome was the first additive screen process to achieve aesthetic and commercial success. This image is a classic representation of the British-colonial style of photography that was used primarily for recording "native types" and "the strange ways of other people" in a stereotypical mode.

© Melville Chater. *Zulu ricksha with passenger in Durban, South Africa.* 1930. 5 x 7 inches. Autochrome.
Courtesy of Volkmar Wentzel Collection.

were still not sensitive to the full range of the spectrum, thus the final image was not able to achieve the look of "natural" color. However, Joly's work indicated that the additive screen process could be a commercially practical way to make color photographs.

Autochrome

In Lyon, France, a major breakthrough in the making of color photographs was patented in 1904 by the inventors of the first practical motion picture projector. Auguste and Louis Lumiére. Autochrome was their improved and modified additive screen process. In the Autochrome system, a glass plate was dusted, in a random fashion, with microscopic grains of potato starch that had been dyed with orange, green, and blue-violet. A fine powder of carbon black was used to fill in any spaces that would otherwise allow unfiltered light to pass through this filter screen, eliminating the need for colored lines to act as filters. A newly developed panchromatic emulsion, which greatly extended the accuracy of recording the full range of the visible spectrum, was then applied to the plate. The exposure was made through the back of the plate, with the dyed potato starch acting as tiny filters. The plate was then developed, reexposed to light, and finally redeveloped to form a positive transparency made up of tiny dots of the primary colors. The Autochrome was a new method of utilizing the same principle articulated by Ducos du Hauron in which the eye mixed the colors, in a fashion much like a pointillist painting, to make a color-positive image (figure 2.6).

Autochrome Characteristics

Autochrome was successfully used from 1907–32, though it did have its problems. Autochromes tended to be dark due to the habitual underexposure caused by the density of the potato starch grains. Since the light had to travel through this filter, exposure times were longer than with black-and-white films. In all the additive processes, it was not uncommon for 75 percent or more of the light to be absorbed by the filters before reaching the film. Recommended starting exposure time was 1 second at f/4 in direct sunlight at midday in the summer and 6 seconds on a cloudy day.

Figure 2.7
The marketing of the Autochrome plate in 1907 offered serious amateurs, such as Charles C. Zoller of Rochester, New York, who often projected his Autochromes to audiences, the opportunity to make their own color snapshots of vernacular scenes.

© Charles C. Zoller. *World War I Support Parade,* circa 1918. 3 1/4 x 4 inches. Autochrome.
Courtesy of George Eastman House.

The randomly applied potato grains tended to bunch up in places, creating blobs of color. Also, Autochromes were difficult to see and were generally looked at in a specially designed viewer and only occasionally projected.

The advantages of this process, however, were numerous. Autochromes could be used in any regular plate camera, without additional filters to produce a color photograph; the image was made in one exposure, not in three; the cost was not overly prohibitive; it gave serious amateurs access to color (figure 2.7); and while the colors were not accurate, they did produce a friendly, warm, soft, pastel image that was considered to be quite pleasing.

By the end of World War I, magazines, such as *National Geographic,* were using Autochromes to make color reproductions for the first time in their publications. Between 1914 and 1938, *National Geographic* published a reported 2,355 Autochromes, more than any other journal, thus taking a leadership role in bringing color photography into mass publication. Autochrome was the first color process to get beyond the novelty stage and to be commercially successful. It cracked a major aesthetic barrier because it was taken seriously for its picture-making potentialities. This enabled photographers to begin to explore the visual possibilities of making meaningful photographs with color.

Finlay Colour Process

Other additive screen processes followed on the heels of Autochrome. Finlay Colour was an additive screen process patented by Clare L. Finlay of England in 1906 and introduced in 1908 as the Thames Colour Screen. This screen was made up in a precise checkerboard fashion of red, green, and blue elements, rather than the random mosaic pattern used in Autochrome. This separate screen could be used with any type of panchromatic film or plate to make a color photograph. In 1909, the Thames Colour Plate was released, which contained an integral screen in which the screen and emulsion were combined to form a single plate. Both of these processes were abandoned after World War I, but improved versions were marketed under the name of Finlay Colour in 1929 and 1931 (figure 2.9). The Finlay Colour processes were to be the major rivals to Dufaycolor until the introduction of the subtractive materials in the mid-1930s.

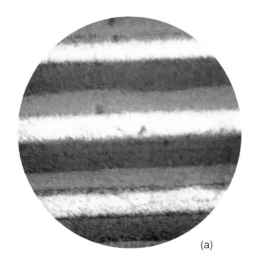

(a)

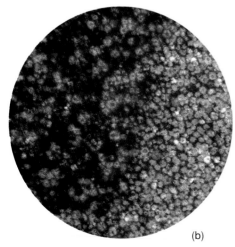

(b)

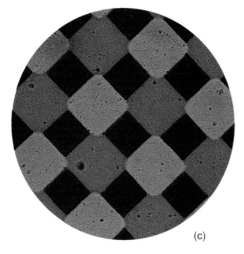

(c)

Figure 2.8

These photomicrographs of (a) Joly Color, magnified 20x, (b) Autochrome, magnified 50x, and (c) Finlay Colour, magnified 50x, allow a direct visual comparison of how each of these additive screen processes constructed a color image.

Courtesy of George Eastman House, Rochester, NY.

Figure 2.9

National Geographic photographers, such as Edwin Wisherd, regularly used the reintroduced Finlay Colour process to illustrate their stories and continued to do so through the mid- 1930s, when Kodachrome replaced all the screen plate processes.

© Edwin Wisherd. *Circus Performers*, circa 1932. Finlay Colour.
Courtesy of Volkmar Wentzel Collection.

Dufaycolor

The Dioptichrome Plate was made by the French firm of Louis Dufay, beginning about 1910. The process was improved and renamed Dufaycolor in the 1920s. Dufaycolor was produced as a roll film, which gave wider public access to color. Dufaycolor eventually became more popular than Autochrome because people preferred the structure of its screen. The screen was a mosaic of alternating blue-dye and green-dye squares that were

Current Applications

Today in color photography, the additive method is sometimes employed in print making. It is in very limited use because the additive enlarger systems are more complex and expensive. To make a full color print with the additive process, the enlarger is used to make three separate exposures, one through each of the three primary-colored filters. The blue filter is first used to control the amount of blue in the print, next the green filter is used to control the green content, and last the red filter is used to control the red in the picture. Some people prefer this additive technique, also known as tricolor printing. This is because it is relatively easy to make adjustments in the filter pack, with each filter controlling its own color.

Television

The additive system is the perfect vehicle for color television since the set creates and then emits the light-forming picture. The color television tube has three electron guns, each corresponding to one of the additive primaries. These guns produce red, blue, or green phosphors on the screen to create different combinations of the three primaries. This creates all the colors that form the images we see on the television set.

The Subtractive Method

Louis Ducos du Hauron not only proposed a method for making color photographs with the additive process in *Photography in Color,* he also suggested a method for making color photographs using the subtractive process.

How It Works

The subtractive process operates by removing certain colors from white light while allowing others to pass. The modern subtractive primaries (magenta, yellow, and cyan) are the complementary colors of the three additive primaries (green, blue, and red). When white light

Figure 2.10
Dufaycolor, introduced in the 1920s, became the most popular of the additive screen processes because it was faster, had an improved screen that provided more realistic color, and, since it was like cut film, was easier to use.

© J. Baylor Roberts. *Pennsylvania Boy Scouts at the World Jamboree in Washington, D.C.*, 1937. 5 x 7 inches. Dufaycolor. Courtesy of Volkmar Wentzel Collection.

crossed at right angles by a pattern of parallel red-dye lines. This design offered greater color accuracy and a faster emulsion; by the mid-1930s exposures of f/8 at 1/25 of a second on a sunny day were possible (figure 2.10). Dufaycolor was marketed until the 1940s. By this time, the quest for an easier-to-use process that would provide more realistic and natural colors brought about technical discoveries that made all the additive screen processes obsolete.

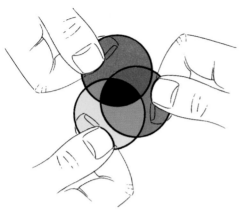

Figure 2.11

The subtractive process allows almost any color to be formed by removing certain colors from white light while permitting other colors to pass. The subtractive primary colors in photography are magenta, yellow, and cyan. They are the complementary colors of the additive primaries, green, blue, and red. Black is formed when equal amounts of all three of the subtractive primaries overlap.

(a)   (b)

Figure 2.12

In Louis du Hauron's Heliochrome process three separate negatives were made on black-and-white plates, using three separate subtractive filters. The negatives were used to make three positives, which were then superimposed to assemble a color photograph. The Heliography method was the first successful use of the subtractive process in the making of color photographs. (A) shows the transparency from the front. (B) presents the transparency from the backside, where the separation of the yellow layer of the assembly print can be seen.

© Louis Ducos du Hauron. *Stuffed Rooster and Parrot*, 1879. Assembly print. 21 x 21.5 cm. Courtesy of George Eastman House.

is passed through one of the subtractive-colored filters it transmits two of primaries and absorbs (subtracts) the other. Individually each subtractive filter transmits two-thirds of the spectrum while blocking one-third of it. For example, a magenta filter passes red and blue but blocks green. When two filters are superimposed, they subtract two primaries and transmit one. Magenta and yellow filters block green and blue, allowing red to pass. When all three subtractive primaries overlap in equal amounts, they block all the wavelengths and produce black. When they are mixed in varying proportions they are capable of making almost any color (figure 2.11). The advantages of the subtractive method over the additive process are twofold: a full-color reproduction on paper is possible, and it dispenses with the previous need for expensive and cumbersome viewing equipment.

Pigments

When working with pigments, as in painting, instead of light, the colors are also formed subtractively. The different colors of pigments absorb certain wavelengths of light and reflect others back for us to see. However, painters generally use red, blue, and yellow as their primary colors. These colors cannot be mixed

from any other colors and are used to make all the other colors. Red and yellow make orange, red and blue make purple, and blue and yellow make green. Green, an additive primary, cannot be used as a primary color in paint because it consists of two colors, blue and yellow.

The Assembly Process: Heliography

In Ducos du Hauron's patented subtractive method, known as Heliography, three separate negatives were made behind three separate filters. He used violet, green, and orange-red for his filters (the correct modern subtractive filters had not yet been established). From these negatives, positives were made and assembled in register to create the final print, known as a Heliochrome. These positives contained carbon pigments of blue, red, and yellow, which Ducos du Hauron believed to be the complementary colors of the filters that were used to form the colors in the original exposure. Color prints or transparencies (figure 2.12) could be made with the assembly process, depending on whether the carbon transparencies were attached onto an opaque or transparent support. The

assembly process is the principle used in the carbo process (see chapter 22).

Exposure Difficulties

Though the subtractive process proved to be practical, it plagued photographers with long exposure times. Ducos du Hauron reported typical daylight exposures of 1 to 2 seconds with the blue-violet filter, 2 to 3 minutes with the green, and 25 to 30 minutes behind the red filter. If the light changed during the exposure process, the color balance would be incorrect in the final result. This problem was solved in 1893, when Frederick Eugene Ives perfected Ducos du Hauron's single-plate color camera.

Direct Viewing Process. Ives's apparatus, the Photochromoscope camera, made three separate black-and-white negatives simultaneously on a single plate through blue-violet, green, and red filters. Positives were made by contact printing. The three glass positives were cut apart and placed on Ives's Kromskop viewer. This viewing system had the same type of colored filters as the camera and a system of mirrors that optically superimposed the three separations creating a color Kromogram. The completed color photograph could only be seen in this viewer (there was no actual object), hence it was called a direct viewing process. While Ives's methods did work, they were complex, time-consuming, and expensive.

Carbro Process

In 1855 Alphonse Louis Poitevin patented a carbon process to make prints from photographic negatives and positives by using an emulsion containing particles of carbon or colored, nonsilver pigment to form the image. The original purpose of this process was not to make colored images but to provide a permanent solution to the fading and discoloration problems that plagued the early positive silver print processes. The carbro process, considered the most versatile of the carbon processes, evolved from Thomas Manly's Ozotype (1899) and Ozobrome processes (1905). The name *carbro* was given to an improved version of the process in 1919 by the Autotype Company to signify that carbon tissue was used in conjunction with a bromide print (car/bro).

Separation negatives were exposed through red, green, and blue filters and used to make a matched set of bromide prints. In the carbro process the image is formed by chemical action when the pigmented carbon tissue is placed face-to-face with a fully processed black-and-white print on bromide paper. When the print and the tissue are held in contact, the gelatin of the tissue becomes insoluble in water in proportion to the density of the silver on the bromide print. After soaking, this sandwich is separated. The tissue is transferred onto a paper support, where it is washed until only a pigment image remains. This is repeated for each of the three pigmented tissues, and the final print is an assemblage of cyan, magenta, and yellow carbon tissues in register, producing a full-color print. Autotype's tricolor carbro process produced splendid color prints from cyan, magenta, and yellow pigmented tissues. Using a bromide print created numerous advantages, including the following: (1) enlargements could be made from

Figure 2.13
Nickolas Muray asserted "color calls for a new way of looking at people, at things, and a new way of looking at color." His 1931 illustration of models in beachwear for the *Ladies Home Journal* became the first color photograph to be published in a popular American magazine. Muray also produced color domestic scenes and portraits for the covers of *McCalls Magazine, Modern Screen Magazine,* and *Time* throughout the 1940s and 1950s.

© Nickolas Muray. *McCalls Magazine Cover,* 1939. 11 x 14 inches, approx. Carbro process. Courtesy of George Eastman House.

small-format negatives; (2) ordinary exposure light sources could be used instead of high-intensity ultraviolet; (3) contrast was determined by the bromide print; and (4) regular photographic printing controls such as burning and dodging could be used. The perfecting of the carbro process demonstrated it was possible to make full-color images from black-and-white materials and was an important step on the path towards a practical chromogenic method for making color images (figure 2.13).

Color Halftones

The first color images to receive widespread viewing were not made by direct photographic means. They were created

indirectly by applying the subtractive principles of color photography on William Kurtz's photoengraver's letterpress in New York in 1892. Using an early halftone process, a scene of fruit on a table was photographed, screened, and run through the press three times (a separate pass for each of the three subtractive colored inks-cyan, magenta, and yellow). The halftone process is a printing method that enables a photographic image to be reproduced in ink by making a halftone screen of the original picture. The screen divides the picture into tiny dots that deposit ink in proportion to the density of the original image tones in the areas they represent. These color reproductions were bound into the January 1, 1893, issue of *Photographische Mittheilungen,* published in Germany. Even

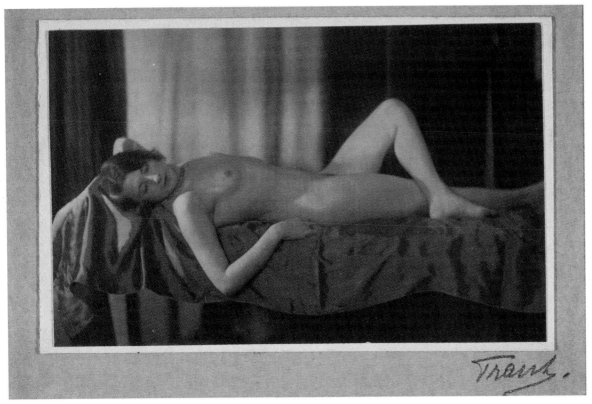

Figure 2.14
The Uvatype, developed by Dr. Arthur Traube, is an example of the imbibition process. In this method, a dye image is transferred from a gelatin relief image to a receiving layer of paper or film.

© Dr. Arthur Traube. *Female Nude*, circa 1920s. Uvatype.
Courtesy of Volkmar Wentzel Collection.

though it was still not possible to obtain color prints from color film in an ordinary camera, this printing procedure pointed a way in which color images could be photographically produced.

Dye-Imbibition Process

In the imbibition process, a dye image is transferred from a gelatin relief image to either a paper or film receiving layer, usually of gelatin. Charles Cros described this method of "hydrotypie" transfer printing in 1880 and suggested it could be used to transfer three dye images in register. The Hydrotype (1881) and the Pinatype (1905) were examples of the early use of this process. One of the notable, but not widely used, relief matrix processes was developed by Dr. Arthur Traube and introduced as the Uvatype in 1929 (figure 2.14). This was an improved version of his earlier Diachrome process (1906) and the dye mordant Uvachrome process (1916). The widest commercial

application of the imbibition process was the Technicolor process for producing motion-picture release prints. The Eastman Wash-off Relief process (1935) was a refinement of the imbibition process, until it was replaced by the improved Dye Transfer process (1946–93).

Subtractive Film and Chromogenic Development

Between 1911 and 1914 Rudolph Fisher of Germany, working closely with Karl Schinzel of Austria, invented a color film that had the color-forming ingredients, known as color couplers, incorporated directly into it. This discovery, that color couplers could produce images by chromogenic development, laid the foundation for most color processes in use today. In this type of film, known as an integral tripack, three layers of emulsion are stacked one on top of another, with each layer sensitive to either red, green, or blue.

Through a process known as chromogenic development, the color couplers in each layer of the emulsion form a dye image in complementary colors of the original subject. During chromogenic development, the dye image is made at the same time as the silver halide image is developed in the emulsion. The silver image is then bleached away, leaving only the dye, which is fixed to form the final image. The problem with this tripack film was that unwanted migration of the dyes between the three layers could not be prevented, causing color inaccuracies in the completed image.

Some black-and-white films, such as Ilford's XP2, also make use of this system to make various densities of black dye.

Kodachrome

In 1930 Leopold Godowsky Jr. and Leopold Mannes, who had been experimenting with making color films in makeshift labs since they were teenagers, were hired by Kodak Research Laboratories. By 1935 they were able to overcome the many technical difficulties and produce the first truly successful integral tri-pack subtractive color reversal film. This film was called Kodachrome and was first marketed as a 16-mm movie film. It was said, only half jokingly, that it took God and man (*God*owsky and *Man*nes) to solve the problem of the color couplers' unwanted migration between the emulsion layers. Their ingenious solution to this problem was to put the color couplers in separate developers during the processing of the film, rather than building them into the film emulsion itself. Unlike all other current color films, Kodachrome continues to be the only color film made without these color couplers in the film emulsion.

Exposure Problems Solved

In Kodachrome film, only one exposure is needed to record a latent image of all three primary colors. The top emulsion layer is sensitive only to blue. Under this is a temporary yellow-dye filter that absorbs blue light, preventing it from affecting the emulsion below. This temporary yellow filter, which dissolves during processing, allows the green and red light to pass through and be recorded in the proper emulsions below.

The Kodachrome Process

Kodachrome is first developed into a negative and then, through reversal processing, into a positive. During the second development, the colors of the original subject are transformed into the complementary dyes of cyan, magenta, and yellow, which are used to form the final color image. Then the positive silver images are bleached away and the emulsion is fixed and washed. This leaves a positive color image that is made up only by subtractive-colored dyes, with no silver.

In 1936 Kodachrome was made for the 35-mm still photography market. Kodak was concerned that nobody would want a tiny slide that had to be held up to the light to be seen. In a brilliant move, Kodak had each processed

Figure 2.15
The introduction of Kodachrome marked the modern era in color photography of accurate, reliable, affordable, and easy-to-use color films. Kodachrome gave a wider variety of photographers the ability to respond in color to subject matter from new points of view and to represent previously unseen subjects and situations.

Unidentified photographer. *Untitled*, circa 1936. 3 1/4 x 4 inches. Kodachrome. Courtesy of George Eastman House.

slide returned in a 2-x-2-inch cardboard mount, which could be projected onto a screen. This gave new life to the Victorian-era Magic Lantern slide exhibitions, which had been in decline. By the late 1930s the union of the small format Leica camera with Kodachrome launched the modern color boom and signaled the end of the additive screen processes such as Autochrome.

Kodachrome was the first film to achieve the dream of an accurate, inexpensive, easy-to-use, and reliable method for making color photographs. The major drawback to Kodachrome is that its complex processing means the photographer is unable to develop the film; it must be sent to a lab that has the necessary equipment. Its use and mastery by artists like Eliot Porter began the modern struggle to have color photography recognized as a

legitimate art form. For over 60 years since its introduction (figure 2.15), Kodachrome was the unmatched standard in accuracy, rendition, contrast, and grain for all color films. Its legendary characteristics were even commemorated in a popular song by Paul Simon. It is only recently that technical improvements have allowed chromogenic films to mount a serious challenge to Kodachrome.

Chromogenic Slide Film

In 1936 Agfa released Agfacolor Neu film, which overcame the migration of the color couplers. This was done by making the color coupler molecules very big. In this manner, they would mix easily with the liquid emulsion during the manufacturing of the film. Once the gelatin that bound them together had set, the color coupler molecules would become trapped in the tiny spaces of the gelatin and would be unable to move. This was the first three-layer, subtractive-color reversal film that had the color couplers built into the emulsion layers themselves and employed a single developer to make the positive image. This simplified process allowed the photographer to process the film. Kodak countered with its own version of the Agfacolor process in 1946 with Ektachrome.

Chromogenic Negative Film

Agfa brought out a color negative film in 1939 from which positive color prints could be made directly on a special companion paper. Kodak followed suit in 1942 with Kodacolor. Kodacolor is considered to be the first subtractive color negative film that completely solved the problem of the color couplers migrating from layer to layer in the emulsion. Kodacolor overcomes the limitation of each image being one-of-a-kind since any number of positive prints can be made from a color negative film.

Chromogenic Negative Development

The processing method used for Kodacolor is, with many improvements, the basis for all color negative film processes in use today (see chapter 8). In this process, currently called C-41, a single developer produces a negative silver image and a corresponding dye image in all three layers of the emulsion at the same time. Bleach is used to remove all the silver, leaving only the dye. The film is fixed, washed, and dried, which completes the process.

When making prints from a chromogenic negative with the subtractive method, the light is filtered in the enlarger before it reaches the negative. Correct color balance can thus be achieved in a single exposure. One of the three dye layers in the negative is usually left unfiltered. Printing is simplified because it is

not necessary to use more than two filters at one time to make a print. The subtractive method also enables pictures to be made directly from slides in a reversal printing process, such as ILFOCHROME Classic and Kodak Type R.

Other Color Processes

Silver Dye-Bleach; Dye-Destruction Process

The silver dye-bleach, also known as the dye-destruction process, is a method of making color prints from positives or negatives. Bleach is used to remove the unnecessary dyes from the emulsion, rather than using chromogenic development to produce dyes in the emulsion. This method was introduced commercially by Hungarian chemist Bela Gaspar as Gasparcolor in 1933 for color motion-picture work. Today's ILFOCHROME Classic materials, introduced as Cibachrome in 1963, make use of this process (see chapter 11).

Internal Dye Diffusion-Transfer Process

Self-processing instant-photography materials, such as Polaroid, make use of the internal dye diffusion-transfer process, which is often called the diffusion-transfer process. It operates by causing the dye-formers to transfer out of the negative emulsions layer(s) to a single receiving layer (also in the material), where the visual positive image forms. The three phases of the process—negative development, transfer, and positive development—happen simultaneously, so that the positive images begin to form almost immediately (see chapter 12).

Digital Imaging

During the 1960s, NASA developed digital technology for recording and transmitting images from out in space.

Digitizing converts an image into a numerical form that a computer can manipulate. Digital cameras use electronic sensors to convert an image into tiny picture elements called *pixels*. The pixels are arranged in a grid format, which can be stored as digital files on a magnetic disk or chip in a computer. Image editing software allows the computer operator to alter any group of pixels, thus color, brightness, and contrast can be seamlessly added or changed and images and text can be combined. Digital information can be rapidly transmitted via telephone lines or microwave signals. Digital images can be produced without the use of conventional photographic film or paper, although traditional prints and transparencies can be produced (outputted) from these electronic files. Images on traditional photographic materials can be electronically scanned and converted into digital form.

In 1981 Sony introduced the first electronic camera for professional use, the Mavica, which recorded an image in analog signals (a continuously variable scale) rather than in digital form. The high cost of the camera and its low quality and expensive output kept its use down. Recently other manufacturers have introduced improved, lower-cost analog and digital cameras, as well as digital backs for conventional film cameras. Advertising and newspaper photographers have been in the forefront of the field with their use of digital cameras for image manipulation and to meet deadlines by saving processing time (see chapter 13). With color image output rising every year, more people will use computers to digitally capture, process, and control their color photographically based pictures (figure 2.16).

Whether working digitally or in silver-based photography, the overwhelming success of color photography is undeniable. In 1993, Kodak estimated that at least 18.4 billion photographs were made and that 95 percent were made on silver halide film in color.

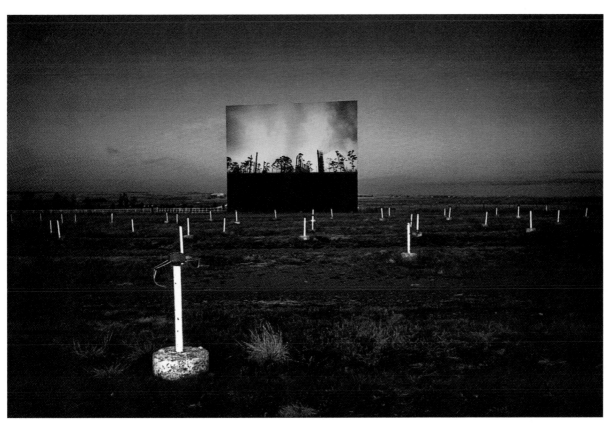

Figure 2.16
Nakagawa does a critical inspection of Western society from his viewpoint, which is "Eastern in origin and Western by immersion." Nakagawa, who spends much of his time divided between Japan and America, uses chemical and digital methods to build an expressive bridge, the frame within the frame, that crosses and juxtaposes both cultures and technologies.

© Osamu James Nakagawa. *Smokestack,* 1994 from the *Drive-In Theater Series.* 26 1/2 x 40 inches. Chromogenic color print.

References

Coe, Brian. *Colour Photography: The First Hundred Years 1840–1940.* London: Ash and Grant, 1978.

Coote, Jack H. *The Illustrated History of Colour Photography.* Surbiton, Surrey: Fountain Press, 1993.

Deribere, M., ed. *Encyclopaedia of Colour Photography.* Watford, England: Fountain Press, 1962.

Eder, Josef Maria. *History of Photography,* 4th. ed. Translated by Edward Epstean. New York: Columbia University Press, 1945; reprinted, New York: Dover Publications, 1978.

Friedman, Joseph S. *History of Color Photography.* Boston: American Photographic, 1944; reprinted, London and New York: Focal Press, 1968.

Gernsheim, Helmet, and Gernsheim, Alison. *The History of Photography 1685–1914.* New York: McGraw-Hill, 1969.

Hornenstein, Henry, with Hart, Russell. *Color Photography: A Working Manual.* Boston: Little, Brown and Company, 1995.

Mees, C. E. Kenneth. *From Dry Plates to Ektachrome Film.* New York: Ziff-Davis, 1961.

Newhall, Beaumont. *The History of Photography from 1839 to the Present,* 5th ed. New York: Museum of Modern Art, 1982.

Ostroff, Eugene, ed. *Pioneers of Photography: Their Achievements in Science and Technology.* Springfield, VA: The Society for Imaging Science and Technology, 1987.

Pantheon Photo Library. *Early Color Photography.* New York: Pantheon Books, 1986.

Rosenblum, Naomi. *A History of Women Photographers.* New York: Abbeville Press, 1994.

———. *A World History of Photography,* New York: Abbeville Press, 1989.

Sipley, Louis Walton. *A Half Century of Color.* New York: Macmillan, 1951.

Stroebel, Leslie and Zakia, Richard (editors). *The Focal Encyclopedia of Photogaphy,* 3rd. ed. Boston and London: Focal Press, 1993.

Wall, E. J. *The History of Three-Color Photography.* Boston: American Photographic, 1925; reprinted, London and New York: Focal Press, 1970.

Welling, William. *Photography in America: The Formative Years 1839–1900.* New York: Thomas Y. Crowell, 1978; reprinted, Albuquerque: University of New Mexico Press, 1987.

Wood, John. *The Art of the Autochrome: The Birth of Color Photography.* Iowa City: University of Iowa Press, 1993.

THREE

Safety in the Color Darkroom

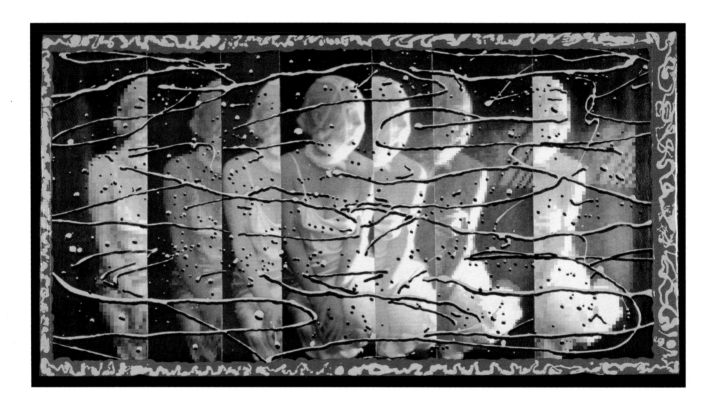

© Frank Rozasy.
She Was Made of Stone, 1990.
12 x 22 inches. Electrostatic prints with enamel paint.

It is of vital importance for all photographers to assume responsibility for protecting themselves when working with any photo-based process. For this reason, this safety chapter is placed before any working procedures or processes are introduced. Making yourself familiar with these suggested guidelines will help to ensure a long and safe relationship between yourself and the practice of making images.

Guidelines for Chemical Handling and Mixing

Every photographer working in a color darkroom needs to be aware of specific health and environmental concerns to ensure and promote a safe working atmosphere. Before beginning to work with any process mentioned in this book, it is necessary for each photographer to become familiar and observe the following basic precautions and guidelines:

1. Read and follow all instructions and safety recommendations on Material Safety Data Sheets (MSDSs) and product literature, which are provided with each product by its manufacturer and in this text, *Before* carrying out any process. This includes mixing, handling, disposal, and storage. Also, obtain any special safety equipment *Before* using the materials you have purchased. MSDSs are available from the manufacturers of each product. The Occupational Safety and Health Administration (OSHA) has a standard MSDS form (see pp. 22 and 23 figure 3.1), which is reproduced to give you an idea of the type of information provided. Each manufacturer prepares its own MSDSs, which typically provide additional ecological, disposal, transport, and regulatory information.

2. Become familiar with all the inherent dangers associated with any chemicals used. When acquiring any chemicals or when working with a new process, ask about proper handling and safety procedures. Obtain MSDSs for all chemicals used. Keep them available in a notebook for easy reference. Learn how to interpret the MSDSs. Right-to-know laws in the United States and Canada require all employers to formally train workers to read MSDSs. Certain color chemicals are more dangerous than others. Para-phenylenediamene and its derivatives, found in some color developers, and formaldehyde and its derivatives, found in stabilizers, are two of the most toxic.

3. Know the first aid and emergency treatment for the chemicals with which you are working. Keep the telephone numbers for poison control and emergency treatment prominently displayed in your working area and near the telephone. Each MSDS has the manufacturer's emergency number on it.

4. Many chemicals may be flammable. Keep them away from any source of heat or open flame to avoid possible explosion or fire. Keep an ABC-type fire extinguisher in the darkroom, which can be used for ordinary combustibles (wood and paper), solvent, grease, and electrical fires in the work area.

5. Protect chemicals from low temperatures (lower than 40°F, or 4.4°C). They may freeze, burst in their containers, and contaminate your working environment. Chemicals that have been frozen may also be damaged and deliver unexpected and faulty results.

6. Work in a well-ventilated space (see ventilation section of this chapter). Hazardous chemicals should be mixed in a vented hood or outdoors. Check MSDSs or the manufacturers for recommended ventilation guidelines for the chemicals you are using.

7. Avoid contamination problems by keeping all working surfaces clean, dry, and free of chemicals. Use polystyrene mixing rods, funnels, graduates, and pails. Use separate mixing containers for each chemical, and do not interchange them. Label them with a permanent marker. Thoroughly wash all equipment used in chemical mixing. Keep floors dry to prevent slips and falls.

8. Protect yourself. Wear disposable, chemical-resistant gloves, safety glasses, and plastic aprons. Find a glove maker who gives information that indicates how long the glove material can be in contact with a chemical before it becomes degraded or permeated. Degradation happens when the glove deteriorates from being in contact with the chemical. Permeation occurs when molecules of the chemical penetrate through the glove material. Permeated gloves often appear unchanged and wearers may be unaware they are being exposed to the chemical. Some chemicals can penetrate chemical gloves in minutes and begin to penetrate the skin. Barrier creams, which can protect the skin from light exposure to specific chemicals, can be applied to your skin. Choose the right cream to block acids, oils, or solvents, and use it exactly as directed. Do not use harsh soaps or solvents to wash your hands. After washing, apply a high-quality hand lotion to replace lost skin oils.

9. Consult the MSDS for the proper type of protection required with each chemical or process. When mixing powered materials, use an NIOSH-approved (National Institute of Occupational Safety and Health) mask for toxic dusts. When diluting concentrated liquid chemicals containing solvents, acetic acid, and sulfites, use a combination organic vapor/acid gas cartridge. Ideally all mixing should be done in a local exhaust system. If you have any type of reaction, immediately suspend work with all photographic processes and consult with a knowledgeable physician. Once an allergic reaction has occurred, you should avoid the chemicals unless your physician approves the use of a respirator. Employers of workers who wear respirators, including dust masks, are required by OSHA to have a written respirator program, formal fit testing, and worker training. People with certain diseases and some pregnant women should not wear them. Check with your doctor.

Figure 3.1

This is the front of the U.S. Department of Labor's Material Safety Data Sheet (MSDS). Manufacturers often create their own forms with additional information. MSDSs can be requested from each product manufacturer.

Material Safety Data Sheet
May be used to comply with
OSHA's Hazard Communication Standard,
29 CFR 1910.1200. Standard must be
consulted for specific requirements.

U.S. Department of Labor
Occupational Safety and Health Administration
(Non-Mandatory Form)
Form Approved
OMB No. 1218-0072

IDENTITY *(As Used on Label and List)*

Note: Blank spaces are not permitted. If any item is not applicable, or no information is available, the space must be marked to indicate that.

Section I

Manufacturer's Name	Emergency Telephone Number
Address *(Number, Street, City, State, and ZIP Code)*	Telephone Number for Information
	Date Prepared
	Signature of Preparer *(optional)*

Section II — Hazardous Ingredients/Identity Information

Hazardous Components (Specific Chemical Identity; Common Name(s))	OSHA PEL	ACGIH TLV	Other Limits Recommended	% *(optional)*

Section III — Physical/Chemical Characteristics

Boiling Point		Specific Gravity (H_2O = 1)	
Vapor Pressure (mm Hg.)		Melting Point	
Vapor Density (AIR = 1)		Evaporation Rate (Butyl Acetate = 1)	
Solubility in Water			
Appearance and Odor			

Section IV — Fire and Explosion Hazard Data

Flash Point (Method Used)	Flammable Limits	LEL	UEL
Extinguishing Media			
Special Fire Fighting Procedures			
Unusual Fire and Explosion Hazards			

(Reproduce locally)

OSHA 174, Sept. 1985

Figure 3.1 (continued)

This is the backside of the U.S. Department of Labor's Material Safety Data Sheet (MSDS). Manufacturers often create their own forms with additional information. MSDSs can be requested from each product manufacturer.

Section V — Reactivity Data

Stability	Unstable		Conditions to Avoid
	Stable		

Incompatibility (*Materials to Avoid*)

Hazardous Decomposition or Byproducts

Hazardous Polymerization	May Occur		Conditions to Avoid
	Will Not Occur		

Section VI — Health Hazard Data

Route(s) of Entry:	Inhalation?	Skin?	Ingestion?

Health Hazards (*Acute and Chronic*)

Carcinogenicity:	NTP?	IARC Monographs?	OSHA Regulated?

Signs and Symptoms of Exposure

Medical Conditions
Generally Aggravated by Exposure

Emergency and First Aid Procedures

Section VII — Precautions for Safe Handling and Use

Steps to Be Taken in Case Material Is Released or Spilled

Waste Disposal Method

Precautions to Be Taken in Handling and Storing

Other Precautions

Section VIII — Control Measures

Respiratory Protection (*Specify Type*)

Ventilation	Local Exhaust		Special
	Mechanical (*General*)		Other

Protective Gloves		Eye Protection

Other Protective Clothing or Equipment

Work/Hygienic Practices

☆ U.S. Government Printing Office: 1987—181-504/64362

10. Follow mixing instructions precisely. Mix chemicals in order and precisely according to directions, including the mixing times. Improper mixing procedures can produce dangerous chemical reactions or give undesirable results.

11. Keep all chemicals off of your skin and out of your mouth. If you get any chemicals on your skin, flush immediately with cool, running water.

12. Do not eat, drink, or smoke while handling chemicals. Wash your hands thoroughly after handling any chemicals. OSHA forbids the consumption or storage of food or drink wherever toxic chemicals are in use or stored. Food should not be stored in the refrigerator next to chemicals and paper.

13. Always pour acids slowly into water; never pour water into acids. Do not mix or pour any chemical at eye level because a splash could prove harmful. Wear unvented chemical splash goggles when mixing acids.

14. Label each solution container to reduce the chance of contamination and/or using the wrong solution.

15. Avoid touching any electrical equipment with wet hands. Install shock-proof outlets (ground fault interrupters) in your own darkroom. Make certain all equipment is grounded. Keep the floor dry. When designing a darkroom, plan to separate wet and dry areas.

16. Follow the manufacturer's instructions for proper disposal of all chemicals. Bleach and fix should be filtered through a small, inexpensive silver recovery unit. This silver can be sold to recoup the cost of the unit. The concentration of silver in such a unit can be highly toxic and must be handled with caution. Each local water treatment facility has its own rules. Photographers need to find out what they are. If you are on a septic system, go to another location. Purchase spill control centers, which contain special "pillows" or other devices that can be dropped on acids, solvents, or caustic chemical spills to immediately absorb them. They are sold by safety supply companies.

    Wash yourself and any equipment that has come into contact with any chemicals. Launder darkroom towels after each session. Specific questions about Kodak products can be answered by their Environmental Technical Services at (716) 477–3194. Ilford provides a similar service at (201) 265–6000.

17. Keep all chemicals properly stored. Use safety caps and/or lock chemicals up to prevent children, friends, and pets from being exposed to their potential dangers. Store chemicals in a cool, dry area away from any direct sunlight.

18. People have varying sensitivities to chemicals. Reduce your risk by keeping exposure to all chemicals to a minimum. Some chemicals cause an immediate and identifiable effect, while others, such as a skin allergy, can take years to develop. Consult your physician if you have a reaction while working with any chemicals. Be prepared to tell your doctor precisely what you were working with and what your symptoms are. Follow the physician's advice about reducing chemical exposure, using respiratory protection, and other precautions. Photographers should consult physicians who are board certified in occupational medicine or toxicology for such advice.

19. If you are planning a pregnancy, are pregnant, are breast-feeding, or have any preexisting health problems, consult your physician. Share with the physician any information from the MSDSs, from this book, or from other sources about possible adverse reactions before undertaking any photographic process. Children, senior citizens, allergy sufferers, smokers, heavy drinkers, and those with chronic conditions and diseases are considered to be more susceptible to the hazards of photographic chemicals.

Specific safety measures and reminders will be provided throughout this book whenever there is a deviation or exception from these guidelines. These instructions are not designed to produce paranoia but to ensure that you have a long and safe adventure in exploring color photography. Remember your eyes, lungs, and skin are porous membranes and can absorb chemical vapors. It is your job to protect yourself.

Ventilation

It is advisable to work in a space that has a light-tight exhaust fan and an intake vent for fresh air. Exhaust fans are rated by their ability to remove air in cubic feet per minute (cfm). A 10-×-20-foot darkroom with a 10-foot ceiling would require an exhaust fan rated at 500 cfm (against 1/4- to 1/2-inch static pressure) to do fifteen air exchanges per hour. Fans that do 500 cfm just sitting on the floor will *not* provide proper ventilation. The amount of ventilation needed varies depending on what chemicals are used, room size, and conditions. Read the MSDSs or contact the manufacturer for suggested ventilation guidelines for chemicals. Figure 3.2 shows how air inlets and outlets should be positioned for maximum effect. This type of ventilation, known as general or dilution, is designed to dilute the contaminated air with large volumes of clean air to lower the amounts of contaminants to acceptable levels and then exhaust the diluted mixture from the work area. Dilution ventilation does not work with highly toxic materials or any particle materials that form dusts, fumes, or mists. These materials require what is referred to as local exhaust ventilation, such as a table slot or fume hood, to capture the contaminants at the source before they escape into the room air. Refer to the reference section at the end of this chapter to carefully research this area before constructing a system.

Available Water Supply

Although water itself does not create a safety issue, it is included in this section because it is the key ingredient in most preelectronic photographic processes. This information applies whenever water is called for in any process discussed in this book.

Use a source of "pure" water. The chemical and mineral composition and pH of your local water source can affect processing results. Color developers are most sensitive to these factors. You can eliminate this variable beforehand by making certain your water source is pure or by using water processed by reverse osmosis. Distilled water often has had certain components (calcium) removed that are required for proper chemical reactions to take place. Water that has gone through a softening process is not recommended for any photographic chemical mixing. Water is usually softened by passing it through a treatment tank containing high amounts of salts. This process alters the chemical composition of the water and can lead to processing irregularities.

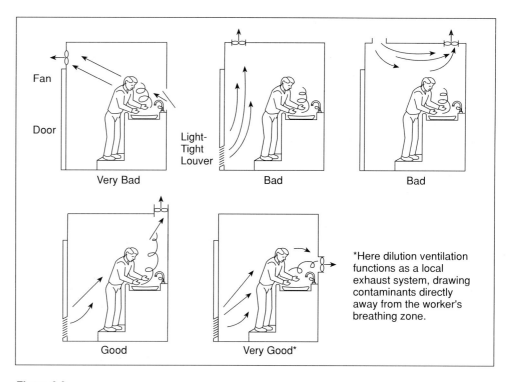

Figure 3.2

These drawings illustrate how the placement of ventilation inlets and outlets affects a local exhaust system in a photographic darkroom.

References

Arts, Crafts and Theater Safety (ACTS), 181 Thompson Street #23, New York, NY 10012. (212)777–0062. (Internet: 75054.25422compuserve.com). ACTS will answer questions about chemicals, work space design, and doctor referral.

The Center for Occupational Hazards, 5 Beekman Street, New York, NY 10038, (212)227–6220 answers questions concerning safety in artists' working space by letter or telephone.

Clark, N., Cutter, T., McGrane, J. A. *Ventilation: A Practical Guide.* New York: Nick Lyons Books, 1987.

Eastman Kodak Co. *Photolab Design.* Kodak Publication K-13. Rochester, NY: Eastman Kodak, 1989.

Eastman Kodak Co. *Safe Handling of Photographic Chemicals.* Kodak Publication J-4. Rochester, NY: Eastman Kodak, 1979.

Freeman, Victoria and Humble, Charles G. *Prevalence of Illness and Chemical Exposure in Professional Photographers.* Durham, NC: National Press Photographers Association, 1989.

McCann, Michael, *Artist Beware,* 2d ed. New York: Watson-Guptill, 1992.

The National Press Photographers Association, 3200 Croasdaile Drive, Suite 306, Durham, NC 27705.

OSHA's Publications Office, Room N-3101, 200 Constitution Ave., N.W., Washington, DC 20210; (202) 523–9667.

Shaw, Susan, and Rossol, Monona. *Overexposure: Health Hazards in Photography,* 2d ed. New York: Allworth Press, 1991.

Tell, Judy, ed. *Making Darkrooms Saferooms.* Durham, NC: National Press Photographers Association, 1988.

Questions about photographic chemicals can be answered by telephoning the following health and safety numbers, some of which operate 24 hours a day:

Agfa (303) 623–5716

Kodak, North America (716) 722–5151

Ilford, North America (914) 478–3131 or (800) 842–9660

Kodak, UK, Europe, and Africa 01–427–4380

Kodak, Australia, Asia, Western Pacific 03–350–1222

Polaroid (617) 386–4846

Your local poison control center.

The Act of Seeing

© Barbara Kasten.
Metaphase 5, 1986.
40 x 30 inches. Dye-destruction print.
Courtesy of John Weber Gallery, New York, NY.

Looking at a photograph is not like looking out a window. It requires a system of thought processes to reach a decision. It is not a mysterious, God-given gift but a process involving visual language that can be taught and mastered.

© Joseph Labate. *Tucson, AZ,* 1986. 15 × 22 inches. Chromogenic color print.

How We See

Seeing is an act of perception. It helps us to ascertain, experience, learn, and understand. It is an individual experience that is conditioned by the traditions and standards of the culture in which we live.

Our Western industrialized culture has always been dependent on literacy to function. It is necessary to be able to read in order to decipher messages that have been put into a written code or language.

When we begin to deal with pictures, another set of skills is needed to interpret the coded information. We must learn to become visually literate.

Visual Literacy

All literacy is based on the quality of our stored information. The more accessible information we have on file, the wider the range of possible responses we have to any situation that arises.

Some of us are afraid to learn to read new images. We tend to accept only the old ways and reject anything that is different or unfamiliar. When we are able to overcome this fear and begin thinking for ourselves, learning becomes a joyful and invigorating experience. This adds to our storehouse of information that can be called upon when dealing with new situations, thereby increasing our range of responses.

Whatever type of communication is in use, the receiver must be able to understand the code. In the past, pictures showed something of known importance. Traditional picture making used the act of seeing to identify subject matter. This is all many of us continue to expect and want of a picture maker. When something different or unexpected appears, we have no data or mechanism to deal with it. What we do not know or recognize tends to make us nervous and uneasy. This hostility manifests itself in the form of rejection, not only of the work but of any new ideas as well.

Looking at a picture is not the same as looking out a window. It requires thinking, sorting, analyzing, and decision making. It is a developed system of thought that can be taught and learned.

Social Values

Once formal education begins, Western society greatly reduces the value it places on learning the visual language. For many in our culture art is simply something that is supposed to be pretty and recognizable. People such as these are not aware of the picture maker's function within society as someone who can perceive, interpret, and offer a wider understanding of reality. Yet it is these same people who crave the products that these explorations often bring forth. We do not make fun of the scientist in the laboratory even if we do not understand what the scientist is doing because society has sanctioned the scientist's activities. The major difference between art and science is that art offers an intuitive approach to explain reality while science insists on an exact, objective, rational set of repeatable measurements. Science says there is only one right answer; art says there are many correct answers. The glory of contemporary art and the contribution of the artist citizen to democracy is diversity.

Visual Illiteracy

The value system of our culture reflects the Aristotelian, scientific mode of thought; achievements have to be measured in terms of words and numbers. The educational system has been primarily interested in teaching the twenty-six symbols of our alphabet and the numerals 0 through 9. This teaching meets the needs of growing industrial nations, but demands change. Education should be a process, not a product. Public education continues to ignore visual literacy and the price that has been paid is that many of us do not have the skills necessary to understand all the messages that surround us in our media-saturated environment. We lack the necessary data to go through a visual decision-making process. We have become "objects" that can easily be manipulated. We simply react to situations by either accepting them or rejecting them. When we cease to question we have been effectively removed from the process.

Photography can enable the imagemaker to comment and interact with society. Pozzi likes to photograph candidly at public events, looking for clues to interpret popular American culture and musing on contemporary values. The visually literate viewer can be in the position of decoding an image and making an intelligent response. This interactive process can stimulate thought and action, bringing about changes in society and making life more meaningful.

© Craig Pozzi. *Oregon State Fair, Salem, OR*, 1988. 9 × 13 1/2 inches. Dye-destruction print.

Visual or Haptic—Which Creative Type Are You?

Have you ever wondered how and why photographers make pictures in a specific style or why viewers of photography react more strongly to certain pictures? This section presents some ideas on this subject, spurs your thinking, and allows you to draw your own conclusions.

The Work of Victor Lowenfeld

The initial work in discovering some of the separate ways that we acquaint ourselves with the environment was done by Victor Lowenfeld in 1939 while he was working with people who were partially blind. Lowenfeld found that some of these people used their limited sight to examine objects when they worked with modeling clay. He noticed that others did not use their eyes but instead used their sense of touch. These observations led Lowenfeld to conduct a study of people with normal vision. He found people with normal vision had the same tendencies: some used their sense of sight, while others used their sense of touch.

Lowenfeld determined that the first group took an intellectual, literal, realistic, quantitative approach to things. He called this group "visual." The second group functioned in an intuitive, qualitative, expressionistic-subjective mode. He labeled these people "haptic." Lowenfeld then set out to determine the major characteristics of each of these two creative types.

Characteristics of the Visual Type

Lowenfeld found that "visuals" tend to produce whole representational images. They are concerned with "correct" proportions, colors, and measurements. The visual-realist likes to become acquainted with the environment primarily through the eyes; the other senses play a secondary role.

The picture maker is an active participant in this decision-making process. Imagemaking offers opportunities for the photographer to interact and comment on what is going on in society. The photographer's work can stimulate others to thought and action. The entire photographic process can make life deeper, richer, more varied, and more meaningful. This process is worth something, even if it cannot be measured in tangible terms.

Seeing is a personal endeavor, and its results depend on the viewer's ability to decode the messages that are received in a symbolic form. A broad, flexible response helps the viewer to understand that our culture determines the hierarchy of subject matter. Keeping the mind open enables us to uncover all the levels and possibilities of new materials and to view the familiar anew.

The Role of the Photographer

Pursuing the role of the picture maker as the "scout," riding out in front of the wagon train, making observations of unknown or hostile territory, and reporting back the findings to the group, requires a mastery of the basic ingredients of all imagemaking. Understanding basic design elements and how light affects objects are crucial in learning how to look at and make pictures.

Becoming visually literate is one small step we can take in accepting responsibility for affirming our own values. Ultimately this could have widespread effects. As people become visually educated, more aware of their surroundings, and able to see the world for themselves, they can participate in making decisions that affect the manner in which the business of society is conducted.

Figure 4.1
Victor Lowenfeld's "visual" types like to make representation images that deal with preserving the illusion of outer reality.

© David Graham. *Mayflower, Philadelphia, PA*, 1984. 24 × 20 inches. Chromogenic color print. Courtesy of Black Star and Laurence Miller Gallery, New York, NY.

Figure 4.2
The "visual" photographer's work often reflects concrete themes and tells a narrative story. Documentary and journalistic work generally fit into the visual's way of seeing. This kind of work lets us see and experience actual events with which we normally would not interact.

© Larry Burrows. *DMZ*, 1966. 11 × 14 inches. Dye transfer print. Courtesy of Larry Burrows Collection and Laurence Miller Gallery, New York, NY.

Visual Photographers

As a generalization, visual photographers prefer to preserve the illusion of the world (figure 4.1). The visual-realist style is an unmanipulated and objective mirror of the "actual" world. It is unobtrusive and concerned with what is there. These photographers use the camera traditionally and tend to be observers/spectators; for them the camera is a recording device. They go for facts rather than for abstract form. The subject is always supreme. In their work they avoid extreme angles and photograph from eye level. Documentary work is the most obvious style. Visual-realists usually attempt to preserve spatial continuity and favor a normal lens. Their style is more open, subtle, recessive, or informal and leans toward the unobtrusive and the familiar.

Working Methods of Visual Photographers. The visual-realists like to print full-frame, uncropped negatives. The code of the visual-realist is that of linear reality. Their pictures reflect concrete themes and often tell a story. The visual-realist uses the "straight" technique. The Zone System is a favorite starting place, with its emphasis on "correct" technique.

The picture is usually created at the moment the shutter is released (figure 4.2). Darkroom work is kept to a minimum. Few or no unusual techniques are employed except what is considered to be in keeping with the current tradition. Visual-realists may not even do their own processing or printing. They use photography to match reality and often use the work to produce motives for change in society. The work enables us to see places and things that we are not able to experience for ourselves.

Characteristics of the Haptic Type

Lowenfeld found that "haptics" were more kinesthetic. Haptic comes from the Greek word *haptos,* which means "laying hold of." Haptics are more concerned with their bodily sensations and subjective experiences. The haptic becomes part of the picture. Emotional and subjective values can determine the color and form of objects, rather than how and what they actually look like (figure 4.3).

Haptic Photographers

Haptic-expressionist photographers often stylize and distort the subject. They participate actively in the photographic process and become part of the picture. The haptics, explorers of the inner self, try to liberate their inner vision rather than reproduce an image of the outer world. They are concerned with the subjective and more personal type of vision. Dealing with spiritual and psychological questions tends to restrict the audience appeal of the work.

Working Methods of Haptic Photographers.   The haptics break with tradition and ritual. Their style is more self-conscious and conspicuous, and the unfamiliar is of importance. The emphasis is on form. They emphasize the essential nature rather than the physical nature of the subject. Haptic-expressionists use the camera flamboyantly. It becomes a tool to offer comment on the subject at hand. They manipulate the image if this will heighten the response. They move and rearrange the given reality to suit their needs. Many times, they fragment real space, preferring a closer, more controlled shot.

Haptics frequently practice postvisualization; they see the darkroom as a creative lab in which to carry on visual research. Experimenting with different techniques and types of film and paper, their darkroom becomes a place for contemplation, discovery, and observation (figure 4.4).

Figure 4.3
Lowenfeld's "haptic" types tend to incorporate themselves into their work. Emotional and personal values can determine the color and form of the final image, resulting in expressionistic work. Younger photographed this scene on black-and-white negative film and used the cliché-verre process to etch outlines of certain areas in the picture. Next, specific areas of the negative were hand-colored with color markers and the result was placed in the enlarger. A pallet of colors was made on a sheet of acetate using color markers, watercolors, and colored acetates. This acetate overlay was contact-printed, along with the projected image, onto color paper. Halfway through the developer step, the warm chemistry was dumped and cold chemistry added to shock the paper and give vibrant colors. The object was to create colors that are symbolic of the experience, expression, and imagination of a child.

© Kent R. Younger. *If You Do All Your Homework, You'll Get Good Grades in School,* 1989/90. 11 × 14 inches. Chromogenic color print.

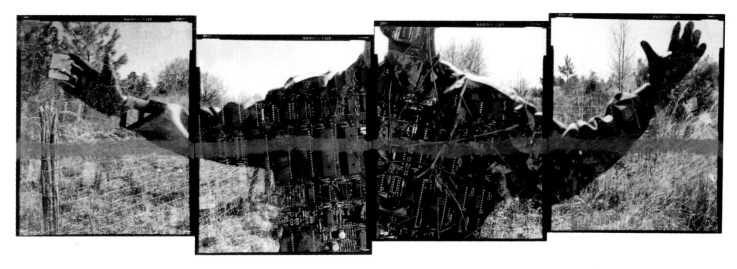

Figure 4.4

The "haptic" photographers actively become part of the photographic process by distorting and stylizing the subject to create a more intense personal response. Kasten says: "My feeling about the subjects I photograph extend from my belief that a tree can talk and a room can float. I have a strong inner response to the mystical qualities of my inanimate surroundings." For this image Kasten made a sequence of shots of himself silhouetted against an empty field. The film was reexposed to a setup of old circuit boards and leaves. The blue line was silkscreened onto the finished panels to add a solid color element that would emphasize the print surface and contrast the photographic depth.

© Bart Kasten. *Self-Portrait with Blue Line*, 1990. 24 × 64 inches. Chromogenic color prints with photo-silkscreen.

Haptics create their own miniuniverse, saturating the image with visual clues and information, attempting to direct and lead the viewer around within the frame.

Photography's Visual Revolution

Photography has brought about a revolution in the arts. It initially freed painters and writers from having to describe objects and happenings and allowed them to move from outer matching to inner matching. It turned art toward the inner processes of creativity in expression, which helped lead to the development of abstract art. This has opened entirely new roads for the human mind to travel upon. The artist is now able to present the entire creative process for public participation.

Photo-based imagemaking has changed so rapidly that it is difficult for many of us to keep up. Most still cling to the same ideas that were presented to us when we were children. This attitude has blocked the path of creativity and slowed the growth of photography. Experimentation in any field is necessary to keep it

alive, growing, and expanding. The photographer should be encouraged to experiment for the pursuit of new knowledge.

As both a photographer and viewer of photographs, it is important to know that there is no fixed way of perceiving a subject, only different ways that a subject can be experienced. Photograph your experience of what is mentally and emotionally important, what is actively in your mind, and what you care about during the process of picture making. When looking at other photographs, especially ones that are unfamiliar or that you do not understand, attempt to envision the mental process that the photographer used to arrive at the final image. The visual photographers are concerned with the "what" and the haptics with the "how."

The Process of Rediscovery

Photography offers a rapid sequence of rediscovery. A new picture can alter the way we look at a past picture. Feel free to use whatever method is necessary to make your picture work, whether it is previsualization, postvisualization, a pre-process idea, or an in-process discovery. In your work you do not think with your

eyes, so give yourself the freedom to question the acceptance of any method of working. Make the darkroom a place and a time for exploration, not a situation in which you display your rote-memory abilities. Do not be too inhibited to walk on the edge. Do not let someone else set your limits. Something unexpected is not something wrong. Enjoy the process of making photographs. Don't turn it into a competition with yourself or others. Randall Jarrell, poet, novelist, and critic, remarked: "A good poet is someone who manages, in a lifetime of standing out in thunderstorms, to be struck by lightning five or six times, a dozen or two dozen times and he is great."

There are major discoveries waiting to be made in photography. Keep your definition of photography broad and wide. If you are able to let your true values and concerns come through, you will be on the course that allows your best capabilities to come forward and be seen. Do not be awed by fashion, for it is no indication of awareness, knowledge, or truth. It is simply a way of being "with it." Talking about photography is just that, talking about photography. Words are not pictures. As a picture maker the ultimate goal should be making pictures.

Figure 4.5
The color key reflects the present fundamental color concerns of the photographer. It is not a constant but varies depending on the concerns, mood, and state of being of the photographer. Fill flash was employed in this theatrically staged portrait to illuminate the subject and separate her from the background activity.

© Bambi Peterson. *Invented Portrait Series: Ray,* 1990. 13 × 18 inches. Chromogenic color print.

Determine whether you possess the more general qualities of either the visual or the haptic way of imagemaking. Choose a subject and photograph it in that manner. Next, turn that switch inside your brain and attempt to think in the opposite mode. Make a picture of the same subject that reveals these different concerns. Compare the results. What have you learned?

The Color Key and the Composition Key

How is the decision reached about which colors to include in a picture? We each have colors we tend to favor. Notice the colors with which you chose to surround yourself. Observe the colors of your clothes or room because they are a good indication of your color key.

The Color Key

Your color key is a built-in automatic pilot. It will take over in situations when you do not have time to think. Everyone has one. It cannot be made; it has to be discovered. The color key reveals the character of a person. It is not a constant; it changes. At one point it is possible to see dark, moody hues; later, bright, happy, and warm colors are prominent. It is all a balancing act that mirrors your inner state of mind. When the picture is composed, the framing establishes the relationship of the colors to one another. These decisions affect how colors are perceived. The colors selected are the ones that the photographer currently identifies with in a fundamental way (figure 4.5).

Figure 4.6
The composition key is an internal sense of design the photographer instinctively uses to structure an image. It reveals the photographer's sense of visual order and style. This sense is not fixed, however, but represents an ongoing visual developmental process. Kuo's late industrial culture images function as icons pointing out the inescapable irony that "the way many of the things in our world which are not *good,* are in fact, rather nice to look at. I see objects like this gas pump as emblems of the aspirations and limits of the culture that produced them."

© Frank L. Kuo. *Gas Pump,* 1981. 15 × 15 inches. Chromogenic color print.

The Composition Key

The composition key is the internal sense of construction and order that is applied when putting the picture parts together. It cannot be forced. Our true sense of design and style is a developmental process. It is a rendition of yourself in terms of picture construction. You are it. It is incorporated into the work and is given back in the final image. Some common compositional keys to begin looking for are the triangle, circle, figure eight, and spiral, along with the H, S, and W forms (figure 4.6).

Recognizing the Keys

Recognizing these keys is a way to make yourself more aware and a better image-maker. The good photographer can learn to make pictures even in bad conditions. The ability to see that there is more than one side to any situation helps make this happen. For example, you could say it is raining and not go out to make a picture, or you could see that it is raining and make this an opportunity to make the diffused, shadowless picture that has been in the back of your mind. Color and composition keys are meant to offer a

guide for understanding how we visually think. They are not hard-and-fast rules for making pictures. They should also show that there is more than one way to see things. When you learn how others view the world, it is then possible to see more for yourself.

Can you identify your personal color and composition keys? Do not expect to find it in every piece. It can be hidden. Doodles can often provide clues to your compositional key. If you are having trouble seeing these phenomena, get together with another photographer and see if you can identify each other's keys.

• ASSIGNMENT •

Go to galleries and museums and look through books, magazines, photo CDs, or on-line collections to find a body of work by a photographer that has meaning for you. Notice the color and compositional devices that this photographer uses in the work. Now make a photograph in the manner of this photographer. Do not copy or replicate this photographer's work, but take the essential ingredients and employ them to make your own photograph. Next, compare the photograph that you have made to the work of the photographer. Last, compare both photographs to your other work. What similarities and differences in color and composition do you notice? What can you see that you did not notice before making these comparisons? Now return to the same subject and make an image your way. Compare the results with what you previously have done. Has your thinking been altered in any way?

Figure-Ground Relationships

What Is Figure-Ground?

Figure-ground is the relationship between the subject and the background. It also refers to the positive-negative space relationship within

Figure 4.7
An example of the figure-ground relationship phenomenon. What do you see first? How can this type of ambiguity affect how the viewer might read and respond to an image? What role does contrast and color play in how you see this image?

Figure 4.8
Complex compositions require careful planning and skillful handling so the audience does not get lost within the figure-ground relationship of the photograph. Teemer comments: "I am endlessly intrigued with space perception. . . . Using a 4-×-5-inch Deardoff camera with a 135-mm lens stopped down and the front board tipped slightly to maximize depth-of-field allows the focus to include both the immediate foreground and the distant Cincinnati skyline forming a juxtaposition between a decorated yard and the modern cityscape. With the entire picture in focus, the field is flattened forming further relationships between color, detail, and their rhythm and patterns across the picture plane."

© Jack D. Teemer, Jr. *Cincinnati*, 1986. 12 × 14 inches. Chromogenic color print.

your picture. "Figure," in this case, is the meaningful content of your composition. "Ground" describes the background of the picture.

Figure 4.7 is a classic example of the figure-ground phenomenon. What do you see first? Can you discern a different figure-ground relationship? What do you think most people see first? Why? What does this tell you about the role of contrast?

Why Is Figure-Ground Important?

When the figure and the ground are similar, perception is difficult (figure 4.8). The viewer might have difficulty determining what is important to see in the picture. This often occurs when the photographer attempts to show too much.

The viewer's eyes wander all over, without coming to a point of attention. The composition lacks a climax, so the viewer loses interest and leaves the image. If you have to explain what you were trying to reveal, there is a strong chance that your figure-ground relationship is weak.

Figure-Ground Strategies

When you observe a scene, determine exactly what interests you. Visualize how your content (figure) and background (ground) are going to appear in your final photograph. Put together a composition that will let the viewer see the visual relationships that attracted you to the scene. Try using different focal-length lenses and angles to alter the areas of focus. Be selective about what is in-

cluded in the picture. Find ways to both isolate and connect the key visual elements of the composition. Try using a higher shutter speed and larger lens aperture to lessen the depth of field. What happens when spacial visual clues are reduced? Do not attempt to show "everything." Often showing less actually tells the audience more about the subject, because they do not have to sort through visual chaos. Try limiting the number of colors in a photograph until you gain more experience. A color photograph does not have to contain every color in the universe. Keep it simple and to the point. Wright Morris, commenting about "the problem" with color photography, said: "By including almost everything within our spectrum, the color photograph forces upon it the ultimate banality of 'appearances.' That is why we tire of

In this series, Brown's choice of camera and lens was intended to distort and confuse. A wide-angle lens held close to the subject distorts the image and minimizes the area of focus. The print size delivers objects that are larger than they are in life, further confusing any direct relationship to reality. Brown says she wants to "evoke an ambiguity of spacial and temporal elements which move through nostalgic references to deeper pyschological concerns."

© Lynne Brown. *Memory References*, 1980. 13 × 19 inches. Chromogenic color print.

them so quickly. The first effect is dazzling; the total effect is wearying. . . . Where everything seems to be of interest, the burden of the photographer is greater, not less. The color photograph not merely says, but often shouts, that everything is of interest. And it is not."[1] Use your abilities to meet the challenge and fulfill the promise that color provides the visual artist.

[1] Wright Morris. *Time Pieces: Photographs, Writing, and Memory.* (New York: Aperture Foundation, 1989), 145.

• ASSIGNMENT •

Make two photographs of the same scene/subject. One should show a clearly definable figure-ground relationship of the scene. The other should portray a weak figure-ground relationship. Then compare and contrast the two. What were some of the methods used to improve your figure-ground relationship? How can they be applied to further picture-making situations?

Thinking in Color

© Robert Hirsch.
Thinking Elvis, 1991.
16 x 20 inches.
Gelatin-silver print with paint, colored pencil, and collage materials.

Photography and Reality

Most people say they prefer color pictures to black-and-white pictures. They claim that color photographs are more "real" than black-and-white photographs. This means that we tend to confuse color photography and reality to even a greater extent than we do with black-and-white photographs. Have you ever seen someone point to an 8-×-10 inch color glossy and say, "There's Betty. She sure looks good, doesn't she?" We all know that isn't Betty, but we expect photography to duplicate our reality for us. This expectation reveals an entire series of problems dealing with the construction of current color materials and our own powers of description and memory. The photographer and the audience must face these problems when working with color.

Standards in Color

In all color processes, the final outcome hinges on how successful the synthetic dyes replicate a "natural" color balance. Each film manufacturer makes emulsions that emphasize different color balances. Certain colors are overemphasized in some and in others their degree of saturation is exaggerated. While these colors may look good, they are not accurate and there is a loss in delicate and subdued colors. There is *no standard!* Some films tend to create a cool, neutral, or even detached look. They emphasize blue and green. Other films give a warm look, favoring red and yellow. These colors seem more intense and vivid. The warmth tends to draw people in and create more involvement.

This lack of a standard color balance is true of all color films, whether negative or slide film. The dyes simulate the look of reality, but they do not reproduce true colors. What you get is an interpretation of the scene. For this reason it is imperative that the photographer work personally with many of the available materials to find one that agrees with his or her personal color sense. By learning the characteristics of films, the photographer will also know what film works best in a given situation.

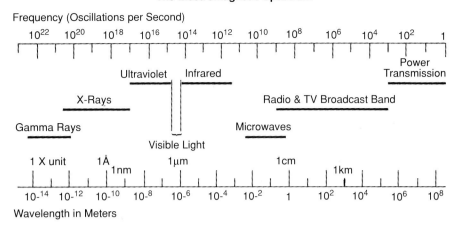

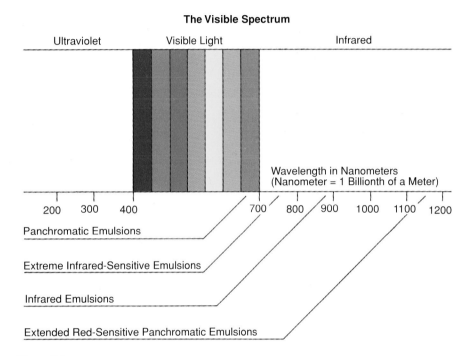

Figure 5.1
The complete spectrum is made up of all forms of electromagnetic energy. Only an extremely limited range of the entire spectrum, called the visual spectrum, or white light, can be detected by the human eye. When white light is broken up into its various wavelengths, the eye sees these wavelengths as separate colors.

Talking About Color

Have you ever noticed how few words there are in the English language to describe colors? Some languages have up to twenty words to distinguish slight differences within one color. Without words to describe, we have a very limited ability to see and distinguish subtle variations in color. Most people simply say a car is red. This covers a great deal of territory. A car dealer may call the same car "candy apple red." Neither term is an accurate description and doesn't give another person much sense of what we are attempting to describe. These vague generalizations cause problems translating into words what we see in pictures.

Color Description—Hue, Saturation, and Luminance

Each color can be defined by three essential qualities. The first is hue, which is the name of the color, such as blue or yellow. It gives the specific wavelength

Figure 5.2
This is an example of color description for red. Notice how this hue's saturation and luminance have been altered, producing a wide variety of color effects.

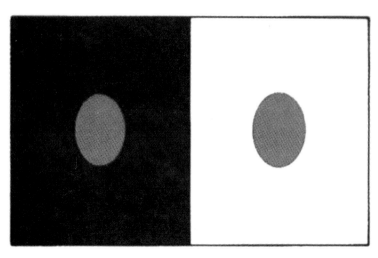

Figure 5.3
The circles in this illustration are the same color. The circle on the right appears to have a greater luminance than the circle on the left because both color luminance and saturation are subjective and dependent on the surrounding colors.

that is dominant in the color source. The second quality is saturation, or chroma, which indicates the apparent vividness or purity of a hue. The spectrum shows perfectly saturated hues (figure 5.1). The narrower the band of wavelengths, the purer the color. Strong, vivid hues are referred to as saturated colors. Almost all colors we see are desaturated by a wider band of other wavelengths. When different wavelengths are present, the hue is said to be weaker, or desaturated.

The third quality of color is luminance, or brightness. Luminance deals with the appearance of lightness or darkness in a color. These terms are relative to the viewing conditions. They describe color as it is seen in individual situations.

Hue, saturation, and luminance can be applied to color description in any situation. Take as an example the specific hue of red, which has the longest wavelength of visible light. Mix it with a great deal of white light and it produces pink, which is desaturated red. Now paint this color on a building that is half in sunlight and half in shadow (figure 5.2). Each side of the building has the same hue and saturation, but each side has a different luminance. If a beam of sunlight strikes an object and makes a "hot spot," then that area is said to be desaturated since

the color has been diluted with a large amount of white light. White is a hue with no saturation but has a high luminance. Black contains no saturation and a very small amount of luminance.

Understanding these three basic concepts helps the photographer translate what is seen by the eye into what will be recorded by the photographic means. It also provides a common vocabulary of terms that we can employ in accurately discussing our work with others.

Color Relativity

Our perception of color is relative. Hue does not exist for the human eye without a reference. A room that is lit only by a red light will, after a time, appear to us as normal. Household tungsten lights are much warmer than daylight, yet we think color balance appears normal under these conditions. When a scene is photographed in tungsten light on a daylight color-balanced film it will be recorded with an orange-red cast.

Stare at a white wall through a red filter. In time, your eyes will stop seeing the color. Now place an object of a different color into this scene. The red reappears along with the new color.

This point is important to remember when attempting to color balance prints. If you stare at the print too long, the color imbalances will appear correct. For this reason it is recommended that a standard reference, such as the Kodak Color Print Viewing Filters with a piece of white paper, be used for determining color balance (see chapter 11).

The color luminance and saturation of an object within a scene appear to change depending on the colors surrounding it. A simple experiment can be performed to see how luminance is relative. Cut two circles from a piece of colored paper. Put one of the circles in the center of a bigger piece of black paper and the other on a piece of white paper (figure 5.3). The circle on the black paper will seem to have a greater luminance than the circle on the white paper, demonstrating how color luminance and saturation are subjective and dependent on the surrounding colors.

This phenomenon, also called simultaneous contrast, will cause the hue and brightness of a color to change. For example, a gray circle will appear yellowish on a purple background, reddish on a green background, and orange on a blue background.

Figure 5.4
Color contrast is created when complementary colors (opposite colors on the color wheel) appear next to each other. This presents the appearance of greater contrast, even if the color intensity is the same. The closer the colors are to each other on the color wheel, the less color contrast will be produced.

© Roger Camp. *The Race,* 1985. Size varies. Dye-destruction print.

Color Contrast

Color contrast happens when complementary colors, opposite colors on the color wheel, appear next to each other in the picture (figure 5.4). Blue next to yellow is an example. The appearance of great contrast is given, even if the color intensity is identical.

The human eye helps to create this impression. Every color is a different wavelength of light. Blue has the shortest wavelength and red the longest. When two primary colors appear next to one another, the eye cannot properly process the color responses. Thus, the colors appear to vibrate, creating contrast. Contrast is the major element that influences balance and movement in a composition. In color photography, unlike in black-and-white photography, contrast does not depend solely on light reflectance.

Color Harmony

Color harmony is a product of both reflected light and the relationship of the colors to each other on the color wheel. A low-contrast picture has colors that are next to one another on the color wheel (figure 5.5). These harmonious colors can reflect greatly varying amounts of light yet still not provide as much visual contrast as complementary colors with closer reflectance values.

In color photography contrast is the result of the amount of light reflected, the colors present, and the relationship of the colors on the color wheel. Complementary colors create a higher contrast and more vibrancy. Harmonious colors produce a more placid scene with lower contrast.

Some Observations About Color

Color Memory

Josef Albers, who wrote *Interaction of Color,* discovered that people have a poor memory for color. Albers asked an

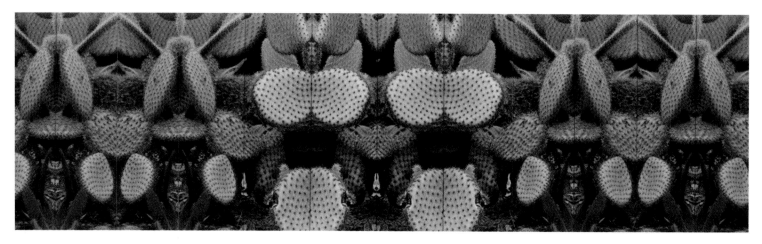

Figure 5.5
Color harmony depends on both the reflected light and the relationship of the colors to each other on the color wheel. The closer the colors are to one another on the color wheel, the more harmonious the color relationship appears. Harmonious colors create less color contrast. Preston became interested in showing, via a still photograph, how the landscape looks when it is seen in motion, as from a passing vehicle. This image was created by making several prints from the same negative and then reversing the negative in the enlarger and making additional prints. These prints were then cut into 2-inch strips and rearranged into the final image. The strips gave Preston the opportunity to create all sorts of anthropomorphic shapes and patterns.

© Judith A. Preston. *Color Pieces Series: Creatures III*, 1991. 7 x 24 inches. Chromogenic color prints.

audience to visualize a familiar color, such as the red on the Coca-Cola logo. Then he showed different shades of red and asked the audience to pick which one was "Coca-Cola red." There was always disagreement. To Albers this indicated that we have a short color memory span. Albers's book will help you gain a deeper understanding of how color interacts with our perceptions.

Color Deceives

To begin to see and use color effectively, it is first necessary to recognize the fact that color continually deceives us. It is possible for one color to appear as two different colors. In figure 5.6, the two halves of the circle are the same color, yet the human eye does not see them as the same.

This tells us that one color can and does evoke many different readings depending on the circumstances. This indicates that it is necessary to experience color through the process of trial and error. Patience, practice, and an open mind are needed to see the instability and relativity of color. Observation will reveal the discrepancy between the physical fact of color perception and its psychological effect. In any scene there is a constant interplay between the colors themselves and between the viewer and his or her perceptions of the colors.

Figure 5.6
The two halves of the circle are the same color, yet the human eye does not see them as the same color. This phenomenon is an example of color relativity.

Color Changes

Colors are in a continuous state of change, depending on their relationship to their neighboring colors and lighting and compositional conditions. The following sections provide a series of visual examples that reveal the flux of color.

Subtraction of Color

In figure 5.7, the two circles in the centers of the rectangles appear to be the same color. To get the best comparison, do not look from the center of one to the center of the other but at a point midway between the two. The small, elongated semicircles at the top and bottom of the figure show the actual colors of the circles in the rectangles. The circle on the white ground is an ocher yellow, while the one on the green ground is a dark ocher. This shows that any ground subtracts its own color from the hues that it possesses.

Experiments with light colors on light grounds indicate that the light ground subtracts its lightness in the same manner that hue absorbs its own

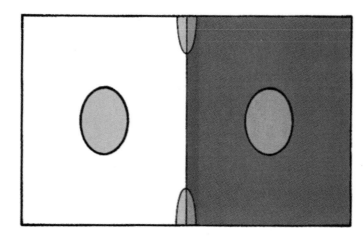

Figure 5.7
The subtraction of color shows how two different colors can be made to look the same.

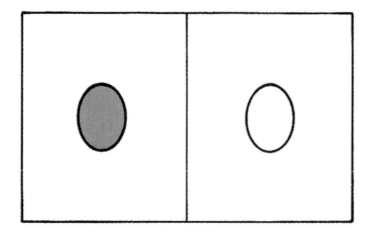

Figure 5.8
Look steadily at the circle on the left for 30 seconds, and then look immediately at the circle on the right. Do you see the afterimage? In an afterimage a color may appear to be different than it is in reality.

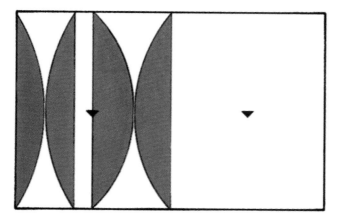

Figure 5.9
Stare steadily at the black inverted triangle on the left, and then quickly shift your focus to the inverted triangle at the right. In the reversed afterimage the white areas of the original will appear as blue and the blue areas as pale orange.

color. The same is true for dark colors on a dark ground. This indicates that any diversion among colors in hue or in the light-dark relationship can either be visually reduced or obliterated on grounds of equal qualities.

The conclusion is that color differences are caused by two factors, hue and light, and in many instances by both at the same time.

Afterimage

Stare steadily at the marked center of the green circle in figure 5.8 for a minimum of 30 seconds, and then rapidly shift your focus to the center of the white circle. Red or light red will appear instead of white. This example reveals how color can appear differently from what it physically is.

Eye Fatigue: Bleaching

Why does this happen? Nobody knows for certain, but one theory is that the nerve endings of the human retina, the cones and the rods, are set up to receive any of the three primary colors, which in turn make up all colors. This theory implies that by staring at green, the blue- and red sensitive parts of the eye become fatigued, causing the complement, red, to be visible. When the eye quickly shifts to white, which is the combination of blue, red, and green, only red is seen, due to the fatigue. Thus red, which is the complement of cyan, is the color seen.

Another theory says that the photopigments of the retina are bleached by bright light. This bleaching process, which is not understood, stimulates the nerves and it takes time for the photochemical to return to normal. When a region of photopigment is bleached, this part of the retina is less sensitive than its surrounding regions and produces visual afterimages.

Reversed Afterimage

Stare at the blue figures with a black inverted triangle in the center in figure 5.9 for at least 30 seconds, and then quickly shift your focus to the square on the right. Instead of seeing the afterimage of the blue figures in their complement the leftover spaces will predominate, being seen in blue. This double illusion is called reversed afterimage, or contrast reversal.

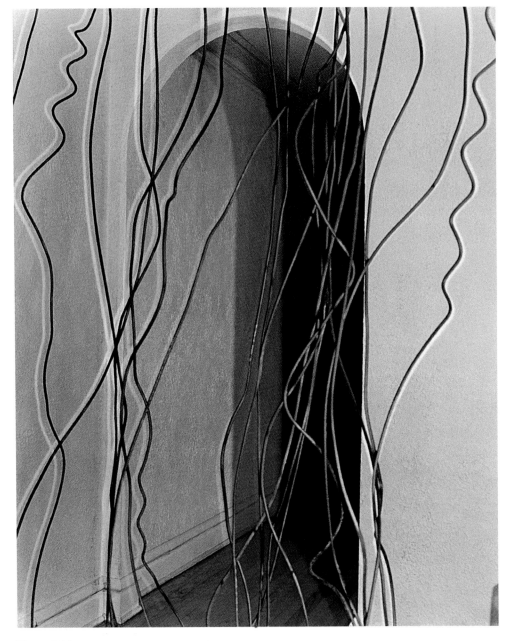

Figure 5.10
To create the effect of seeing an afterimage, Minnix first made a straight color print that was used as a paper negative in the making of the final image. This was accomplished in the following manner. A new sheet of color paper was exposed to the original negative for a predetermined time in the enlarger. This paper was left in the easel. The first straight print was then laid over the top of this newly exposed print. The enlarger was turned on for a brief time with the straight print lined up with, and then slightly offset from, the projected image. The negative was then removed and replaced by a clear orange negative mask. A brief exposure was then made through the paper negative (the straight print) onto the paper in the easel. This created a light exposure of the image in reversed tone and negative color.

© Gary Minnix. *Untitled*, 1985. 24 x 20 inches. Chromogenic color print.

retina and optical nerve after stimulation.

The phenomena of afterimage, reversed afterimage, and positive afterimage show us that the human eye, even one that has been trained in color, can be deceived by color. The conclusion is that colors cannot be seen independently of their illusionary changes by the human eye (figure 5.10).

Cooking with Color

Learning to work with color has many similarities to learning how to cook. A good recipe is no guarantee of success; the secret is often in preparation. The cook must constantly sample, taste, and make adjustments. The colors in a scene can be thought of as the ingredients that make up the picture; their arrangement and mixture will determine the final result. Two cooks can start off with the same ingredients yet produce a completed dish that tastes quite different. Simply by making small changes in quantity, one of the ingredients will lose its identity while another dominates. Cooking teaches that a successful meal involves more than reading a recipe. The same holds true for the photographer. Changes in color placement within a composition cause shifts in dominance, which can alter the entire feeling or mood of the picture. Also remember that properly presented food/photographs show that the cook/photographer has thought about every stage of the dining/visual experience and set the psychological stage for the diner's/viewer's response.

Positive Afterimage

When the eye has been "adapted" to a bright light (a light bulb viewed with the eye held steady or an electronic flash) a dark shape, of the same form as the adapting light, appears to hover in space near the light source. This floating shape appears dark when seen against a light-colored background. It may appear very bright during the first few seconds, especially if it is viewed in darkness. This is known as positive afterimage and is caused by the continuing firing of the

Color Is a Private Experience

Learning about color is a step-by-step process of observation, memory, and training that teaches us that seeing is a creative process involving the entire mind. What is ultimately learned is that color continues to be private, relative, elusive, and hard to define. Our perception of color is hardly ever as it actually

Figure 5.11
By studying the work of master photographers it is possible to gain insight into their sensitive handling of color relationships.

© Eliot Porter. *Waterfall Hidden Passage, Glen Canyon, Utah,* 1962. Dye Transfer print.
Courtesy of Amon Carter Museum, Fort Worth, TX.

appears in the physical world. There are no standard rules because of mutual influences colors have on one another. We may know the actual wavelength of a certain color, but we hardly ever perceive what the color physically is.

In photography this problem is compounded by the fact that the registration and sensitivity of the retina in the human eye is not the same as that of photographic materials. In the world of human vision, colors are busily interacting with each other and altering our perceptions of them. This interaction or interdependence keeps colors in an active, exciting state of flux.

• ASSIGNMENT •

Study the works of the visual masters of color to gain an artistic understanding of what they knew about color relationships and how they applied them (figure 5.11). This is not done to copy, compete, or revive the past. The aim of any study is to understand the past and create new work that reflects present-day concerns, directions, and ideas.

References

Albers, Josef. *Interaction of Color,* rev. ed. New Haven and London: Yale University Press, 1975.

Arnheim, Rudolf. *Art and Visual Perception: A Psychology of the Creative Eye,* rev. ed. Berkeley: University of California Press, 1993.

Gregory, Richard L. *Eye and Brain: The Psychology of Seeing,* 4th ed. Princeton: Princeton University Press, 1990.

Rock, Irvin. *Perception.* New York: Scientific American Books, 1984.

von Goethe, Johann Wolfgang. *Theory of Colours.* Cambridge, MA: M.I.T. Press, 1970.

Defining the Light/Exposure Methods and Techniques

© Lynn Saville.
Graphic Dancer, 1989.
16 x 20 inches.
Chromogenic color print.

An Exposure Starting Place

Without proper exposure, nothing is possible in photography. Exposure technique is the prerequisite to the process of transforming ideas into photographs. The exposure guidelines in this chapter are offered as basic starting points for those still learning exposure control. They will produce acceptable exposures under a wide variety of conditions without an extensive amount of knowledge, testing, or frustration. As you gain experience and confidence, more advanced exposure and development procedures can be employed (see chapter 14).

Determining the correct exposure with color materials is essentially the same as it is for black-and-white. Transparency film requires the greatest accuracy because the film itself is the final product; its exposure latitude is not wide, so small changes can produce dramatic results. In general, underexposure of slide film by up to 1/2 f-stop produces a richer, more saturated color effect. With negative film, overexposure of up to a full f-stop produces similar results. Good detail in key shadow areas is needed to print well. Negative film has a much wider exposure range, plus the printing stage allows for further corrections after initial exposure of the film.

Camera Meters

Camera meters are the device most of us initially employ to make our exposure calculations. Now almost every contemporary 35-mm SLR camera has a thru-the-lens (TTL) metering system. These systems provide accurate results under even light and they are convenient, but it is up to the operator to make them perform to obtain the desired pictures. The more you know about the camera's metering system, the greater the likelihood you will use it to achieve the desired exposure. All meters are partially blind; they see only the middle gray of 18 percent reflectance as it appears on film. (See the tear-out 18 percent gray card at

· TABLE 6.1 ·
Basic Metering Guidelines

1. Check to see that the ISO film speed matches the meter setting.
2. Perform a battery check before going out to take pictures.
3. When taking a reflected light reading, point the meter at the most visually important neutral-toned item in the scene.
4. Get close to the main subject so that it fills the metering area. Avoid extremes of dark or light when selecting areas on which to base your general exposure.
5. If it is not possible to meter directly from the subject, place your hand in the same light as the subject and compensate the exposure by opening up one f-stop, or place the 18 percent gray card from the back of this book in the same type of light and meter off it.
6. In situations of extreme contrast and/or a wide tonal range, consider averaging the key highlight and shadow areas or take a reading off an 18 percent gray card under the same quality of light.
7. For an incident reading, fit the light-diffusing dome over the cell and point the meter at the source of the light so the meter is in the same lighting conditions as the subject in relationship to the camera position.

the back of the book, which you can use to help determine the proper exposure.) The reflectance reading tells the photographer that if the object the meter is reading is a middle gray or averages out to be a middle gray, this is how the camera should be set for an average exposure. The meter is a tool that measures only the intensity of the light; it does not judge the quality of the light or the feeling and mood that the light produces upon the subject. The best exposure is not necessarily the one the meter indicates is the correct exposure. The meter is a guide that reads the signs. It is up to the photographer to see, respond to, and interpret the light and decide what exposure will deliver the color, detail, feeling, and mood needed to express and convey the situation to the audience. Some basic metering guidelines are summarized in table 6.1.

Figure 6.1
A reflective light reading is made by pointing the light meter directly at the subject. A reflective reading measures the light that is bounced off, or reflected from, the subject. Most in-camera meters can only measure reflected light.

Reflective and Incident Light

There are two fundamental ways of measuring the amount of light in a scene. Virtually all in-camera meters are designed to read reflective light. Reflective light is metered as it bounces off the subject. This is accomplished by pointing the meter directly at the subject (figure 6.1). A reflected reading from low midtones and high shadows delivers good general results with negative film.

Incident light is measured as it falls on the subject. The meter is not pointed at the subject but toward the camera or main light source (figure 6.2). Incident meters are not influenced by the multiple reflectance values of a subject; therefore, they do not require as much expertise to achieve satisfactory results. Most in-camera meters cannot read incident light without a special attachment that fits over the front of the lens. This adapter permits incident reading with most TTL metering systems. Incident readings work well with slide film, as does reflected reading of key highlights, if areas containing shadow detail are not visually critical.

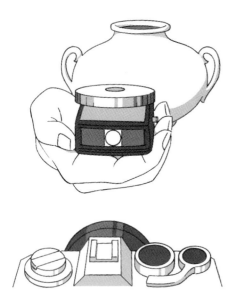

Figure 6.2
An incident light reading measures the light that falls on the subject. To make an incident reading, the photographer stands in front of the subject and points the meter at the camera or main light source. The meter is not pointed toward the subject. Most meters require a special light-diffusing dome attachment to read incident light.

Gray Card

Both reflective and incident meters can be easily fooled if there is an unusual distribution in the tones of a subject. For this reason it is often desirable to ignore the subject completely and take your meter reading from an 18 percent gray card (as found in the back of this book). The gray card provides a neutral surface of unvarying tone that is only influenced by changes in illumination. In this respect, it is like an incident reading, only it is measured by reflective light. The gray card is designed to reflect all visible wavelengths of light equally, in neutral color, and to reflect about 18 percent of the light striking it. To obtain accurate results, be certain the gray card is clean and not bent. Position the gray card to avoid highlight or shadow emphasis. Point your reflective meter to fill as much of the gray card as possible; avoid casting any shadows in the area being metered.

In color photography, the gray card can be photographed in the same light as the subject and included at the edge of the frame or on a separate exposure. This can provide a standard neutral reference guide for evaluating the filtration requirements when making prints or additional slides or in photomechanical reproduction. It is a popular misconception that the gray card represents the average reflectance of an ideal subject, for the average reflectance of a normal subject is about 9 percent.

Basic In-Camera Metering Systems

There are five basic metering systems currently in use (figure 6.3).

The Center-Weighted System

The center-weighted system has its light-sensitive cell located in the back of the pentaprism, providing the center of the frame with the greatest sensitivity to light. This sensitivity decreases toward the bottom and top of the frame.

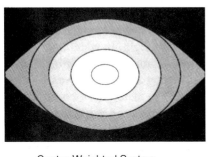

Center-Weighted System

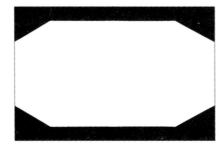

Overall System

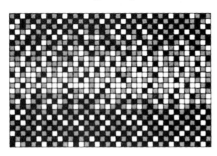

Averaging System

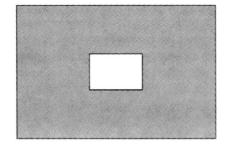

Spot System

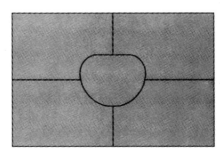

Matrix System

Figure 6.3
How five basic in-camera metering system patterns are set up to determine exposure.

The Overall System

In the overall system the cells read the entire frame as it is reflected from the shutter curtain or the film. It tends to provide a bias of sensitivity toward the center of the frame.

The Averaging System

The averaging system has two cells in the pentaprism that read different parts of the frame. Their readings are averaged together with a bias towards the center of the picture area.

The Spot System

The spot system measures light from a small zone in the center of the frame. It requires care and skill to make use of the spot. It must be pointed at crucial areas of detail in the picture to obtain proper results. Averaging is often employed when working with a spot meter. For instance, the light is measured in the key shadow and highlight areas, and then these two readings are combined and averaged to get the exposure. When it is not practical for the photographer to get up close to measure the light on a subject, as with a distant landscape, a sporting event, or an animal in the wild, the spot meter has the advantage of being able to measure the light from any number of key areas of the scene from a distance.

Matrix Metering

Many modern 35-mm cameras have computer-assisted matrix metering. With this feature, the meter is programmed to recognize common lighting situations and adjust the exposure accordingly. For example, the Nikon F4S divides the scene into five zones and compares the scene being metered to the light patterns from 100,000 photographs in its memory. It switches automatically between sensitivity patterns, depending on whether the camera is held horizontally or vertically. It also chooses between four different meter programs depending on the light: center-weighted, highlight- or shadow-biased, and a five-segment average.

Common Metering Problems

Having a TTL metering system does not guarantee good exposures. Unusual lighting conditions can still easily fool the meter. The most common errors occur when the subject is not in the main area that the system is reading, if there is a very dark or light place in the metered area, if the quality of the light is not even and is striking the subject from the front, or if the light is overly bright or dim. Knowing which type of metering system the camera uses allows the photographer to frame the proper areas within the metered zone to get the desired outcome.

How the Meter Gets Fooled

Scenes containing large amounts of light areas, such as fog, sand, snow, or white walls, give a meter reading that causes underexposure because the meter is fooled by the overall brightness of the scene. Additional exposure of between one and two f-stops is needed to correct the meter error.

Scenes with a great deal of dark shadow produce overexposures. This happens because the meter is designed to reproduce an 18 percent gray under all conditions. If the major tones are darker or lighter the exposure will not be accurate and must be corrected by the photographer. A reduction of one to two f-stops is needed for dark subjects. An incident reading performs well in these situations because it is unaffected by any tonal differences within the subject (figure 6.4). Bracketing is a good idea in both these situations.

Bracketing

Bracketing is done by first making what is believed to be the correct exposure. Then an exposure 1/2 f-stop under that exposure and finally one more exposure 1/2 f-stop over the original exposure, totaling three exposures of the scene, are made. In tricky lighting situations, bracket two 1/2 f-stops in each direction (over- and underexposure) for a total of five exposures of the scene. With slide film it is often better to bracket in 1/3 f-stops because a more accurate exposure is needed than with negative film.

Do not be afraid to use a few more frames of film. Bracketing can help the photographer gain a basic understanding of the relationship between light and exposure. Analyze and learn from the results so next time a similar situation is encountered, bracketing will not be necessary.

Handheld Meters

When acquiring a handheld meter be certain it can read both reflected and incident light. Incident light readings are accomplished by fitting a light-diffusing attachment over the meter's cell. The meter can then be pointed at the light source rather than at the subject. Since it measures the light falling on the subject and not the light reflected by the subject, the incident reading is useful in contrasty light or when a scene has a large variation in tonal values (figure 6.4).

Handheld spot meters are also available. As with the in-camera spot system, the main danger of using the spot meter is it reads such a tiny area that taking a reading from the wrong place can easily throw off the entire exposure. For this reason the spot meter should be used with care until confidence and understanding is gained of how and where to meter. Some handheld meters have attachments that allow them to make a spot reading.

Manual Override

Cameras that have fully automatic exposure systems without a manual override reduce the photographer's options. The machine decides how the picture should look, how much depth of field it should have, and whether to stop the action or to blur it. If you only have access to an automatic camera, see if it can be fooled by adjusting the shutter speeds, altering the film-speed setting, or using the back-light control to change your lens aperture. Learn to control the machine and not be its prisoner.

Batteries

Most in-camera meters are powered by small silver-oxide or lithium batteries. They tend to fail without much warning, so carry spare batteries when you go out to photograph. Older mercury cell equipment can be run with newly designed zinc-air batteries (see section on batteries in chapter 17).

Basic Methods of Reading the Light

The Brightness Range of the Subject

The brightness range of a subject (the difference in the number of f-stops between the key highlight and key shadow area of a scene) is one way to determine exposure. The brightness range method can be divided into four broad categories: diffused, even, or flat light; average bright daylight with no extreme highlights or shadows; brilliant, contrasty, direct sunlight; and dim light.

Diffused Light 3 f

Overcast days offer an even, diffused quality of light. Colors appear muted, quiet, and subdued. Both highlights and shadows are minimal (figure 6.5). Whenever the scene is metered, the reading usually remains within a range of three f-stops. The apparent brightness range and contrast can be increased through overexposure.

Average Daylight 7 f range

In a scene of average bright daylight the colors look more saturated, the contrast is more distinct, the highlights are

Figure 6.4
Scenes containing larger areas of dark shadows or bright highlights can easily fool the meter. In this scene of great contrast, Noble used a handheld meter to take an incident light reading to help determine the exposure he wanted so the highlight areas would retain maximum detail.

© Peter Noble. *Pushkar Morning Shave*, 1990. 24 × 36 cm. Chromogenic color transparency.

Figure 6.5

Under diffused light, colors appear to be muted and the difference between highlights and shadows are minimal. Trolinger's work not only shows the aftereffects of the great fire in Yellowstone National Park but reveals how even in color the combination of light and subject can produce a minimalist color palette—black-and-white in color.

© Charlotte Trolinger. *Swan Lake Flats.* Yellowstone National Park, September 11, 1988. 11 × 14 inches. Chromogenic color print.

brighter, and the shadows are darker with good detail in both areas (figure 6.6). Meter reading from different parts of the scene may reveal a range of about seven f-stops. Care must be given to where meter readings are taken. If the subject is in direct sunlight and the meter in the shadow, overexposure of the subject is the result.

Brilliant Sunlight

Brilliant, direct sunlight causes the deepest color saturation while also producing conditions of maximum contrast (figure 6.7). The exposure range can be twelve f-stops or greater, which stretches or surpasses the ability of the film to record the scene.

These conditions result in black shadows and bright highlights. Color separation is at its greatest; white appears at its purest. Determining which areas to base the meter reading on is critical for obtaining the desired results. These effects can be compounded when photographing reflections off glass, polished metal, or water. Selective exposure techniques such as averaging, use of incident light, or spot reading may be

needed (see section on unusual lighting conditions later in this chapter).

Dim Light

Dim natural light taxes the ability of the film to record the necessary color and detail of the scene (figure 6.8). Colors can be flat and monochromatic and contrast is often problematic. Contrast can be extreme when artificial light sources are included within the scene. Contrast can also be lacking, with details often difficult to determine. Low levels of light mean long exposures, a tripod, a high-speed film, or

Figure 6.6

In average bright daylight, contrast is greater, colors are more saturated, and there is good detail in both key shadow and highlight areas. Because all the dishes in this area faced the southeast, and Freeman didn't want any shadows on the satellite dishes, he photographed only in the late afternoon. Freeman said the dishes opened up the communications frontier for rural areas. "It makes me think of when I was a kid in Chicago, in 1948. Our family had the first television set on the block and every Sunday night there'd be twenty people from the neighborhood sitting in our living room, watching 'Ed Sullivan.' That's what dishes have done for the country."

© Roger Freeman. *Satellite Dish Series: Allegeny County, NY,* 1984–85. 20 × 24 inches. Chromogenic color print.

Figure 6.7

In brilliant sunlight, contrast and color saturation are at their maximum. The exposure must be carefully thought out so the needed detail is produced in the key subject areas.

© Eduardo Del Vaile and Mirta Gómez. *Ixtlan de los Hervores, Mexico,* 1989. 11 3/4 × 17 1/2 inches. Chromogenic color print.

Figure 6.8

Dim light can strain a film's ability to record the necessary color and detail. Colors can appear monochromatic and the contrast range is often extreme, with either not enough contrast or too much contrast. Artificial light sources can supply unusual and/or dramatic effects.

© Jan Staller. *Taxi, New York City*, 1985. 15 × 15 inches. Chromogenic color print. Courtesy of Lieberman and Saul Gallery, New York.

amounts of either dark or light tones can give incorrect information if the exposure is based on a single reading (figure 6.10). When making a picture of a general outdoor scene, the correct exposure can be achieved by taking two readings and then averaging them. For example, you are photographing a landscape, it is late in the day, the sky is brighter than the ground, and detail needs to be retained in both areas. First meter a critical highlight area (sky) in which detail is required. Let's say the reading is f/16 at 1/250 second. If the exposure was made at this setting, the sky would be rich and deep, but the ground detail would be lost and might appear simply as a vast black area. Now meter off a key area in the shadow area of the ground. Say it is f/5.6 at 1/250 second. This would provide an excellent rendition of the ground, but the sky would be overexposed and appear white, completely desaturated of color, and with no discernible detail. To get an average reading, take the meter reading of the highlight (sky) and the shadow (ground) and halve the f-stop difference between the two readings. In this case, an average reading would be about f/8½ at 1/250 second. It is permissible to set the aperture in between the click stops with most cameras. The final result is a compromise of the two situations, with acceptable detail and color saturation in each area.

When working with negative film, it is often possible to take the meter reading from the ground, let the sky overexpose, and correct by burning it in when a print is made.

If the subject that is being photographed is either a great deal darker or lighter than the background, such as a dark-skinned person against a white background or a fair-skinned person against a black background, averaging will not provide good results. If there is more than a five f-stop range between the highlight and shadow areas, there will be an unacceptable loss of detail in both areas. In a case like this, let the background go or use additional lighting techniques such as flash fill to compensate for the difference.

additional lighting are often required to make the picture.

Metering for the Subject

Metering for the subject is another way to determine proper exposure. When in doubt about where to take an exposure reading, decide what the subject is in the picture and take a reflected reading from it (figure 6.9). For instance, when making a portrait, go up to the subject and take the meter reading directly from the face, open up one f-stop for fair skin or close down one f-stop for dark complexions, and then return to

the chosen camera position. When photographing a landscape in diffused, even light, an overall meter reading can be made from the camera position. If the light is hard (not diffused) or directional, the camera meter can be pointed up, down, or sideways to emphasize the sky, the ground, the highlights, or the shadows. These readings can also be averaged.

Exposing for Tonal Variations

Exposing for tonal variations is another method that can be used in calculating the exposure. A scene that has large

Figure 6.9
When exposing for the subject, a reflective reading is made directly from the most important object in the scene. Proper detail is then retained where it is required and the meter is not fooled by areas of bright light or deep shadow. To make her circus series Saville used a handheld Nikon F with a 135-mm lens. The 200-speed negative film was intentionally overexposed for greater color saturation and shadow detail. Saville says, "I use slow shutter speeds and let the movement paint itself onto my film. . . . The use of quick shutter speeds, to freeze the movement, would artificially separate these performers from their actions, leaving them high and dry in an *instant* that never really existed for the spectator."

© Lynn Saville. *White Liberty Horses*, 1991. 16 × 20 inches. Chromogenic color print.

Basic Flash Fill

A basic flash-fill technique involves first taking an available-light meter reading of the scene, setting your camera's shutter to the correct flash synchronization speed, and then determining the f-stop. Now divide the exposure f-stop number into the guide number (GN) of your flash unit. The result is the number of feet you need to be from your subject. Shoot at the available-light meter reading with the flash at this distance. For example, the meter reads f/16 at a synchronization speed of 1/125. Your flash unit has a GN of 80. Divide 16 (f/16) into 80 (GN). The result is 5, the distance you need to be from the subject with an exposure of f/16 at 1/125.

A second flash-fill method is to set the camera to make a proper ambient light exposure, using the correct synchronization speed. Note the correct f-stop that is required. Position or adjust the flash unit to produce light that is the equivalent of one or two f-stops less exposure, depending on the desired effect. If the flash produces an amount of light equal to the original exposure, the shadow areas will be as bright as the directly lighted areas, and the modeling effect will be lost (see section on flash and slow shutter speed in chapter 20).

A third technique is to determine the correct ambient light exposure at the proper flash synchronization speed and then vary the output of the flash by using the different power setting (half- or quarter-power) so the amount of flashlight is correct for the subject-to-flash distance. If the flash does not have a power setting, the output can be reduced by putting a diffuser or neutral density filter in front of the flash head.

Figure 6.10
Twilight, when this image was made, can pose exposure difficulties because at this time scenes often contain large amounts of dark and/or light areas. Exposing for tonal variations is one way to arrive at the correct exposure. Durante says he is interested in documenting the "social iconography" that defines our society. "This image of a cowboy's shadow cast on the gate of a stock pen accentuates the role of the cowboy in American cultural myth (i.e., the Marlboro Man), as a symbol—a faceless Western everyman."

© Alfred Durante. *Gladewater, TX,* 1989. 11 × 17 inches. Chromogenic color print.

You can also improvise by putting a clean white handkerchief in front of the flash head; each layer of cloth reduces the output by about one f-stop. Most newer dedicated (designed to function with a particular camera) flash units can make automatic flash-fill exposures. Flash fill can also be employed selectively to provide additional illumination or with filters to alter the color of specific areas in the scene (figure 6.11).

Red Eye

When photographing any living being with a flash unit attached to the camera or with a ringlight around the lens, red eye can happen. If your subject looks directly at the camera, and the light is next to the lens axis, light passes directly into the pupils of your subject's eyes and is strongly reflected back to the camera. With color film, this is seen as a pink or red spot in the center of the eye because the light illuminates the blood vessels in the retina of the eye. If this effect is not desired, try one of the following: have the subject look to one side of the camera, bounce the flash light, or move the flash unit some distance (6 inches or more) from the lens axis. This can be done by elevating the flash on a commercially available extender post or by getting a long flash synchronization cord and holding the unit away from the camera with one hand.

Figure 6.11

Colburn states: "With the exploration of small town events it becomes increasingly important to me to establish the sense of inclusion and membership that forms the structure of these events. The nature of the event and the context in which they occur presents an opportunity to make images that celebrate shared values and a sense of identity and membership. The images should be seen in contrast to the many exclusive experiences of contemporary life. These exclusive experiences reinforce the perception that we are, at best, members of a subgroup never to be a part of the whole. My photographs are premised on what we hold in common." Fill flash was used in the early evening light to give a theatrical look, to provide more detail on the subjects, and to separate them from the background. The negative film was also overexposed one f-stop to give extra color saturation.

© Richard Colburn. *Mr. and Mrs. Nevis Pageant, Muskie Days, Nevis MN*, 1990. 18 1/4 × 18 1/4 inches. Chromogenic color print.

Unusual Lighting Conditions

Unusual lighting conditions cause exposure problems: uneven light, light hitting the subject from a strange angle, backlight, glare and reflections, areas with large highlights, or shadows such as inside doorways and windows. The wide range of tones in such scenes is often greater than the ability of the film to record them. The photographer must decide what is important to record and how to get it done.

Subject in Shadow

When the subject is in shadow, decide what is the most important area of the picture, which colors have the most interest, and what details need to be seen. If the subject is in shadow, take a reflected meter reading from the most important shadow region. This provides the correct information for that key area. Other areas, mainly the highlights, will experience a loss of color saturation and detail due to overexposure, which can be corrected by burning in these areas when the print is made (figure 6.12). At other times, there may be a key highlight striking the subject in shadow. The exposure can be made based on the highlight reading, letting the remainder of the subject fall into obscurity. Additional light, by means of flash and/or reflective fill-cards can be used to put more illumination on the subject.

Subject in Bright Light

Should the main point of interest be in a bright area, take a reflected reading from the key highlight area or use an incident reading. A contrasty subject dealt with in this fashion provides dramatic, rich, and saturated color along with good detail in these bright areas (figure 6.13). The shadows will lack detail and not provide much visual information. Anything that is backlit becomes a silhouette with no detail at all under these circumstances.

Alternative Solutions

If it is not acceptable to lose the details in the shadows, there are other alternatives. These include averaging the reflective reading, bracketing, using additional lighting techniques such as flash fill, or combining both a reflective and an incident reading. This last method is done by taking an incident reading directed toward the camera of the light striking the subject. This reading is not affected by extreme highlights. Then take a reflected reading with the meter aimed at the key subject area. Now average the two and bracket for insurance. When in doubt, the best insurance is to bracket.

Figure 6.12

A proper exposure can be calculated when the subject is in shadow by taking a reflective reading from the key area from which detail needs to be retained. Other parts of the picture can experience loss of color saturation and detail. To make this photograph a slide image of a model was projected onto a rear projection screen. A model then positioned herself to create a silhouette, and the image was photographed from the front of the projection screen.

© Joyce Roetter. *Personal Shadow.* 1989. 24 × 36 cm. Chromogenic color transparency.

Reciprocity

What is the reciprocity law? It is the theoretical relationship between the length of exposure and the intensity of light. It states that an increase in one is balanced by a decrease in the other. For example, doubling the light intensity should be balanced exactly by halving the exposure time. In practical terms, this means that if you meter a scene and calculate the exposure to be f/8 at 1/250 second, you could obtain the same exposure by doubling your f-stop opening and cutting your exposure time in half. Thus, shooting at

f/5.6 at 1/500 second should produce the same results as shooting at f/8 at 1/250. You could also double your exposure time and cut your f-stop in half, so that shooting at 1/125 second at f/11 is the same as shooting at 1/250 second at f/8. Table 6.2 shows some of the theoretical exposures that would work the same if your exposure was f/8 at 1/250 second.

Reciprocity Law Failure

Unfortunately, the reciprocity law does not hold true in every situation. When we make either very long or very brief

• T A B L E 6 . 2 •

Theoretical Exposure Equivalents (based on a starting exposure of f/8 at 1/250 second)

f-stop	Time in Seconds
f/16	1/60
f/11	1/125
f/8*	1/250*
f/5.6	1/500
f/4	1/1,000

*Starting exposure.

exposures, reciprocity failure can take place. Depending on the type of film used, exposures at about 1/5 second or longer and those faster than 1/10,000

flash goes faster than 1/50,000

second begin to show the effects of reciprocity failure. At about 1 second or longer, the normal ratio of aperture and shutter speed underexposes the film. Since only specialized cameras are capable of speeds higher than 1/10,000 second, most photographers do not need to worry about high-speed reciprocity failure. Some electronic flash units, when set on fractional power, can achieve exposures that are brief enough to cause reciprocity failure. Films such as Fuji Provia claim no exposure correction is necessary for exposures between 1/4,000 and 16 seconds. Check the manufacturer's suggested guidelines to keep up with the rapid changes in film technology.

Reciprocity Failure and Its Effect on Color Materials

With black-and-white film we can simply increase the exposure time to compensate for the slow reaction time and avoid underexposure of the film. The problem with color materials is that the three emulsion layers do not respond to the reciprocity effect in the same manner. This can produce a shift in the color balance of the film or paper. If you wish to correct for reciprocity failure, follow the exposure and filtering instructions provided with the film or paper. These are merely starting points, and you must experiment to discover what works best in a particular situation.

The problem with filtering is that by adding filters you make the exposure even longer, which in turn can cause the reciprocity effect to be even more pronounced. When using a single lens reflex (SLR) camera the filters add density, which can make viewing and focusing more difficult in a dimly lit situation.

Figure 6.13
When the subject is in bright light, exposure can be determined by taking a reflective reading from the key highlight area, causing a loss of detail in the shadows. If this is not acceptable, try one of the alternative solutions. An incident reading can often be used in this situation to provide an acceptable exposure.

© Eduardo Del Valle and Mirta Gómez. *Merida, Mexico*, 1989. 16 × 10 3/4 inches. Chromogenic color print.

Figure 6.14

Reciprocity failure creates the intense colors found in Zaitz's images. He has this to say about his work: "The technique I use for transforming my landscapes is time. On the average each exposure is 1 hour long, with some going 2 1/2 hours. I never use any filters or lighting equipment with colored gels. All the light sources were different types of ambient street light mixing with the slowly changing early morning light."

© Dan Zaitz. *Places I've Dreamed of #18*, n.d. 16 × 20 inches. Chromogenic color print.

Common Reciprocity Failure Situations

Some typical times that you will run into reciprocity problems are before sunrise, after sunset, at night, and in dimly lit interiors. Fortunately, the quality of light at these different times tends to be strange. That is, there is no standard by which we can judge whether or not you have succeeded in producing an acceptable color balance. Accurate color does not always mean good color. At times like these you may want to take a chance that the combination of light and reciprocity shift will work in your favor to create an unusual color balance that gives your picture impact that would be impossible to achieve in any other fashion (figure 6.14). Apply what you have learned from this experience to future situations.

<hr>

· ASSIGNMENT ·

Keep Making Photographs

Do not let reciprocity law failure stop you from making pictures. Try some exposures with the recommended filters, some with nonrecommended filters, and others with no filters at all. Be sure to bracket your exposures to ensure that you get acceptable results. Film is your least expensive resource. Do not be afraid to use it. If that extra roll produces a satisfying result, you won't be thinking of the extra time or expense; you will be happy that you produced something good. It is very difficult to be a photographer if you do not expose film. Do not expect every frame to be a work of art. Ansel Adams is reported to have said he was happy if he could produce twelve good photographs in a year.

Color Transparency Film

© Michael W. Davidson.
Mount Franklin (El Paseo del Norte), 1990.
24 x 36 cm.
Chromogenic color transparency.
In this photomicrograph vitamin C crystallites represent the plants, sugar xanthan was used as mountains,
a blue filter portrays the sky, defocused Cibachrome bleach crystallites are the clouds.
Courtesy of the Institute of Molecular Biophysics,
Center for Materials Research and Technology (MARTECH),
The Florida State University,
Tallahassee, FL.

Characteristics of Color Transparency Film

Advantages

Color transparencies, also known as color slides, are positives that are made on reversal film. Each image you look at on transparency film is the original piece of film that was exposed in the camera. What you see is what you get. Prints, on the other hand, are second-generation images, made by enlarging a negative onto color printing paper. The old rule that says the fewer generations we have to go through for a final image the better the quality holds true. Slides are looked at by transmitted light that passes through the image only one time. Prints are seen by light that is reflected from them. The light bounces off the base support of the print and passes through the image in the emulsion twice, coming and going. This effect doubles the density, which in turn reduces what can be seen within the print itself. Due to this "double density effect," slides have certain advantages over prints made from negatives, including the sharpest grain structure, maximum color separation, the best color saturation (intensity), and more subtlety in color and detail.

The viewer can distinguish a wider tonal range because the slides are viewed by transmitted light. A high-contrast slide image can have a "readable" tonal range, from the whitest white to blackest black, of about 400:1 when projected, and even more when viewed directly. This ratio is an indicator of how well the detail and color saturation are clearly separated in the key highlight and key shadow areas. A color print viewed in normal room light can have a tonal range of about 100:1. It is usually closer to 85:1 due to light scattering by the surface of the print. It is said that an "average" daylight scene has a brightness range of 160:1 or higher. This means that slide film can do a superior job of capturing a fuller range of tones in many situations.

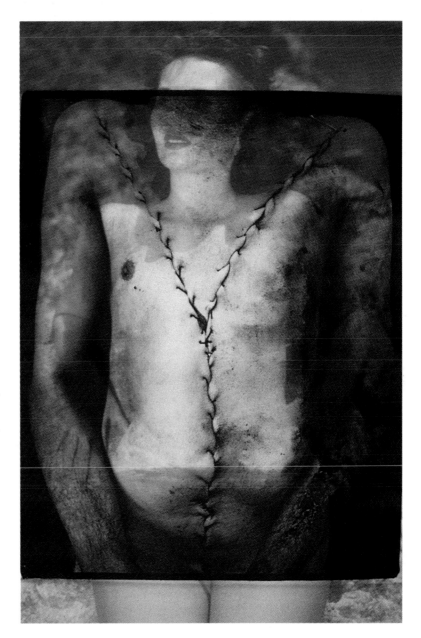

Silverthorne takes advantage of the ability of transparency film to let the imagemaker instantly see what happens when two pieces of film are sandwiched together. Working on the theme of death and the body, Silverthorne examines the thin line that separates Eros and Thanatos. His work often simultaneously juxtaposes attraction and beauty with the forbidden and the repulsive. In this dialogue between life and death, Silverthorne has stated: "I wanted to show that there was no way around this incident of death."

© Jeffrey Silverthorne. *Mother and Father,* 1988. 24 x 20 inches. Dye-destruction print. Courtesy of the Visual Studies Workshop Gallery, Rochester, NY.

Transparency film's wider tonal range translates into higher contrast. This contrast gives the slide film increased color saturation, most noticeable in the slower films, and helps its ability to differentiate details in the highlight areas. This is most noticeable in the difference between diffuse and specular highlights, the classic example being a white flower with water droplets. The white petals reflect light in all directions (diffused highlights), while the water droplets directly reflect light as a bright catchlight (specular highlights). Slide film clearly shows the difference between the two; in a print the subtlety of the separation can be lost.

Generally, transparency film is exposed to produce acceptable detail in the key highlight areas of a scene. Both color saturation (vividness) and density increase proportionately with less exposure. For this reason many photographers intentionally underexpose their slide film by changing the manufacturer's standard ISO (International Standards Organization) rating. For example, a film rated at ISO 64 could be modified in the range of ISO 80 to 120. Experimentation by bracketing in 1/3 or 1/2 f-stops is desired.

The processing of slide film provides the user with a finished product without any additional steps, and because no printing is involved in producing the final image, slide film can be processed at home without a great deal of specialized equipment. Their small size makes transparencies easier to sort, index, and store. The cost per final image is between 20 and 30 percent less than with negative film. Transparencies are the choice for photographic reproduction, because printers can make color separations directly from them. They are also ideal for direct digtial translation via a film scanner.

Disadvantages of Transparencies

Despite their good points, slides do have their disadvantages. They are small and difficult to see; generally a projector and a screen are required for proper viewing. Since the final image is contained on the film base itself, each slide is unique and must be handled with care to prevent damage when being viewed. Both of these characteristics can make slides less convenient to use than prints.

Unlike negative film, transparencies can only be manipulated slightly through development to effectively alter the range of contrast. This is because the color balance of the film is directly affected by development. The biggest disadvantage to someone who is learning to work in color is that there is no second chance to make corrections with slides as there is when making a print. Transparency film has a much narrower exposure latitude than negative film. An exposure error of even a 1/2 f-stop can ruin

Images made on transparency film can be directly translated into digital form on a scanner. Weintraub developed an approach of layering image fragments for a series dealing with artificial light and vernacular elements of urban architecture. "For me, digital imaging is a means to control image processing, so that the image can be made totally mutable and plastic. The process I use for repeated layering and dissolves is directly connected to my intent to develop an image that evokes a complex architectural space, and which conveys the ambiguous and sometimes paradoxical multiplicity of messages of the urban environment . . . . The unnatural and artificial color spectrum, while 'cheerful' and engaging, underlines a troubling separation from nature and accentuates the desolation of the made environment."

© Annette Weintraub. *Night Sight,* 1993. 31 x 47 inches. Tiled phase-change prints.

the picture since both the color and density of the completed picture are determined by exposure. It is possible to make corrections by recopying the slide, but this adds contrast and takes away the initial advantages of slide film.

If a print is made from a slide via an internegative, there are twice as many color and tonal distortions to deal with as when working with negative film. Prints made through a direct-positive process, such as ILFOCHROME Classic, can suffer from color distortion due to the lack of a corrective mask on the slide film. These prints also tend to be more contrasty than normal and may require a mask to print correctly (see chapter 11).

How Transparency Film Works

Transparency film makes a positive, rather than a negative, image. The film uses the "tripack" structure, a sandwich of three gelatin layers that contain light-sensitive silver halides. During exposure,

each layer records one of the primary colors of light. White light, which is a mixture of blue, green, and red, creates a latent image on all three layers. Other colors formed by mixing the light make latent images only in those areas that are sensitive to those colors. For instance, yellow, which is a mixture of green and red, makes a latent image only in the green and red layers. It is not recorded by the blue layer. Imagine a large red ball. In the final picture, it appears red because the dyes of the colors complementary to blue and green were formed in two layers of the film during development. When the slide is viewed in white light, the blue and green are subtracted from the light, which leaves only red to be seen. Slide film, unlike negative film, has no color mask to correct inherent imperfections of the green-sensitive and red-sensitive layers of the film.

Recent technical advances in color negative films are being applied to slide material. For example, Fuji's Provia 100 Professional film contains at least three sublayers in each of its three color-sensitive emulsion layers having different sizes and shapes of silver halide crystals to enhance color quality and improve gradation and tonal rendition. Provia also is the first slide film to use developer inhibitor releasing couplers (DIRs). These compounds work during first development to boost saturation, control contrast, and improve sharpness.

Processing

Almost all the current color transparency films make use of a standard chromogenic development process (E-6) to produce the cyan, magenta, and yellow dyes in their three-layer emulsion structure.

In chromogenic development the first step is similar to black-and-white processing. A silver-grain negative image is developed in each of the layers of the emulsion. The silver appears where the film has been struck by light. White light affects all three layers, while red, for example, forms silver only in the red-sensitive layer. No colored dye is formed during this stage of the process.

Next, the first development is halted and the film is "fogged" either through chemical action or exposure to light so that the silver grains can be formed throughout all layers of the emulsion.

During color development the remaining silver is developed and the subtractive primary dyes are produced in the emulsion layers in proportion to the amount of silver that is formed. These dyes make up the final image. At this stage the film looks black because it has metallic silver in all the emulsion layers and color dyes in many places.

To be able to see the dye-positive image, the film has to be bleached. The prebleach, which replaces the older conditioner step, contains agents that enhance image stability. It contains only trace amounts of formaldehyde, thus reducing the possibility of user contact with free formaldehyde. The bleach changes all silver into silver halide crystals. The fixer then removes all the silver halides from the film, leaving

only the dye-positive image. Some processes combine the bleach and the fix into one step.

The wash takes away the remaining fixer. The final rinse is the last step, which is mainly a wetting agent used to reduce water spotting and prompt even film drying. The final rinse replaces the old stabilizer step and is free of formaldehyde. Its concentration can be varied to accommodate various drying conditions.

Temperature Control

All color processes are extremely sensitive to time, temperature, and agitation. New technical advances, such as multi-layered coating used to create up to seventeen-layer emulsions, mean the latest generation of slide films are even more "process sensitive" than their predecessors. Time and temperature are critical to obtain correct color balance and density. For optimum results, you must maintain the correct range of temperatures throughout the process. If this is not possible, have a professional lab develop the film.

In the Kodak E-6 process, the developing steps are the most sensitive. Tolerances for consistent results follow:

First Developer
Time: plus/minus 5 seconds
Temperature: plus/minus 0.5°F (0.3°C)

Color Developer
Time: plus/minus 15 seconds
Temperature: plus/minus 1.1°F (0.6°C)

Water Bath

To maintain these critical temperatures, a water bath is recommended. Fill a deep tray or pail with water so that it is equal to the depth of the solution in the storage containers. Bring the water temperature slightly above the actual processing temperature (100.5°F, or 38°C) to allow for cooling due to ambient room temperature. Allow the containers and loaded film tank to stand in the water until they reach operating levels.

Measure the temperature inside the solution containers without having the thermometer touch the container wall. Be certain the thermometer is accurate. When not agitating, keep the processing tank in the water bath. Keep the wash temperature the same as the bleach and fixer.

Handling and Agitation

Load film in total darkness. Handle the film only by its edges and ends. Use a light-tight processing tank so that processing can be done under room light.

Proper agitation is crucial with all color processing. Too little or too much agitation causes uneven or unusual color balance and/or density effects in the processing of the film. Proper agitation in the developer is a must. It is done by inverting the tank, rotating the tank, or rotating the reels. Follow agitation instructions based on the type of tank used. If only one roll of film is being processed in a multireel tank, place the loaded reel in the bottom and fill the tank with the empty reels.

Stainless steel tanks and reels are recommended because they can be inverted, offer a clean and even agitation pattern, do not absorb chemicals, are easy to clean, and are durable. However, they are more expensive, initially harder to load, and require practice to correctly get the film put onto the reel.

Almost all contemporary transparency color films can be developed in one standard process called E-6 (table 7.1). To determine whether a film can be developed by this method, simply read the label on the film box or cassette.

Allow film to hang and naturally air dry, undisturbed, in a dust-free environment. The final rinse can be mixed with distilled water. Shake the loaded film reel over the sink to break the surface tension. This will permit the final rinse to flow freely and run to the lower end of the hanging film. A lint-free, disposable paper towel, such as a Photo-Wipe, can be gently used on the nonemulsion side of the film.

Troubleshooting E-6

Table 7.2 lists some common E-6 processing problems, their probable cause, and possible corrective actions. Follow all safety recommendations when handling chemicals.

Processing Adjustments for ISO

Most E-6 process films can be exposed at different speeds and still produce acceptable results (figure 7.1) if the first developer time is adjusted to compensate (table 7.3). Use the standard times for all other solutions. Adjustments in processing can allow film exposed at the wrong ISO rating to be saved. However, when film is push processed it can suffer a color balance shift, a change in contrast, and a decrease in exposure latitude. Highest quality is achieved when normal speed rating and processing are observed.

Special Processing

The majority of transparency films, such as Agfachrome, Ektachrome, and Fujichrome, can be processed at most laboratories or by yourself. The quality of these laboratories varies tremendously. Check them out before giving them any important work to do. Some films, notably Kodachrome, have to be returned to the manufacturer or a major laboratory to be processed. This is because the dye couplers are not found in the emulsion of these films but in the processing chemicals. This process (K-14) is very exacting and is carried out by expensive machinery. Processing kits for Kodachrome are not available to the general public (figure 7.2).

Brands

Transparency film is available in many brands and in different speed ranges. Each manufacturer uses its own dyes, yielding noticeable variations in the colors produced. Certain brands emphasize distinctive colors; others may have an overall cool (blue) or warm (red and yellow) bias. Brands also differ in their contrast, grain structure,

· **TABLE 7.1** ·

Kodak E-6 Process

Step	Time in Minutes*	Temperature (°F)†
The First Three Steps Must Be Carried out in Total Darkness		
First developer	6‡ (1) and (2)	100.4 +/−0.5
Wash	2	92 to 102
Reversal bath	2	92 to 102
The Remaining Steps Can Be Carried out in Room Light		
Color developer	6	100.4 +/−2
PreBleach	2	92 to 102
Bleach	7	92 to 102
Fixer	4	92 to 102
Wash	6	92 to 102
Final Rinse	1	92 to 102
Dry	as needed	up to 140

Note: Before beginning to process, read and follow all manufacturer's warning, mixing, and disposal instructions to ensure your health and that of the environment.
*All steps include a 10 second drain time.
†For best results, keep all the temperatures as close to 100° F as possible.
‡Development time changes depending on the number of rolls that have been processed. Check the capacity of the solutions with the instructions. Mixed solutions have a limited life span. Follow manufacturer's recommendations for storage and useful time limits of all solutions. Times will also change when film is processed in a rotary processor.
(1) *Initial Agitation*: For all solutions, tap tank on a 45-degree angle to dislodge any air bubbles. No further agitation is needed in the reversal bath, prebleach, or final rinse.
(2) *Additional Agitation*: Subsequent agitation is required in all other solutions. After tapping the tank, agitate by slowly turning the tank upside down and then right side up for the first 15 seconds. For the remaining time of each step, let the tank rest for 25 seconds and then agitate for 5 seconds. Keep the tank in a water-tempering bath to maintain the temperatures for both first and color developers.
    With noninvertible tanks, which cannot be turned upside down, tap the tank on 45-degree angle to remove air bubbles, and rotate the reels at indicated times to achieve proper agitation.

saturation, and overall sharpness. Be aware that different lenses, especially older lenses, deliver distinct color rendering. New multi-layer coating techniques allow modern lenses to provide a greater standardized color response. Since these characteristics cannot be compensated for during a secondary step like printing, it is important that the photographer choose a transparency film whose bias fits both the aesthetic and technical concerns of the situation.

The manufacturers have been busy making changes in almost every film currently on the market. For this reason, it is futile to attempt to describe the characteristics of each film because this information becomes rapidly outdated. Contact the major film manufacturers (table 7.4) and ask for brochures on their current products. The only way to keep up is to use the different films and evaluate the results for yourself. You can read test reports and talk with other photographers, but choosing a film is a highly personal matter. Experience is the best guide. Try different films in noncritical situations to

learn their strong and weak points. After some experimentation you will most likely discover that there is one type of film you prefer. It is worth the time to work with one film and learn its personality, because this will be helpful in obtaining consistent and pleasing results.

· **ASSIGNMENT** ·

Differences in Films

Shoot a different brand of film than you have used before and then answer the following questions: What differences do you notice when you compare this film to what you had previously used? Look at the color balance. Is it warmer or cooler? Is the color saturation similar? What about the contrast? Is it higher or lower? Are the grain pattern and structure the same? Compare flesh, neutral, and white tones to see how they differ. Which film do you prefer? Why? Is there a time when you would prefer to use one of these films instead of the other? Why?

· TABLE 7.2 ·

E-6 Troubleshooting Guide

Problem	Cause and Correction
Improper color balance	Solution contamination. Clean all equipment thoroughly. Organize and label solutions to ensure proper sequencing.
Overall blue color cast	Improper color developer mixing or incorrect color developer alkalinity (pH). Use reverse-osmosis treated water or add 1 Ml/L of sodium hydroxide per 5 units more yellow wanted in color balance (equivalent to about a CC05Y filter). Be sure to adhere to safety rules for working with sodium hydroxide.
Green shadows	Exhausted reversal bath. Replace with fresh solution.
Overall green color cast	Reversal bath omitted.
Red specks	Improper bleaching. Rebleach in fresh solution.
Overall red cast	Insufficient bleach aeration. Rebleach with vigorous agitation.
Overall yellow color cast	Improper color developer mixing or incorrect color developer alkalinity (pH). Use reverse-osmosis treated water or add 1 Ml/L of sulfuric acid per each 5 units more blue wanted in color balance (equivalent to a CC05B filter). Follow all safety rules when handling sulfuric acid.
Yellow or muddy highlights	Exhausted fixer. Refix in fresh solution and repeat wash and final rinse steps.
Images appear both negative and positive or very light color	Developer exhausted. Replace with fresh solution. Color developer temperature too low. Check thermometer. Process at correct temperature.
Images too dark	Underexposed film. Check camera meter and review exposure methods. Or first developer time too short, temperature too low, or lack of proper agitation.
Images too light	Overexposed film. Check camera meter and review exposure methods. First developer time too long, temperature too high, overagitation. Color developer temperature too low.
Dirt, dust, and spots	Mix final rinse with distilled water. Hang in dust-free area and allow to air dry undisturbed. Gently wipe nonemulsion side of film with a soft, disposable, lint-free paper towel (such as Photo-Wipes).
Light crescents	Kinked film. Practice loading developing reels with unwanted film. Don't force film onto reels.
Streaks or blotches	Make sure film is properly loaded on the reel. Poor agitation. Follow correct agitation methods for each step.
Dyes fade after short time	Prebleach step skipped.

· TABLE 7.3 ·

Starting Points for First Developer Time Compensation

Camera Exposure* Time	First Developer in Minutes†
One stop overexposed	4
Normal exposure	6
One stop underexposed	8
Two stops underexposed	11½
Three stops underexposed	16

*Color slide film that is more than one f-stop overexposed or more than two f-stops underexposed will not deliver normal color balance or density.

† Time based on first roll in fresh solutions.

Figure 7.1

Most color slide films can be push processed one f-stop and still deliver acceptable results. Wanting to handhold the camera in a very low light situation, Lincoln pushed 1600 speed slide film to 3200. Her film was given additional time in the first developer to compensate (see table 7.3).

© M. L. Lincoln. *Waiting For the Subway*, 1990. 16 x 20 inches. Dye-destruction print.

Figure 7.2
Even though Kodachrome cannot be processed without expensive equipment, it has been a traditional favorite in terms of delivering maximum contrast and clear color separation, especially with photographers who do magazine work. According to Glassman this series of ordinary children in one small park in New York City is meant to examine aggressive play and question its implications in issues of war and peace. Kodachrome was selected for this project as a means of contrasting the brightly colored toys and clothes of childhood with the darkness of the action. Fill flash was employed to accentuate the colors, keep shadows around the face to a minimum, and give the series a uniform look. The print was produced from an internegative made from the slide.

© Carl Glassman. *Child's Play #6*, 1987. 14 1/2 x 22 inches. Chromogenic color print.

Film Speed

Each brand offers a selection of different film speeds. The speed, or light sensitivity, of a film is determined from a set of procedures established by the International Standards Organization (ISO). Films can be divided into four basic categories based on their speed: slow films have an ISO below 100, general-use films possess an ISO of between 100 and 200, fast films have an ISO of 200 to 400, and ultrafast films have an ISO of 400 or more.

In general, the slower the film the greater the color saturation, the tighter the grain structure, and the better the color contrast, all of which make the image appear sharper. Slower films also have less tolerance for exposure error. Faster films look grainier and do not have as much color contrast or saturation. They have a greater ability to handle small exposure errors and limited mixed lighting conditions. In low light conditions faster films are able to capture a greater variation in hue and tone than print film, by sacrificing grain and sharpness. (For a more detailed discussion of grain see section on brands, grain, and speed in chapter 8).

As the speed of a film increases there is a drop-off in quality (color rendition, grain, sharpness). These effects are much more noticeable in slide film than with print film. But ISO 400, print film shows a clear superiority. In the ISO 1000 to 1600 range print films have an overwhelming edge. This is because print films use ingredients such as developer inhibitor releasing (DIR) couplers to prevent overdevelopment and grain buildup. The DIR technology is now in use with some of the slow slide films, and we can expect to see improvements in the faster films in the next few years. Print film also uses integral masks, which are dyes that help to improve color saturation and cancel out unwanted color shifts.

Choose film with care so that it will work for your situation. Try not to get into the position of making the film fit the circumstances.

Amateur and Professional Films Compared

Both amateur and professional films have similar color quality, grain characteristics, image stability, and sharpness. The main difference is in the color balance of the films. As all color film ages, the characteristics of its color balance change.

An amateur photographer typically buys a few rolls of film at a time. The film might remain in the camera at various temperatures for months before it is processed. Allowances for this type of use are built into the film during manufacturing. For example, if a film's color balance shifts toward yellow as it ages, the color balance of the emulsion is made in the complementary direction, blue, to compensate. This allows time for the film to be shipped, stocked, and sit in the camera. By the time the film is finally shot and processed its color balance should still be close to optimum.

Professional films are manufactured at their optimum point for accurate color balance and consistent speed. These films are designed for refrigerated storage by both the dealer and user. They should be processed immediately after exposure.

Lighting Conditions: Using Daylight, Tungsten, and Type A Films

The color performance of a film varies depending on the lighting conditions in which it is used. Slide materials work best when properly matched to the type of light under which they are exposed (see chapter 9). Daylight films work best in daylight and with electronic flash. Tungsten slide film is designed to be balanced with photo floodlights. Type A film is balanced for 3400 K bulbs. Type B film is balanced for 3200 K bulbs.

Make certain the film used matches the light under which it is going to be exposed, because any mismatch between film type and light source will be dramatically evident. Daylight slide film

Streetman's homage brings together the disparate elements of the real and the unreal. Streetman began this image by photographing the scene on 4-x-5-inch daylight balanced transparency film and making a 20-x-24-inch print. Next she made a detail of the same subject, shot out of focus, and printed 11 x 14 inches. This smaller print was cut to match the contour of the rock face and collaged onto the larger print. An airbrush was used to add a white reflective veil of acrylic paint. Two yellow "syrup" figures (a Holmes trademark) were hand-painted so that the paint stands in relief. Figure shadows were added with the airbrush.

© Evon Streetman. *Tribute to Henry Holmes*, 1975. 20 x 24 inches. Dye-destruction prints with mixed media.

exposed under floods or household bulbs comes out an orange-yellow-red; tungsten slide film shot in daylight comes out blue. This can be corrected at the time of exposure through the use of the proper filter over the lens (see chapter 10).

Under mixed light conditions, situations illuminated by daylight and artificial light or scenes with both tungsten and fluorescents, there is no way to simply color correct the scene if the slide is the finished product. Even if a print is made, corrections will probably be limited in scope.

In open or deep shade, or in overcast daylight, the film may record the scene with a cool, bluish cast. A warming filter, such as an 81A, can be used to correct this.

In contrasty lighting, slide film can produce bleached-out highlights and dark, inky shadows.

Transparency Duplication

Once transparency film has been exposed and processed, the major method to make corrections and/or modifications is by slide duplication (dupes). It is possible to change colors and combine images for effect but at the expense of an increase in contrast and loss of subtle detail. Most 35-mm cameras accept a rigid-tube copying accessory that replaces the lens. The slide is placed in front of a light diffuser in the copying tube and is lighted either by daylight or electronic flash. Thin plastic CC filters are used to adjust or modify the color balance. This is an excellent tool for experimentation, especially when naturalistic color rendition is not a priority. Making your own color-accurate dupes can be difficult and requires a number of test rolls to determine correct exposure and filtration. Unless you make dupes frequently and in large quantities, you are better off having them made by a professional lab.

Commercial duplication makes use of a specialized copying stand with diffused electronic flash and built-in color filters. Commercial labs should use special low-contrast duplicating films that are designed specially for both E-6 or K-14 (Kodachrome) films. When accurate copy slides are required, use only a first-class professional lab because the quality of dupes can vary greatly (also see the section on copy work in chapter 15).

Viewing Transparencies

In order to critically judge the quality of a color transparency it is necessary to have a viewing light source (illuminator) that possesses specific characteristics, that is, a correlated color temperature of 5000 K (see chapter 9). Light sources that range in color temperature from 3800 K to 5000 K are satisfactory for general viewing by the public if they emit adequate amounts of light in the blue, green, and red portions of the spectrum. If a transparency is viewed with a tungsten light source it will have a red-yellow color bias. If it is viewed against a blue sky it will likely be biased in the blue direction.

Ideally transparencies should be shown in a projector with a high-intensity color-corrected lamp. The most popular projectors use the round, slotted Kodak Carousel trays that hold 80 or 140 slides. The 80-slide trays are less vulnerable to

Exploring issues of Chicana ideology is of primary importance to Montoya. "In my own evolving ideology I question my identity as a Chicana in occupied America, and articulate the experience of a minority woman in the West. I work to understand the depth of my spiritual, political, emotional, and cultural icons, realizing that in exploring the topography of my conceptual homeland, Aztlan, I am searching for configurations of my own vision." For this image Montoya sandwiched a Kodalith and 4-x-5-inch transparency, producing a moiré pattern, and rephotographed the resulting sandwich on a slide duplicator.

© Delilah Montoya. *Sapagonia*, 1995. 24 x 36 cm. Chromogenic color transparency.

jamming and can accommodate thicker cardboard, plastic, or glass mounts. For correct viewing, hold slide in its proper orientation (how the scene looked in reality), turn the slide upside down, and drop it in the slot in the tray. The emulsion side of the film should be facing the lens and screen.

Storing and Handling Color Films

All color films, both slide and negative materials, should be stored in a cool, dry place in original packing, away from color processing chemicals and substances that contain formaldehyde. New and simulated leather and cellular foam products can release small amounts of formaldehyde and should not be used as film bags. All color films should be exposed before the expiration date indicated on the film package and processed as soon as possible.

Do not leave film in strong sunlight or in a hot location, such as near a heating duct or in the glove compartment of a car. Load and unload the camera in subdued light.

When processing film, especially sheet film, avoid touching the emulsion surface. Handle film by its edges. If necessary, wear clean, lint-free cotton gloves.

X-ray equipment, such as that used in airport security systems, can fog film. The effect is increased with the intensity of the X-ray, the cumulative number of inspection exposures, and the sensitivity of the film. Films having an ISO film speed rating of 400 or higher are more susceptible than slower films. Ask for a hand inspection of your camera equipment. Carry film in a special lead shield pouch designed to protect film against low-dose X-ray inspection units. Visual inspection is the only protection against high-dose X-ray machines used in some foreign countries. Film fogging can occur around any radiation source, including doctor's offices, medical labs, hospitals, and factories.

Protect film against cleaners, industrial gases, motor exhaust fumes, mildew and fungus preventatives, paints, processing chemicals, and solvents.

For consistency, store film in the refrigerator at less than 55°F (13°C). When film is removed from the refrigerator, allow it 1/2 to 1 1/2 hours to warm up to room temperature before removing it from its original packing. This prevents condensation from forming on the film surface.

Exposed film should be processed as quickly as possible. If a delay is unavoidable, put the film in a resealable food storage bag and place it in the refrigerator. Allow it to reach room temperature before processing.

Processed color film is subject to color fading from light (especially UV), high temperatures, and humidity. To avoid the adverse effects of heat, light, and moisture, processed film should be kept in mounts or archival sleeves and stored in a cool, dark, and dry location with good ventilation. Temperature should be kept below 77°F (25°C) with a relative humidity of 30 to 60 percent. For long-term storage, temperature below 50°F (10°C) with a relative humidity of 30 to 50 percent is recommended.

For more information on storage of color materials, especially prints, see chapter 15.

· **TABLE 7.4** ·

Major Film Manufacturers

Agfa Film
100 Challenger Road
Ridgefield, NJ 07660

Eastman Kodak
343 State Street
Rochester, NY 14650

Fuji Film
555 Taxter Drive
Elmsford, NY 10523

Ilford Photo
70 West Century Road
Paramus, NJ 07653

Konica USA
440 Sylvan Avenue
Englewood Cliffs, NJ 07632

Polaroid
575 Technology Square
Cambridge, MA 02139

Scotch Films-3M Color Systems
Building 223-4N-11
St. Paul, MN 55144

Note: Many manufacturers offer on-line information.

Color Negative Film and Prints

© Brent W. Phelps.
Carrollton, TX, 1983.
30 x 40 inches.
Chromogenic color print.

Color Negative Film Characteristics

Color negative film is the first part of a flexible two-stage process for making prints on paper. The method is similar to that used for transparency production, except that film is processed into a negative instead of a positive. This means that areas in the original that were dark appear as light and colors show as their complement (opposite) on the film. Color negative film possesses an orange integral mask (a color mask) to correct for deficiencies in the green- and red-sensitive layers of the film.

Advantages

Color negative film is easier and quicker to process than transparencies. It is convenient because unlimited prints can be produced, once the additional printing equipment is acquired. Prints are easy to store, send, and display without the need for such additional equipment as a slide projector, screen, and darkened room. Prints allow intimate contact with the work, enabling the viewer time to become involved with the image.

Negative films offer greater exposure latitude than slide films and they give the photographer another opportunity to interact with the work. Exposure latitude is a film's ability to provide acceptable results when less than optimum exposure was made. Both the color saturation (degree of color intensity) and density increase with more exposure, which is the opposite of transparency film. Negative film should be exposed to produce acceptable detail in the key shadow areas. When in doubt about the proper exposure, it is usually best to slightly overexpose the film. Many photographers intentionally overexpose their negative film by decreasing the manufacturer's ISO film speed rating. For example, a film with an ISO of 100 might be rated at 80, while an ISO 400 film could be shot at 200. Bracket in 1/2 f-stops to discover what works best for your situation. Slight

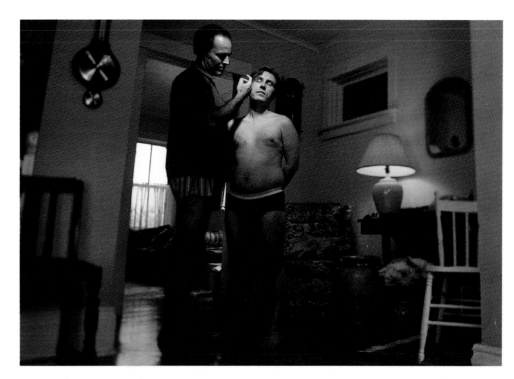

Figure 8.1

"To give my photographs a surreal quality," Hafkenscheid says, "I like to emphasize the colors. Lush, bold colors add to the drama of the scene, giving it a sense of hyper-reality. By utilizing mixed lighting (mixing flash and available light: tungsten, fluorescent, and daylight) on daylight negative film, colors can be created which are normally not apparent to the naked eye. The fleshtones of the person(s) photographed are usually highlighted and corrected during the printing process. The rest of the room is underexposed and not corrected for the daylight film and therefore reflects the color of whatever light source is available. This creates deep saturated colors which add an extra dimension to the theatrical scene."

© Toni Hafkenscheid. *Andrew and Rod*, 1995. 30 x 40 inches. Chromogenic color print.

overexposure can also produce a tighter grain pattern. This is because the final image is made up of color dyes rather than silver.

Negative film has a wide latitude for overexposure, which can be corrected when the print is made. If the film is greatly underexposed, the result is a weak, thin negative that produces a flat print lacking in detail and color saturation/richness (see chapter 6). Changing the color balance, contrast, density, and saturation is possible during the printing process, which can produce a final piece that is a more accurate reflection of the photographer's concerns. For these reasons, negative film tends to work better in contrasty and mixed-light conditions (figure 8.1).

Disadvantages

The major disadvantages of color negative film are that more time and

equipment are required to get the final image and the quality of the obtainable color is not as high as transparency film. If a normal print and a slide of the same scene are compared, the transparency will have more brilliance, greater detail, deeper saturation, and more subtle color because the transparency film itself is the final product and it is viewed by transmitted light. The negative requires a second step, printing, to get to the final image, resulting in a loss of quality because the print paper is viewed by reflected light. The paper absorbs some of the light, known as the *double density effect,* causing a loss of color and detail. If a print is the desired end product, the negative/positive process offers the most accurate color rendition. This is because the negative film contains an integral mask (a color mask) that corrects deficiencies in the green- and red-sensitive layers of the film.

Construction of Negative Film

Think of color negative and reversal film as a sandwich that is constructed on a single piece of bread. The bread in this case is called the base. Three different silver halide emulsions that are sensitive to blue, green, and red light form what is called the tripack on this base (see figure 1.6).

Each emulsion layer is coupled to the potential dyes, magenta, yellow, and cyan, which are used to form the color image. These dyes are the complements of the green, blue, and red hues that made up the original scene. When the film is exposed, a latent image is created in each layer. As an example, red light is recorded in the red-sensitive layer of the tripack, but it will not affect the other two layers (figure 8.2).

Colors that are made up from more than one primary color are recorded on several of the layers of the tripack. Black does not expose any of the emulsion, but white light is recorded on all three layers (see figure 1.7).

Chromogenic Development of Negative Film

During the chromogenic development process both the full-black silver image and the color dye image are formed simultaneously in the tripack. Next the film is bleached, which removes the unwanted black silver image. This leaves the three layers of dye showing the scene in superimposed magenta, yellow, and cyan, each one being a complement and a negative of the green, blue, and red from the original scene. Now the film is fixed, during which the unexposed areas of the emulsions are made permanent. Washing then removes all the remaining unwanted chemicals. Last, it is stabilized for maximum dye life and then dried (see figure 1.8). The final color negative has an overall orange mask. The orange color is due to

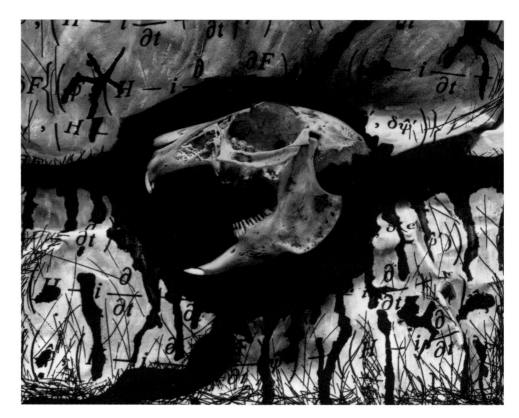

Figure 8.2

This image is the result of negative manipulation in which Murphy mimicked the method used to make a normal color negative; 4-x-5-inch black-and-white film was shot, processed, and then hand-colored with color markers. The final colors are complements of the color applied to the negative; thus orange becomes blue, and cyan becomes red. The background of the skull is a crumpled photocopy, and the black lines are scratch marks made directly on the negative. This series evolved when Murphy learned a close friend was terminally ill. The work reflects upon the complexities of hope, desideration, and desire in the rational and spiritual questioning of death. For Murphy the skull (bones) has developed a renewed spiritual quality in an attempt to suspend the finality of extinction.

© Jeff Murphy. *Rabbit Skull,* 1990. 24 × 30 inches. Chromogenic color print.

colored couplers that are used to improve color reproduction by reducing contrast and maintaining accurate color during the printing of the negative.

Most current negative films can be developed in the C-41 process (table 8.1). To be sure that the film you are using is compatible in C-41, check the box or cassette. Many of the latest films are extremely process sensitive and require very accurate temperature control or color shifts, lack of color saturation, changes in contrast, and increase in grain may result. Read and follow the sections in chapter 7 on temperature control and handling and agitation. Read and follow all manufac-

turer's safety warnings, mixing, and disposal instructions to ensure a safe and healthy working environment. C-41 negative films are stored and handled in the same manner as E-6 slide films (see chapter 7). In the future, expect to see a modification in the stabilizer step when the formaldehyde is removed from the process.

Troubleshooting C-41

Table 8.2 identifies some of the basic C-41 processing problems, their probable cause, and their possible correction.

· TABLE 8.1 ·
Kodak C-41 Process

Step	Time in Minutes*	Temperature (° F)†
The First Two Steps Must Be Carried out in Total Darkness		
Developer	3 1/4‡ (1) and (2)	100 +/– 0.25
Bleach	6 1/2	100 +/– 5
The Remaining Steps Can Be Carried out in Room Light		
Wash	3 1/4	75 to 105
Fixer	6 1/2	100 +/– 5
Wash	3 1/4	75 to 105
Stabilizer (3)	1 1/2	75 to 105
Dry	As Needed	Up to 140

Note: All times and temperatures are for small tanks—not more than four reels. If using a rotary-type processor, such as the Jobo, changes in time will be necessary.

*All steps include a 10-second drain time.

†For best results, keep all temperatures as close to 100°F as possible. When not agitating the solution, keep the processing tank in water bath. Before processing, warm the tank in water bath for about 5 minutes. See water bath section in chapter 7.

‡Development time changes depending on the number of rolls that have been processed. Mark the number of rolls processed on the developer storage container. Check the capacity of the solutions with the instructions. Mark the mixing date on storage bottle. All solutions have a limited storage life. Check the instructions to determine how long solutions will last under your storage conditions.

(1) *Initial Agitation*: For all solutions, tap the tank on a 45-degree angle to dislodge any air bubbles. No further agitation is needed in the stabilizer.

(2) *Additional Agitation*: Subsequent agitation is required in all other solutions. After tapping the tank, agitate by slowly turning the tank upside down and then right side up for the first 30 seconds. For the remaining time in the developer, let the tank rest for 13 seconds and agitate for 2 seconds. Since the time in the developer is short, proper agitation is a must or uneven development results. For the remaining time in the bleach and fixer, let the tank rest for 25 seconds and agitate for 5 seconds. When using noninvertible tanks, which cannot be turned upside down, tap the tank on a 45-degree angle to remove air bubbles, and rotate the reels at indicated times to achieve proper agitation.

(3) Stabilizer may be mixed with distilled water. Shake your loaded film reel over the sink to break the surface tension. This allows the stabilizer to flow freely and run to the lower end of the hanging film. A lint-free, disposable paper towel, such as a Photo-Wipe, can be gently used on the nonemulsion side of the film to remove excess stabilizer, dust, and processing debris. Allow film to hang undisturbed and naturally air dry in a dust-free environment.

How the Chromogenic Color Print Process Works

A chromogenic color print is made when light is projected through a color negative onto color printing paper. The light is filtered at some point before it reaches the paper. The paper, like the film, has a three-layered tripack emulsion composed of silver and dyes that are used to form the image. Each layer is sensitive to only one color of light, which is complementary to the dyes found in the negative. When the print is made, the colors from the negative are reversed. For instance, a red ball would be recorded in the cyan layer of the negative. When light passes through the negative, only green and blue light are transmitted. This exposes only the layers in the paper emulsion that are sensitive to green and blue light, releasing the complementary magenta and yellow dyes in the paper. The magenta and yellow dyes recreate the red ball from the original scene. Where there is clear film in all the emulsion layers, white light produces a latent image in each of the layers of the print emulsion. This produces black when the print is processed (figure 8.3).

· TABLE 8.2
C-41 Troubleshooting Guide

Problem	Cause and Correction
Negatives too dark	Overexposure. Check camera and meter. Review exposure methods. Overdevelopment. Time too long or temperature too high. Check thermometer for accuracy. Review temperature, time, and agitation procedures. Contaminated or incorrectly mixed developer.
Negatives too light	Underexposure. Check camera and meter. Review exposure techniques. Underdevelopment. Time too short or temperature too low. Check accuracy of thermometer. Review temperature, time, and agitation procedures. Developer exhausted, incorrectly mixed, or contaminated. Check mix date, number of rolls processed, and storage conditions. Out-of-date film.
Dense with high contrast	Bleach time too short. Unaerated bleach. Bleach temperature too low. Bleach incorrectly mixed or overdiluted.
Clear film with no edge marks	Bleached before development. Film was not a C-41 process film.
Clear film with edge marks	Unexposed film.
Dark crescent-shape marks	Kinked film. Practice loading unwanted film on reels. Only handle the edges and ends of the film. Do not force film onto reel.
Unusual color balance and contrast	Solution contamination. Dump and remix contaminated solutions. Clean all processing equipment after each use. Mix and store all solutions in clean containers. Clearly label all containers. Return chemicals to proper containers.
Dust, dirt, and spots	Mix stabilizer in distilled water. If water is extremely hard, follow stabilizer bath with Kodak PhotoFlo 200 Solution mixed in distilled water. Allow film to dry naturally in an undisturbed, dust-free environment. To facilitate the free flow of the stabilizer, shake your loaded film reel over the sink to break the surface tension. A lint-free, disposable paper towel (such as Photo-Wipes) may be used to gently wipe the nonemulsion side of the film.

Figure 8.3

Calvin chose 4-×-5-inch Type L negative film with exposure times from 2 to 10 minutes in this series. Using a drum processor to make the print, she increased the developing time to 5 minutes to saturate and make the colors more expressive and subjective. To produce this image Calvin says, "I assembled and photographed a combination of slide projections and objects alluding to ideas and mysteries contained in interior spaces. Beginning with traditional icons of domestic space, I add mysterious, jarring, and unsettling elements which evoke associations and feelings of tension or claustrophobia. The space is ambiguous; perspective is disorientingly shifting; scale is inconsistent. All combine to produce domestic space which is anxious, dark, and chaotic, instead of lyrical or comforting."

© Jane Calvin. *Woman, Window, and Chair Series #38*, 1990. 20 × 24 inches. Chromogenic color print.
Courtesy of Ehlers Caudill Gallery Ltd., Chicago, IL.

Developing the Print

When the print is developed, each of the three layers of the exposed emulsion develops into a positive black-and-white silver image that represents the third of the spectrum it recorded (red, green, and blue). Wherever the silver is deposited, dyes that correspond to that color are formed. For example, where blue light strikes the paper, only the yellow layer of the tripack, which is complementary to blue, is affected. The blue light forms a positive silver image and a directly corresponding yellow dye. After development, the paper contains

the exposed tripack of positive silver and dyed images. Next the print is bleached. This converts the silver to silver halides, which the fix then removes. Usually the bleach and fix are combined so that this process takes place more or less at the same time. This leaves only a positive dyed image that is washed and then dried. Since the image is formed by dyes, these prints are called dye coupler prints.

The colors in the resulting image are those that are reflected back to the eye from the light falling on the print. An object that is red looks red because the yellow and magenta dyes in the print

emulsion absorb the blue and green wavelengths from the light falling on it, reflecting back only the red.

What Is This Type of Print Called?

Prints made from negatives in the C-41 process use chromogenic development to produce the cyan, magenta, and yellow dyes in their emulsions and are known as chromogenic or dye coupler color prints. The term *chromogenic* was coined by Rudolph Fisher, who patented the use of color couplers in 1912 and 1914 (see section on subtractive film and chromogenic

Edwards relied on the characteristics of color negative film to explore the chaotic family life of Gypsy children. Edwards recalls: "Their everyday life was full of casual hysteria and occasional violence. I used motion and saturated colors to express these ideas and feelings. I used an open flash and a combination of ambient light (fluorescent and window light). I picked a basic drugstore film (Kodacolor 400) and greatly overexposed and overprocessed it. I felt the grain and exaggerated palette caused by the existing colors in their homes, the flash/ambient light, and massive overexposure/overprocessing of the film were important expressive elements."

© Jennifer Edwards. *Frankie Flying (from Gypsy Families)*, 1984. 16 × 20 inches. Chromogenic color print.

development in chapter 2). Prints from these processes are commonly called chromogenic color prints (because there is a black-and-white process; see later section on chromogenic black-and-white film) or dye coupler prints. Color prints may also be referred to by the specific paper they were made on, such as Ektacolor. The opposite method for making color prints is the dye-destruction process, or silver dye-bleach method, in which all the color dyes are built into the emulsion and selectively removed during processing (see sections on dye-destruction process and ILFOCHROME Classic in chapter 11).

Many people and organizations still call all modern color prints Type C. This widely used misnomer is not an accurate description for the current materials.[1] Type C was actually a specific product, Kodak Color Print Material, Type C, that was introduced in 1955. In 1958 Kodak introduced Ektacolor Paper, Type 1384 to replace Type C in photofinishing applications. Type C continued to be avail-

able for professional use for some time but has not been made during the past two decades. Today C-print is a slang term that refers to just about any color print made from a color negative, thereby distinguishing them from prints made from slides.

Brands, Grain, and Speed

Follow the same guidelines for film selection as outlined in chapter 7. Exposing for key shadow detail is the basic starting guide with negative film. Beware of using a film with a higher speed than necessary for the conditions; this can result in the loss of highlight detail in the final print.

Grain

The look of a final print is linked to the film speed and format size of the negative. Slower films appear sharper, possess greater color saturation, and have a fuller tonal range and less apparent

graininess. Faster films appear less sharp, with less color saturation and more apparent graininess. The larger the film size, the less apparent the visible grain. The Advanced Photo System, introduced in 1996, is about 40 percent smaller than 35mm. Designed for amateurs, it allows camera manufacturers to make smaller cameras and lenses. The reduction in film size produces more visible grain in enlargements of 8 × 10 inches or greater. The format has a magnetic layer that allows a camera to record a variety of information linked to each frame that includes format type (regular or panoramic), text, exposure, and potentially sound.

Processed black-and-white film is made up of particles of metallic silver called grain. Graininess is the subjective perception of a mottled random pattern. The viewer sees small, local-density variations in an area of overall uniform density. Although color negatives and transparencies contain no silver, they do exhibit graininess. This is because undeveloped color films contain silver compounds, which are removed by the bleach and fix, that help form the color dyes as they are developed. As the color dyes are created, dye clouds form around the silver particles and remain even after the silver is removed, retaining the silver grain pattern. These clouds of dyes form the grain in a color negative or transparency. Kodak's print grain index is a way to subjectivity evaluate the perceived print graininess from color negative films by using a uniform perceptual scale based on a diffusion enlarger. For details about this assessment system and a copy of the Kodak grain ruler, contact Kodak and request their publication E-58.

Many photographers intentionally overexpose color negative film by 1/3 to one full f-stop to improve shadow detail and saturation and to reduce graininess (see chapter 14). Others take advantage of the two-step process and purposely slightly overexpose and overdevelop in order to heighten contrast for dramatic effect. Slight to moderate overexposure of color negative film, unlike black-and-white, creates larger dye clouds in each of the emulsion layers. As the dye clouds

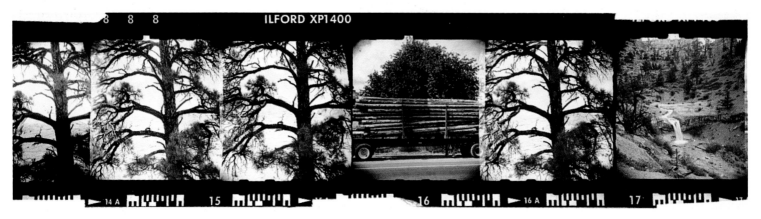

Heller shot black-and-white chromogenic film in a stereo camera and made monotone prints on color paper. This limited palette helps to unify the narratives between and among the frames of these sequences. Heller points outs that the "images are shot in the order they appear. As a result, the narratives reflect a passage of both time and place. In some instances, days or weeks may interrupt one frame from the next."

© Steven A. Heller. *Trees, Logging Truck: Utah,* 1995. 15 × 40 inches. Chromogenic color print.

expand, they overlap and fill in from layer to layer, lending the appearance of less graininess.

Type S and Type L Films

Some manufacturers design films specifically for different exposure situations. For example, Kodak's "Professional" color negative films come in two versions. Type S, for short exposures, is balanced for daylight and designed for an exposure time of 1/10 to 1/10,000 of a second. Type L, for long exposures, is balanced for tungsten light (3200 K) and for exposure times of 1/50 to 60 seconds (see figure 8.3). If exposure time and/or the color temperature of the light do not match the film, filters are necessary to correct the color temperature. Small mismatches can be corrected when making the print.

Prints and Slides from the Same Film

There are motion-picture film stocks such as Kodak 5292 that can be processed to give both slides and prints from the same roll of film. It is generally

fine for snapshooting, but it does not deliver the accurate quality that film designed for these specific purposes is capable of doing. Motion-picture stock is designed to be exposed at 1/50 of a second (the equivalent of twenty-four frames per second) and can suffer from reciprocity failure when exposed at other speeds. These stocks lack an antiscratch overcoat on the emulsion side of the film, which makes them susceptible to scratching problems with winders or motors that advance or rewind the film. These films must be processed in ECN-2 motion-picture process rather than in C-41 or E-6 processes because the rem jet backing (film lubricant) must be removed during processing and would contaminate C-41 solutions.

Chromogenic Black-and-White Film

Ilford XP2 is an ISO 400 film, available in 35-mm, 120 roll, and sheet formats, and is the second generation of monochromatic negative material (the first was Ilford XP1) to make use of new chromogenic color coupler technology. Special DIR (developer inhibitor releasing) couplers yield ultrafine grain, high-acutance

images. Ilford XP2, like regular color negative materials, produces finer grain when overexposed. This film has an extremely wide exposure latitude (ISO 50 to 800), allowing it to capture subjects with a wide brightness range while producing excellent highlight detail with no grain.

Ilford XP2 is designed to be processed in standard C-41 chemistry alongside all other color negative films. No special handling is required because times and temperatures remain the same and the film will *not* contaminate the chemicals in any way. After processing, the negative is composed solely of stable dyes and is completely silver-free. This means that this film may be processed and printed by any lab offering C-41 service. XP2 prints better on color paper and has slightly more contrast, a broader tonal rage, and finer grain than its predecessor, XP1. If prints show a slight color cast when made on regular color paper, have the printer use an unexposed strip of processed color film to provide the orange mask to correct this situation. XP2 is handled like a conventional black-and-white negative when printed on black-and-white paper. Store unexposed and exposed film in the same manner as any color film. For more information see Ilford Technical Information Catalog #9444.

Nine

Filtering the Light

© William Lesch.
Red Mountain and Clouds, 1989.
Size varies: 16 x 20 through 30 x 40 inches.
Dye-destruction print.
Courtesy of Etherton/Stern Gallery, Tucson, AZ.

Our Sun: A Continuous Spectrum Source

Our sun radiates "white" light, which is a continuous spectrum of all the visible wavelengths that are produced by the elements burning on the sun's surface. As these wavelengths are separated out by absorption and reflection we see them as color. The shortest wavelengths appear as violet, the longest as red, and all the other colors fall somewhere in between these boundaries. The human eye can only detect a tiny portion of the electromagnetic spectrum known as the visual spectrum. The ultraviolet (UV) wavelengths occupy the range just beyond the blue-violet end of the visual spectrum and are too small to be seen by the human eye. The infrared (IR) part of the electromagnetic spectrum begins just beyond the visible red wavelengths, which are too long to be seen with the human eye.

Color Temperature and the Kelvin Scale

The balance of the amount of colors that are contained in a continuous spectrum source of light, having all the visible wavelengths (red, orange, yellow, green, blue, and violet) in various amounts, is measured as color temperature. Color temperature is expressed on the absolute (Kelvin) scale. The Kelvin scale starts at absolute zero, minus 273.15°C on the centigrade scale (usually rounded off to minus 273°C). Absolute zero is the temperature at which all molecular motion theoretically stops. The degree symbol is not used when expressing the color temperature of a light source in Kelvins (K). The Kelvin temperature is determined by adding 273 to the number of degrees centigrade to which a black metal radiator would have to be heated to take on a certain color. A black body is used as a standard gauge since it does not reflect any light falling on it and only emits radiation when heat is applied to it. The Kelvin scale is to the color of light as the

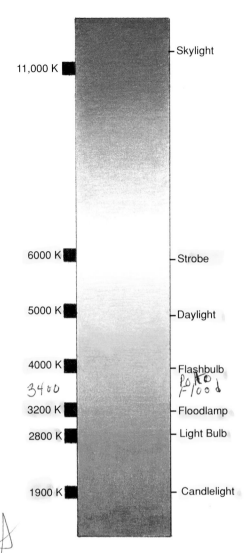

Figure 9.1
The Kelvin scale is how color temperature of light is measured. The bluer the light, the higher the Kelvin temperature. The chart gives common illumination sources and their approximate Kelvin temperature.

ISO scale is to the sensitivity of film (figure 9.1).

Table 9.1 provides the Kelvin temperatures for common daylight and artificial sources.

Color Temperature Meters

The photographic color temperature of a light source can be measured by a color temperature meter. The most reliable and expensive meters compare the relative amounts of red, blue, and green energy in the light. They work well with sunlight and incandescent light sources but are not as accurate for measuring fluorescent

light. This is because light sources, such as fluorescent light, that do not radiate color continuously and evenly throughout the spectrum cannot be given a color temperature. These discontinuous sources are assigned color temperatures on the basis of measurement with a color temperature meter and/or on the visual response of color film to these discontinuous light sources.

To operate a digital color meter, set the film type (daylight or tungsten), position the meter near the principal subject and point it at the camera and/or main light source, and read the temperature and filtration recommendations in the meter's display window. Its suggested filtration should work with negative film, but transparency film may require a test roll for accurate results (see section on testing for a critical neutral color match in this chapter).

The Color of Light

Although we think of daylight as being "white" it usually contains some color depending on the time of day, the time of year, and the weather. Artificial light is rarely white. Our brain remembers how things are supposed to look and makes us believe that the light is white even if it is not. It interprets the scene for us.

How Film Sees Color

Unfortunately, color film cannot yet do this. It simply records what is present. Each color film is designed to accurately record the quality of light for a certain manufactured "normal" color temperature. If you use a film that does not match the color temperature of the light, the picture will have an unnatural color cast to it. Silver-based photographic materials have an inherent sensitivity to the blue wavelengths of the visual spectrum and to all the shorter wavelengths. Their sensitivity can be extended to green, yellow, and red visible wavelengths as well as into part of the infrared portion of the spectrum.

· TABLE 9.1 ·

Common Light Sources and Their Approximate Color Temperatures

Daylight Sources*	Color Temperature (K)
Skylight	12,000 to 18,000
Overcast sky	7000
Noon sun with clear sky (summer)	5000 to 7000
Noon sun with clear sky (winter)	5500 to 6000
Photographic daylight	5500
Noon sunlight (depends on time of year)	4900 to 5800
Average noon sunlight (Northern hemisphere)	5400
Sunlight at 30-degree altitude	4500
Sunlight at 20-degree altitude	4000
Sunlight at 10-degree altitude	3500
Sunrise and sunset	3000

Artificial Sources†	Color Temperature (K)
Electronic flash	5500 to 6500
Blue-coated flashbulbs	5500 to 6000
White flame carbon arc	5000
Zirconium-filled clear flashbulbs (AG-1 & M3)	4200
Warm white fluorescent tubes	4000
Aluminum-filled clear flashbulbs (M2, 5, & 25)	3800
500-watt 3400 K photolamp (photofloods)	3400
500-watt 3200 K tungsten lamp (photolamps)	3200
200-watt household lamp	2980
100-watt household lamp	2900
75-watt household lamp	2820
40-watt household lamp	2650
Gaslight	2000 to 2200
Candlelight (British Standard)	1930

*All daylight color temperatures depend on the time of day, season of the year, and latitude and altitude of the location.
†The age and the amount of use of bulb, lamp, or tube affects the color temperature.

Daylight Type Film

The most common color film is designed to give an accurate representation of a scene in daylight. At midday the Kelvin temperature of outdoor light is about 5500 K. Daylight films are designed to give faithful results between 5200 K and 5800 K. Daylight has a predominately blue color content. If you make pictures at other times, such as early in the morning or at sunset, the light has less blue in it. When the color temperature drops below 5200 K, daylight film begins to record the scene as warmer. The more you drop below 5200 K, the greater the color cast will be. In artificial tungsten light, daylight film produces a warm orange-reddish-yellow cast.

In winter light, everything appears slightly cooler or bluish. Light reflected off colored walls or passing through translucent objects creates a color cast that influences the entire scene. This is known as color contamination (see section on monochrome in chapter 19 for more information).

Tungsten and Type L Films

Tungsten Type B slide film and Type L negative film are color balanced at 3200 K. They are designed to be used with 250- to 500-watt photolamps or spots. Using tungsten film in daylight produces a blue cast. If you use it with a light source of a lower (redder) color temperature, such as a household bulb, the result is yellower.

If these shifts in color are not desired, they must be filtered out. The most critical results are generally obtained when filtering at the time of exposure, rather than attempting to correct the shifts later.

What Does a Filter Do?

A photographic filter is a transparent device that can alter the quality and quantity of light. It is placed in front of the camera or enlarging lens or in the path of the light falling on the subject. Filters that go in front of the lens must be of optical quality or they can degrade the image quality. Filters used in front of a light source or with a color enlarger do not have to be of optical quality, but they must be able to withstand high heat without becoming distorted or faded.

How Filters Work

Most filters are colored and work subtractively, absorbing the wavelengths of light of their complementary (opposite) color while transmitting wavelengths of their own color. The color of a filter is the color of the light it transmits. For example, a red filter is red because it absorbs blue and green light while transmitting red light. Although a filter transmits its own color, it also passes all or parts of the colors next to it in the spectrum while absorbing part or most of all other colors. A red filter does not transmit yellow light, but it does allow some light from yellow objects to pass. This occurs because yellow is made up of green and red. The red filter passes the red portion of the yellow while blocking the green.

Filter Factor

Filters are normally uniform in color but may differ in density (color strength). The amount of light absorbed depends on the density of the filter. Because filters block some of the light, they generally require an increase in exposure to make up for the light lost due to absorption. This compensation is known as the filter factor and is indicated as a number, followed by an X sign, which tells how much the exposure must be multiplied. A filter factor of 2X

• TABLE 9.2 •

Filter Factor Adjustments

Filter Factor	Exposure Adjustment
1.2X	+1/3 stop
1.5X	+2/3 stop
2X	+1 stop
2.5X	+1 1/3 stops
3X	+1 2/3 stops
4X	+2 stops
5X	+2 1/3 stops
6X	+2 2/3 stops
8X	+3 stops
10X	+3 1/3 stops
12X	+3 2/3 stops
16X	+4 stops
32X	+5 stops

Note: Cameras with through-the-lens meters should automatically make the correct filter factor adjustment. When using a handheld meter, you'll have to manually make the adjustment. The aperture of a lens may be set in-between the standard click stops to achieve accurate exposure adjustment.

means that one additional f-stop of exposure is needed; 2.5X shows 1 1/3 additional f-stops are necessary; 3X means an extra 1 2/3 f-stops are needed; 4X indicates two additional f-stops of exposure. To simplify matters, many manufacturers indicate how many f-stops to increase the exposure.

Most thru-the-lens (TTL) camera metering systems give an accurate reading with a filter in place; otherwise the film speed can be adjusted to compensate. For example, if you are using a film with a speed of 100 and a filter with a 2X factor you change the film speed to 50. This provides the film with one additional f-stop to compensate for the filter factor. Some TTL meters can be fooled and give faulty readings with certain filters. Bracket your exposures when using a filter for the first time. Autofocus systems may not operate properly with heavy filtration, diffusion, or certain special effects filters. If the system balks, switch to manual focus. Table 9.2 shows the effect of filter factors on exposure.

Dichroic Filters

Dichroic filters, such as those found in many color enlargers, act by interference. A thin coating on the surface of the filter

Figure 9.2
Parker made use of Kodak Wratten filters, numbers 24, 59, and 47, in producing this image. Parker comments: "I borrow ways of doing things in the darkroom from film, printmaking, and graphic design. I devise my way of thinking from fiction, poetry, philosophy, and painting. My sense of when it works comes from jazz. I use several enlargers and a large stereo system. The sheet of color paper and I walk around collecting projections. At the end of the exposure the sheet looks exactly as it did when I started. An odd thing the latent image is, in a visual art media. I do some small time chemistry in a Jobo CPP2 processor and see what happened and go around again, retracing my spiral travels until I pull the cork from the bottle."

© Bart Parker. *Stone Daughters, Departed Sons, No. 15*, 1987. 20 × 16 inches. Chromogenic color print.

causes certain wavelengths to be reflected, and thus canceled out, while permitting other wavelengths to pass through it.

How Filters Are Identified

Filters are described and identified in a variety of systems. The most widely used is the Kodak Wratten number system in

which filters are simply identified with a number, such as 85B (figure 9.2).

In color photography filters are employed to make changes in the color balance of the light that creates the image. The color of a light source is described in terms of its color temperature, measured in degrees Kelvin (K). If the color temperature of the light does not match that of the film,

Figure 9.3

4-×-5-inch Type L negative film was chosen for its ability to deal with a mixed light situation. Lauritzen made four separate exposures of this scene to combine natural and artificial light and to minimize contrast. First, a short exposure was made for the hills and the sky; second, an exposure was made for the entrance lights; third, an exposure was made for the neon; and fourth, an exposure was made for the street lights. Even with such exacting exposure controls this print still required extensive dodging, burning, and localized color corrections.

© Erik Lauritzen. *The Gem,* 1989. 16 × 20 inches. Chromogenic color print.

the final image will contain a color cast. A color temperature meter can be used to provide a precise reading of the Kelvin temperature of the light source when extremely accurate color correction is needed.

Match the Film to the Light

It is always best to match the light and the film with the correct filter at the time of exposure. Negative film allows for some correction when the print is made, but slide film is unforgiving. For this reason, filtering at the moment of expo-

sure is critical. Manufacturers have made it easier by supplying slide film for daylight (5500 K), Type A (balanced for photo-flood lights at 3400 K), and Type B (balanced for studio lights at 3200 K). Type A and Type B film exposed in sunlight produce a strong blue cast, while daylight film exposed in artificial light has a distinct red-orange-yellow cast.

There are about one hundred different correction filters available to deal with the range of color temperature encountered.

Filter Categories Used with Color Films

The following are general categories of filters that are commonly employed with color films (figure 9.3).

Color Compensating Filters

Color compensating filters (CC) are used to make slight and precise corrections in one or two colors of the light.

• TABLE 9.3 •
Conversion Filters for Color Films

Color Film Type	Designed for	Daylight (5500 K)	Lighting Conditions Photolamp (3400 K)	Tungsten (3200 K)
Daylight type (5500 K)	Daylight, blue flash, electronic flash	No filter	80B	80A
Type A (3400 K)	Photolamps (3400 K)	85	No filter	82A
Tungsten Type B (3200 K)	Tungsten (3200 K)	85B	81A	No filter

• TABLE 9.4 •
Exposure Compensation with Conversion Filters

Filter	Changes Color Temperature From	To	Film	Exposure Increase In f-stops*
80A	3200K	5500K	Daylight	2
80B	3400K	5500K	Daylight	1 2/3
80C	3800K	5500K	Daylight	1
80D	4200K	5500K	Daylight	1/3
85	5500K	3400K	Tungsten (Type A)	2/3
85B	5500K	3200K	Tungsten	2/3
85C	4650K	3400K	Tungsten (Type A)	1/3

*These are suggested starting points. For critical work, especially with color slide film, a visual test should be conducted.

• TABLE 9.5 •
Light Balancing Filters

Subject Conditions	Filtration for Daylight Films (5500 K)	Filtration for Tungsten Films (3200 K)
Sunrise, sunset	80B or 80C (blue)	82 (blue)
Two hours after sunrise or before sunset	80D (blue)	81 + 81EF (yellow)
Average noon sunlight	None	85B (orange)
Overcast	81A or 81B (amber)	85B + 81B
Open shade	81B or 81C (amber)	85B + 81A

Note: Sky conditions vary dramatically depending on the time of day, the weather, and location. While these filters may not always fully correct the color, they should provide much better results than if no filter was used at all.

CC filters counteract small color shifts and correct minor color casts and are usually used to control the primary colors. For example, a red CC filter reduces blue and green light. A filter of one of the secondary colors affects its primary complement. Thus a magenta filter reduces green light, a yellow filter reduces blue light, and a cyan filter reduces red light.

The amount of light reduced depends on the filter's density. CC filters come in various densities of blue, cyan, green, magenta, red, and yellow. Their density is indicated by numbers like CC10R—the 10 represents a density of 0.10 and is commonly referred to as ten units or points of red. CC filters are also employed to gain proper balance when color printing.

Conversion Filters

Conversion filters are used to make large changes in color balance. Generally they correct a mismatch of film type and illumination, but they can be employed to create a deliberate color shift. They consist of 80 series (dark blue) and 85 series (amber/dark yellow) filters (see table 9.3). The common 80 series filters are used with daylight film to color correct it with tungsten light. The 85 filters correct tungsten film when it is used in daylight. See table 9.3 to determine the correct combination of film and filter for common lighting situations. All these filters reduce the amount of light entering the camera lens and require an increase in exposure. They can also make focusing more difficult, reduce the depth of field, and extend shutter speeds to unacceptably long times. See table 9.4 for exposure corrections when working with common conversion filters.

Light Balancing Filters

Light balancing filters make smaller changes in the color balance than conversion filters. They are used to match an artificial light source more closely with a tungsten film (table 9.5). Filters in the 81 series have a yellowish or amber color, to counteract excessive blue light, and lower the color temperature. Use an 81A or 81B filter to reduce excessive blue in aerial, marine, and snow scenes. It is also effective on overcast and rainy days, in open shade, and directly after sunset. An 81C can be used in daylight conditions having an inordinate amount of blue. Filters in the 82 series possess a bluish color, to counteract excessive yellow, and raise the color temperature of the light. An 82A filter is used to reduce the warm cast in early morning and late afternoon light.

Correcting Color Balance with Electronic Flash

Electronic flash has a color temperature equivalent to bright daylight, usually about 5600 K to 6000 K. Each unit is

Figure 9.4

Colored filters or gels can be placed in front of a flash or other light source to create color changes within a scene. In this photograph about seventy-five colored flashes were combined with daylight. This helps to lead the eye around and make visual connections within the composition.

© Michael Northrup. *Strobacolor Series: House Frame*, 1984. 16 x 20 inches. Chromogenic color print.

different; some tend to be cooler and bluer than others. Electronic flash also produces ultraviolet wavelengths that can appear as blue on color film. If your flash is putting out light that is too cool for your taste, a yellow CC or CP Print filter of slight color value can be cut and taped in front of the unit. Usually a filter with a value of 05 or 10 will make the correction. Filters can be intentionally used to provide creative lighting changes within a scene (figure 9.4). Flash can also be employed if you are shooting daylight film in tungsten light. The flash can help to offset the tungsten light and maintain a more natural color balance.

· ASSIGNMENT ·

Expose a portion of a roll of film under lighting conditions that do not match the type of light for which the film was designed. Then, under the same mismatch of light and film conditions, take corrective actions using filters and/or flash to make corrections. Compare your results. Discuss the emotional effect that is created when the film and light do not match.

Observe problem situations that you keep encountering that a filter would help to solve. Base your purchases on your own shooting experiences and get the equipment that lets you make pictures you desire.

Neutral Density Filters

Neutral density filters (ND) are applied to reduce the intensity of the light by absorbing the same amount of all the wavelengths. ND filters will not affect the color balance or tonal range of the scene. They have an overall gray appearance and come in different densities (ND2, ND4, and ND8) that will cut the light by one, two, or four f-stops. An ND2 transmits 50 percent of the light, ND4 25 percent, and ND8 12.5 percent. Kodak's Wratten ND filters, available in dyed gelatin squares, come in thirteen different densities, ranging from 0.1 (needing 1/3 f-stop more exposure) to 4.0 (needing 13 1/3 more f-stops of exposure). The Kodak density (logarithmic) values are *not* the same as the ND filters labeled with simple filter factors.

An ND filter can be used anytime the light is too bright to use a slow shutter speed and/or large lens opening. An ND filter can be used to reduce the depth of field. This can be effective in outdoor portraiture because it permits you to use a large aperture to put the background out of focus, thus giving more emphasis to the subject. ND filters can be employed in order to get a slower shutter speed and produce intentional blur action shots. For instance, a slow shutter speed would let the movement of cascading water be captured as a soft blur. Another example would be moving zoom lens control during exposure, for which a shutter speed of 1/15 second or slower is necessary. They can also be useful in making pan shoots or when you have to use a very high-speed film in extremely bright light (see chapter 20).

Reflections: Polarized and Unpolarized Light

Normally a light wave moves in one direction, but the light energy itself vibrates in all directions perpendicular to the direction of travel of the light wave. Such light is said to be unpolarized. Polarizers, such as the naturally occurring mineral called Iceland spar, transmit only the part of each light wave vibrating in a particular direction; the rest of the light wave is refracted away from its original direction. The portion of the light that is transmitted is called polarized light.

What a Polarizing Filter Can Do

A polarizing filter is made up of submicroscopic crystals that are lined up like a series of parallel slats. Light waves traveling parallel to these crystal slats pass unobstructed between them. Light waves vibrating at different angles are blocked by the crystal slats. Because the polarized light is all at the same angle, the polarizing filter is designed to be rotated so it can block the polarized portion of the light.

The polarizing filter is a device used to polarize the light in photography. Modern polarizing materials such as Polaroid, first produced in 1932 by

Figure 9.5

It is the imagemaker's job to pay attention and control reflections. Bringing a virtual studio to the wilderness, Streetman superimposed a silver grid to make use of the reflection that shifts from silver to gray depending on the viewer's position. The clouds were painted on the underside of two large sheets of mylar. By placing the rocks under and over the mylar Streetman produces gestural marks with the reflections on the surface. Streetman says she designed visual invitations that cause the more curious observer to discover the deception and to be reminded of the traditional value of the artist as craftsperson.

© Evon Streetman. *Landscape and Systems*, 1984. 24 × 30 inches. Dye-destruction print with mixed media.

Dr. Edwin Land, have replaced the naturally occurring Iceland spar crystals. Polarizers are usually a gray-brown color.

Polarizers are used to eliminate reflections from smooth, nonmetallic, polished surfaces such as glass, tile, tabletops, and water, and they can improve the color saturation by screening out the polarized part of the glare. This can make a clear blue sky appear deeper and richer and have more contrast without altering the overall color balance of the scene. The increase in saturation results from a decrease in surface

glare. Since most semismooth objects, such as flowers, leaves, rocks, and water, have a surface sheen, they reflect light, thus masking some of the color beneath the sheen. By reducing these reflections, the polarizer intensifies the colors.

A polarizing filter can also be more effective than a haze filter for cutting through haze with color film because it reduces more of the scattered blue light and decreases reflections from dust and/or water particles (figure 9.5). The net effect is the scene appears to be more distinct and sharp while also increasing the visual sense of depth and adding to the vividness of the colors. When copying original art and reproductions from books or when photographing glossy-surfaced objects, maximum glare control can be obtained by using polarizers in front of the light sources as well as in front of the camera lens. Evaluate each situation before using a polarizer, as there are situations where the purposeful inclusion of reflections strengthen the photographer's underlying concept.

Using a Polarizer

When using a polarizing filter, focus first; turn the filter mount until the glare decreases and the colors look richer; then make the exposure. The filter factor will remain the same, regardless of how much the filter is rotated. The filter factor varies, from about 2X to 3X, depending on the type of polarizer used.

The amount of the effect is determined by how much polarized light is present in the scene and the viewing angle of the scene. At an angle of about 35 degrees from the surface, the maximum reduction in reflections can be achieved when the polarizer is rotated to the correct position.

A polarizer may also be combined with other filters for special effects. There are polarizers with color available. These combine a gray and a single colored polarizing filter. Any color, from gray to the full color of the other filter, can be achieved by rotating the filter frame ring. There are also multicolored polarizers that combine a single gray polarizing filter and two colored polarizing filters. The colors are altered by rotating the filter frame ring.

Linear and Circular Polarizers

There are now two types of polarizers used in photography: the traditional linear and the newer circular model. If your camera has a semisilvered mirror (this includes all current auto-focus SLR cameras), the linear filter will produce

underexposed and out-of-focus pictures. Circular filters work on all SLR cameras without producing these undesirable side effects but are considerably more expensive. A linear model can be used with a semisilvered mirror camera by (1) determining the exposure without the filter on the camera, (2) manually setting the exposure to compensate for the filter factor (give more exposure) before attaching the filter to the front of the camera's lens; or (3) manually focusing the camera. Do not rely on the auto-focus.

Special Purpose Filters/Ultraviolet

Special purpose filters include ultraviolet, haze, and skylight filters. All of these absorb ultraviolet (UV) radiation, reducing the effects of scattered light, which adversely affects the color dyes (often giving a blue cast). This produces a more accurate and natural rendition on the film. Typically, a UV filter is effective with landscapes, especially photographs of mountains, the seashore, or snow scenes in which UV radiation is intense. UV filters can also help to ensure optimum quality when doing copy work, close-ups of plants (figure 9.6), and objects with bright colors such as porcelain ware. UV filters are not effective in reducing the excess amount of blue light in scenes containing shade (81 series should be used). The UV filters have no filter factor, and many photographers leave one in front of their lens most of the time to protect the surface of the lens from dirt, moisture, and scratches. Infrared filters that transmit infrared wavelengths are used with special infrared films.

Special Effects Filters

Special effects filters produce unusual visual effects. Exercise care and thought before using one. They are overused and are a visual crutch of unthinking photographers who lack real picture-making ideas. Most pictures made with them appear

cliché. Special effects filters include the following (figure 9.7):[1]

- *Center spot:* diffuses the entire area except the center.

- *Changeable color:* used in combination with a polarizing filter. Rotating the filter changes the color, from one primary, through the midtones, to a different primary color. Available in yellow to red, yellow to green, green to red, blue to yellow, and red to blue.

- *Close-up:* fitted with a normal lens to permit you to focus closer than the minimum distance the lens was designed to accommodate.

- *Color spot:* center portion of filter is clear with the surrounding area colored.

- *Color vignette:* filter with colored edges and clear center.

- *Cross screen:* exaggerates highlights into star shapes.

- *Diffraction:* takes strong highlights and splits them into spectral color beams.

- *Diffusion:* softens and mutes the image and color. Available in varying strengths to give different degrees of softening effect.

- *Double exposure:* masks half the frame at a time.

- *Dual color:* each half of the frame receives a different color cast.

- *Fog:* delivers a soft glow in highlight areas while lowering contrast and sharpness. Available in several grades. Effect varies depending on aperture of the lens; stopping down reduces the effect.

- *Framing:* masks the frame to form a black or colored shape.

- *Graduated:* half the filter is colored and the other half is clear. The colored portion fades to colorless toward the center line of the filter.

[1] Filter kits that utilize a universal holder and gelatin squares provide an economical way to work with a variety of filters.

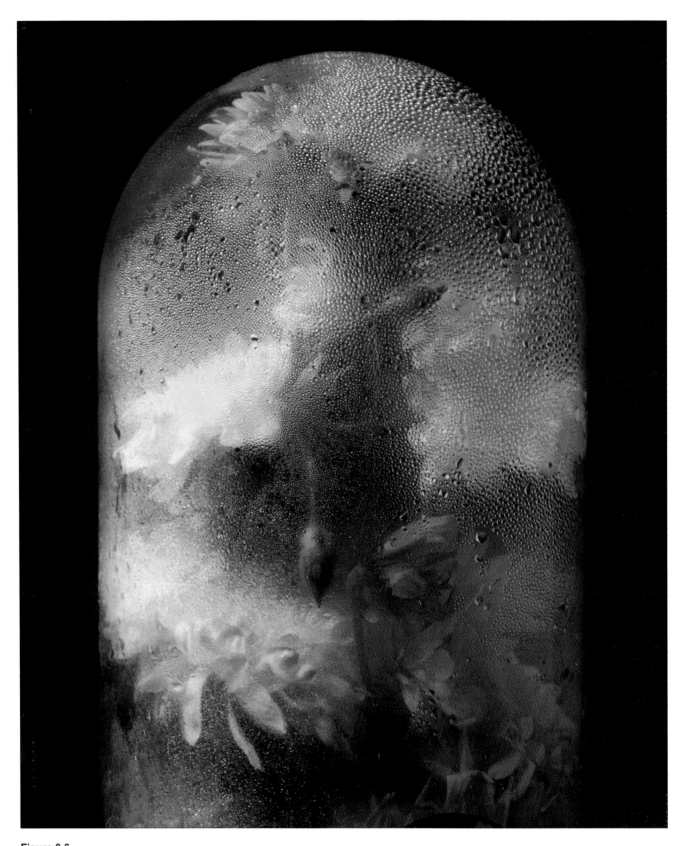

Figure 9.6

To obtain an accurate color rendition, Moninger used a UV filter. The UV filter absorbs UV radiation and reduces the effects of light scattering that can produce a light blue cast in the color dyes of the film. Moninger tells us about his *Nightflowers Series*: "I am intrigued by the concept of 'obscuration' of the photographic subject. In these images, the metaphor is the limitation of human perception, the eternal barriers to aspiration. The flower forms are fractured by a veil of lens-like water beads. Extending the location work (New York City flower shop windows late at night) into a few studio setups, #21 was executed by placing cut flowers in a glass bell jar. The mist formed naturally."

© Jim Moninger. *Nightflowers #21*, 1987. 16 × 20 inches. Chromogenic color print.

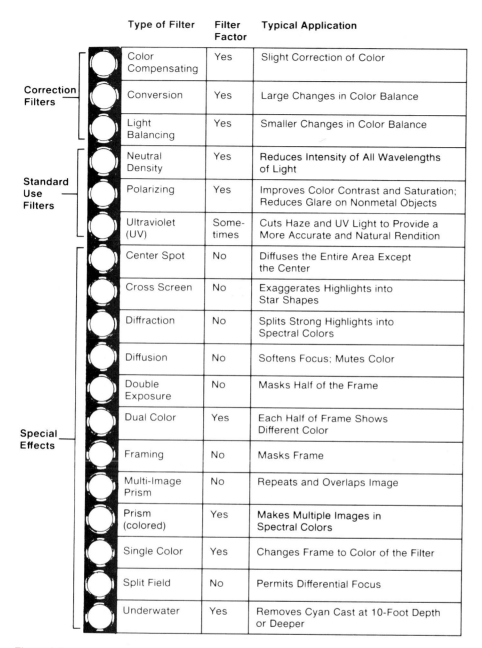

	Type of Filter	Filter Factor	Typical Application
Correction Filters	Color Compensating	Yes	Slight Correction of Color
	Conversion	Yes	Large Changes in Color Balance
	Light Balancing	Yes	Smaller Changes in Color Balance
Standard Use Filters	Neutral Density	Yes	Reduces Intensity of All Wavelengths of Light
	Polarizing	Yes	Improves Color Contrast and Saturation; Reduces Glare on Nonmetal Objects
	Ultraviolet (UV)	Sometimes	Cuts Haze and UV Light to Provide a More Accurate and Natural Rendition
Special Effects	Center Spot	No	Diffuses the Entire Area Except the Center
	Cross Screen	No	Exaggerates Highlights into Star Shapes
	Diffraction	No	Splits Strong Highlights into Spectral Colors
	Diffusion	No	Softens Focus; Mutes Color
	Double Exposure	No	Masks Half of the Frame
	Dual Color	Yes	Each Half of Frame Shows Different Color
	Framing	No	Masks Frame
	Multi-Image Prism	No	Repeats and Overlaps Image
	Prism (colored)	Yes	Makes Multiple Images in Spectral Colors
	Single Color	Yes	Changes Frame to Color of the Filter
	Split Field	No	Permits Differential Focus
	Underwater	Yes	Removes Cyan Cast at 10-Foot Depth or Deeper

Figure 9.7
Common filters and their typical applications in color photography.

- *Macro filter:* typically, when attached to a 50-mm lens on a 35-mm SLR camera, it permits 1/2 magnification; when attached to a 100-mm lens, it enables 1/1 magnification.

- *Prism/multiimage:* repeats and overlaps the image within the frame.

- *Prism/colored:* makes multiple images with spectrum-colored casts.

- *Split field:* allows differential focus within the frame.

- *Tricolor:* filter has three sections, red, green, and blue, in a single filter element.

- *Underwater:* removes the cyan cast that appears at a depth of 10 feet or more.

Homemade Filters

Making your own filters can save money and free you from using only manufactured materials. By using your ingenuity it is possible to create your own filters for artistic control of color. Although homemade filters may not match the quality of commercially manufactured filters from optical grade materials, they can produce results that are not only acceptable but even desirable. A universal filter holder, attached in front of the lens, permits you to experiment with a variety of materials.

Homemade Colored Filters

All that is necessary to make a colored filter is some type of transparent material. Colored cellophane and theatrical gels provide simple starting places. The greatest versatility can be achieved by marking clear acetate with color felt-tipped pens. When held or taped in front of the camera, they are excellent at producing pastel-like colors. The pastel effect can be heightened by photographing a light-colored subject against a bright background. There are endless possibilities, since you can make split-field filters with numerous color combinations.

By photographing through transparent objects, such as stained glass or water, it is also possible to transfer color(s) to a subject (figure 9.8).

Homemade Diffusion Filters

Diffusion filters can be made from any transparent material. Each material creates its own unique way of scattering the light and produces a different visual effect. Although most photographers use a diffusion filter at the time of camera exposure, it is also possible to employ one in front of your enlarging lens when printing. Test some of the following methods to see which suit your needs:

- *Cellophane:* Crumple up a piece of cellophane, and then smooth it out and attach the cellophane to the front of your lens with a rubber band.

- *Matt spray:* On an unwanted clear filter or on a plain piece of plexiglas or glass, apply a fine mist of spray matt material.

Baker Hall used a No. 2 close-up filter with his Leica rangefinder camera to make this image based on a picture from his family photo album. Baker Hall releases "the shutter only when what I see on the ground glass looks familiar, though I have only a few sketchy recollections from that traumatic time of my life. I appear to be working within the lineage of cave painting, unearthing images from the buried walls of my mind, remembering without the aid of memory."

© James Baker Hall. *Untitled,* 1995 from *Family Album series.* 26 1/2 × 40 inches. Chromogenic color print.

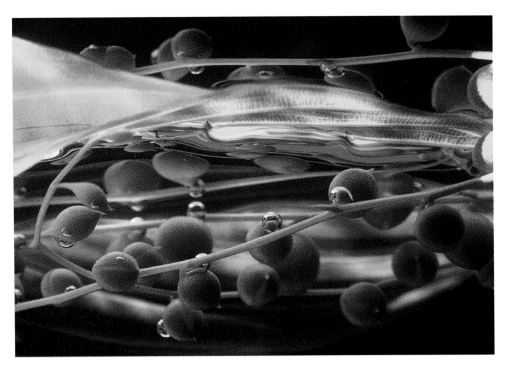

Figure 9.8
Camp tells us: "My work in color grew out of my beginnings as a poet who was writing imagist poems, but wanted to deal with color in a more tangible form than that expressed in words. . . . I was influenced by Steichen's *Heavy Roses* into using dead and dying flowers as subject matter . . . to escape the bounds of the traditional still life I made the transition from a vase to a bowl to an aquarium in which to float flowers in order to free them from the frozen specimen looking appearance so many still lives possess. Water has many properties of its own, one of which is that it picks up colors that are in proximity to it. I discovered stained glass would act as a filter, transferring its color to the surface of the water as well as to the flowers themselves."

© Roger Camp. *Water Music #24,* 1995. 16 x 20 inches. Dye-destruction print.

- *Nail polish:* Brush some clear nail polish on a piece of clear glass or an unwanted UV filter. Allow it to dry and it's ready to use. Painting different patterns and/or using a stipple effect will deliver a variety of possibilities. Nail polish remover can be used for cleanup.

- *Petroleum jelly:* Carefully apply the petroleum jelly to a clear piece of glass or a UV filter with your finger, lint-free towel, or a brush. Remove any that covers the sides or the back of the support so it won't get on your lens. The direction of application and the thickness of the jelly will determine the amount of diffusion. Cleanup is done with soap and warm water.

- *Stockings:* Stretch a piece of fine-meshed nylon stocking over the front of the lens and attach it with a rubber band. Use a beige or gray color unless you want the color of the stocking to influence the color balance of the final image. White stockings scatter a greater amount of light, thus they considerably reduce the overall contrast of the scene.

- *Transparent tape:* Apply a crisscross pattern of transparent tape on a UV filter. The amount of diffusion is influenced by the width and thickness of the tape.

· ASSIGNMENT ·

Using one or more of the methods discussed in this chapter, or one of your own design, make a series of photographs that derive their emotional impact through the use of filters.

Fluorescent and Other Gas-Filled Lights

Characteristics of Fluorescent Light

A fluorescent light source consists of a gas discharge tube in which the discharge radiation causes a phosphor coating on the inside of the tube to fluoresce. Although fluorescent light may appear to look like light from that of another artificial source it is not. Fluorescent light possesses both a discontinuous and unbalanced spectrum. The color of the light depends on the type of phosphor and gas used. It has peak outputs in the green and blue regions of the spectrum, valleys or deficiencies in red, and gaps of other wavelengths, and its intensity varies as the gas moves in the tube. This makes it a discontinuous source, lacking the full range of wavelengths that are present in the visible spectrum. Fluorescent light is generally unsuitable for naturalistic color photography.

What Happens Without a Filter?

If you photograph using daylight film under fluorescent light the resulting image will have a green cast. This is not generally attractive, especially if you are making pictures of people; they will have a green cast to their skin. If this is not what you had in mind, corrective action is required.

Unnumbered filters are available to make general adjustments for the excessive blue-green cast of fluorescent lights. With daylight film use a FL-D filter under daylight-type fluorescent lamps and a FL-W filter with warm white or white-type fluorescent lamps. With Type B tungsten film, use an FL-B filter.

Here are additional corrective actions that can be taken:

1. Use a shutter speed of 1/60 second or slower to minimize the flickering effect of the fluorescent lamp.
2. Replace all the fluorescent lights with tungsten lights or with tubes that are designed to give off light closer to daylight. (This is generally too expensive.)

Figure 9.9

Concerns with exposing the myth of the document have led Jude to deal with the absurd placement of animals and objects in natural history museums. He wants to create "an awareness of the *straight* photograph's value not as a reliable formal document, but as a visual catalyst of thought." Public places, such as the museum in this picture, are often lighted by fluorescent lights that can prove difficult to color correct. An FLD filter was used at the time of exposure. Jude states: "The flat lighting, along with a slight underdevelopment of the daylight transparency film, produced an acceptable level of contrast in the Cibachrome print. I find it best to somewhat compromise the quality of the transparency in order to avoid the usually harsh contrast of Cibachrome."

© Ron Jude. *LSU Natural History Museum*, 1990. 6 1/4 × 8 inches. Dye-destruction print.

3. Place plastic filters over the tubes that will make them closer to daylight. (This isn't often practical.)
4. If possible, shoot a fast daylight negative film that has a speed of 400 or more. This provides two chances to make corrections. Once at the time of exposure and again when making the print. The higher speed films have a greater tolerance for this type of light.
5. Experiment with the filter pack when making a print with a daylight negative film. Sometimes it is possible to get more naturalistic color with the use of only one filter, usually yellow. To color correct in printing, it may be necessary to set the magenta filter to zero in order to compensate for the excess of green cast. Results

depend on the type of fluorescent tube, film, and enlarger.

6. Use a fluorescent filter. They are available for both daylight and tungsten films and can be used with either slide or print film. These generally make a big improvement (figure 9.9). If critical results are needed, run tests using CC filters to determine the exact filtration. You will usually need a magenta or a combination of magenta and blue filters. With daylight film, start with about CC30 magenta and add additional filtration if needed.

7. Match tubes to film. Certain tubes photograph more naturally with specific films. For instance, daylight and color-matching tubes look more natural if you use a daylight-type film and filter. Warm white tubes are more suitable with tungsten films and filters.

8. Use an electronic flash as a fill light. This will help to offset some of the green cast and make the scene appear as our brain tells us it should be.

9. Use a special film, such as Fujicolor Reala, with an additional emulsion layer that responds to blue and green light (which forms a magenta dye image) and generates developer inhibitors that act on the red-sensitive emulsion layers to enhance the reproduction of blue-green colors. With proper printing filtration, people photographed under cool-white fluorescents can have natural-looking skin tones.

High-Intensity Discharge Lamps/Mercury and Sodium Vapor Sources

High-intensity discharge lamps, such as mercury and sodium vapor lights, fit into the category of gas-filled lights. These bright lamps are generally used to light industrial and public spaces. They are extremely deficient in many of the wavelengths that make up white light, especially red, they are difficult to impossible to correct for,

and they require extreme amounts of filtration (table 9.6).

Testing for a Critical Neutral Color Match

Achieving a neutral color match with any discontinuous light source requires running tests with heavy filtration (this same test can be used in any situation requiring critical color balance). Shoot a test roll of transparency film, bracketing in 1/3 f-stops, with and without selected correction filters of the subject under the expected lighting conditions. Use a color temperature meter or see table 9.3 for suggested starting filters. Include a test target, such as the color reference guide in the back of this book, in the scene with the same light as the principal subject. Keep a record of each frame's exposure and filtration. Process and examine unmounted film on a correctly balanced 5000 K light box. Placing filters over the film lets you determine their effect. Putting a 20M filter

over the film has the same effect as adding 20M in front of the camera lens when reshooting with film having the same emulsion batch number (printed on the side of the film box).

Using the Color Reference Guide

Place the color reference guide next to the transparency on the light box. Look at the gray scale first, since it is usually easier to see which color is in excess. For example, if the gray scale has a slight blue cast, add a slight yellow filter (05Y) over the transparency. Scan rapidly back and forth between the color reference guide and the image to see if it looks correct. If it does, it indicates a 05C filter should be used to achieve a neutral color balance with the same film emulsion batch and processing chemicals. This same procedure can be used with negative film, bracketing in 1/2 f-stops and producing test prints to be compared to the color reference guide.

• **TABLE 9.6** •

Filtering for Discontinuous Light Sources

Fluorescent Bulbs

Lamp Type	Film Type		
	Daylight	Tungsten	Type A
Daylight	50R	No. 85B + 30R + 10M	No. 85 + 40R
White	40M	50R + 10M	30R + 10M
Warm white	20B + 20M	40R + 10M	20R + 10M
Warm white deluxe	30C + 30B	10R	No filter needed
Cool white	30M + 10R	60R	50R
Cool white deluxe	10B + 10C	20R + 20Y	20Y + 10R
Unknown	30M	50R	40R

High-Intensity Discharge Lamps

Lamp Type	Film Type		
	Daylight	Tungsten	Type A
Lucalox	80B + 20C	30M + 20B	50B + 05M
Multivapor	20R + 20M	60R + 20Y	50R + 10Y
Deluxe white mercury	30R + 30M	70R + 10Y	50R + 10Y
Clear mercury	70R	90R + 40Y	90R + 40Y

Note: These general recommendations should only be used as starting points. For critical applications testing is necessary. Filters will vary from one kind of film, for instance Ektacolor and Ektachrome, to another.

With an exposure time of 20 minutes that combined ambient and light painting with a 1.5-million candle power spotlight and Rosco colored gels, color shifts were inevitable. Working with subject matter makes reference to the imposition of humans on the landscape. Darby says: "I enjoy the entire process of building-up of the exposure on the film. I like the idea of control and also the unpredictable surprises that can occur. The film is alive . . . [and] capable of so much with the element of time and the physical involvement of the artist."

© Patrick T. Darby/Trevor C. Davis. *Moon River #1*, 1995. 8 × 20 inches. Chromogenic color print.

· ASSIGNMENT ·

Shoot part of a roll of film under fluorescent light with no correction. Next, under the same fluorescent conditions, try one or more of the suggested corrective actions. Compare the two. Which do you favor? Why?

W hy a Color May Not Reproduce Correctly

The dye layers of color film are designed to replicate what the film designers believe is an agreeable rendering for most subjects in a variety of situations. There can be times when it is impossible to recreate a specific color, even when the film has been properly manufactured, stored, exposed, and processed. Film designers concentrate on trying to reproduce flesh tones, neutrals (whites, grays, and blacks), and common "memory" colors such as sky blue and grass green well under a variety of imagemaking situations. This results in other colors, such as yellow and orange, not reproducing as well. Color films are not sensitive to colors in precisely the same way as the human eye. For example, color film is sensitive to ultraviolet radiation. A fabric that reflects ultraviolet energy appears bluer in a color photograph than it does to the human eye. This is why a neutral garment, such as a black tuxedo made of synthetic material, may appear blue in a color print. This effect can be reduced by using an ultraviolet filter.

Other fabrics absorb ultraviolet radiation and reemit it in the blue portion of the visible spectrum. Since the human eye is not exceptionally sensitive to the shortest (blue) wavelengths of the spectrum, this effect, known as ultraviolet fluorescence, is often not noticed until viewing a color print. White fabrics, such as a wedding dress, which has had brighteners added during manufacture or laundering to give it a whiter appearance, are the most likely candidates to appear with a blue cast in a color photograph. Unfortunately a filter over the lens will not completely correct the problem. An ultraviolet absorber, such as a Kodak Wratten Filter No. 2B, is needed over the light source of an electronic flash for accurate correction.

Another trouble spot is anomalous reflectance, which results from high reflectance at the far-red and infrared end of the spectrum, where the human eye has almost no sensitivity. This is commonly observed in color photographs of certain flowers, such as blue morning glories and gentians, which reproduce badly because color films are more sensitive to the far-red portion of the spectrum than is the human eye.

Also, some organic dyes used to color fabrics, especially synthetic materials, often have high reflectance in the far-red portion of the spectrum. The effect is most frequent in medium- to dark-green fabrics, which may reproduce as neutrals or warm colors. There is no effective correction.

Color Crossover

A color crossover occurs when the highlight and shadow areas of a color transparency or negative are of different color balances. This condition is almost impossible to correct without retouching. Crossovers can be produced by using an incorrect film under a specific light

Figure 9.10
Try making photographs even if the film does not match the exact lighting conditions. The mismatch can create a lively interchange of unexpected color combinations, thus producing images with striking color balances and a heightened sense of mystery. Graham exposed 4-x-5-inch Type S negative film at about 9:00 P.M. and supplemented it with multiple pops from a portable flash unit.

© David Graham. *The Sea Missile Motel, Cocoa Beach, FL,* 1989. 30 × 40 inches. Chromogenic color print.
Courtesy of Black Star and Laurence Miller Gallery, New York, NY.

source, longer or shorter exposure times than the film was designed for, improper storage, and/or out-dated film. While often unwanted, color crossovers can produce unexpected visual excitement by creating an unreal color palette.

Take a Chance

Do not be afraid to make pictures even if your film does not match the color temperature of the light. Sometimes you can get an evocative color mood piece when this mismatch occurs. Often the combination of different light sources enlivens and creates surprise in your picture (figure 9.10). When in doubt, take it and see what it looks like. At worst you will learn what does not work for you. At best, you may have interacted with the unexpected and come away from the situation with something Jean Cocteau would have referred to as "astonishing." If you are going to be a photographer, you have to make pictures. Use your film. It is your cheapest resource and provides you with a springboard for not only your current work but future ideas as well. "Art is about taking chances. Danger and chaos—those are the real muses an artist must court," said Robert Rauschenberg. Be a visual explorer and see what you can discover.

Printing Color Negatives

© Patrick Nagatani.
Kwahu/Hopi Eagle Kachina, White Sands Missile Range, NM, 1989.
17 x 22 inches.
Chromogenic color print.

Basic Equipment and Ideas for Color Printing

Some photographers are afraid to try color printing. If you can make a successful black-and-white print, you can make a successful color print as well. The methods presented here are designed to teach the basic concepts and techniques that are necessary to make a color print with a minimum of equipment.

There are always new methods appearing on the market. Once you learn these basic principles, you will be ready to adapt to any future changes in technology without difficulty. There are some differences between working in color and black-and-white that you need to know.

The Safelight

The standard OC black-and-white safelight fogs color paper, so a #13 filter is used in the safelight when printing from negatives (slides are printed in total darkness without a safelight). The #13 filter can be used with any type of safelight that has a screw- or slide-in filter slot. The latest generation of LED (light-emitting diode) color safelights provide even more light. Since color paper is sensitive to all colors of light, safelight handling should be kept to a minimum; it is possible to fog your paper even under a #13 filter. Safelight fog first appears as a cyan stain in the white borders and highlight areas of the print.

A small pocket flashlight with an opaque paper shade is a great help in getting about and setting things up at your station (figure 10.1). For a modest investment, there are mini-battery-powered safelights that can be worn around the neck.

Color materials are extremely sensitive to light, therefore use care when pointing the flashlight or turning on any white-light source in the darkroom. Do not turn on the enlarger light if the head is raised.

Multiple station darkrooms are places of collective activity and require

responsible behavior to protect the efforts of all concerned. If an individual darkroom is available, printing can be done in total darkness when a #13 filter is not available and the paper can be processed in a drum under full illumination.

Ambient Light

Color paper has a broader spectral sensitivity than black-and-white paper, thus it is more prone to fogging and color shifts caused by ambient light. Ideally, the walls and ceiling around the color enlarger should be a matt black. Ambient light may come from such sources as light leaks in the enlarger negative stage, illuminated timers having both digital and luminous readouts, electrical devices with red "on" lights and/or illuminated dials, and reflections from shiny apparel and/or other darkroom equipment including burning and dodging tools.

Mask all potential ambient light sources with black felt, black tape, or opaque weather stripping. Make certain timers are safe or turn them away from the easel area. Make all darkroom tools out of opaque materials.

The Easel

Most easels are painted yellow by the manufacturer, which works well for black-and-white printing because the yellow color reflected onto the paper during exposure does not affect it. This is not the case with some color papers, which can be sensitive to the reflected yellow light; the papers can be fogged by it. However, papers with opaque backings, such as IL-FOCHROME Classic, are not affected by reflected color. The problem of paper being fogged by a yellow easel can be overcome by spray painting the easel baseboard with a flat-black enamel or covering it with opaque paper.

The Enlarging Lens

Use the best enlarging lens you can afford. Inexpensive lenses, with four or fewer elements, may not produce a flat

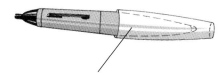

#13 Amber Safelight

Opaque piece of paper that acts as an aperture control device for the penlight.

Figure 10.1
Because color paper is sensitive to a wider range of wavelengths of light than black-and-white paper, it requires a different safelight in order not to fog the paper. A small pocket-style flashlight, with an opaque piece of paper wrapped around it to act as an aperture control, can provide additional light for setting up at the enlarging station.

field of focus, thus making it impossible to get both the center and edges of the image sharp. They also may not be accurately color corrected. Poorly made lenses can produce spherical aberrations, which lower image definition and cause focus shift. This means there is a loss of image sharpness when the lens f-stop is changed from wide open (during focusing) to its stopped-down position (for exposure). High-quality lenses have six or more elements and are better corrected for color. The best are labeled APO (apochromatic). Make sure the lens is clean and there is no light flare from light leaks around the enlarger. Most enlarging lenses provide optimum sharpness when stopped down two to three f-stops from their maximum aperture (f/8 or f/11).

The Enlarger

There are two basic types of enlargers: condenser and diffusion.

Condenser Enlarger

A condenser enlarger uses one or more condenser lenses to direct the light from the lamphouse into parallel rays as it goes through the negative. This type is widely used in black-and-white printing because of its ability to produce greater apparent sharpness and because it matches the standard black-and-white contrast grades of paper extremely well. Condenser enlargers are easily used to make color prints using color printing filters.

Diffusion Enlarger

In a diffusion enlarger, which is commonly employed in making color prints, the light is mixed in a diffusing chamber. With this type of enlarger the light is traveling in many directions (diffused) as it reaches the negative. The diffusion process ensures the proper mixing of the filtered light, offers a suitable contrast for color printing, makes defects in the negative less noticeable, and softens the final print. There are black-and-white and color diffusion enlarger light sources.

Both condenser and diffusion heads offer advantages and disadvantages. When the opportunity presents itself, try each type, compare, and see which is more suitable to your needs.

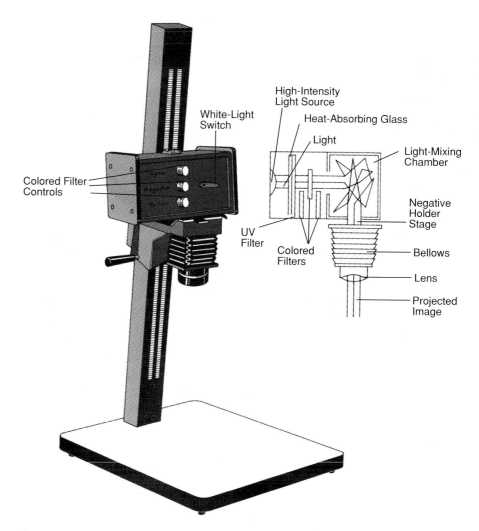

Figure 10.2
A composite dichroic diffusion color enlarger is a self-contained system that features separate colored filter controls, a color-corrected high-intensity light source, a UV filter, heat-absorbing glass, and a white-light switch.

Dichroic Systems for Printing Color

The best color enlarging system is the dichroic colorhead, which is a self-contained system with filters, a color-corrected high-intensity light source balanced for color papers, a UV (ultraviolet) filter, heat-absorbing glass, and a white-light switch (figure 10.2). Collectively, the filters are known as the color pack. They are used to adjust the color of the white light during printing in order to properly color balance the print. This colorhead normally contains three filters (cyan, magenta, and yellow) made with metalized dyes. These enable the printer to work more accurately. The dichroic head also enables you to make moderate changes in the filter pack without affecting the printing time. Most modern dichroic systems are in diffusion-type enlargers. Black-and-white printing can be done on any color enlarger by dialing the filter setting to zero.

Converting Black-and-White Enlargers

Many black-and-white enlargers can be converted to color by replacing the black-and-white head with a dichroic head. A less expensive method is to use CP and CC filters.

CP Filters. CP (color print) filters can be used with enlargers that contain a filter drawer. The CP filters change the color of the light before it reaches the negative. They are only available in the subtractive primary colors and are not as optically pure as the CC filters, but they do cost less. The major advantage of the CP filters is they go above the lens, eliminating the focus and distortion problems associated with CC filters, which are located below the lens. A UV filter and heat-absorbing glass are needed with both CC and CP filters to protect the film and shield the paper from UV exposure. Both filters can be used with either condenser- or diffusion-type enlargers but *not* with a cold-light enlarging head. The cold-light system uses coils or grids of glass gas-filled tubing that produces a colored light that is not suitable for color printing.

CC Filters.   CC (color correction) filters work well for occasional use, but they are problematic and more expensive. CC filters are optically pure gelatin acetate filters that are placed in a filter holder under the enlarging lens. They are available in both additive and subtractive colors and in a wide range of densities. CC filters change the light after the image has been focused, which can cause problems in loss of image contrast, distortion of the picture, and a reduction in overall sharpness. Economic use of filters (i.e., one CC20 filter, not four CC05 filters) helps to alleviate these problems. Wear thin cotton gloves when handling these filters in order to prevent the filters from getting dirty and scratched. Avoid leaving the enlarger light on when it is not needed, because prolonged exposure to light causes the filters to fade. The use of CP filters under the lens is not recommended because they will likely overly diffuse the image.

The disadvantages of using nondichroic filters include the need to recalculate your exposure after changing filters and their susceptibility to scratching and fading.

The Voltage Stabilizer

Regardless of the type of enlarger or filter system, a voltage stabilizer (figure 10.3) is needed. Some of the dichroic systems have a voltage stabilizer built in. Any changes in the voltage to the enlarger during exposure produce changes in the color balance. To prevent this from occurring and to have consistent results, a voltage stabilizer is connected between the timer and the power outlet.

Notebooks

Keep a notebook to record final print information. This establishes a basic starting point that will make it much easier to make a print when a similar situation occurs with a certain type of film. It also makes reprinting quicker. Commonly recorded information is provided in table

A properly produced image from a color negative enables the viewer to fully participate in the photographer's presentation of an event.

© Len Jenshel. *World Trade Center*, 1971. 16 × 20 inches. Chromogenic color print.
Courtesy of Laurence Miller Gallery, New York, NY.

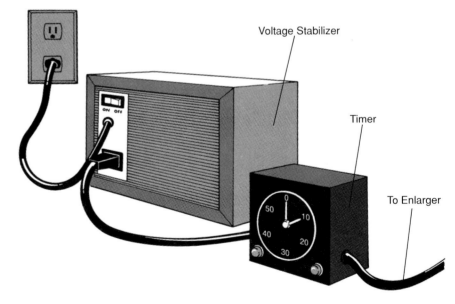

Figure 10.3
A voltage stabilizer is needed when making color prints because power fluctuations during exposure may produce changes in the color of the light source. This may cause changes in the color balance of the print, making corrections and consistency difficult to achieve.

10.1. A color printing notebook can be established by copying this table, punching it with a three-hole paper punch, and inserting it into a loose-leaf binder.

Each color enlarger has its own time and filtration differences, but the information in your notebook will help you to arrive at a final print with more ease. In a group darkroom, find an enlarger that you like and stick with it. Learn its quirks and characteristics so that you are comfortable working with it.

· TABLE 10.1 ·
Color Printing Notebook

Date: _____

Type of film used: _____

Subject or title of print: _____

Negative number: _____

Type of paper used: _____

Enlarger used: _____

Enlarger lens: _____

Enlarger height or print size: _____

f-stop of the lens: _____

Exposure time: _____

Yellow filtration: _____

Magenta filtration: _____

Cyan filtration: _____

Burning and dodging instructions: _____

Date: _____

Type of film used: _____

Subject or title of print: _____

Negative number: _____

Type of paper used: _____

Enlarger used: _____

Enlarger lens: _____

Enlarger height or print size: _____

f-stop of the lens: _____

Exposure time: _____

Yellow filtration: _____

Magenta filtration: _____

Cyan filtration: _____

Burning and dodging instructions: _____

Temperature Control

Temperature control is necessary for most color processes. Being off by as little as .5°F can cause a change in the color balance. Check your thermometer against one known to be accurate. The Kodak process thermometer is an excellent standard of comparison. Corrections can be made if yours is off. If the standard reads 100°F and yours says 101°F, simply process at 101°F instead of 100°F based on your thermometer's reading.

The least expensive method of temperature control is the water bath (see chapter 7). Chemicals are put into cold or hot water until they reach operating temperature. The temperature must be maintained, which requires constant monitoring. This method makes accuracy and consistency difficult to maintain.

If you can afford it, buy a temperature control storage tank or make your own using a fish tank heater and an old soda pop cooler. The consistency of the results, plus their convenience, offsets the cost. If you are fortunate enough to work in a lab with an automatic print processor, it takes care of temperature control, replenishment rate, and processing.

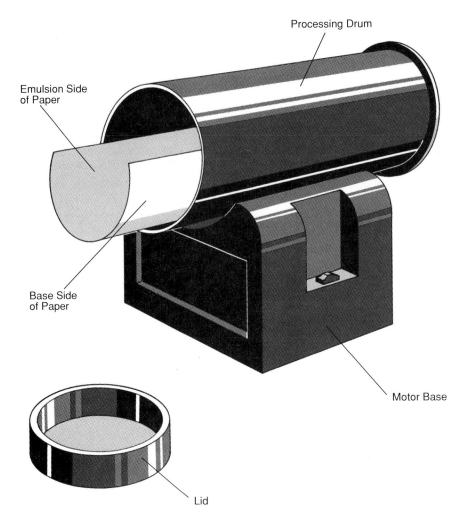

Figure 10.4
A processing drum mounted on a motor base is a convenient and inexpensive tool for making color prints. The base of the paper is placed in contact with the interior wall of the drum, with the emulsion side of the paper curling inward.

The Drum Processor

A drum processor (figure 10.4) rotates with the appropriate chemicals inside the drum and is the best alternative to an automatic color print processor. Processing can be carried out in room light with a minimal amount of chemistry. A motor base can aid in attaining proper agitation and consistency, which in turn will make printing easier, simpler, less costly, and more enjoyable. There are many types and styles of drums and bases available. Check them out and see which you prefer. The ILFOCHROME Classic-style drum has no feet or big lips to get in the way, and it rolls easily on a level surface. Drums are available from 8×10 inches to 16×20 inches. More than one print can be processed at a time in a drum. For instance, the 16-×-20-inch model can do up to four 8-×-10-inch prints. Read the

manufacturer's suggestions for use, processing times, and amounts of chemicals (see chapter 11). Kodak publications usually refer to the drum as a "tube." Prints may also be tray-processed with excellent results.

What to Photograph

Begin with a simple composition, shot on daylight-type negative film with an ISO of about 100 in normal daylight outside conditions. Do not shoot under any type of artificial light, including flash. Be sure to include a human flesh tone by shooting someone with whom you are familiar and can refer back to if need be. Many photographers also include a gray card (such

as the one in the back of this book) and a color chart for reference (on the reverse side of the gray card). Others like to incorporate a black and a white object as well to get the correct color balance. Include any colored objects that you think will be helpful in your learning process.

Photographing color references is not necessary, but it can be helpful for making impartial decisions. It is necessary to remain objective, but keep in mind that color photography is highly interpretive and therefore subjective as well. There are no standard formulas for color balance that can be applied to every situation. It is either the color that you want and like or it isn't. It makes no difference how accurately you can render the gray card if the colors do not do what you have in mind.

It is not a math problem you must solve, it is a visual one. There is more than one correct answer, but do not use this as an excuse for ignorance. You must learn technique and be able to control it in order to be proficient in the craft of imagemaking. Likewise, do not let equipment or technique get in the way of making photographs.

Keep in mind there are things to look at and things to photograph. Sometimes things we look at are worth photographing and sometimes they are not. Just because something is worth looking at does not mean it will translate well into a photograph. Other things that may be problematical to look at can make exciting pictures. How do you know the difference? By photographing and determining for yourself. In 1974 Garry Winogrand wrote an essay about his work, entitled "Understanding Still Photographs," in which he said: "I photograph to see what things look like photographed."

The Qualities of White Light: Principles of Subtractive Printing

White light is made up of blue, green, and red wavelengths, known as the additive primary colors. The three colors that are produced by mixtures of the paired additive primaries are cyan (blue-green), magenta, and yellow, called the subtractive primary colors. We will work with the subtractive method because it is the most widely used. Each subtractive primary represents white light minus one of the additive primaries (cyan equals white light minus red, magenta equals white light minus green, and yellow equals white light minus blue).

Subtractive primaries are the complements (opposites) of the additive primaries. Thus cyan is complementary to red, magenta is complementary to green, and yellow is complementary to blue. When you determine your filter combinations for printing, think of all the filters in terms of the subtractive colors. This means blue equals magenta plus cyan, green equals yellow plus cyan, and red equals yellow plus magenta.

Additive colors are converted to their subtractive equivalents in the following manner:

10 Red = 10 Magenta + 10 Yellow
20 Red = 20 Magenta + 20 Yellow

Filters of the same color are added and subtracted normally:

10 Magenta + 10 Magenta = 20 Magenta
30 Magenta − 10 Magenta = 20 Magenta

Neutral Density

Whether you work with the dichroic, CC, or CP filters, they all contain cyan, magenta, and yellow. Each of the three subtractive filters blocks out one of the three components of white light—blue, green, and red. If all three filters were used at once, not only would the color balance be changed, but some of all three would be eliminated. This also builds extra density (gray), which requires extended printing time. This effect is known as neutral density. The same color changes can usually be achieved without affecting the print density by using only two of the subtractive filters.

The general rule for printing color negatives is to use only the magenta and yellow filters. Leave the cyan set at zero. This also eliminates one-third of the filter calculations and makes printing faster and easier. Whenever possible subtract colors from your filter pack rather than add them. Most printing materials deliver that optimum response with a minimum of filtration.

Figure 10.5 shows what happens as white light is passed through the different subtractive filters.

General Printing Procedures

These are the general steps for color printing:

1. Select a properly composed and exposed negative.
2. Clean the negative carefully. Use film cleaner and soft, lint-free paper towels such as Photo-Wipes. If there are problems with dust or static, use an antistatic device. If you want to avoid the radiation contained in a static brush, get a static gun such as a Zerostat, which is sold in music stores. The static gun and a good sable brush will get the job done and eliminate unnecessary spotting of the print later. Using canned air can create more problems than it solves. The propellant can come flying out onto the negative, making a bigger mess than was already there. If you use canned air, carefully follow the manufacturer's working guidelines. Use a product that is environmentally safe, containing no chlorofluorocarbons.

    If the film has been improperly processed or handled and is noticeably scratched, apply a liquid no-scratch substance such as Edwal's No-Scratch. Clean the negative and paint No-Scratch on the entire non-emulsion side. If the negative is badly scratched, paint it on both sides. This treatment diffuses the image slightly. After printing, be sure to remove all the No-Scratch with film cleaner and Photo-Wipes. If you lose the little brushes that come with the No-Scratch, cotton swabs are a wonderful substitute.
3. Turn on the power to the enlarger.
4. Remove all filters from the light path. Many dichroic enlargers have a white light switch that will do this.
5. Open the enlarging lens to its maximum aperture. Having as much white light as possible makes composing and focusing easier because this has to be done through the orange mask of the negative film.

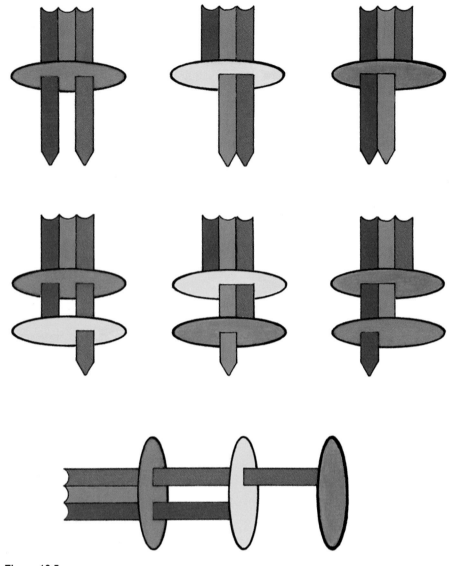

Figure 10.5
A graphic presentation of how white light is affected as it passes through the subtractive primary color filters, illustrating the basic principles of subtractive color printing.

6. Set the enlarger height, insert the negative carrier, and focus using a focusing aid. Have a piece of scrap printing paper at least the same size as the print in the easel to focus on. This makes composing possible on a black easel and ensures the print will have maximum sharpness.

7. Place the starting filter pack, based on past experience or the manufacturer's suggestion, into the enlarger. If you forget to put the filters back into the enlarger after focusing and then print with white light, the print will have an overall reddish-orange cast.

8. Set aperture at f/5.6.

9. Set timer for 10 seconds.

10. Place the unexposed paper, emulsion side up, in the easel. The emulsion side looks dark bluish gray under the safelight. The paper generally curls in the direction of the emulsion. Most paper is usually packed emulsion side up in the box. Many are packaged with only one piece of cardboard, and it is facing the emulsion side of the paper. If the paper looks white under the enlarging light, you have probably printed on the wrong side; throw it away and start again. Printing and processing through the wrong side of the paper results in a fuzzy reversed image with an overall cyan cast.

Take your time. Do not worry about making a mistake. That is part of the learning process.

11. Have an opaque sheet of cardboard that is at least the same size as the printing paper. Cut away one-quarter of it. It should look like a fat L (figure 10.6). Place it firmly on top of your printing paper. This one-quarter is now ready to be exposed.

12. Expose this first quadrant at f/5.6 for 10 seconds.

13. Move the cardboard L to uncover a different quadrant while covering the one that was just exposed. Stop the lens down to f/8 and expose for 10 seconds.

14. Repeat this process two more times until you have exposed each of the four quadrants one time at a different aperture for 10 seconds. Upon finishing this process there will be four different exposures. They will be at f/5.6, f/8, f/11, and f/16, all at 10 seconds, which is the ideal exposure time for a color negative.

Any setting within the 8- to 20-second range is fine. Color paper can suffer reciprocity failure during extremely short or long exposure times. Whenever possible, adjust the aperture so that the exposure time is as close to 10 seconds as possible to avoid color shifts due to reciprocity failure. Changes in the number of seconds used for the exposure are more likely to produce shifts in color than changes made by using the aperture. Some timers are inaccurate at brief exposures. If there appear to be inconsistent exposures, check the timer against one that is known to be true.

15. Follow the instructions for whichever process you are working with. The current industry standard is Kodak's RA-4, which offers faster dry-to-dry times, a wider selection of printing paper contrasts, a slight increase in print stability, cleaner chemicals (less tar buildup), and is more environmentally friendly (no benzyl alcohol) than its EP-2 predecessor.

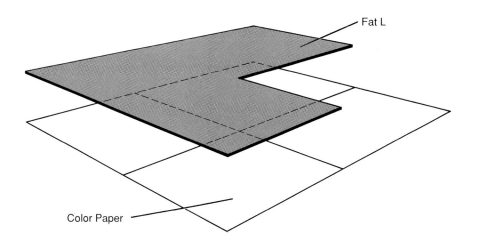

Fat L is moved so that each quarter of the paper is uncovered for its own separate exposure.

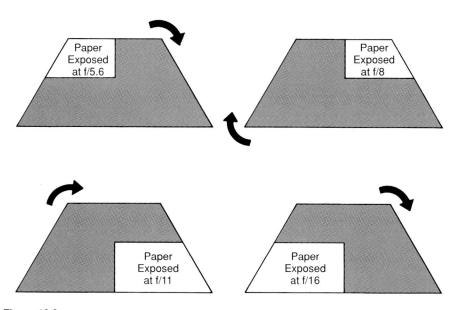

Figure 10.6
The fat L is used to find the proper exposure of color paper. Each quarter of the paper is exposed using a different f-stop with the same exposure time for all four exposures. Changes in the amount of exposure time may cause changes in the color balance.

16. Dry and evaluate. When drum processing, a handheld blow dryer speeds drying of test prints but can leave drying marks. If this is a problem, air dry the final print by hanging it from one corner on a wire line in a clean, dust-free area. Do not try to determine any accurate information about the print until it is completely dry. Color balance is not correct while a print is wet. It usually has an overall blue cast and the density appears darker until after it is dried. There are a number of common problems that occur in the processing of prints. The troubleshooting guide (table 10.2) and the manufacturer's instructions can help solve these difficulties.

The Kodak RA-4 process (table 10.3) provides a standard by which you can compare the other negative-to-print processes in a drum processor. Many institutions have small print processors that may operate with different chemicals, times, and temperatures. The automatic print processors offer ease and reliability

by providing constant processing times, temperatures, and replenishment rates. Whatever the process, be consistent so that repeatable results are achieved. It is necessary to have clean working conditions or you run the risk of contaminating the chemistry.

Color Paper Selection

There are fewer choices of color printing papers compared to black-and-white papers. There are no fiber-based papers. All the regular materials are resin-coated (RC), with a thin, water-resistant, plastic coating that facilitates rapid processing and drying. Some special-use materials have a heavier polyester base. You will want to experiment, since each manufacturer's paper delivers differences in contrast, color balance, and surface texture. Papers come in matte, semimatte (also known as luster or pearl), glossy, and textured finishes. The glossy surface reflects light and gives the impression of highest color saturation, contrast, detail, and sharpness. Is also reveals any surface defects, especially fingerprints, and is highly reflective. Color papers are generally available in only a limited range of three contrasts. There is an all-purpose version for general use, a lower-contrast paper for portrait work, and a slightly higher-contrast version. The difference in contrast is only equal to about half a grade of black-and-white paper contrast. No variable-contrast papers are available, so contrast is most easily controlled by the initial exposure of the film and the film's development time.

Handle Color Paper with Care

Handle the paper by its corners and from the base side. If you touch the emulsion you will leave a fingerprint the FBI could easily use to track you down. Handle paper with clean, dry hands. If problems continue with fingerprints, get a pair of thin cotton gloves to wear when handling the paper. Be sure to wash the gloves periodically.

• TABLE 10.2 •
Troubleshooting/Prints from Negatives

Problem	Possible Cause
Unrealistic color	Incorrect filter pack
Overall red/orange cast	Exposure with white light
Reddish fingerprints	Emulsion touched prior to processing
Light crescents	Paper kinked during handling
Very light print	Emulsion facing wrong way in drum
Light and dark streaks	Prewet not used Not enough agitation in developer Drum not on level surface Paper stuck in machine rollers
Light streaks or stains in paper feed direction	Paper feed tray damp
Blue or magenta streaks	Stop bath is not working
Pink streaks	Water on print prior to processing
Red streaks	Lack of prewet
Bluish appearing blacks	Developer is too diluted Developer time is too short Not enough drain time after prewet
Black specks and marks	Tar buildup in developer
Cyan stain	Developer contaminated by bleach-fix Paper fogged by safelight
Overall reddish cast	Developer heavily contaminated by bleach-fix
Pinkish highlights	Developer temperature too high
Yellow-greenish highlights	Presoak too hot
Dark specks or spots	Rust in the water supply
Lack of contrast	Developer temperature is too low Developer is too diluted Development time is too short Lack of agitation Not enough developer solution Developer is exhausted Chemicals outdated
Cream-colored borders	Too high developer temperature Too long development time Improper mixing of developer
Bluish magenta stain	Stop bath exhausted Wash rate is too slow
Grayish purple metallic haze	Bleach-fix exhausted
Scratches to print emulsion	Paper put into processor emulsion side up
Ivory-colored print borders	Paper has expired

Changes in Paper Emulsion

Each batch of color paper has different characteristics that affect the exposure and filtration. Because of this the paper is given an emulsion number that is sometimes printed on the package. In order to avoid the problems associated with changing emulsions, try to buy paper in as large a quantity as is affordable. It is better to buy a one-hundred-sheet box of paper than four twenty-five-sheet packages that may have been made at four different times. Each time the emulsion number is changed it is usually necessary to correct the exposure and filter information. As the manufacture of color papers has improved, there is a less noticeable difference in color balance from emulsion to emulsion.

Storage

Color paper keeps better if refrigerated. It can be frozen it you do not expect to use it for some time. Allow enough time for the paper to reach room temperature before printing or inconsistency results. It takes a one-hundred-sheet box of 8-×-10-inch paper about 3 hours to warm up.

Check the expiration date on the paper box before buying. Purchase paper from a source that regularly turns over its stock. With a permanent marker, write on the box the date you acquired your paper. Most properly stored paper lasts at least 12 to 18 months after opening. Keep paper away from high temperature and humidity. Paper that has started to deteriorate will deliver ivory borders instead of white.

Making a Contact Print

Due to the orange mask of color negative film, most photographers find it difficult to "read" what is in their negatives. The contact print provides the opportunity to see the negative in a print form. You can see what was done right and wrong in the coverage of the subject, both aesthetically and technically; you can see things that may have been missed in the examination of the negative; and it can point the direction toward the pursuit of an idea or improvement of a technique.

Richard Avedon said: "I learned from [Alexey] Brodovitch to learn from myself, from my accidents and dreams. Your next step is most often in your false step: Never throw away your contacts. The photographs you took when you were not thinking about taking photographs—let them be your guide."[1]

Follow these steps to make a contact print:

1. Place a neatly trimmed strip of paper, emulsion side up, under the enlarger. Make sure the enlarger is

[1] "Richard Avedon," *American Photography* 2, no. 4, July/August 1991, 60.

· TABLE 10.3 ·

Kodak Ektacolor RA-4 Drum Processing Steps at 95°F.

Processing Step	Time* min:sec	Temperature (°F)
Prewet	0:30 +/–0:05	95 +/– 2
Developer	0:45†	95 +/– 0.5
Stop	0:30 +/– 0:05	95 +/– 2
Wash	0:30 +/– 0:05	95 +/– 2
Bleach-Fix‡	0:45†	95 +/– 2
Wash*	1:30**	95 +/– 2
Dry	As needed	Not over 205

*Each step includes a 10-second drain time.
†Changes in time of 1 second less or 5 seconds more than normal may produce color shifts.
‡After bleach-fix, paper can be handled under room light.
*When possible, remove print from drum and wash in a tray or print washer with a continuous water flow that provides a complete change of water at least every 30 seconds.
**Longer wash times are acceptable and even desirable to remove unwanted chemicals.

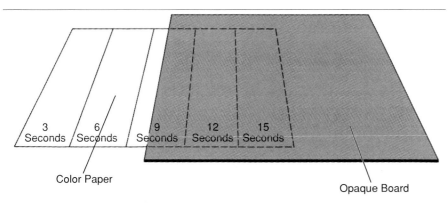

Figure 10.7
Some people do not like the fat L method for determining exposure for a contact print and instead use an opaque piece of board to block the light. In this method, like in black-and-white printing, the exposure time is varied while the f-stop remains unchanged. Once exposure is calculated, it is adjusted so it is in the 10-second range, and any additional exposure changes are made by adjusting the f-stop.

high enough that the beam of light will completely cover the paper of the full contact print evenly. If you are using a color print processor, be sure the paper is big enough to go through the machine's rollers without jamming. When making an 8-×-10-inch contact print set the enlarger to the proper height used to make an 8-×-10-inch print. This will give a closer idea of the actual enlarging time for the finished print.

2. Place the film emulsion side down on top of the paper. Cover with a clean, scratch-free piece of glass or use a contact printing frame. If safelight conditions are dim or nonexistent, leave the negatives in their protective sleeves. Check the protective sleeves to make certain they do not affect the clarity and color balance of the contact print or the filter information from the contact may not be correct when it is applied to making the final print.

3. Set the starting filter pack (based on filtration determined from previous experience, manufacturer's guidelines, or standard test negative). If you have no previous information, use 60Y and 40M as a ballpark starting point.

4. The fat L can be used to determine correct exposure, following the method previously outlined in making the print. Some people do not like using the fat L for contact prints. Instead, a piece of cardboard is used to block the light and move it across the paper to create six separate exposure increments as in black-and-white printing (figure 10.7). Try exposing at f/8 in 3-second increments (3, 6, 9, 12, 15, and 18 seconds). If the entire test is too light, open the lens to f/5.6. If it is too dark, stop the lens down to f/11 and repeat the procedure.

5. Process, dry, and evaluate.

6. Pick the area that has the best overall density. Recalibrate the time so it is in the 10-second exposure range. For example, if the best time was f/8 at 6 seconds, adjust the exposure so that the new exposure is f/11 at 12 seconds. Make any changes in the filter pack based on the information obtained in the area of best density. To avoid reciprocity failure, which produces color shifts, try to maintain exposure times in the 8- to 20-second range.

7. Make a new contact print of the entire roll based on these changes.

8. Process, dry, and evaluate.

Reading the Contact Sheet

The information from the contact print should make it easier to choose the best negative to print. If the selection looks too magenta on the contact print, begin to correct for this by adding more magenta to the filter pack before making the first test. This step begins the process of making that perfect print even more rapidly. In general, the information obtained from an 8-×-10-inch contact print (exposure and filtration) can be applied as a starting place for the creation of the 8-×-10-inch enlargement.

Evaluating a Print

People often ask, What is the correct type of light for evaluating prints? The answer is that it depends. A print may be deemed color correct in normal daylight conditions, but when displayed under artificial light, the color balance may not appear acceptable. For the most accurate results the print should be examined under lighting conditions similar to those under which the finished print will be viewed. For prints to be viewed under average daylight conditions, a print viewing area can be constructed that has two 4-foot 5500 K full-spectrum fluorescent lamps about 4 to 5 feet from the viewing surface.

Follow these steps when evaluating a print:

1. Make sure the test strip or print is completely dry. Is the exposure correct? First determine the best overall density because changes in it will affect the final color balance. It is troublesome to determine correct color balance in a print that is over- or underexposed. Look carefully at sensitive areas such as facial and neutral tones. This helps to determine which exposure will give proper treatment for what you have in mind. Disregard extreme highlights and shadow areas; they will need burning in or dodging. Underexposure makes areas of light tones lose detail and appear white. Overexposure of light tones produces unwanted density, a loss of color separation, and an overall grayish look.
2. After deciding what is the best density, determine which color is in excess. It is easier to see the incorrect color in a middle-tone area. If there is a face in the picture, the whites of the eyes are often a key spot to make this determination. Avoid basing the color balance on shadow areas, extreme highlights, and highly saturated colors.
3. The most effective way to tell which color is in excess is by using Kodak Color Print Viewing Filters (figure 10.8). One side of the filter set is designed for negative printing and the other side for positive (slide) printing. Use the appropriate side.

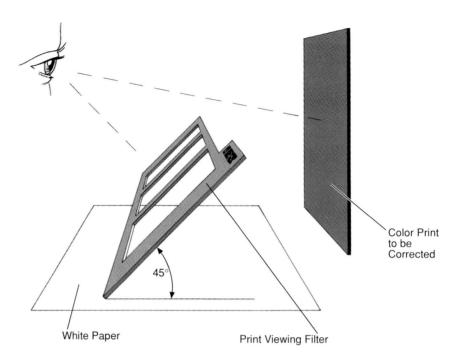

Figure 10.8
Colored print viewing filters are an effective method to learn how to recognize all the basic colors used in color printing and may be employed to make visual corrections of color prints. The correction method shown here demonstrates one technique for determining which color is in excess. Be certain the light striking the correction filter and the print is of equal intensity and quality.

Methods for Using Viewing Filters

There are a number of different ways to use viewing filters. One or a combination of the following methods should be helpful in determining the color balance of the print.

Filters Next to the Print

Under lighting conditions similar to those under which the final print will be seen, place a piece of white paper next to the area of the print to be examined. The filters are available in six colors: magenta, red, and yellow (the warm colors) and blue, cyan, and green (the cool colors). Half of these can be immediately eliminated by deciding if the print is too warm or too cool. Then glance rapidly back and forth between the key area and the white piece of paper to see if the color in excess can be determined.

The white paper is a constant to avoid color memory (see section on color memory in chapter 5). If this does not work, take the green filter and place it on the white paper at a 45-degree angle so that the light passes through the green filter and strikes the white paper, giving it a green cast. Glance rapidly back and forth between the color that the filter casts onto the white paper and the key area being examined in the print in order to see if the color cast matches. If it does, the excess color is green. If it does not, follow the same procedure with the blue filter. If the blue does not match, try the cyan. If there is a problem deciding between green and blue, it is probably neither. It is most likely cyan, the combination of blue and green light. Printing experience has shown that cyan is in excess more than either blue or green. Notice if one color appears regularly in excess in your printing, and be on the lookout for it.

Now use the viewing filter to determine the amount of excess color by judging which of the three filter strengths the color cast comes closest to. Is the excess slight (a five-unit viewing filter), moderate (ten units), or considerable (twenty units)? If the change is moderate, requiring a ten-unit, viewing filter, make a ten-point correction in the filter pack.

The dichroic head makes it possible to fine-tune a print with small changes in the filtration of two or three points. Moderate changes in filtration of ten to twenty units, generally will not affect the print density with the dichroic head. When working with CC and CP filters changes in filtration must be compensated for by adjusting the exposure time. An increase in filtration requires an increase in exposure to maintain proper print density. Use the manufacturer's suggestions until experience is gained.

Filters over the Print

Another method of making filter corrections with color print viewing filters involves looking at the print through the filter that is the complement (opposite) of the color that is in excess. To use this method, flick the filter over the print and look through it at the key examination area. Keep the filters about 6 inches from the print surface. Do not put your eye directly against the filter because it will adapt to that color. Do not let the light that is illuminating the print pass through the filter on its way to the print. Whichever filter and density combination neutralizes the excess color and makes the print appear normal is the combination on which to base the corrections. If the print looks too blue, it should appear correct through a yellow filter. Make the determination as rapidly as possible. Do not stare too long, because the brain's color memory takes over and fools you into thinking the scene is correct (an example of color adaptation). The brain knows how the scene is supposed to look and will

attempt to make it look that way, even if it does not. When in doubt, go with your first judgment.

The Ring

The "ring-around" is a popular method of evaluation in which the print is compared to a series of standard selections. The ring includes a "correct" print along with a series of "incorrect" prints made from the same negative. This includes an under-and overexposed print and one print with each of the six colors printed in varying degrees of excess. The ring can be created from your own standard negative or purchased in a commercially prepared format.

Discover the Method That Works for You

Traditionally, the ring has been used because it seemed to be the most logical way to learn how to tell the differences in color balance. The problem that arises is that we do not necessarily learn to recognize color differences in a logical manner. Most of us are able to learn just as rapidly by diving in and making a print. Making the ring is time-consuming and not particularly interesting. Our ability to learn new information remains higher when we continue to print from new and stimulating negatives. The ring can be of value to those working at home, alone, without someone experienced in color printing to act as a guide.

Ultimately, it makes no difference which method is used. We see things in our own way and in our own time. Try one of these methods; if it does not work, try another. Discover which does the job for you. You may even come up with a better way.

Françoise Gilot, the French painter and printmaker who dared to love and then leave Picasso, said:

I had to find my own path toward artistic freedom. This did not mean having less regard for the gods and demigods atop Mount Olympus, but simply recognizing that, each human experience

being unique, each artist has the burden and the privilege to bear witness, thus adding something to the wealth of human culture. Since for generations women have been notoriously silent, it was incumbent upon me and my female contemporaries to revel an as-yet-unfathomed side of the planet—the emergence of a sunken continent of thoughts, emotions, and wisdom.

In color printing, each one of us must find our own way.

Changing the Filter Pack

When modifying the filter pack (figure 10.9) a filter of the same color can be added, although it is more desirable to subtract a complementary filter. This is because the paper responds better with a minimum of filters and also because it is best to keep the exposure time in the 10-second range. In most cases use only the magenta and yellow filters. Leave the cyan set on zero. Do not have all three in the pack together because doing so produces unwanted neutral density (gray). Avoid extremes of exposure to prevent reciprocity failure.

Memorizing table 10.4 is helpful because this information is needed every time a change in the filter pack takes place. It provides the answers to the six most commonly asked questions in color printing.

Burning and Dodging

Just as in black-and-white printing, burning in, giving the print more exposure, makes it darker, and dodging, giving the print less exposure, makes it lighter. In color printing it is possible to not only change the density of a print but also the color balance of selected areas by burning and dodging. If you burn in an area with more yellow light, you reduce the amount of yellow in that area. Waving a CC or CP filter below the enlarger lens during exposure is another way to

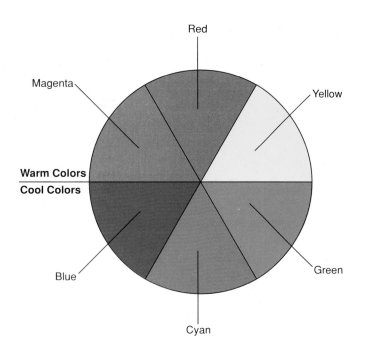

Figure 10.9
The basic rules for making changes in the filter pack. (*a*) It is first determined from the color wheel if the print is a cool or warm color, and then it is decided which color it is. Using the colored print viewing filters, it is decided how much correction is needed. (*b*) The chart is a reference to determine how much and which filters must be used to make the desired correction.

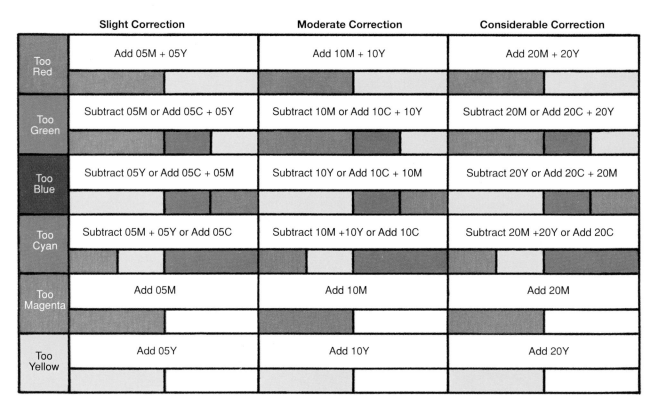

	Slight Correction	Moderate Correction	Considerable Correction
Too Red	Add 05M + 05Y	Add 10M + 10Y	Add 20M + 20Y
Too Green	Subtract 05M or Add 05C + 05Y	Subtract 10M or Add 10C + 10Y	Subtract 20M or Add 20C + 20Y
Too Blue	Subtract 05Y or Add 05C + 05M	Subtract 10Y or Add 10C + 10M	Subtract 20Y or Add 20C + 20M
Too Cyan	Subtract 05M + 05Y or Add 05C	Subtract 10M +10Y or Add 10C	Subtract 20M +20Y or Add 20C
Too Magenta	Add 05M	Add 10M	Add 20M
Too Yellow	Add 05Y	Add 10Y	Add 20Y

change the color balance for a specific area. For instance, a yellow filter can be waved across the projected sky area to make the sky bluer or a blue filter can be waved across the color shadow areas of a projected image to make it warmer (more yellow). Start with ten units of whatever color you want to work with.

Be prepared to add exposure time to compensate for denser filters. Too much burning and/or dodging can cause a color shift to take place in those areas.

A "dodger" can be made by cutting a piece of opaque cardboard in the shape of the area that will be given less exposure and attaching it to a dowel, pencil, or

wire with a piece of tape (figure 10.10). Keep the dodger moving during the exposure or an outline will appear on the print. A ballpark range for dodging is about 10 to 20 percent of the initial exposure. An area being dodged can seldom tolerate more than a 30 percent dodge before the differences between the overall exposure and the area being dodged become apparent. For example, a black area will turn gray with a color cast.

A "burning" tool can be produced by taking a piece of opaque cardboard that is big enough to cover the entire print and cutting a hole in it to match the shape of the area to be given more exposure (figure 10.11). Keep it in constant motion during exposure to avoid the outline effect. Generally, burning in requires more time than dodging. Bright highlight areas, such as skies, often require 100 to 200 percent of the initial exposure time. Reciprocity failure can occur while burning in, producing color shifts that may require a change in the filter pack for the area being given the extra time.

Save These Tools

After a while your collection of opaque burning and dodging tools will meet most printing needs, saving construction time and speeding darkroom work. Some photographers do most of their burning and dodging with their fingers and hands. Others prefer to purchase commercially prepared tools. Do whatever works best for your needs.

Final Decisions and Cropping

Once the correct filter pack and exposure are determined, check the print for exact

Dodging and burning tools may be made in a variety of forms. Flynt made his own "dodging matts" in order to emphasize various areas of the composition and surface integrity of the print. During this process, the print received a number of exposures, each with a different filter pack. This idea is clarified by Flynt's statement: "I work primarily with dancers and performers who are equally interested in the movement possibilities afforded underwater. The additional elements superimposed in the darkroom further distance the viewer from the traditional perception of the photographed figure in space. The overlays provide an ironic element of *place* or structure that the original underwater setting lacked. The pool provides the neutrality of the studio, combined with the spontaneity of the street."

© Robert Flynt. *Untitled,* 1989. 11 × 14 inches. Chromogenic color print.

cropping. A handy way to determine whether the print has been cropped properly is to cut out a pair of Ls from a piece of white board. These Ls can be overlayed with one another on the print to determine the exact cropping of the final picture.

Look at the Print in a Mirror

If the print still does not look the way you wish, try an old painter's method for seeing the work in a different fashion: look at the print in a mirror. Reversing the image allows you to momentarily forget your original idea and see the work as a viewer might or in a totally different manner than before. This could provide the clue to the direction you need to take to let the picture deliver its message to its future audience.

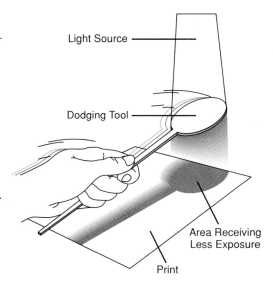

Figure 10.10

A "dodger" is employed to give an area of a print less exposure. It is necessary to keep the dodger in motion during exposure to avoid creating an outline of the tool.

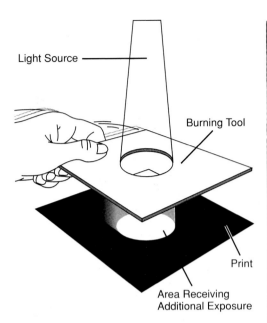

Figure 10.11
A "burning" tool is used to give an area of the print more exposure. It must be kept in motion during exposure or a dark halo effect will be visible around the edges of the area receiving more light.

Color Analyzers

Color analyzers are exposure meters for the darkroom that measure color in addition to brightness of a projected color image. The information they provide is used to help determine the correct exposure and filter pack of the print. To be of use, the analyzer must be programmed. This is done by finding (by trial and error) the proper exposure and filtration for a standard reference negative, generally containing a gray card and/or average skin tone (you can make your own or buy one from Kodak) for a specific paper. This information is put into the analyzer and becomes the standard by which the machine bases its decisions.

When a print is made from a new negative, a probe is used to read comparative areas such as skin tone or a gray card from the new negative. The machine then compares the information and tells what the difference is between the two. This data is then used to make adjustments in the exposure and filter pack of the enlarger to bring the new negative in line with the standard. An an-

Scales prefers working with 400 speed negative film in the 6-×-6-centimeter format because of the latitude and flexibility it gives him when printing his scenes of everyday life in New York City. "I try to make images that allude to the reality of being Black in America. The photographs are descriptions of my perceptions of ordinary places and people—in the complexities of living. I do not pretend to understand them, each person. In fact, the discoveries are most often within myself, observing these documents of my own sights."

© Jeffrey Henson Scales. *Grant's Tomb*, 1993. 19 × 19 inches. Chromogenic color print.
Courtesy of the Visual Studies Workshop Gallery, Rochester, NY.

alyzer can be very useful in production work, where the same type of film is exposed under the same type of illumination. Color labs use analyzers with specific programs for use with specific films. Problems can arise when a new negative does not contain a suitable standard reference area for the analyzer to read.

What a Color Analyzer Cannot Do

An analyzer can be a benefit under certain conditions, but it can prove to be problematic for beginning photographers who want to learn and understand the basic concepts and principles of color

printing. An analyzer can leave the photographer out of the fundamental creative visual process of achieving the perfect print. With the analyzer, you do not even have to know what filters are in the pack or how changes in the relationship of filters affect the print. Printing is a private, individualistic, subjective, and time-consuming activity. It requires the photographer to make visual decisions based on the merits of each picture situation and not on a predetermined machine response. At times it seems an analyzer mainly teaches the operator how to program and reprogram a machine. Some photographers become dependent on this unnecessary piece of equipment. They use the machine's brain instead of their own to make pictures. For some beginners the analyzer offers the illusion of freedom, independence, and self-sufficiency. But once you learn to make all printing decisions visually, with your own eyes and mind, the possibilities increase. You can do anything you like to the print, anywhere, at any time. Consider John Ruskin's advice in "On the Nature of Gothic Architecture" from *The Stones of Venice:* "The painter should grind his own colours; the architect work in the mason's yard with his men; the master-manufacturer be himself a more skillful operative than any man in his mills."[2]

As with almost anything else in photography, there are those who would offer a different opinion. When the opportunity presents itself, try an analyzer and see what you think. They can be fun, but do not be seduced by pure technology. Make a judgment based on your experience and actual needs. Until then, do not run out and purchase an analyzer for color printing.

There are other devices, such as the visual color matrix, that are designed to help determine the correct filter pack. Although less expensive, these devices tend to be imprecise, providing at best a general starting place for the filter pack.

Following the methods outlined in this chapter, most people can make a correct color print from a properly exposed negative within three attempts (test strip, first print, second corrected print) while at the same time learning the basic concepts and principles of color print making.

Internegatives

A color print can be made directly from a slide using a separate positive printing process (see chapter 11) or with a regular color negative print processing method by first making what is called an

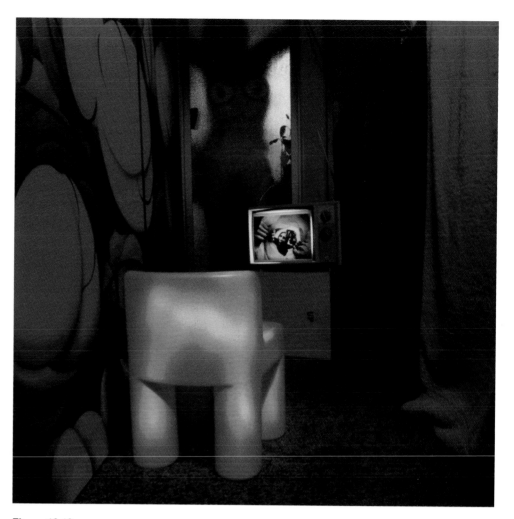

Figure 10.12
De Marris is involved in constructing sets, much like stage setting for plays, in which all items are precisely chosen and arranged. Long exposures, lasting minutes, give her the chance to enter the scene during the actual taking of the photograph to light very specific areas. Flood lamps and/or light bulbs of various colors, mixed with flashlights, modeling lights, and strobes with colored gels provide a surreal color scheme. Duraflex printing materials allow De Marris to make very large and rugged prints, with the presence of a painting on a wall, that reveals the importance highly saturated color plays in her imagery.

© Pamela De Marris. *Renunciation # 4*, 1990. 50 × 50 inches. Chromogenic color print.

internegative (figure 10.12). An internegative is a negative made from a transparency, usually by projecting the image onto sheet film. One method of accomplishing this is through the use of one of the family of Kodak's Vericolor Internegative Films. These are available in 35-mm 100-foot rolls and in sheets of 4-×-5-inch, 5-×-7-inch, and 8-×-10-inch film. Fuji also makes a complete line of internegative materials. All are tungsten-balanced (3200 K) films that can be processed in C-41 color negative chemicals. If the source of exposure is not 3200 K, use filters to correct it. Internegative films offer a long tonal range and excellent color separation, and they

do not have much trouble with reciprocity failure. These films can give the photographer more control over color and detail in the final print than is sometimes possible with a direct slide-to-print process (positive-to-positive). Development time can be altered by up to +/− 20 percent from normal to increase or decrease contrast without causing much of a color shift.

Making Internegatives on 4-×-5-inch Film

Place a clean, properly exposed slide in the enlarger. Take a clean 4-×-5-inch sheet-film holder and slide in a piece of

[2] John Ruskin, *The Works of John Ruskin*, vol. X. Edited by E. T. Cook and Alexander Wedderburn (London: George Allen, 1903–12), 201.

Using a 4-×-5-inch camera and straight negative printing methods, Whaley blends the languages of photography and painting to evoke a theatrical state between the imaginary and the real. Under the guise of the still-life genre, Whaley's *Natura Morta* (Dead Nature) series reflects the anxieties that are between our civilization and the natural world. Whaley states: "Through Western art historical references and the juxtaposition of the beautiful and the unexpectedly morbid, or the serious and the whimsical, the work explores the ironic tensions between these two worlds and the time-bomb inherent in that conflict."

© Jo Whaley. *Communication Theory*, 1994. 20 × 24 inches. Chromogenic color print.
Courtesy of the Robert Koch Gallery, San Francisco, CA.

exposure. Once this is established, make any future changes by either opening or closing the lens; changes in time could alter the color balance.

Film is developed in a standard C-41 process, and it can be processed in a drum as with a piece of paper. Use 3 ounces of each chemical for the 8-×-10-inch drum and increase the development time by 10 to 20 percent. Take the negative out of the drum for washing. If there is a blue streak down the middle of the film, it indicates that the tank wall prevented the developer from washing away the antihalation dyes. This streak should wash out.

Kodak makes internegatives at a modest cost that deliver acceptable results for most general daylight situations. For critical work, a custom internegative is probably necessary. Since internegatives are a generation removed from the original they tend to produce prints that do not match the color accuracy and/or sharpness of a print made directly from an original camera negative.

Copying a Slide onto Negative Film

A slide can be copied onto color negative film with the use of a copying tube. The tube fits over the front of the camera lens and holds one slide at a time. Point the camera at a bright light source that matches that color balance of the film being used, and then focus and set the exposure. Use a camera that has thru-the-lens (TTL) metering because it will easily give the correct exposure. Still, it would not hurt to bracket the exposures. Next, process the film and print in the regular manner.

plain white paper. Focus the image to the required size. Check to be certain that there are no light leaks or reflections coming from the enlarger that can fog the film. Close down the enlarging lens until the shadow values start to lose detail and merge together, usually at about f/11. In total darkness, remove the white piece of paper and replace it with a piece of film. Be careful not to move the

holder. A tape marker can be used to indicate where the holder should go and can be felt in the dark. If the holder has been moved, put the dark slide in over the film, turn on the enlarger, and reposition the holder. See the instruction sheets that come with each type of film for suggested exposure and filter starting points. When establishing a starting pack, a test strip can be made to determine proper

Display and Print Materials

Kodak Duratrans, Duraclear, and Duraflex materials allow you to make large-scale color transparencies directly from color negatives and internegatives. Duratrans RA Display Material is durable and translucent, making it ideal for backlit transparencies on illuminators without dif-

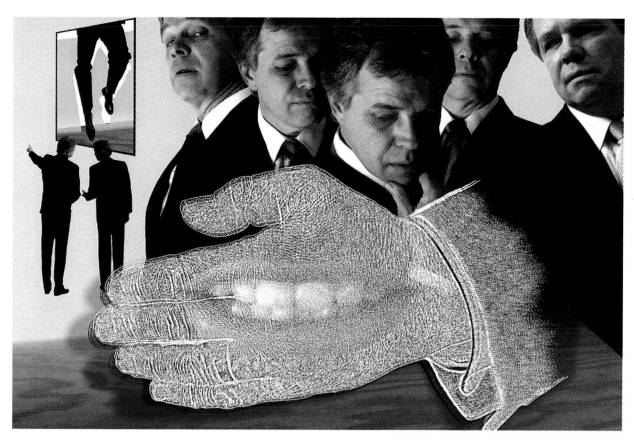

According to Hallman, "This work relates to the production of gender defining images produced by women beginning in the late 1970s. The considerable attention given these issues by female artists was often met by men with a disregard that ignored the impact of those very issues upon their own lives. As men. Those whom the structure favors are not inclined to question or examine that structure. It is not surprising that there has been a lack of interest by many of us [men], with the notable exception of gay men, in exploring what men are . . . [and the] largely invisible patterns within this culture that inhibit or influence many of the choices made in our lives." This image was processed using Adobe PhotoShop software. The original negatives were scanned onto Kodak CD-ROM.

© Gary Hallman. *Committee II (Wise Guys)*, 1994. 24 × 36 inches. Inkjet print.

fusers. Kodak Duraclear RA Display Material is a clear-based transparency material designed for use on illuminators with built-in diffusers. Kodak also makes plastic-based Duraflex RA print materials, which are designed to make reflection prints. Typically they are used to make ID cards, postcards, and sales presentation portfolios, which require durability. Artists use these materials to make very large prints because of their sturdiness (figure 10.12).

These products are processed in a regular RA-4 setup but do require longer processing times than normal RA-4 papers.

Ilfocolor Deluxe

Ilfocolor Deluxe, formerly marketed as Ilford Colorluxe, is a color negative print material on a polyester base. It is useful when a durable image base is required. It has an extremely high-gloss surface with ILFOCHROME Classic-like color saturation. It is available for the RA-4 process and does not require any changes in processing times (Nagatani's chapter opening photograph is an example of Colorlux).

All of the previously mentioned display materials should be handled in total darkness and may be intermixed in the same chemistry as other color print materials without any ill effects.

References

For more information about color negative chemicals, equipment, or materials contact:

Agfa
100 Challenger Road
Richfield Park, NJ 07660

Charles Beseler Company
1600 Lower Road
Linden, NJ 07036

Fuji
514 South River Street
Hackensack, NJ 07601

Ilford Photography
West 70 Century Road
Paramus, NJ 07653

Jobo Fototechnic
P.O. Box 3721
Ann Arbor, MI 48106

Kodak Information Center
Department 841
R2-Riverwood
Rochester, NY 14650

Unicolor
Photo Systems, Inc.
7200 Huron River Drive
Dexter, MI 48130

ELEVEN

Making Prints from Color Transparencies

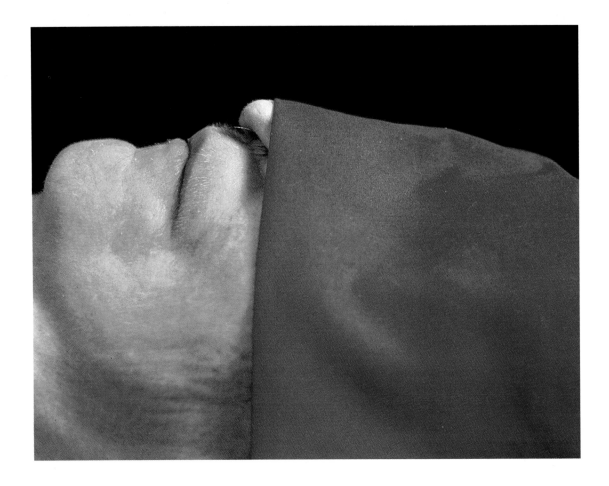

© Andres Serrano.
The Morgue (Infectious Pneumonia, 1992).
49 1/2 × 60 inches. Dye-destruction print with silicone, plexi-glass and wood frame.
Courtesy of Paula Cooper Gallery, New York, NY.

Working in the straightforward fashion of a studio photographer, Serrano looks closely at subjects most people would prefer to ignore. Serrano confronts our anxiety concerning scopophobia, the fear of looking and the fear of being seen. Serrano is not interested in transcending his literal subject matter; his images are about what they are of, and any allegorical capacity hinges on the significance of what is before the lens. Serrano favors the dye-destruction process because it is "particularly well suited for such colors as reds and yellows which coincidentally have figured prominently in my work."

Improvements in processing techniques now enable you to produce a high-quality print directly from a color transparency (aka slides). There are advantages of transparency film over negative film. First, processed transparency film produces a direct-positive image to view. This makes it much easier to tell which transparency has the preferred color and exposure without making a contact sheet. Since there is no orange mask to get in the way, what you see is what you get. Next, transparency material is capable of showing a wider range of tones than a negative, though this advantage is lost when a print is made from a slide. Last, a transparency gives better results if the picture is to be reproduced using any type of photomechanical printing process—that is, prints for publication—since separations can be made directly from the transparency without making an additional generation (the print).

The Processes

There are a number of companies that manufacture the materials for making prints from transparencies. Rapid changes in this area cause products to appear, change, and disappear in a short period of time. At the moment, there are two common processes in use that appear to be similar but are not interchangeable.

The Chromogenic Process

In the chromogenic process the colors are made by a chemical reaction with the developer. The Kodak Ektaprint R-3000 process with its Ektachrome 22 and Radiance papers are examples of this process. Note: There is also an R-3 process that is *not* recommended for drum processing because it requires reexposure to a 100-watt bulb at a distance of 2 feet during the last 40 seconds of the first wash. The Agfachrome CRN and CRH papers and Fujichrome Color Paper Type 35 are compatible with the R-3 process. Table 11.7, toward the end of this chapter, outlines the basic starting steps for drum processing with the R-3000 process.

Casebere does not work in direct response to an actual subject (such as a real prison) but by contemplating it through images, texts, and popular beliefs and then constructing a visual interpretation of his finding. Casebere's model of the panopticon, the *ideal* prison of the nineteenth century, elicits an unsettling sense of edgy mystery. This emotional response is provoked by how Casebere directs his studio lights to produce deep shadows. His camera placement does not reveal the real size of his model. The shiny surface of the dye-destruction print calls attention to the lone light in the window and makes the viewer speculate what is going on inside.

© James Casebere. *Panopticon #2*, 1992. 40 × 30 inches. Dye-destruction print.
Courtesy of Michael Klein Gallery, New York, NY.

The Dye-Destruction Process

In the second process, known as dye-destruction or silver dye-bleach, all the dyes are present in the emulsion. Processing destroys the dyes that are not needed to make the final image. Utocolor, a dye-destruction process introduced in 1909, was the first method for making prints from color slides. Gasparcolor, unveiled in 1933, was a movie film in which the subtractive color image was formed by bleaching out the unwanted dyes instead of forming them in the emulsion. The IL-FOCHROME Classic P-30P process and paper is based on the Gasparcolor process and can be used in a home darkroom. This process was originally known as Cibachrome. In 1992 Ilford changed the name of Cibachrome materials to IL-FOCHROME Classic, adding lower-contrast materials to the product line. At present it is the most widely used reversal process and is covered in depth later in this chapter (see table 11.4 for review of this process).

There are other processes available. Each has its own strengths and weaknesses. Since there is such a great variety of processes and since technical changes occur with great frequency, it is most important to read the manufacturer's instructions *before* you begin to work.

Basic Reversal Printing Principles and Equipment

In the midst of all these technological transformations there are some basic principles that can be applied to reversal printmaking.

Safety

Follow the manufacturer's instructions and the guidelines found in chapter 3. Wear Neoprene gloves, which repel acids and bleach, when handling chemicals. Obtain Material Safety Data Sheets (MSDS) from each manufacturer. Work in a well-ventilated area. Avoid breathing any chemical fumes. If you are sensitive to fumes, wear a protective organic vapor mask. Read Ilford publications *Disposal of Photoprocessing Wastes* (1992) and *Procedure for Neutralizing Ilford, ILFOCHROME Classic and ILFOCHROME Rapid Bleach Solutions* (1994).

The "Ideal" Transparency

The most important step in reversal printmaking is the selection of the "ideal" transparency since all the results are based on it. Generally, a slide with a greater-than-normal color saturation produces superior results. This means a slide that has been slightly underexposed by 1/3 to 1/2 of an f-stop. A contrasty slide is difficult to print, because the process itself adds more contrast to the finished print. A slide that might normally be considered a little flat often prints surprisingly well.

What to Photograph: Keeping It Simple

For first attempts at making prints from slides, work from a simplified transparency. Avoid the use of a lot of different colors. Make slides that show predominantly one, two, or three colors. This does not mean that you make a picture with only one color in it; one color should have the greatest visual influence, authority, or force in the picture.

Next, make photographs that have uncluttered compositions. Emphasize shape; look for rectangles, circles, squares, triangles, and other geometric formations.

Start out using a daylight balanced film. Properly exposed warm-toned films tend to print with little difficulty on reversal papers. Once you gain experience and confidence, move ahead to more complex compositions and color arrangements.

A "standard" slide, like the standard negative discussed in chapter 10, having a flesh tone, gray card, and color patches, is an effective guide for some photographers for learning the basics of reversal printing.

Lack of an Orange Mask

Because slides do not have the orange mask to compensate for inadequacies in the negative/positive system, expect to lose a certain amount of detail and subtlety in the tone and color of the reversal print.

No Safelight

The sensitivity of these materials is such that safelights cannot be used. The paper must be handled in total darkness until it is loaded in a drum, which is the easiest way to process these materials.

Determining the Emulsion Side of the Paper

It can be difficult to determine which is the emulsion side of the paper in total darkness. Here are four ways to tell which is the emulsion and which is the base side of the paper:

1. The paper has a tendency to curl, with the emulsion on the outside of the curve.
2. Use the glow from a luminous timer dial or a strip of luminous tape on the darkroom wall. The paper reflects light on the nonemulsion side. This will not fog the paper.
3. Ilford suggests rubbing both sides of the paper while holding it up to your ear. The emulsion side makes a different sound than the base side. If this method is used, be careful not to damage the paper and have clean hands to avoid leaving fingerprints. With ILFOCHROME papers, the emulsion comes facing the label on the inner light-tight package.
4. If all else fails, cut an edge from a piece of the paper and look at it under white light to determine the emulsion side.

Keep a Record

Keep a written record of your lab work (see notebook model in chapter 10). Once the proper exposure and filtration for a type of film in a certain lighting situation (daylight, tungsten, mixed) are established, you have a basic starting filter pack the next time this situation is encountered. As in negative printing, the perfect print is best discovered through a visual process of trial and error. Different films, enlargers, lenses, and paper all produce changes in the filter pack.

Temperature Control

If the process requires temperature control, warm the chemicals in their sealed bottles in a water bath (see temperature control and water bath sections in chapter 7). Clean glass baby food jars make good one-shot chemical containers. Put tape on the side and label a separate jar for each step. Make a mark on the side of the jar to indicate the proper amount of chemical needed for each step.

It is important to be able to make a print directly from a slide. The image can then be viewed in a wider variety of surroundings. It also affords the photographer the opportunity to interact with the picture and to make changes and corrections. Here Troeller combined a monochrome palette, limited depth of field, and dye-destruction's naturally high contrast to make a vibrant illusion in space. She adds: "Photographing nudity at healing sites and spas required using a fast slide film because much of the work was in non-window interiors where flash was invasive. I found Kodachrome 200 very sensitive to reds and skin tones in this light."

© Linda Troeller. *Contrexeulle Spa*, 1989. 16 × 20 inches. Dye-destruction print.

Making a Print

To make a print, remove the slide from its mount and clean it carefully because dust spots will appear as black spots on the final print, making spotting difficult. Now insert the slide into the negative carrier. Tape may be applied along the sprocket holes to keep the piece of film in place. In most of the processes the emulsion side goes down, but check the process instructions to be sure. Place the carrier into the enlarger and turn it on. Compose and focus the picture on a scrap piece of the same type of paper with which you are working. Unless the paper has an opaque backing, it can be fogged by an easel with a yellow base. Avoid this problem by spray painting your easel with flat black enamel or taping a piece of black paper securely to the easel base. If you have difficulty focusing on your target paper, remove all the filters from the pack to get white light.

Be sure to return the filters to the pack before printing. Some enlargers have a white-light switch that does this automatically. Set the filtration according to past experience or the manufacturer's recommendations, and then make a test strip of a key area, the same as you would for a print from a negative.

Response to Time and Filtration

One major difference in reversal papers is their response to time and filtration. You must be bolder in your changes to affect the print. Starting test strip times could be 5, 10, 20, and 40 seconds at about f/8 or f/11.

When making filter corrections, often there will be little difference in changes of three or five units of a color. Leaps of ten, fifteen, or even twenty units at a time are not unusual.

Before processing, recheck the manufacturer's procedures and times.

Processing

Processing may be carried out in a drum or small tabletop processor such as those made by Jobo. The drum is a good starting place because it is inexpensive and easy to use since the steps can be carried out in white light. Tray processing also works fine, but be sure there is adequate ventilation.

Using the Drum

When using a processing drum, be sure it is clean and dry. When loading the drum, place the base of the exposed paper against the wall of the drum, with the emulsion side curling inward upon itself. Be certain the lid is secure before turning on the white light. Process on a flat, even surface covered with a towel for good traction. A motor base for the drum can be obtained to make processing easier if a great deal of printing is planned. The ILFOCHROME Classic-style drum, with no legs sticking out the sides to get in the way, is the best for rolling on a flat surface. The drum rotates with the chemicals inside (see figure 10.5).

General Preprocessing Procedures

Have all the chemicals warmed to temperature and ready to go before exposing the paper. If tray processing, be certain to have enough chemicals to completely cover the entire print. Note that Ilford does not recommend tray processing for ILFOCHROME materials. Avoid contamination by always using the same bottles for the same solutions. Have a container ready for proper disposal of chemicals. Check and maintain proper temperature or your results will be chaotic and not repeatable. Presoak the paper for 60 seconds in a water bath to help ensure even development. Drain times are considered to be part of the normal processing times. If the presoak is 60 seconds and it takes 10 seconds to drain the drum or tray, start to drain at 50 seconds.

"During the later part of the 1980s," Simmons says, "I was dealing [often using dollhouse-size figures] with the superficiality, with the exterior mode we inhabit, with the confusion between ourselves and our possessions: a self-image based on what we do and where we live and how we function and certain kinds of cold disappointments in terms of truth and lies. One of the things I'm working on in my new work is imagining the daydreams and the night dreams and the fantasies of the characters that I've created. Now I'm concerned about what's going on inside . . . it's important for me to address their inner lives."

© Laurie Simmons. *Cafe of the Inner Mind: Dark Cafe*, 1994. 35 × 53 inches. Dye-destruction print. Courtesy of Metro Pictures, New York, NY.

Proper Agitation

When rolling the drum on a flat surface, make the pattern of agitation uneven during the first 30 seconds. Lift the drum up slightly on one side, roll it, and then lift it up on the other side.

Print Drying

Exercise care in handling a wet print because the emulsion is very soft and easy to damage. After processing, dry the print with a handheld hair dryer or in an RC paper print dryer. Do not dry it in a regular dryer that was designed for fiber-based papers because this will melt the plastic coating on the print and leave a mess on the dryer. To avoid getting hair dryer marks, air dry the final print by hanging it on a wire line from one corner in a warm, dust-free area.

Evaluating a Print

For best results compare the test strip with the original slide or a similar slide of the same subject. Look at it in the same type of light that you expect to view your finished print. Pick the exposure that you like the best and check for color balance in key areas. If possible, look at a white or neutral area when deciding which color is in excess. Use the Color Print Viewing Filters on the side-labeled prints from slides as a guide.

The guideline for determining proper density is to print for the key highlight area, thus ensuring the retention of highlight detail. If there is more than about a six f-stop difference between the key highlight and the key shadow (a brightness range of 1:64), burning in the shadow areas (and maybe masking) is usually a necessity. Another point to consider is that slide films were designed for projection and not for printmaking. No

reversal paper is capable of retaining the total range of density and color that was in the original slide.

The main thing to remember when printing from slides is that all the rules of negative printing must be turned around (table 11.1). This could prove to be a bit confusing if you have been negative printing. Take a little extra time and think before you act. It could save time, money, and a great deal of anger. They don't call it reversal for nothing.

Reversal Exposure Starting Points

Having determined the correct number of seconds required for exposure, make future exposure changes, whenever possible, using the aperture of the enlarging lens (table 11.2). Changing the amount of seconds can affect the established color balance. This procedure can reduce the need for making additional corrections to the color pack.

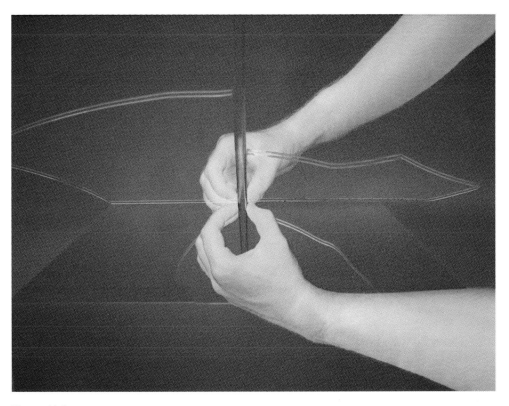

Figure 11.1

This piece is part of a series of dye-destruction prints made from color negatives, instead of color slides. It was made in the studio using broken glass and mirrors. According to Dzerigian: "Using the negative image and its subsequent reversal of values and hues established the abstraction and light from within qualities I was looking for in this symbolic still life."

© Steve Dzerigian. *Union*, 1984. 8 3/4 × 13 inches. Dye-destruction print.

Color Corrections

To remove the excess color cast from a print, remove that color from the filter pack. This means all the negative printing filter rules also apply in reverse. Depending on the process, cyan filters may be employed. Be sure to have only two colored filters in the pack at once or unwanted neutral density will be produced. Refer to table 11.3 to avoid confusion.

Work in units of about five to ten for a slight change in color, ten to twenty for a moderate change, and twenty to forty for a considerable effect. Generally, changes of five units or fewer are hardly noticeable in reversal printing, except when trying to match subtle color tones in a final print. Be bolder with corrections than in negative printing. A general rule is to double the corrections in reversal printing, based on your negative printing experience. Unlike printing from color negatives, it is possible to make prints with white light and all the filter settings on zero.

After making the appropriate changes, make a new test print and reevaluate following the same procedures.

Local Color Correction

It is possible to selectively add colors to a print during exposure. Hold a color printing (CP) filter under the lens so that it covers the area you wish to alter. A CP filter can be cut into smaller pieces and attached to a support wire to filter smaller areas of a print. The amount of filtration depends on the effect desired. With reversal papers, filter densities up to fifty units may be used for dramatic effects.

Variations. ILFOCHROME Classic material can be exposed directly in a camera, resulting in a direct-positive color image. Filters can be placed in front of the lens at the time of exposure to make color corrections and changes. Another possibility is to print color negatives instead of slides. The outcome is a negative color print instead of a positive color print (figure 11.1).

• TABLE 11.1 •
Some Reversal Printing Rules

- More exposure gives you a lighter print, not a darker one.
- When looking at your test strip, keep in mind that the darkest strip has actually had the least amount of exposure.
- To darken an area, give it less exposure.
- To lighten an area, give it more exposure.
- To make a print darker, give it less exposure.
- To make a print lighter, give it more exposure.

• TABLE 11.2 •
Using the Aperture of the Enlarging Lens to Control Exposure

- If the print is slightly dark,
  open the enlarging lens about 1/2 f-stop.
- If the print is dark, open the aperture of the enlarging lens about one f-stop.
- If the print is slightly light,
  close the enlarging lens about 1/2 f-stop.
- If the print is light, close the aperture of the enlarging lens about one f-stop.

• TABLE 11.3 •
Reversal Filter Pack Changes

Print Is Too	Add	or	Subtract
Blue	Yellow		Cyan and magenta
Yellow	Magenta and cyan		Yellow
Green	Magenta		Cyan and yellow
Magenta	Cyan and yellow		Magenta
Cyan	Magenta and yellow		Cyan
Red	Cyan		Magenta and yellow

• **TABLE 11.4** •

Review of ILFOCHROME Classic Process P-30P

For making an 8-×-10-inch print at 75°F with 2.5 ounces of chemical per step

Step	Time
1. Presoak	30 to 60 seconds
2. Develop	3 minutes
3. Rinse	30 seconds
4. Bleach	3 minutes
5. Rinse	15 to 30 seconds
6. Fix	3 minutes
7. Wash	3 minutes minimum
8. Dry	As needed

ILFOCHROME Classic: The Current Standard

There are many processes available for making prints directly from slides. Many color printers believe the dye-destruction process offers superior color, resolution, and sharpness; greater dye stability; fewer processing steps; and easier-to-maintain processing temperatures. Since its introduction in 1963 as Cibachrome, ILFOCHROME Classic has become the standard for the other processes to be compared and matched against. For this reason, the ILFOCHROME Classic Process P-30P is offered as a starting place for making prints from slides. IL-FOCHROME Classic is noted for its vivid color intensity, with exaggerated red sensitivity. It is not the only process. If you try it and find it is not to your satisfaction, use another process.

The ILFOCHROME Classic Process P-30P

The ILFOCHROME Classic Process P-30P (table 11.4) is carried out at 75°F (24°C) plus or minus 2°F. Follow all safety procedures recommended by Ilford and this text. Avoid getting chemicals on your skin; when mixing and using the processing solutions, wear protective eye gear and gloves; work in a well-

House explores various legends of sea goddesses by constructing a special tank, 4 feet x 6 feet x 18 inches deep, in order to shoot figures in water in the studio. The tank is plexiglas, so backdrops of different colors can be placed underneath and lights with gels can be illuminated from the sides as well as through the water. The brilliant red glow of "water on fire" was created by wrapping the strobes with red cellophane. Salome's veils were replaced by sea anemones whose fluorescent colors were enhanced by leaving the shutter open, turning off the strobe's modeling lights, and exposing the image to black light for about 45 seconds at f/32. ILFOCHROME, with its exaggerated red, provides the vehicle to deliver a startling large-scale exhibition print.

© Suda House. *Salome from the Aqueous Myths,* 1986. 40 × 30 inches. Dye-destruction print.

ventilated area. Process P-30P[1] developer and fixer contain chemical ingredients common to typical black-and-white developer and fixer formulations. The bleach, however, is unique and contains

p-toluene sulfonic acid, which is very acidic in solution and is a strong irritant to the skin and eyes. The acidity is easily neutralized when the bleach waste is added in equal quantities to developer waste during the processing sequence. After neutralization the mixture is easily biodegraded in a properly operating secondary sewage treatment plant. The P-30P waste fixer solution contains

[1] The following information on Process P-30P is from a letter to the author from Warren L. Mauzy, Manager of Environmental Safety and Technology, Ilford Photo Corp., February 6, 1991.

photographic silver, which must be removed before disposal in most municipal sewage treatment facilities. The silver can be recovered by metallic replacement or electrolytic methods.

To make an 8-×-10-inch print with an ILFOCHROME Classic drum, pour 2.5 ounces (75 ml) of each solution into a separate clean container and place them in a tray of water at 78°F (25.5°C). This will maintain a proper average processing temperature because temperature drifts in a downward direction under normal room conditions. Process P-30P can be replenished one time by adding 1.25 ounces (37 ml) of fresh chemical to an equal amount of used chemical. Temperature must be adjusted to maintain 75°F. Be careful to avoid contaminating the chemicals.

Follow these steps when using the ILFOCHROME Classic process:

1. *In total darkness, place exposed paper in a clean and dry drum.* Be certain the ends of the drum are securely attached. Now processing can take place in white light.
2. *Presoak.* Stand the drum on end and pour water (75°F) into the funnel opening. The water will flow into the cap, but it will not come in contact with the paper until the drum is tipped over on its side. Set the timer for 1 minute and start it going. On a level surface immediately lay the drum on its side and begin rolling it rapidly back and forth, making more than one complete revolution each way. At the end of the minute, drain the water into a *nonmetal* container that will be used to dispose of all used chemicals.
3. *Developer.* Following the same steps as the presoak, pour the developer into the top of the drum. Set the timer for 3 minutes and begin to process. During the first 15 seconds agitation should be rapid, vigorous, and somewhat irregular to avoid creating a uniform pattern that can produce staining. At the end of the development time drain the used solution into a clean container for partial reuse.
4. *Rinse.* Pour 3 ounces (90 ml) of water into the top of the drum. Agitate

the water rinse for 30 seconds and drain into the disposal bucket.

5. *Bleach.* Pour bleach into the top of the drum. Set the timer for a minimum of 3 minutes and begin agitating the bleach in the same manner as the developer. The bleaching time may be increased up to 5 minutes if highlights do not look clear. When bleaching is completed, drain the used solution into a clean container for partial reuse.
6. *Rinse.* Pour 3 ounces (90 ml) of water into the top of the drum. Agitate the water for 15 to 30 seconds and drain into the disposal bucket.
7. *Fix.* Pour fixer into the top of the drum. Set the timer for 3 minutes and begin agitating the fixer in a gentle and uniform manner. At the completion of fixing drain the used solution into a clean container for partial reuse.
8. *Wash.* Carefully remove the print from the drum; it is easy to damage the wet emulsion. Wash the print in a tray for at least 3 minutes in rapidly running clean water at 75°F.
9. *Dry.* Remove surface water with a squeegee or clean chamois cloth. Drying can be accomplished in a number of ways: the print can be hung up, laid flat (emulsion side up) on a blotter or drying rack, dried in a print dryer designed for resin-coated papers, or dried with a blow dryer. Prints must be completely dry before they are evaluated for proper color balance and exposure.
10. *Cleaning the drum.* After processing is complete, take the drum apart and thoroughly wash and dry all its components, inside and out, before processing the next print.
11. *Replenishment.* To reuse the chemicals one time, save 1.25 ounces (37 ml) of each solution. Pour the remainder into a plastic, not metal, container. All the chemicals must be mixed together so that they can neutralize one another before they are discarded.
12. *Chemical disposal.* When the printing session is complete, add all the chemicals together into the plastic container in the following order to

neutralize: developer, bleach, and fix. Do not dispose of the chemicals individually. Adding the chemicals in a different order produces sulfur dioxide fumes. Then pour the neutralized mixture down the drain with running water. For additional information call the Ilford Emergency Hotline at (800) 842-9660.

Processing Problems

There are a number of common mistakes that occur when working with ILFOCHROME Classic materials. The troubleshooting guide shown in table 11.5 and the manufacturer's instructions should help you to get back on the right track.

Dye Chrome K-2 Chemistry for ILFOCHROME Classic Materials

There are other manufacturers who make chemicals for processing ILFOCHROME Classic materials. Dye Chrome Research's K-2 chemistry permits you to vary the contrast of any ILFOCHROME Classic material (table 11.6). This is done by dividing the bleach step into two parts: a dye-bleach step and a silver-bleach step.

In the ILFOCHROME Classic P-30P process a single bleach step attacks the negative silver image, formed during development, destroying the unwanted dyes and leaving only those needed to form the final image. The dye-bleach can only function in the presence of the silver, but the silver must then be completely bleached in order for the fixer to clear the highlights and produce a true white. In the single bleach bath, both the dye- and silver-bleach functions are interdependent and must be finished when each emulsion layer contains the right amount of residual dye to form the image. When the silver is depleted, the bleaching action ceases. Print exposure is the key that determines the amount of silver deposited and, consequently, the action of the bleach step. The more

• TABLE 11.5 •

Troubleshooting ILFOCHROME Classic

Print Problem	Possible Cause
Light flare	Paper fogged
White, yellow, or bluish streaks across print	Loose drum end cap Processor not properly closed
Overall reddish cast	Light fog from stray (red) light
Dark with red-orange cast	Exposed through back of print (lustre)
Black with no image	Exposed through back of print (glossy)
Irregular color streaks	Wet drum
Blue border/gray highlights	Developer contaminated
Orange cast/blacks bluish	Developer contaminated with fixer
Uneven tones/gray areas	Not enough chemicals used
Flat contrast and dark	Development time too short
No blacks and light	Development time too long
Print is black	Development step skipped Developer exhausted
Dull and milky	Bleach time too short
Gray highlights	Bleach exhausted Bleach too cold Bleach time too short
Black with faint image	Bleach defective Bleach step omitted
Brown-red borders	Bleach carried over into fixer Not fixed long enough
Dark, dull fogged	Print fixed before it was bleached
Flat and yellow	Print not fixed
Yellow edges	Lack of agitation
Pink-magenta borders	Overagitation
Greenish borders	Outdated paper Paper improperly stored
Reticulation	Inconsistent temperatures

• TABLE 11.6 •

Dye Chrome K-2 Drum Processing of ILFOCHROME Classic Materials (85°F with 3 ounces of solution per 8-×-10-inch print in an 8-×-10-inch drum)

Step	Time in Minutes*
Developer	3
Rinse	1
Dye-bleach	3†
Rinse	1
Silver-bleach	2‡
Fixer	3**
Wash	3 to 5
Dry	As needed

*Includes drain time.

†Times typically vary between 3 and 4 minutes with 3 1/4 being an average starting place. A 15-second change in time alters the contrast but generally doesn't require an exposure adjustment.

‡Time may be extended to 3 minutes.

**May be extended to 4 minutes.

exposure the material receives, the more developed silver there is to work with, thus producing a greater bleach reaction, which results in a lighter picture.

In the K-2 process, the silver-conversion and dye-bleach reactions do not have to compete for silver, thus the dye-bleach step time can be lengthened or reduced. Dye-bleaching is proportional to the silver image density. When a shorter dye-bleach time is used, less dye is broken down. Thus, the resulting image is darker and has less contrast, and there is a decrease in printing speed.

This can be useful in reducing the high natural contrast of ILFOCHROME Classic materials. When the dye-bleach time is extended, more dye is broken down so the print is lighter and has more contrast and the printing speed is increased. The silver-bleach then converts any unused silver back to silver halide, and the fixer removes it, as in the regular ILFOCHROME Classic process. Contrast can be reduced by about a grade and a half or increased by close to a full grade, based on conventional black-and-white papers. These changes *do* require adjustments in filtration and print exposure.

K-2 is extremely process-sensitive, and requires tight temperature control (85°F within 1/2°F or 29.4°C). Temperature errors in the developer and bleach steps can produce a color shift of about 5CC per degree. The K-2 developer, like many black-and-white developers, is a Metol-hydroquinone formula. Be sure to wear gloves if you are sensitive to Metol. For more details about the K-2 process contact Dye Chrome Research Company, Inc., Box 969, Lake Placid, FL 33852.

K-2 is *not* disposed of in the same manner as ILFOCHROME Classic P-30P. The following are Dye Chrome's specific disposal steps: Collect all solutions except the dye-bleach into a single container. Save the dye-bleach in a separate container. Do not combine it with any other of the chemicals. First dispose of the dye-bleach by carefully pouring it down a toilet without splashing, and then flush the toilet. Next, pour the

• TABLE 11.7 •

Kodak Ektachrome R-3000/General Drum Processing Guidelines Using a Motor Base
(8-×-10-inch print at 93°F with 3 ounces of chemical per step)

Processing Step	Time in Minutes*	Temperature (°F.)†
Prewet	1 1/2	90 to 100
First developer	1 3/4‡	93 +/- 1
First wash (§)	1 3/4	90 to 100
Color developer	2 1/4**	93 +/- 2
Second wash (§)	3/4	90 to 100
Bleach-fix	2 1/2	93 + /- 2
Third wash (#)	2 1/2	90 to 100
Dry	As needed	Not to exceed 150

*Drain time is included.

†Keep the temperatures of all solutions as similar as possible for most accurate results.

‡Time may be adjusted since the first developer is affected by type of drum, rotation speed, and solution volume.

§Drain drum every 20 seconds and replace with fresh water.

**Color developer time may be increased up to a maximum of 2 3/4 minutes.

#For most effective final wash, remove print from the drum and wash in a tray. Washing time may be increased.

other combined solutions down the toilet and flush.

Other Direct-Positive Material

Ilford's Omnipro system with its P-4 chemicals allows you to produce direct-positive color, continuous tone black-and-white papers, and graphic arts materials in a single chemical process. In the Omnipro processor ILFOCHROME Rapid direct-positive material can be processed in 3 1/2 minutes dry-to-dry. Ilford's black-and-white Multigrade variable contrast papers and Ilfospeed RC Deluxe graded paper along with Graphic Arts Rapid Access materials can be processed in 3 1/2 minutes; ILFOCHROME Rapid Overhead Transparency film takes 6 minutes, all in the same chemicals.

Masking for Contrast Reduction

Due to the lack of graded papers and various developer formulas that can be used in black-and-white printing, controlling the contrast of a color print can be problematic. You will probably encounter a slide that turns out to be difficult to print and cannot be corrected by burning, dodging, or using IL-FOCHROME Classic low-contrast paper. You may want to try a *contrast mask* when subtle detail must be retained. To make a mask the original slide is contact-printed, along with diffusion material to keep it slightly out of focus, onto panchromatic black-and-white film. This film is processed and then placed in register with the original slide and a print is made in the usual manner. The higher densities of the mask "fill" the lower densities of the original slide to reduce the overall density range.

The effect of the mask is generally most evident in the reduction of excessive contrast in the highlight areas. An increase in detail should be visible in the key shadow areas as well. The purpose of a mask is to make a good print better and not to "save" a badly exposed slide. The following method for masking has been provided by Scott Vlaun, a color printing consultant and former master printer for Portland Photographics in Maine. For simplicity's sake, this description only deals with slide film, but the method may also be used with color negative material.

Making a Contrast Reduction Mask (CRM)

1. *Preparing the originals.* Thoroughly clean *all* working surfaces including the glass and your original film. Using a metal ruler and an X-Acto knife blade, cut a support window (slightly larger than the image area of the original slide) into a scrap piece of film the same size as the Kodak Pan Masking film you plan to use. This film is available in 4-×-5, 5-×-7, and 8-×-10-inch formats (other slow, fine-grain films may be substituted). Working on a light table, use 3/8-inch silver photographic tape to attach your original slide, which has been removed from its mount (emulsion side down) to the support window. Do not crop the image or permit light to leak around the film's sprocket holes. Grouping the originals according to density, up to four 35-mm or two 120 originals can be put on one 4-×-5-inch sheet.

2. *Preparing the chemistry.* Set up seven trays in the sink, using a tray size larger than the film size. The processing temperature is 68°F (20°C) with at least 1/2 inch of solution in all trays. Mix Kodak HC-110 developer with water, according to instructions, 1:3 (one part developer to three parts of water) to make a stock solution. Take this fresh stock solution and dilute it 1:9 for the first tray of developer and 1:15 for the second tray of developer. The third tray is for stop bath, the fourth for rapid film fixer, the fifth for a rinse, the sixth for hypo-clear (such as Perma-Wash), and the seventh for washing.

3. *Exposing the masking film.* Attach a piece of mat drafting mylar to the support window to cover the base (shiny) side of the original(s). *Clean all surfaces!* Go into the darkroom

Dunitz concentrates on the spectral qualities that can be created on sheets of stainless steel and titanium. Changes in the surface are effected by using a torch, a wire brush, and/or an electric grinder. Alternations are also made by wiring an insulated paintbrush to a DC converter and voltage regulator. The image is rendered with water and baking soda as controlled changes in the voltage alter the colors. The dye-destruction process provides a direct and dramatic translation of the results.

© Jay Dunitz. *Pacific Light # 28,* 1985. 48 × 64 inches. Dye-destruction print.

and set the enlarging lens at 24 inches from the printing surface. Make sure the enlarger is not focused on any debris on the condenser or diffusion box. Turn off all the lights and allow your eyes to adjust to the darkness. Turn on the enlarger and put a clean piece of white paper on the baseboard to make sure the light is even and clean. Place a clean piece of black paper on the baseboard and turn off the enlarger. In total darkness, lay the masking film (emulsion side up) on the black paper. Place the window support and diffusion material (emulsion side up,

diffusion material down) on top of the masking film. Cover this sandwich with a clean piece of heavy plate glass or use a contact printing frame. Using a digital timer, expose at f/8 for 3 seconds with white light. Put this piece of exposed film in a light-tight box and repeat this process so you will have two sheets of film with identical exposures.

4. *Processing the masks.* Simultaneously process the two pieces of exposed film in the two separate trays of developer, with different dilutions, for 3 minutes with constant agitation. This will give you two masks with

different contrast. Fix and wash as you would for normal black-and-white film. In order to keep grain to a minimum, avoid temperature fluctuations and use a hypo-clearing agent to reduce the wet time. The grain of the CRM can show up in the highlight areas of large prints. Do not heat dry the CRM as slight shrinkage of the emulsion can make registering with the original impossible.

5. *Evaluation.* Examine the wet masks to determine if you need to open or close the lens to get the proper density and to be sure there is no dust. Generally, a good mask will look

like a thin (underexposed) black-and-white negative. The amount of density needed will depend on the degree of contrast reduction desired. It is better to slightly undermask (use a thinner mask) and to make up the difference by dodging and burning. Experience will have to act as your guide since there most likely will never be a single perfect mask.

6. *Registering the mask.* On a clean light table, tape down the original, in the support window (emulsion side down), to keep it from sliding around. Place the CRM (emulsion side up) on the original. Using a loupe, carefully align the two. Tape the CRM to the support with the silver tape (cut the tape beforehand so you can hold the CRM with one hand and tape it with the other). Run the tape only along one side so the package can be opened like a book allowing you to clean the inner surfaces.

7. *Printing.* To ensure maximum sharpness, use a glass negative carrier to print the masked original. With some enlarger systems, you can make a cardboard or metal jig to sit on the bottom of the negative stage. Put a piece of glass on top of the jig followed by your package of original slides and diffusion material and another piece of glass on top. If you use a 4-×-5-inch glass carrier to print 35-mm or 2 1/4-inch roll film, mask off the extra space by cutting an opaque piece of thin board and place it on top of the glass. Do *not* put tape on the glass carrier. The window, showing the masked film, must be in the precise center of the glass or the image may not be evenly illuminated. Print following normal procedures, but expect to need two to three f-stops more exposure because of the CRM. If there is still too much contrast, the mask is too thin. If the print appears flat or muddy, the mask is too dense.

For more detailed information see Ilford's technical information guide entitled *Masking and Advanced Printing Techniques for Cibachrome* (ILFOCHROME Classic) *Materials.*

Internegatives

If you are not happy with the way that the slide has printed, try making an internegative from the slide and see if it will deliver more desirable results (see section on internegatives in chapter 10).

TWELVE

Instant Processes: The Polaroid System

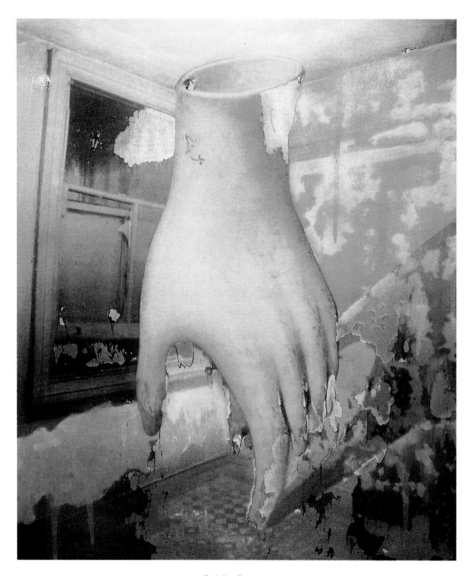

© John Reuter.
Balance, 1995.
20 × 24 inches. Diffusion image transfer with dry pigment and pastel.

For this image, a homage to René Magritte, Reuter outputted the images to a 4-x-5-inch film recorder and printed it as an image transfer using a 20-x-24-inch Polaroid studio camera. Reuter says the image-transfer process "can alter, transform, and move the image to a level of image artifact . . . a physical object that has interest beyond the image it carries. The elements of color, texture, and scale contribute to the power of the piece as it is perceived as the viewer stands in front of it. . . . Reworking is the final step and I use it to enchance the emotional elements of the image that I experienced in its original creations."

Modern Instant Photography

Modern instant photography began in 1948 with the marketing of Edwin Land's first Polaroid process. The first full-color instant film, known as Polacolor, was introduced in 1963. This revolutionary product was a diffusion-transfer, peel-apart color print film that developed itself and produced a color print in 60 seconds (see the section on the diffusion-transfer process later in this chapter). It was an immediate success with both amateur and professional photographers. In 1976 Kodak launched its own line of instant products but 10 years later was forced to withdraw them when Polaroid won patent infringement suits against Kodak's design. Polaroid and Fuji collaborated on a Fuji peel-apart instant film that was sold in Japan. By 1991, when many of the original Polaroid patents expired, Fuji began selling this instant film in Europe. At this writing it is only available through the "gray" market in America.

It Is Not What You Think

Most people associate instant films with family snapshots. Do not be fooled by instant films' innocent faces. It is possible to make beautiful, intimate, and unique color photographs with these films. They are convenient and fast and can provide immediate feedback in any shooting situation. Professional photographers routinely use Polaroid to check composition, lighting, reciprocity, and the working order of their equipment. The information gained from the Polaroid can help the photographer make corrections and create a stronger image. Commercial photographers even use Polaroids for their final presentations and for direct photomechanical reproduction. Polaroids are also great icebreakers when photographing people because they are a familiar and nonthreatening object in our culture. The prints make wonderful gifts to provide your model at the completion of any picture-making session. Don't underestimate the Polaroid's potential. It

Figure 12.1
This Polaroid SX-70 photograph is part of a 10-year project documenting nightlife in New York City as seen by a "camera girl" who was simultaneously earning a living selling Polaroid pictures to clubgoers. Smith tells us: "Using a Polaroid SX-70 camera with a sonar focusing device enabled me to simultaneously image and project onto film the important information in a dark and densely populated space. Working quickly and intuitively, I could grab and materialize fleeting impressions of people who came to experience the 1980s version of mass modern electronic entertainment and decor in the nightspots of the most hyped-up city in the world during that time."

© Sharon Smith. *Cigarette Girl, The Ritz, New York*, 1980. 3 1/4 × 3 1/4 inches. Diffusion transfer print.

is fun to work with and it is always a thrill watching the image come up. The artistic use of the material has helped it gain acceptance as a valid medium.

Polaroid SX-70: Time-Zero

In 1972 the Polaroid SX-70 system was introduced. It is a color diffusion-transfer process that is self-developing in natural light and is the basis for almost all self-processing instant photography materials. SX-70 and its heirs are the dream-come-true vision of Dr. Edwin Land's one-step instant pictures

at your fingertips (figure 12.1). Although the SX-70 is now defunct, Time-Zero (with an ISO of 150) is an integral color-positive film that can be exposed in a Polaroid SX-70, under an enlarger, or with a special film back (see NPC, Four Designs Company, and Graphic Center in references at end of this chapter). They are not compatible with a conventional camera.

Late in his life, Walker Evans became very rhapsodic about the SX-70 camera and wrote: "But a year ago I would have said that color is vulgar and should not be tried under any circumstances. . . . I'm very excited about that little gadget (the SX-70) which I thought

(a)

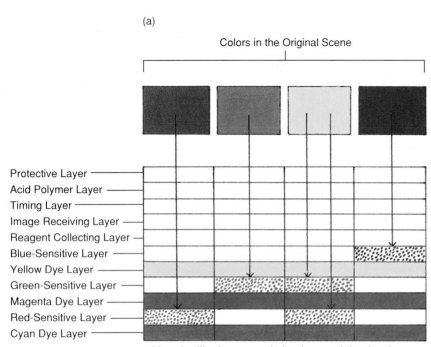

Colors in the Original Scene

Protective Layer
Acid Polymer Layer
Timing Layer
Image Receiving Layer
Reagent Collecting Layer
Blue-Sensitive Layer
Yellow Dye Layer
Green-Sensitive Layer
Magenta Dye Layer
Red-Sensitive Layer
Cyan Dye Layer

After the film is exposed, the dyes and the developers are released and become activated.

Figure 12.2

Typical diffusion-transfer process: (*a*) Film exposure; dye developers begin to diffuse upward. (*b*) The exposed silver blocks upward diffusion of corresponding dyes. For example, the exposed blue-sensitive layer blocks the yellow dye. (*c*) The dyes not restrained by the silver continue diffusing upward to form the image.

(b)

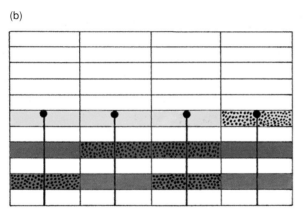

Exposed silver blocks upward diffusion of corresponding dyes. For example, exposed blue-sensitive layer blocks yellow dye.

(c)

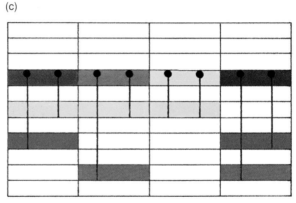

Dyes not restrained by silver continue to diffuse upward to form the image.

was just a toy at first. . . . [I use it to] extend my vision and let that open up new stylistic paths I haven't been down yet. . . . A practiced photographer has an entirely new extension in that camera. You photograph things that you would not think of photographing before. I don't even yet know why, but I find that I'm quite rejuvenated by it."[1] Evans went on to comment that the streamlined SX-70 process put all the responsibility on the photographer's mind and eye, leaving nothing to be added by technique. Quite a recommendation from one of the masters of modernist black-and-white photography.

Handheld Instant Cameras

The Spectra System, introduced in 1986, is a group of automatic handheld cameras with a few manual overrides. The Spectra film has an ISO of 640 and the overall picture size is 4 × 4 1/16 inches. It produces an image area of 3 9/16 × 2 7/8 inches, which is larger and more rectangular than the SX-70. The image appears seconds after exposure by diffusion-transfer subtractive color chemistry, which is very similar to the SX-70 process. Polaroid also makes a series of cameras that use the 600-type film, producing an image area of 3 1/8 × 3 1/8 inches, plus Captiva single lens reflex (SLR) cameras delivering an image of 2 7/8 × 2 1/8 inches.

Diffusion-Transfer: The Polaroid Process

The Polaroid SX-70 and Spectra development processes use the diffusion-transfer method (figure 12.2). After the shutter is pressed, the motor drive, which is powered by a battery in each film pack, automatically ejects the film through a set of rollers that break a pod of reagent located at the bottom of each piece of film. Development is then automatic and requires no timing. The best results are obtained at about 75°F (24°C). If it is colder, the color balance can shift to the cool direction. This can be compensated by putting the film inside your shirt to keep it warm while it is developing. Development can take place in daylight because the light-sensitive negative is protected by opaque dyes in the reagent. Both the positive and negative images are contained within each sheet of film.

As the picture forms, a number of things occur at once. First the silver halides are reduced to metallic silver in the exposed areas of each of the three additive primary light-sensitive layers. As this happens, the complementary subtractive primary dye developers move through the layers of the negative and the opaque reagent to form a white background for the picture. Now the dye developers are prevented from moving up to the positive image area by the developing silver. This layer will now only pass certain colors through. For example, the blue layer blocks the yellow dyes but not the cyan and magenta. Within a few minutes all the dyes that have not been blocked travel through the white opaque layer and become visible. The process automatically completes and stabilizes itself, resulting in a completed dry print.

Color Balance

These films are balanced for daylight and electronic flash, but they can be exposed under any light source by placing CC filters in front of the lens of the camera or the exposure sensor in the case of automatic cameras. It is also possible to correct for differences in color balance from one pack of film to another with the CC filters.

Exposure

Exposure is automatically determined by the Polaroid camera. This can be controlled to a limited degree by adjusting the exposure wheel on the camera to either the darker or lighter setting.

Storage

Store film in its sealed box. Keep it cool and dry. For prolonged life, this film can be refrigerated above 34°F (1°C), but do *not* freeze. Let film warm to room temperature before use.

Levinthal creates a world in miniature by placing this world on a screen through a video camera and then recording scenes from it on Polaroid SX-70 film.

© David Levinthal. *Modern Romance*, 1985. 3 1/4 × 3 1/4 inches. Diffusion transfer print.

Instant Manipulation

The dyes beneath the print's plastic coating of Polaroid Time-Zero film are the most malleable both during and after development. Spectra and Captiva prints can be manipulated, but not to the same extent. Altering the print as the image is developing lets you interact with the picture during the part of the process that is supposed to be automatic with no human intervention. Any type of stylus can be used to push and pull the dyes under the plastic covering (figure 12.3). Pencils, dowels, clay-working tools, dental tools, burnishing tools, spoons, butter knives, coins—anything that can apply pressure directly to the print surface is worth

trying. The secret of a good manipulation is knowing when to stop. Do not get carried away. Avoid creating more chaos; we already have enough of it in this world. Make some extra pictures to play and loosen up with before you get down to business.

Time-Zero Manipulation Approaches

If you have never attempted this process, try photographing a still life or a scene that is repeatable. There are several ways to manipulate this film. The easiest is to allow the image to develop for only about 15 seconds. As soon as the outlines of the image become visible, you make your

Figure 12.3
Pompe shot this self-portrait on Polaroid Time-Zero film indoors with both sunlamp and 3200 K light sources to alter the normal color balance. A nutpick was used as a stylus to manipulate the dyes under the surface of the film. A 4-x-5-inch intertransparency was made from which a dye-destruction print was created.

© Kathleen Pompe. *Self-Portrait*, 1989. 20 x 20 inches. Dye-destruction print.

Compositions that are predominantly one color don't offer as much opportunity to alter. Look for a picture that can provide a variety of shapes and tones for experimentation. As for color relationships, the film responds strongly to blue, green, and red. Take your time. Be gentle. Do not rush. It is okay to be subtle. The entire print does not have to be manipulated. The final picture will be textured with bumps and waves. Do not forget it is fine to ignore all this and just jump in and see what can be discovered.

Another method of manipulation involves puncturing a small hole behind the image during the initial development stage and, while watching the image develop, moving the dyes around using a needle or paper clip inserted through the hole.

Another possibility is to use an X-Acto or other utility knife to cut open and peel a fully processed image apart. Next, run cool water over the image to remove the white, chalky coating. The longer you wash, the more image will be removed. Now apply water-based dyes, such as Dr. Martins, with a brush or cotton swab. Color markers can also be used. These images are best viewed as transparencies. Build small light boxes for display so they can be lit from behind. Boxes can be constructed so the images can be interchanged, combined, or shown in small groups. Wear gloves when disassembling this film as it contains a caustic developer gel. If you get any developer on your skin, immediately wash with running water. This process should be performed by children only if they are under direct adult supervision.

Also note that the backside of Polacolor film can be manipulated by applying pressure to selective areas during development by using the same tools as in Time-Zero manipulation.

Later Manipulations

It is possible to wait a couple of hours after you have shot to begin alterations. It will be necessary to soften the dyes again. This is done with the application of heat. A home hand iron works great. Hair and print dryers, hot plates, and dry

choices as to which areas to work on and how to alter them. This method is the quickest and relies on your first inclinations. For a general blurring and softening of the entire image, begin lightly manipulating the surface with a blunt tool before the image becomes visible. As the image develops use a more pointed tool for outlining areas and objects. Different amounts of pressure can produce black or white lines. New colors can be blended by applying a slightly heavier, pointed pressure to mix the layers underneath. Blues and reds can be produced during this time. During the next 5 minutes, use a blunt- or fine-tip tool to blend, distort, and stretch the image. Try varying the pressure and using both circular and short stroke motions.

If you prefer a more contemplative method, make a number of exposures and allow one to remain unmanipulated as a guide. Permit the print to fully develop. Then take a stylus and gently trace over the image to see which areas are the most receptive to manipulation. Gently start rubbing, in a circular motion, on the background and light-colored areas before tackling the more detailed aspects of the picture. Wherever pressure is applied, it loosens the dyes and bring to the surface a bit of white reflective pigment that is under the picture. Rubbing on dark colors tends to turn these colors a gray-white. Consider leaving a dark area unmanipulated to create contrast and juxtaposition with the altered part of the image.

mount presses work too. But be careful; too much heat causes the plastic surface to bubble, buckle, or crack. If you do not want these effects, cover the picture with some clean, smooth sheets of paper. Then apply low heat for a few seconds at a time until the dyes soften.

Reentering the Process

Manipulation lets the photographer reenter into part of the photographic process from which they had been excluded. It gives the photographer more freedom of choice in determining the final outcome of the picture and increases the options. Avenues for subjective feeling are now able to enter into an automatic technical process. The artist can build more time into the picture. Instead of 1/125 second of time, the photographer can continue to be involved with the image for longer blocks of time. This can give the photograph more life and involve the viewer for longer periods of time.

Copies

Because these images are one-of-a-kind and small (SX-70s are about 3 1/4 × 3 1/4 inches and Spectras about 4 × 3 inches) they can be copied onto conventional film to make more prints or enlargements.

Most Polaroid materials duplicate well onto 4-×-5-inch transparency film, and these "interpositives" can make great small-sized prints.

Polachrome

In 1976 Polaroid introduced the first instant movie system, known as Polavision. With only a 2 1/2-minute playtime, Polavision was not seen as a good value when compared with super 8 movie film, plus the introduction of new home video systems by Sony and JVC ensured its demise. The thinking behind the project was redirected, and in 1983 Polachrome, the first Polaroid instant film designed to be used with a standard 35-mm camera, was introduced. Polachrome is a

It is important for imagemakers to work with materials that respond to their aesthetic and conceptual concerns. Erickson, who specializes in photographing flowers with Polachrome, says: "Since 1983, Polachrome film and I have had a love-hate relationship. I love to use it and hate when I am away from it. I go through stages in my work where I use this medium, then take a break from it. Every time I go back, I can't believe I left!"

© Wendy Erickson. *Birds of Paradise,* 1993. 12 × 17 inches. Dye-destruction print.

diffusion-transfer, additive-color, line-screen, positive-transparency film similar to the type introduced by Charles Joly in 1894. A screen is formed on one side of the film by alternating lines of red, green, and blue. When you make your exposure the light passes through these colored lines, which act like color separation filters for the single layer of high-resolution panchromatic black-and-white emulsion. The film is developed in a

manual or automatic Polaroid Processor. The film is wound onto a spool and then placed back inside the processor. It is a dry process; the chemicals that are required for development come with each roll of film. Both the exposed film and developer box are placed into the processor when you are ready to develop.

Polaroid also makes High Contrast Polachrome, which is actually the same film, which provides more highly saturated colors than regular Polachrome by using a different reagent (processing fluid) and an extended developing time (2 minutes). This film has a bold, intense palette, like that of fresh acrylic paint. It is useful when you want exaggerated or saturated colors.

The Process

During development both a negative and a positive black-and-white image are produced in a silver-diffusion process. Then the negative and other processing layers are removed. What remains is a black-and-white positive that is filtered by the color screen. Thus, the final transparency is created by the additive process of blending light and not by the subtractive method.

The entire development process can be carried out in minutes at normal room temperature. You do not need any power source with the manual processor or a darkroom. There are no chemicals to mix and nothing to wash. The film comes out dry and ready to mount.

Characteristics

Polachrome does have some characteristics that make it different from conventional slide material that you should be aware of before you make use of it. Compared with conventional slide material this film is slower, grainier, has less accurate color rendition, possesses a reduced brightness range, is not able to separate dark tones, and has little margin for exposure error. The surface of Polachrome is more fragile than conventional film and requires greater care in mounting and handling. If you have a camera that has an OTF (off-the-film) meter, it may give faulty exposures due to the different reflectance of this film. Read the precautions enclosed with the film.

This film was designed for projection. For best results, use a flat-field lens on a glass-beaded screen and avoid lenticular screens, which might make a moiré pattern.

The additive screen adds neutral density and becomes visual at magnification of 6X to 10X. Prints made from this material that are 8×10 inches or larger reveal the filter screen lines of the film. This can also be quite evident if the transparencies are reproduced photomechanically or when photographing a television screen.

You may find that the color balance of this film is not suitable for all applications; it is different (pastel-looking) than most of the E-6 process films. While the colors can be vivid, they often have a soft look reminiscent of the early Autochrome process. Try a roll and see.

General Information

- *Exposure.* Start at a film speed of 40. Do not be afraid to alter the speed rating if the results are not to your liking. This film is different from traditional slide film, where it is important to avoid overexposure. With this film, avoid *underexposure.* Polachrome has less shadow detail than regular slide film and becomes grainier as exposure decreases. When in doubt, give it *more* rather than less exposure. Some photographers will alter the ISO from 40 to 32 or 25 in order to overexpose the film.

- *Color Balance.* This film is designed for a daylight color balance (5500 K). With a tungsten color balance (3200 to 3400 K) use a Wratten 80A or 80B filter.

- *Reciprocity Failure.* For a 1-second exposure, increase your exposure 2/3 f-stop; at 10 seconds, increase one f-stop.

- *Resolution.* In low humidity, film curl may cause a loss of sharpness. Use a smaller aperture to compensate.

- *Film Rewinding.* Do not rewind film completely back into the cartridge. Leave the leader, or tongue, of the film out of the cartridge. If you forget and rewind the film completely, use the film extractor provided with

the processors to fish out the film leader. You need the leader to process the film.

- *Processing.* Make sure the film cartridge and processing pack contain the same type and number of exposures. The film is available in twelve and thirty-six exposures. Starting development time is 75°F (24°C) for 60 seconds. Film can be processed between 60° and 85°F (15° and 29°C). Changes in time and/or temperature can produce color shifts and changes in density. Many photographers extend the developing time, as underdevelopment produces grainy and muddy results. For more exact processing procedures see the instructions with the AutoProcessor. They are clear and easy to follow.

- *Projection.* Because the base density of Polachrome is greater than conventional subtractive transparency films, use the high-power lamp setting on the projector to achieve normal screen brightness.

- *Storage/Handling.* Keep the film and processing pack in temperatures below 70°F (21°C). Refrigerate both, if possible, for longer life and stability but do *not* freeze. Let the film and pack warm up before use. Development should be carried out as soon as possible after exposure.

This film scratches very easily. Avoid touching it with a loupe or with your fingers. Avoid slide-in type mounts, which can easily damage the fragile emulsion. Polaroid makes clip-down slide mounts for this type of film. For optimum protection, use glass slide mounts. Do *not* use film cleaner on the emulsion (silvery) side of the film.

Polaroid and the View Camera

Polaroid makes possible the rapid use of color materials for larger-format cameras. Polacolor is a family of color print materials, available in 3 1/4-×-4 1/4-inch

Bresler recounts how she "suddenly recognized my studio windowpanes as a transparent membrane separating inside and outside. I began to paint and draw on the glass. . . . Photographing through the glass . . . I am able to join together the inner layer of personal expression to the existing cityscape. The result is a hybrid vision that exemplifies the camera's ability to join together disparate elements into a unique and therefore unseen whole. This series of miniatures is called *A Book of Days*. It is an important ritual of marking the days—of continually re-exploring and representing the metaphors of interior versus exterior space."

© Edie Bresler. *April 20, 1994*, 1994. 4 1/2 × 3 1/2 inches. Diffusion transfer print.

Larger-Format Polaroid Materials

Polaroid also makes a print film (Polacolor ER) and overhead projection transparency material (Colorgraph Type 891) for use with an 8-×-10-inch view camera. It requires its own special Polaroid film holder and processor for development. Color materials are available for other special uses, such as the Polaroid 20-×-24-inch cameras, which can be rented from Polaroid and used at one of their studios.

Polaroid Transfers

The transfer process allows a previously made image to be relocated onto another receiving surface. Magazine transfers, the kind often done in grade school, are the most familiar. Postmodernistic trends have brought about a renewed interest in transferring images. The Polaroid transfer method is capable of producing soft, fully rendered images or fractured, partially rendered images. Other postvisualization methods, such as handcoloring, can be incorporated into the process of transforming the image to provide a more subjective response to the subject. Although any size Polaroid film can be used, Polacolor (3 1/4-×-4 1/4-inch and 4-×-5-inch) films provide a simple avenue to begin experimentation. The Polacolor ER films, such as Type 669, 59, 559, or 809, as well as Polacolor 64 Tungsten, deliver the most constant transfer results. Type 59 is excellent for beginners while Polaroid Pro 100 is not recommended for transfer applications.

and 4-×-5-inch sizes. They are designed to be exposed in special Polaroid film holders instead of the camera's regular film holder. Check with Polaroid to ascertain the correct film holder.

The Polacolor ER (extended range) films have an ISO of 80, are balanced for daylight and electronic flash, and will produce a print in 60 seconds at 75°F (24°C).

The Polacolor ER Type 59 sheet film, 559 (4-×-5-inch), and 669 (3 1/4-×-4 1/4-inch) pack films accommodate a brightness range of up to 1:48 and are recommended for commercial studio and location shooting. Type 88 (3 1/4-×-4 1/4-inch) film is

designed to give a more contrasty print with more subdued colors than the Polacolor ER film. All these films must be used with the appropriate Polaroid film holder.

Changes in time and/or temperature alter the outcome of the final print. An increase in temperature makes the colors appear warmer, while decreasing temperature produces cooler hues. Extending the development time can increase color saturation and overall contrast. A drop in development time can flatten or mute the colors while reducing contrast. Filtering at the time of exposure is necessary to alter or control the color in the final picture.

Polacolor Transfer Method

The Polaroid transfer process can be carried out under ambient light. A few simple safety precautions are in order since Polaroid did not design their films to be used for this purpose. Wear gloves during this process; the film contains a caustic developer gel. If you get any developer on your skin, immediately wash it off.

Parker's enigmatic work mingles pictorial clarity with thematic ambiguity. Through a process of recontextualization, Parker bestows "human implications" upon her constructions. By placing prosaic materials in unfamiliar situations and surprising juxtapositions, Parker allows viewers to infuse them with their own inventive meaning.

© Olivia Parker. *Exit*, 1991. 24 × 20 inches. Diffusion transfer process.
Courtesy of the Polaroid Collection, Cambridge, MA.

For this reason this process is not recommended for children. To transfer an image from Polacolor film to another surface follow these suggestions:

1. Select a receiving support, such as watercolor paper, but different support materials, such as vellum, rice paper, wood veneer, or even other photographs. Cold-press papers, which have large pores, deliver more texture and less detail. Heat-press papers, which have smaller pores, provide a smoother image with more detail. Paper may also be treated with a gelatin for enhanced detail. For the sharpest possible image with the most color saturation, tape down the receiving support material before starting the transfer process. Natural fabrics, such as broadcloth, linen, silk, and even wood, can be used. They may require more wetting and pressure. Additional pressure can be applied by putting a heavy weight, such as a brick, on top of the transfer after you have completed the rolling process. If you do not want the characteristic "ooze" of excess developing chemicals around the outside of the image to show, use tape or rubber cement to mask out the nonimage area.

2. Immerse the paper in a tray of distilled water (100°F, 38°C) for about 60 seconds for 80-lb. paper, 2 minutes for 140-lb. paper, and 5 minutes for 300-lb. paper. Differences in the pH level of the water will affect the outcome. Remove the paper and drain. Place the paper on a flat, dry surface, and use a squeegee to remove the excess water. Other methods include using a brush, cotton ball, or portable steamer to dampen the paper. If the paper is too wet, the dyes can liquify and run. Try dry paper to see the different effect it makes.

3. Make sure the rollers and exit slot of the film holder are clean. Wipe them down with a damp, lint-free cloth before processing. Expose the Polacolor film and pull it through the film holder. Cut off the clipped end of the film pack, known as the trap end, with a pair of scissors. Wear gloves and avoid getting any of the processing chemicals on your skin.

4. Try variations in the processing time. Many workers prematurely peel the film apart to stop the migration of the dyes. For example, if the film is peeled apart after about 10 to 15 seconds (at 70°F, 21°C), the negative retains almost all the cyan dye, about half of the magenta, and almost no yellow. This is why the Polacolor transfers look cyan. This can be corrected by using 10CC to 20CC red filtration at the time of exposure. If you peel sooner than 10 seconds the negative may be fogged by light. Do not touch the negative at this time as the heat from your fingertips can produce fog marks (white ovals).

5. Normally you would save the positive and throw out the negative, but in this case save the negative for transferring. Immediately place the

Hock is one of the artists who pioneered the artistic use of the Polaroid transfer process. It has recently become very popular, with Polaroid even marketing its own transfer process kit. The transfer process enables the imagemaker to photograph original and appropriated scenes and combine them to produce a juxtaposition that is only possible in the visual world.

© Rick Hock. *Monkey Business*, 1987. 40 × 56 inches. Diffusion transfer image transfers on paper. Courtesy of Jayne H. Baum Gallery, New York, NY.

negative, face down, onto the receiving material and apply an even, medium pressure with a hard roller (soft rubber brayer) or squeegee (waiting causes the dyes to dry out). Do this four to six times in one direction, rolling smoothly, and stop just before the end of the Polaroid image. After placing the negative on the receiving material, cover it with a piece of clean, smooth paper, which acts as a buffer and delivers a more even and complete transfer. Shadow areas may require more pressure than highlight areas to transfer. Controlled levels of pressure can be applied to specific areas with a smooth, round tool, such as a spoon. Too much pressure can distort the darker areas while too little pressure can create tiny white dots.

6. Wait about 2 minutes. Keeping the negative warm, with low heat from a hair dryer, prevents the image from lifting off when you peel the negative back. Then carefully and slowly peel the negative back diagonally from one corner to reveal the transfer image. Don't let the negative fall back onto the receiving material. The blade of a utility knife can be gently slipped under a corner of the negative to lift the corner from the receiving material in order to reduce smudging and keep the edge of the image clean. Allow to air dry.

7. Consider doing posttransfer work. While the image is still wet, a foam brush can be used to clean up the edges and remove excess dyes. A knife can be used to scrape away designated areas. Watercolors can be applied while the surface is wet or after it is dry. Permit the transfer to dry on a flat surface. Once dry, fine sandpaper can be used to eclipse areas of the image while graphite can be applied to highlight others. Colored pencils and pastels work well on dry images. A neutral acrylic mat varnish may be used to protect and seal the finished work. Brighter colors can be obtained by immersing the finished transfer in a working

Doukas has been a pioneer in refining the emulsion-transfer process. The original image was made on 4-x-5-inch transparency film. This was then exposed onto four sheets of Polaroid Type 809 film (4 x 5 inches) in the darkroom. Finally, each piece of film was transferred onto Arches Aquarelle Satine paper.

© Michael Doukas. *Untitled*, 1994. 16 × 20 inches. Emulsion transfer to paper.

solution of stop bath or distilled white vinegar diluted one part vinegar to four parts water. Agitate for 30 to 60 seconds. Rinse for 2 to 5 minutes. If bubbling occurs, reduce the time in the acid or increase the dilution ratio.

8. Obtain a copy of *The Polaroid Guide to Instant Imaging/Advanced Image Transferring* for extended details about this process, including 8-×-10-inch transfers. For information on other transfer processes, see *Photographic Possibilities* by Robert Hirsch.

Polaroid Emulsion Transfer

Emulsion transfer is a process for removing and transferring the top image layer of Polaroid ER films (Types 108, 669, 59, 559, 809) or Polacolor 64 Tungsten onto another support surface. European imagemakers began experimenting with the process during the 1980s, but it did not gain access into American photographic practice until the 1990s. Basically an exposed sheet of Polaroid ER film is submerged in hot water until the emulsion can be separated from its paper support and then transferred onto another surface, including ceramics, fabric, glass, metal, and wood. Three-dimensional surfaces can also be used. The process removes the image from its normal context and destroys the traditional frame, while adding a sense of movement and elements of the third-dimension into the image. The following steps are provided as a gateway to this nontraditional process.

Robbennolt's constructed tableaux present personal struggles. All the manipulation takes place prior to shooting. In her studio Robbennolt starts "by doing a painting on a sheet of corrugated cardboard. Holes are cut into the painting at the appropiate places and models insert the appropriate parts of their bodies from behind the painting."

© Linda Robbennolt. *Touched*, 1988. 20 × 24 inches. Diffusion transfer print.

The Emulsion Transfer Process

Emulsion transfers can be made onto any clean, smooth surface, including glass or sheet metal. Fabric support should be stretched and mounted, since folds in the material can produce cracking when the emulsion dries. The emulsion can be transferred in sections by tearing it with your nails or cutting it while soaking. The print can also be cut into pieces before its first submersion. All steps may be carried out under normal room light. (See figure 12.4 for visual outline of this process).

1. Expose and process Polaroid Type 669, 59, 559, or 809 film and let it dry for 8 to 24 hours or force-dry with a hand hair dryer. Besides using a camera, exposures can be made onto positive transparency film and projected onto Polaroid ER. This can be done with the Polaprinter, the Vivitar slide printer, the Daylab II, a colorhead enlarger, or a copystand.

2. Cover the backside of the print with plastic contact paper or with a coat of spray paint and allow to dry. This prevents the back coat of the print from dissolving during the submerging process. Trim the white borders of the print if you do not want them to transfer.

3. Fill one tray, larger than the print, with 160°F (71°C) water. Fill a second tray with cold water. Place a sheet of acetate or Mylar on the bottom of the cold water tray.

If transferring onto watercolor paper, use a foam brush to moisten (but do not soak) the paper with room temperature water. Put the paper on a clean, smooth piece of glass and squeegee it onto the surface, taking care to remove bubbles and/or wrinkles.

4. Submerge the print face up in the tray of hot water for 4 minutes with agitation. The water should be allowed to cool. Using tongs, remove the print from the hot water and place it in the tray of cold water. This quick dunk, just prior to placing the emulsion down, provides a lubricating layer helpful for manipulation.

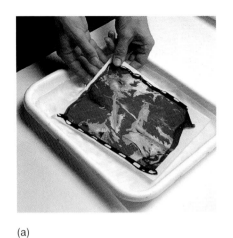

(a)

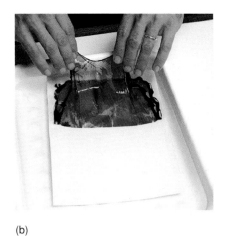

(b)

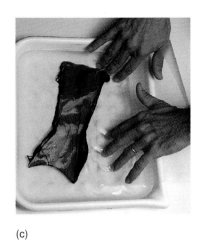

(c)

(d)

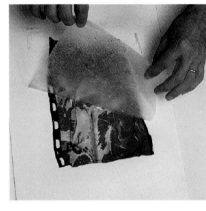

(e)

Figure 12.4

These images visually outline the procedures involved in making a Polaroid emulsion transfer.

Polaroid Emulsion Transfer Process.
Courtesy of Polaroid Corporation, Cambridge, MA.

(f)

(g)

5. Lightly massage the emulsion with a pushing motion from the edges of the print toward the center. (See figure 12.4a.) Slowly and carefully lift the emulsion and peel it away from its paper support base. (See figure 12.4b.) Keep the emulsion that is being released from its support under the water. Now reverse the image (so it will not appear backwards when transferred) by bringing the emulsion back over itself (like turning down a bedsheet). Leave the emulsion floating in the water and dispose of the paper support. Hard water can make the emulsion difficult to remove. If this is a problem try using bottled spring water.

6. Take hold of two corners of the floating emulsion with your fingers and clamp it on the bottom of the tray. (See figure 12.4c.) Holding the emulsion, lift the acetate in and out of the water several times to stretch the image and remove the wrinkles. (See figure 12.4d.) Repeat this on all four sides, always holding the top two corners. Once stretched, you can dunk the image to purposely let the water curl and fold it. When you are satisfied with the image, remove it from the water and place it onto your transfer surface, making sure the acetate or carrying material is on top.

7. Rub the image with your fingers and carefully remove the acetate. (See figure 12.4e.)

8. Smooth and straighten the image until it looks the way you want it. (See figure 12.4f.) At this point the emulsion can also be resubmerged in and out of cold water to perform

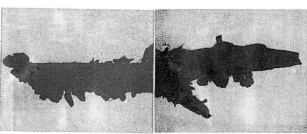

Crane made direct photograms, using a 40-watt light bulb, directly onto Polaroid Type 809 film. The objects, an axe, a stick with fungies, and the large mushroom, were placed on the Polaroid 8-x-10-inch film and exposed. Then they were transferred to wet Fabriaro watercolor paper in sequence. Crane investigates the interaction of process and the artist's hand while echoing themes of nature and technology.

© Barbara Crane. *Fungigram with Axe*, 1994. 11 × 32 inches. Diffusion transfer image transfers. Courtesy of Ezell Gallery, Chicago, IL.

additional manipulations. When completed, roll the image with a soft rubber brayer from the middle outward. (See figure 12.4g.) Begin using only the weight of the roller and gradually increase the pressure after all the air bubbles and excess water have been removed. Generally the operation is considered complete when all the folds appear to be pressed down. However, other rubbing tools and techniques may be used to achieve different effects.

9. Hang to dry. The transfer may be flattened in a warm dry-mount press.

References

Polaroid provides toll-free telephone technical assistance at (800)225-1618, Monday through Friday, 8 A.M. to 8 P.M. (Eastern time). Polaroid also offers *Polaroid 35mm Instant Slide System: A User's Manual* by Lester Lefkowitz, which provides in-depth technical information, *Instant Projects* by Robert Baker and Barbara London, which contains a wealth of ideas and information on using their instant materials, and "Creative Uses for Polaroid Materials: A Guide to Image Transfer, Emulsion Transfer, and Time-Zero Manipulation." Write Polaroid Corporation, 575 Technology Square, Cambridge, MA 02139. Also see the Polaroid chapter in *Photographic Possibilities* by Robert Hirsch.

Four Designs Company, 9444 Irondale Ave., Chatsworth, CA 91311 and Graphic Center, P.O. Box 818, Ventura, CA 93002 are sources for used SX-70s and customized film backs. Four Designs Company converts old Polaroid 110A/B roll film cameras to use the new pack films. NPC Corporation, 1238 Chestnut St., Newton Falls, MA 02164 makes an SX-70 back for the Mamiya RB-67.

THIRTEEN

The Digital Image

© Pedro Meyer.
Truths & Fictions, A Journey from Documentary to Digital Photography, 1994.
CD Rom.

This screen shot shows the original images Meyer used to digitally construct his final representation.
"Today more than ever the artists should re-establish the role of a demiurge and sow doubts, destroy certainties, annihilate convictions so that, at the other end of confusion, a new sense and sensibility can be created."
Joan Fontcuberta, introduction to the print version of *Truth & Fictions.*

Using captured images and Adobe PhotoShop software, Lê has been examining history from his perspective of an American born in Vietnam. "Hyper-History examines what we know today about the Vietnam War as a combination of images from movies, such as *Apocalypse Now, The Deer Hunter,* and *Platoon,* and what we remember from newspaper articles and the evening TV news broadcasts. [These images exist] between the truth and a lie, but never-the-less [they are] the history in our mind's eye when we think about the Vietnam War."

© Dinh Q. Lê. *Hyper-History (copters),* 1995. Variable size. Digital file.

What Is a Digital Image?

Since camera-based images were being made centuries before the invention of photography, photography itself can be viewed as a progression in the evolution of camera images. Although the digital image shares many characteristics of the silver-based photograph, a debate continues as to whether digital imagery can be classified as photography or should be considered a separate system of representation. The technology that forms the digital image is intrinsically different from the silver-based photographic image. It exists as numerical information and does not necessarily have to be represented as a physical entity. The computer stores and processes information, such as an image, as a set of instructions known as binary code and displays it on a screen. This code like a light switch, operates in two states, "on" and "off." The use of binary code allows the digital image to be easily manipulated and stored.

The Defining of an Aesthetic

The computer provides a junction between photography, video, illustration, painting, and music in a way that changes the viewer's response to each separate media. The building of any aesthetic involves the discovery of a medium's advantages and limitations, while determining how to work within those parameters. While the paths of traditional and digital media continue to be linked, they ask fundamentally different critical questions, requiring the creation of a new "digital aesthetic."

In creating a digital aesthetic the importance of "craft," the knowledge and skill the maker brings to the physical nature of the work, is redefined. In many digital works the processes we have traditionally described as craft appears to be assumed by the machine. This can be the computers greatest asset as well as a source of criticism that can separate digital work from the traditional dialogue of art.

Some people believe the computer is a magic box that will do all the work and make them instant imagemakers. It is important to understand that computers work by human direction and do not accomplish tasks on their own. Without human guidance the computer will apply a pre-programmed set of solutions to every problem. Each decision artists allow the computer to make takes them further away from the imagemaking equation. The worthwhile image takes time and effort, even on a computer. The computer is no different than any other tool, like a hammer you have to figure out how best to hold it and then what to hit.

Looking at Digital Images

Simply using a digital camera to take a traditional picture does not take advantage of digital imaging's inherent strengths. It is the alterations and the way they are made that separate the digital image from the traditional photograph. When looking at a digital image one of the things we are looking at are these changes.

The camera and the computer are mediated ways of seeing; but historically the camera has been considered an objective observer that makes no subjective assertions. The digital image does not make this claim. The informed viewer knows that the digital image is about fabrication.

Surrealists, such as Salvador Dali and René Magritte, distorted scale and perspective while juxtaposing commonplace objects in unusual contexts. In these images the viewer is asked to make connections they would not normally make. The computer artist, by changing the context or content of images, can ask the viewer to make associations that are normally not possible or that are difficult to produce with traditional photographic methods.

· ASSIGNMENT·

What happens when you scan an image and apply a preprogrammed effect, such as a Fresco or Van Gogh filter, to it? What is the result? Is it a creative act?

The author gratefully acknowledges the assistance of John Valentino in the preparation of this chapter.

Parker uses a computer as a natural extension of her way of making images. "I can make objects that never existed but still have something of the odd relationship to reality that a photograph does," Parker says. "A digital image differs from a photograph in that it is fluid; it can change to another then another version." Parker can choose to keep or destroy the generations of change and seldom uses filters that radically change the image. "Fortunately I already had a group of themes and ideas underway when I gained access to a computer. Otherwise the question would have been: now that I have the freedom to do anything I want to with images, what do I do?"

© Olivia Parker. *Nijinsky's Cat as Seen by Diderot,* 1995. Variable size. Digital file.

Every Image Is an Original

When copies of digital files are made, the specific code that describes the image is exactly copied, allowing the digital image to be reproduced infinitely and perfectly. The computer image, unlike the film-based image, exists as data and is not as susceptible to many of the harmful effects of age or use.

As the writer/philosopher Walter Benjamin stated: "Even the most perfect reproduction of art is lacking in one element: its presence in time and space."[1] Since there is no physical difference between copies of digital images, every image can be considered an original. If every image is an original then every digital image is a reproduction, since there is no way to determine which version came first.

A student of economics can tell you that what makes an object valuable is its scarcity. The monetary value of an image can affect our opinion and appreciation of it. If the digital image resists being a commodity it could affect how people accept and react to these images. The continued use of digital images could cause a new questioning of the meaning and value of the original.

The Computer and Popular Reality

Since the invention of the daguerreotype we have been altering photo-based images. Everyday we are bombarded with images that have been modified. Framing and cropping by the photographer can alter the content of the image and therefore the meaning of the picture. The average viewer has been taught to trust the photograph, especially ones in the media, as an accurate representation of reality. There was a public outcry when *National Geographic* moved the Pyramids on its February 1982 cover. The print media has reacted to digital manipulation with internal rules and proposed codes of ethics. Despite these

[1] Walter Benjamin. "The Work of Art in the Age of Mechanical Reproduction," in *Illuminations.* Edited by Hannah Arendt. (New York: Harcort, Brace and World, 1968), 222.

Role playing and a sense of theater dominate Adams's collage investigation of gender issues. Here Adams has fabricated and then in stages photographed a classic stag party scenario. An assortment of males leer at the stripper's pixelated breasts (a computer printout suspended in front of the figure). The illusion is shattered when the viewer of the collage realizes that Adams is playing all the characters. While this image was not computer generated, a computer was used extensively in its production. To make the red curtains, a photograph of a red curtain was scanned, then the Mosaic function in Adobe PhotoShop software was used, a large print of it made, and the wall was painted from that print. Adams comments: "This elaborately simulated digital manipulation adds an additional level of mediation and artifice, and suggests that parts of the picture were not only photographed at different times, but perhaps were never present at all."

© Bill Adams. *Bachelor Party, Version 2*, 1995. 48 × 64 inches. Color chromogenic prints.

Yoshida addresses her concerns with the body, mythology, spirituality, the connection between woman and nature, and the mysterious conjunction of power and pleasure in intersubjective sexual relations. Focusing on women's rights and censorship issues, Yoshida points out that a woman has never appeared on U.S. paper currency.

© Barbara Yoshida. *The Three Graces*, 1995. 6 6/16 × 7 13/16 inches. Iris ink jet print.

tales of photographic deception, people continue to believe in the authority and veracity of the photograph. Digital images that look like traditional photographs betray that trust because all of the separation between media has been removed. The traditional set of rules established by our culture to discriminate between media no longer applies when the digital image enters the equation. This fosters a sense of digital anxiety. The degree of postcamera control offered by digital editing has been seen as a threat to our notion of photographic identity as it has been established through a fragile social contract between subject and the imagemaker (see sections on a View from Within and the Portrait as Social Identity in chapter 21.)

Appropriation

From ancient to modern times, imagemakers have "borrowed" from others to produce work. The use of source material should be examined on an individual basis, taking into account the concepts of fairness, originality, content, and the motivation of the artist. When appropriating images we can ask, Does the appropriation change the meaning in a significant way?

By appropriating images, artists, such as Sherrie Levine and Barbara Kruger, challenge the notion of authorship and originality. In these cases the original was directly referenced, but the ideas expressed by the appropriation differed from the originals. This validates the appropriation and legitimizes the work in the postmodern art world.

Copyright and the Digital Image

Photographers have fought to define the legal status of the photographic image. In the United States copyright generally belongs to the person who pressed the shutter. In some situations, such as with many photojournalists, the image may belong to the newspaper or client who paid for its production (known as work for hire).

Legally an idea cannot be copyrighted; only the expression of an idea may be protected. Generally we can assume that if an appropriated image is so

Drawing on the methods and strategies of advertising, Kruger reuses studio-type images and text to deal with capitalism, patriarchal oppression, and consumption. Kruger attempts to deconstruct consumerism, the power of the media, and stereotypes of women by showing how images and words can manipulate and obscure meaning. About her work, Kruger states: "The thing that's happening with photography today vis-a-vis computer imaging, vis-a-vis alteration, is that it no longer needs to be based on the real at all. . . . Photography to me no longer pertains to the rhetoric of realism; it pertains more to the rhetoric of the unreal rather than the real or of course the hyperreal."

© Barbara Kruger. *Untitled*, 1990. 143 × 103 inches. Photographic silk-screen on vinyl.
Courtesy of Mary Boone Gallery, New York, NY.

far removed from the original that it is unrecognizable, then the new image is not an infringement of copyright law (see chapter 15).

Using appropriated sources create an image(s) that alters the context of the original. Discuss how the two images differ. Would the image carry the same message if the materials were not appropriated?

The Digital Impression: Intangibility

Although computer programmers attempt to simulate a tactile experience with tools that replicate an airbrush, paintbrush, or pencil, they are still imitations that respond differently from traditional tools. One of the greatest difficulties new computer users encounter is their inability to apply real-world intuition to the machine. When working with any new tool, users must develop a set of intuitive actions based on their experience on the machine.

Information on a computer is never truly in a fixed state. The computer image, because of its immateriality, is constantly in a state of flux, waiting to be changed. Only the printed image(s) can be thought of as permanently fixed.

The data displayed on a computer screen often carries more information than can be outputted. An understanding of the final product is necessary for deciding when an image is finished. Knowing why you started making the image is another indicator of when it is finished. The adage less is more can also be applied to digital images. There comes a point where further alterations can become confusing. Since many viewers will be looking for the digital changes, those alterations should have a purpose that furthers the image's content/context.

Itagaki's computer-altered images symbolize how individuals in a materialistic civilization cannot be separated from technology. His computer-generated images, made on transparency paper, are burned, painted, and mounted on bases made of canvas stretchers and plywood. A thick transparent resin is then poured on the mounted image. The finished work has a thickness of about 2 inches with the base and resin.

© Yoshio Itagaki. *Daniel in Yellow*, 1995. 16 × 11 × 2 inches. Ink jet print with mixed media.

Artist as Programmer

One criticism of the digital image is that it is made by the program writer as opposed to the imagemaker. This phenomenon is not without historical precedent. The camera has shaped our system of photographic representation. Its monocular vision, seeing the world from a single linear viewpoint, is a construct at the heart of classical Aristotelian thinking. The development of flexible roll film and the handheld camera has defined an entire way of seeing.

Many of the existing digital tools were created to suit someone else's needs or were designed for general use. Imagemakers have always found ways to make tools fit their personal vision. Programs are available that give digital imagemakers the ability to author software and customize imagemaking tools.

Dichotomy Between Screen and Output

We have been conditioned to accept the wall on which an image is displayed as neutral space; under this paradigm the wall should not affect how the viewer reads the content/context of a piece. Work that exists on a computer screen does not operate under this assumption. The physical apparatus of the machine has an entirely different set of connotations that include all of the other uses of a computer (word processor, telephone, checkbook). Work that exists on a computer's screen has to overcome this limitation. Digital images that are printed out as photographs or lithographs begin to take on the characteristics and connotations of those mediums.

• ASSIGNMENT •

Place an image in an unexpected or nontraditional location. Can an image's surroundings affect the content/context of an image?

Hardware

Why a Computer?

As a camera condenses a three-dimensional scene into a two-dimensional representation, the computer seamlessly combines different media into a virtual representation, retaining the qualities of some and eliminating the qualities of others. Anything that can be done with a camera, paintbrush, or drafting set can be done on a computer.

The computer is a powerful tool for experimenting with ideas and design. But the computer is not always the best way to produce an image. Images stored on silver-based film continue to carry more information than most digital media. Currently few digital mediums can compete with film in terms of cost or economical storage. If you are not planning on significantly manipulating the image, the wise choice may continue to be the silver-based image.

Computer Economics

While it is possible to get started in photography for a couple of hundred dollars, the computer artist must begin with a substantial investment, making institutional affiliation almost a must. The economic benefits are long term since the computer is an endless store of art supplies. Digital images may exist only on a monitor and do not have to be printed out onto paper. Getting the image off the computer can be done at moderate cost at a service bureau (see section on service bureaus). Once the image is complete it can be printed out without the test print process used in photography. Old versions of projects are simply erased. Editions of images can be easily made on demand.

Computer technology is developing and changing so rapidly that it is impossible to know what will be in use during the next decade. When acquiring a computer the best advice is to buy the fastest machine (to reduce image processing time), with the most memory, highest resolution, and capacity for future expansion that you can afford. Your machine may be in the avant-garde for only a few months before it is replaced by something new, but this form of marketing does not make your machine obsolete or affect its performance.

Working on the Machine

Resolution

A computer, like film, offers a variety of resolutions for different applications. Films with an ISO of 50 deliver finer grain than ones with an ISO of 400, but there is a trade-off; the lower ISO films require more light and longer shutter speeds. When working with a digital image you will be asked to trade image quality for speed and hard-drive space. Large, high-resolution images require additional processing time and more hard-drive space.

How the Screen Approximates Resolution   The average monitor has a resolution of 72 pixels per inch. Most programs describe the size of an image in terms of

Gottlieb digitizes her color slides by scanning them onto a Photo CD, which she then imports into her computer for manipulation. Gottlieb intends to "challenge the viewer by experimenting with color, light, and perspective to alter reality and stimulate new perceptions. The intent is to inspire a wide spectrum of emotion by utilizing contradiction, mystery, and vivid, sensual color."

© Jane Gottlieb. *Picasso's Dancers*, 1995. 29 × 42 inches. Ink jet print.

a ratio displayed in the title box at the top of the screen. A ratio of 1:2 means each screen pixel equals four outputted image pixels. Although two images may appear as the same size on the screen, their resolution and therefore their relative size may be different, making cutting and pasting difficult.

The Color Monitor

There is an inherent visual difference between images seen on your monitor, other monitors, and output devices. Sophisticated monitors allow for color correction as well as contrast and brightness adjustments, but these only affect how the image appears on *your* monitor. It will appear differently on another monitor and/or paper output. Hardware and software are available to help control the color balance between monitors and output.

All monitors use an additive color system where red, green, and blue (RGB) are added to make white. Any combination of the light primaries always produces a lighter result. Since light is transmitted from the image, the colors tend to be more saturated and luminous. The printed image uses a subtractive color scheme where cyan, magenta, and yellow pigments are layered on a sheet of paper. Any increase in pigment density subtracts the initial amount of light, producing a darker result.

Color Systems

Depending on the type of machine and monitor and the amount of video memory (VRAM) it is possible to manipulate millions of colors on the computer (see section on memory). Image-processing programs allow color manipulation in several distinct ways, the most important of which is the **RGB** setting. All video monitors represent color by displaying minute RGB bars. Other on-screen colors are computer simulations or approximations of these color schemes. In addition to color, images can be produced as a **gray scale,** which produces 256 shades of gray, or **bitmap** images, which are purely black-and-white.

The Pixel   The building blocks of the digital image picture elements (pixels) are arranged as a grid on a monitor. Pixels create an image in a way very different from the dots in a halftone image or grains of silver in a black-and-white photograph. Pixels are more like the individual tiles in a mosaic. Each pixel contains complete information about hue, lightness, and saturation of a particular point of an image. The more pixels an image has the finer the image appears and the larger the file size.

What Is 2/4/8/16/24/32 Bit Color?

Bit depth used to describe the number of bits (the smallest unit of information on a computer) that is assigned to each pixel, refers to the number of shades of gray or the number of colors that can be represented by a single pixel. The greater the number of bits (1, 2, 4, 8, 16, 24, or 32) the greater the number of colors and tones a computer can simulate. Both 24 and 32 bits account for color variations well beyond the range of human perception. Displayed bit depth is governed by a special set of memory chips, called video RAM, or VRAM, which is dedicated to displaying text and graphics.

If a computer does not have enough VRAM to display a particular color it can perform a function called *dithering.* Dithering is only possible if the software permits it and the user selects it. By placing different colored pixels next to one another the computer can produce up to 5,000 colors in a way that is similar to CMYK (cyan, magenta, yellow, black) printers. On a monitor these images often produce a noticeable moiré pattern that many people find distracting.

Other Digital Colors

Many software applications allow for the manipulation of color according to its hue, saturation, or luminosity (**HSL**) or through a licensed color system such as **Truetone®** or **Pantone®.** These last two systems allow for the most understandable color manipulation on the computer.

Process color, or CMYK, is the traditional printing method of lithographic printers. This set of subtractive primaries is the color system used by most color printers. Many output devices cannot print all of the colors the computer is capable of processing. Some software packages warn you if the color selected cannot be printed by a particular device. Computer users can make

Hallman uses the computer, with its fluid technology of pixels, as a stage for critical examination of his own experience as a man in this culture. By using himself as principal actor, Hallman neutralizes the issues surrounding the representation of individuals and focuses attention on ideas. "Partly because of the tableau methodology, and the flexible range of computer color, I feel more responsible for the meaning and expression carried by color in this work. It is a pleasure and powerful seduction, requiring a new and constant mindful attention."

© Gary Hallman. *Cul de Sac Pas de Deux #3,* 1995. 24 × 36 inches. Ink jet print.

Nakagawa scans his black-and-white and color photographs into the computer, manipulates them with Adobe Photo-Shop software, outputs his results as a 4-× 5-inch color negative, and prints them as traditional color images. The colors used for these exterior spaces are duo-tones and allude to a sense of the past. Nakagawa critiques Western society from his viewpoint, which is Eastern in origin and Western by immersion. Nakagawa explains his selective use of color: "By intensifying certain colors within an image, I intentionally call attention to the comparison of nostalgia with explicitly political messages."

© Osamu James Nakagawa. *Hiroshima, Point Zero, from the TV Screen Series,* 1993. 26 1/2 × 40 inches. Chromogenic color print.

color separations for printing using this mode. When switching from RGB to CMYK the computer dulls the screen colors to simulate a subtractive print. **Duo-tone** effects, applying a second accenting color, are also possible.

Memory

RAM

When a program is begun, its contents are loaded into random access memory (RAM). Instructions the computer needs to perform its tasks are stored and processed in a series of chips called single in-line memory modules (SIMMs) or dual in-line memory modules (DIMMs). DIMMs are faster than their SIMM counterparts. The amount of RAM a computer has directly affects its performance and capabilities. RAM is easily expanded.

Many computers and programs allow the use of virtual memory, an operation in which the computer uses the hard disk as RAM. This process is extremely slow compared to using real RAM. Certain procedures require large amounts of memory and may necessitate the use of virtual memory.

How Much Memory Do I Need?

Most software applications include minimum memory requirements on their printed material. However, to run the program effectively you may need much more. It is prudent to research programs before purchasing them. One major factor that has made specific computer models obsolete is their inability to add more RAM.

ROM

Permanently installed in the computer, read only memory (ROM) contains the basic instructions the computer needs to start up and to draw objects on a screen. Unlike RAM memory, ROM is unalterable.

Hard Disk

The hard disk, usually installed inside the computer, is where applications and files are stored. Since image files are often larger than the available RAM, some software applications use the hard disk to temporarily store information. The program shuffles information from the hard disk (the scratch disk) into RAM, where it is processed. This enables the program to complete complex operations and functions, such as "undo" and "preview." The scratch disk can take up to five times as much space as the original image because it stores several different versions of the image. The computer's hard disk must have enough free space to accommodate these temporary files.

Major File Types

It is essential to know how to store information. Different file types are best for different applications. Here are the major types:

- TIFF: An acronym for tag image file format, TIFFs are currently the standard in the graphics field. Known as an interchange format, it is (usually) easily opened on any platform and is considered one of the most reliable file formats for storing data without losing information. TIFF files offer a compression option that may inhibit the ability to open them with other platforms and cause a loss in image quality.

- EPS: Short for encapsulated post script, EPS files were designed for saving high-resolution illustrations on Adobe software. EPS files are difficult or impossible to alter.

- PICT: Encoded in the Macintosh's native graphics language, PICT files can also be opened on the DOS platform. This file type is easily opened and saved in most software applications (see section on software later in this chapter).

- Raw: Raw files are straight binary files with information pertaining only to one color. Raw files can be difficult to work with and may destroy data if not configured correctly. Their main advantage is their ability to open up unknown file types and their compact size.

- Program Specific: Program-specific file types are native formats that contain the maximum amount of information about an image. Several times larger than similar files, certain operations can only be conducted on a file saved in its native format. To change the file type to a nonnative format the image must be streamlined, layers combined, and certain formatting information eliminated.

Storing the Image

Compacting Algorithms

Compression algorithms, a set of program instructions, allow the user to compact or segment a large file into smaller pieces that can more easily fit onto storage mediums. There are many types of file compression schemes; some cause files to lose information, and others compress files without sacrificing information. Before using any type of compression software be sure to know how it will affect your image.

No-Loss Compression

No-loss compression programs create an archive of a selected file in which the information describing the item is converted to a form that takes up less space. When the file is used again it must be uncompressed, a process that returns the file to its original state.

There are a number of these software applications, each with its own advantages and disadvantages.

JPEG Compression

The JPEG algorithm takes the redundancy out of an image by manipulating tonal values. This compression technique mathematically represents similar tones and eliminates some information as a means of saving space. JPEG offers several choices governing compression size and quality.

Storage Mediums

In addition to hard drives, there are a number of expandable and portable devices that can aid in the storage and transportation of information. In the 1970s and early 1980s, the 5 1/4-inch floppy disk and the smaller 3 1/2-inch disk were the standard for storing files. Each disk held 400 to 800 kilobytes (KB) and 1.4 megabytes (MB, or 1,433 KB) of information. At that time

Golding discusses how this picture is a hybrid of traditional and digital processes. Digital imaging allows Golding to "coalesce these materials into a singular image devoid of the 'thumb print' of any one process." This picture began as black-and-white images that were scanned, manipulated, outputted to negative, and printed on black-and-white paper. Golding applies a sepia wash and hand colors the prints before rescanning them. Due to their large file size (50 to 60 MB) he electronically cuts them in half and works on them as separate images. Many of the elements in the picture, such as the Katcinas, were created digitally. As a final step he combines the pictures and digitally lights them to get the desired aesthetic effect. The result is outputted to a 4- × 5-inch slide and printed on ILFOCHROME. This picture raises the issue: Do you have to be a member of a particular group in order to fairly photographically represent it?

© Stephen Golding. *Dioramas of the Old West: Indians, Settlers, and Katcinas*, 1993. 8 × 23 1/2 inches. Dye-destruction print.

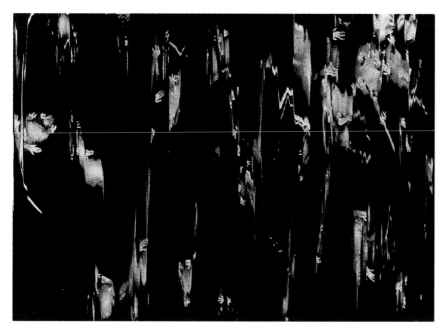

According to Selter: "This image was made by five mice running around on a flatbed scanner while I performed a scan at 200 ppi (pixels per inch). The combination of the moving animals and the moving scanner bar resulted in this unique pattern of motion, a pattern that seems to proclaim the 'essence' of mouse: rapid, bouncy, punctuated by brief pauses of the feet. . . . I began to see that each kind of animal [scanned] produced a pattern somehow typical of its type of locomotion. The visible halftone dots serve to 'atomize' the image, so the closer you look the less information you get. Only by standing back and taking in the whole scene does an image emerge. . . . This is an argument against reductionism as the answer to the secret of life."

© Carol Selter. *Mice*, 1995. 28 1/2 × 39 inches. Chromogenic color print.

you could keep a copy of the software application and a small number of files on a single floppy. Then a typical word processing file might require 8 KB. Today an image file can easily need 8 MB, (a hundred times larger file) requiring most high-quality images to be spread out on several disks to be moved. Floppy disks are also not the most reliable storage mediums and are not recommended for long-term storage of data. Storage devices are continually being developed and improved. These are just a few that have made a major impact on the digital medium.

CD-ROM

Currently, compact disk read only memory (CD-ROM) disks hold over 600 MB of data and are the industry standard for the commercial distribution of large amounts of data. Standard CD-ROM drives can only read disks, but devices are available for one-time imprinting of disks. Data cannot be altered once imprinted. CD-ROMs are one of the most archival means for saving data. Data can be copied off a CD with ease.

Magneto Optical

Through the use of a laser, magneto optical or erasable optical drives store data by changing the polarity of small portions of the disk. These high-cost storage devices have the advantage of being rewriteable. They have a life span of at least 10 years.

Removable Hard Drive

Similar to the hard drive inside your computer, removable hard drives, or SyQuests, are made up of an aluminum disk coated with iron oxide. The SyQuest disk, one of the first removable storage devices, is presently the industry standard among commercial printers and service bureaus (see following section on service bureaus).

Input: Scanning

Input devices called scanners take information off of printed or photographic materials in a way similar to photocopiers. Light is reflected off (or through) an image or object and interpreted by light sensors. Color scanners use RGB filters to read an image in single or multiple passes. Most scans need correction to adjust color and contrast or to crop an image.

Flatbed, Film, and Stock

Flatbed scanners, capable of digitizing images in a variety of resolutions, are the most common way to digitize a document. These devices allow the user to preview the image and make minor corrections before scanning. Although designed to digitize prints, some flatbed scanners can handle transparencies.

By transmitting light through an image, **film scanners** are designed to capture the minute details of small negatives and transparencies. These devices usually cost more than flatbed scanners but are designed to treat transparent media with greater precision and care.

Prepackaged **stock images** are available as photo CD-ROMs and can be downloaded in different resolutions. Many stock image packages include reproduction and alteration rights in the cost of the CD; others require usage fees and may not allow alterations to the image. Remember, the use of copyrighted images without permission is illegal (see previous section on appropriation).

Drum Scanners

Currently the most accurate way to digitize flat media is on a drum scanner. The image is read on a glass drum while being spun at several thousand revolutions per minute. Scans made on these devices are generally more precise and translate images with greater detail than other scanners. These high-end scanners work with both prints and transparencies.

Capturing Images

Internal video cards and other external devices can convert a video signal to a format that the computer can process. With these devices you can capture (grab) images from broadcast television or videotape. Since the individual video image is only on the screen for a moment and does not need to be of high resolution, screen-capture images will also generally be low resolution.

Using the capture technique, image-makers can use video cameras to collect original material. Specially designed video-capture cameras (often called array cameras) are capable of producing higher-resolution images. Although commercially broadcasted images are copyrighted, artists interested in commenting on popular culture and the media often use these images.

"As an artist working in an institution and society laden with written and visual information, I am inundated with imagery that attempts to 'mean' something. Seeing an alternative to all of this 'information imagery,' I began exploring flower arrangements." Rich creates her images on a Hewlett Packard scanner and outputs to a Lasergraphics film recorder. After scanning the arrangements, Rich sometimes makes minor alterations, digitally extending some flower petals and eliminating others. Floral forms take on human characteristics, echoing aspects of life such as sexuality, love, conflict, and decline. "The work, like the garden, is about life cycles; the process of generation and growth and its inherent contradictions."

© Felicity Rich. *Denuded-2,* 1994. 17 × 12 inches. Chromogenic color print.

With the advantages of being both quick and reusable, filmless **still video** cameras are attached to a computer or contain a storage disk for images. While film cameras continue to capture more information in a cost-effective manner, still video cameras are becoming more accessible and are improving in resolution and quality. Digital cameras, which permit captured data to be directly input into the computer, may become the standard means of making a digital picture as they become more affordable (note: none of the artists whose work appears in this chapter mentioned using a digital camera).

Service Bureaus

Service bureaus, commercial printers, and many copy centers will scan images and download them onto paper, film, or disk. The quality of the output depends on the skill of the operators as well as the type and maintenance of equipment. General rule: if it's not done to your satisfaction ask them to do it again.

Georgiou uses the computer to make images that can't be photographed to speculate how future civilizations might perceive our present culture. This faux-documentary presents recurring forms of the "power-glyphs" found in monolithic ruins and petroglyphs across North America. Georgiou created this image using a combination of digitized photographic images and live capture video images that have been manipulated together in digital form.

© Tyrone Georgiou. *Plug Ruins, Utah from Unexplained Archaeology of North America,* 1991. Variable size. Digital file.

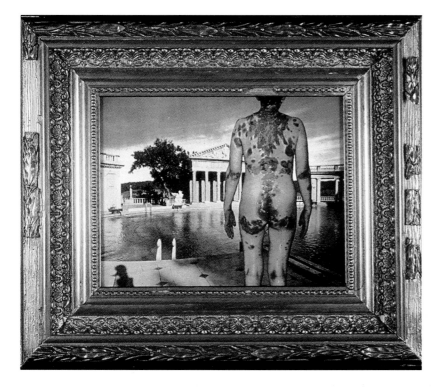

Working with a film recorder and Adobe PhotoShop software, Lentz combines "the scientific aesthetic of medicine with the narrative characteristics of gothic fiction. The result is a revision of domestic horror, where melancholy is written on the skin" (allusions to AIDS).

© Huey Lentz. *San Simeon,* 1995. 12 × 14 inches with frame. Chromogenic color print.

Output: Presenting the Digital Image

Film Recorders

A film recorder transfers a digital image onto ordinary color or black-and-white film that you can view, print, and store as a traditional photograph. For color imaging, exposures are made through red, green, and blue filters to provide image data in raster or bitmap form. Many output devices, such as film recorders, have their own RAM (as with your computer) in which the image is loaded and stored during printing. Output devices with limited memory may not be capable of producing large, high-resolution images.

Thermal Printing

Dye-sublimation printers, currently the most direct way to produce digital prints, work with RGB, CMYK, and gray-scale images. In this process the pigments, contained in thin plastic sheets, are turned into a gas and transferred onto a piece of specially coated paper. The colors are not laid side by side as in a halftone process but are blended to create a continuous tone print. Depending on the support material (paper base) and storage conditions, these prints can be expected to last about 10 years before fading is noticeable.

    Thermal-wax printers, similar to dye-sublimation printers, melt thin coatings of pigmented wax onto paper. Some thermal-wax printers print on a variety of papers. Their life span is shorter than dye-sublimation prints.

Printing with Ink

Ink-jet printers, as the name implies, work by spraying minute amounts of cyan, magenta, yellow, or black ink onto a page. As with all plain-paper printers, better-quality paper will yield higher-quality images. Ink-jet prints are impermanent and can, without protection, fade within 6 months.

    An **Iris** print is a type of ink-jet print that is produced by spraying fine dots of CMYK ink onto paper. Created on a spinning drum, these gallery-quality

The Iris ink-jet printer allows an imagemaker, such as Erickson, to transform a scanned image to printmaking paper. For Erickson, "The digital image becomes a new form, no longer a photograph as we know it, but hybrid. The Iris prints are like velvet to the touch, and the colors positively glow. The closest way I could describe these prints would be platinum prints in color."

© Wendy Erickson. *Cowboy Room,* 1994. 24 × 24 inches. Iris ink jet print.

be solely photo-based. The program's own internal tools, coupled with devices such as pressure-sensitive graphic tablets, let the user simulate the effects of other media as well as create unique digital images.

Different software packages may be used at different stages in the imagemaking process. Imaging applications can be classified under the following categories: draw, paint, image processing, animation, video editing, 3-D modeling and rendering, page layout, and interactive multimedia authoring or scripting. Some software applications specialize in one of these, and others combine two or more feature categories. Currently there is no single application software on the market capable of performing all of these functions well. A single application can provide adequate tools for an imaging project, but it is often necessary to combine the strengths and tools of other software to create desired effects.

Raster/Bitmapped Software

Most programs that process photo-based pictures operate with raster (bitmapped) images. The advantage of the bitmapped image is its ability to be edited pixel by pixel. Photo-based or raster image programs do not keep individual objects as separate entities. Items must be applied to a background/layer at which time any alteration will affect surrounding areas, replacing data or leaving holes. Increasing the size of an image increases the number of pixels, spreading out data. Reducing the size of an image eliminates pixels and reduces image quality.

Vector Graphics Software

Vector graphics (object-oriented) programs offer a wide range of options for manipulating lines and polygons. Vector graphics programs treat objects as separate entities that can be colored, stacked, reshaped, or moved without affecting the background or any other object. Designed for drafting and illustration purposes, vector software is not ideally suited for photo-realistic images.

prints can be made on a variety of materials that will accept ink. Depending on the type of ink, paper, and coating, these images have a life span ranging from as little as 6 months to decades.

Toner/Electrostatic Printing

Using colored toners in a CMYK halftone process, **Cactus** printers do not use a fixed pattern of dots as in traditional printing but a software-driven, varying dot pattern. Although the dots are visible to the naked eye (making them inappropriate for most fine or intricate work), Cactus prints are an inexpensive way to make large-scale, mural-sized digitized prints.

Using a laser beam to charge a photoelectric drum, **laser printers** utilize toner to create an electrostatic image. Once the charged toner is attracted to the drum, it is transferred to the paper and sealed by a hot fuser roller. Laser prints produce black-and-white and color prints of photocopier quality.

Software

Types of Digital Images

While the computer is a powerful tool, it is a blank slate, dependent on the instructions contained in software applications. Images created on a computer need not

Manual renders objects with wood textures "to stand in for Nature, . . . and to represent the synthetic and seductive world of computing and technology in comparison to the material (wood)." *The Constructed Forest,* an installation, represents the encounter between two distinct worlds within hyperspace. The base image was made on a 6-×-7-centimeter negative, scanned, and adjusted in Adobe PhotoShop. The three-dimensional figure of the sphere, bisected by a rectangle, was rendered in Strata Vision software (now Strata Studio Pro).

© Manual (Suzanne Bloom and Ed Hill). *Community Forest,* from *The Constructed Forest,* 1993. 24 × 36 1/2 inches. Chromogenic color print.

Campus's combinations of computer ingenuity psychologically insinuate the notion of disease or mutation of the natural world. Campus tells us: "My process involves the interaction of opposites: the inner (me) and the outer (my subject) meeting through the camera/computer; the natural (a leaf or flower or stone) and the synthesized (fabricated patterns made in the computer); the physical (made of irregular shapes and forms) and the mental (lines, squares, patterns derived from mathematical formulae). I am often dealing with issues of decay and regeneration . . . but always symbolically. Nature is vast and neutral, so I can load my images [via Adobe PhotoShop software] with complexity that might not be possible otherwise."

© Peter Campus. *burning,* 1992. 39 13/16 × 50 5/16 inches. Dye destruction print.
Courtesy of Paula Cooper Gallery, New York, NY.

Produce an image that cannot be created photographically or manually with pen or paint. You should have an idea why you are making the image on a computer as opposed to other mediums. Relate to Walter Benjamin's "Art in the Age of Mechanical Reproduction" (see footnote 1 earlier in this chapter).

Basic Digital Tools

Cutting and Pasting

The capacity to replicate and move information is the essential power of the computer. Cutting and pasting is possible between files made on different pieces of software as well as between documents made on the same software. But the data structure of the information is not always compatible. Most well-developed software applications have a set of procedures for converting and opening files produced by different applications.

Shape

An object can be manipulated through one of the toolbar items such as a brush, blur, or eraser tool. These affect the portion of the image directly surrounding the tool icon and allow for a selective and precise manipulation of an image.

Digital Filters   An image can also be manipulated through tools called **filters.** Filters can be added to a program to create effects that emboss, enhance, or pinch. In the nineteenth century photographers turned to the aesthetic strategies of painting for guidance. Today software manufacturers have done the same; producing effects packages that transform digitized images into simulated paintings. As imagemakers discover an original digital aesthetic there will be less of a reliance on older mediums, and filters that simulate them, allowing an authentic digital syntax to emerge.

Forming Good Computer Habits

- Save Often: Problems with the power supply or misread data can cause the computer to malfunction. Frequently saving data is often the only way to avoid problems. Once every 15 minutes is not too much. When working on large, important projects make copies on a reliable removable medium for safekeeping.

- Delete old files: A drive filled with old, no longer used files can become a liability by preventing you from having an adequate scratch disk.

- Back Up: Make periodic backups on an external storage device. Although uncommon, files can be corrupted by everyday use or by a computer virus (a devious program designed to infect computers and destroy or interrupt data).

Protecting Yourself and Your Computer

- Monitor emissions: Extremely low frequency (ELF) and very low frequency (VLF) emissions are types of electromagnetic radiation created by monitors. Some research studies have linked these emissions to an increased risk of cancer or miscarriage. Keep your eyes at least 18 inches away from the screen and avoid prolonged exposure. Low-emissions monitors are available as well as filters for the screen.

- Eye strain: Eye strain can be reduced by working in a well-lit room and by keeping the screen free of dust and clear of reflections.

- Take breaks: Taking a 15-minute break every 1 or 2 hours helps keep you sane as well as prevents fatigue. Try mixing noncomputer-related activities into your digital routine.

- Carpal tunnel syndrome: Carpal tunnel syndrome, caused by repetitive movements and improper keyboard and mouse use, is characterized by numbness and tingling in the wrists and hands. In advanced stages, the syndrome can cause permanent nerve damage. Keeping your wrists flat, straight, and at a height equal to your elbows helps prevent injury.

- Proper posture: Make sure you are comfortable and that your feet are on a footrest or are flat on the floor. The top of the monitor should be at eye level.

- Power surges: Power surges, called spikes, occur when the power to your home or studio is restored after an interruption. These surges can damage the sensitive circuitry in your computer. Surge suppression devices are designed to protect a computer and peripherals from a spike.

Scale and Size

Scale, one of the primary clues to depth perception, can be manipulated to change the context or to create an image that challenges the viewer's assumptions. An image can be foreshortened to simulate perspective or stretched to fit into a defined area.

Program controls usually refer to image size or canvas size. Both make the image larger or smaller, but the canvas size allows for the creation of blank drawing space (or crops the image) while altering the image size affects the overall dimensions of the image.

• ASSIGNMENT •

Using the noise filter and the toolbar on your image manipulation program, create a color image without using any of the programmed filters; use the concepts described in chapter 18.

The Computer as Multimedia Tool

Moving Images

Moving images, or video, address time in a different way than a still image. With video the viewer tends to be involved within the flow of events, while the still image is an abstraction calling for a more concentrated viewing and interpretation. The assembling and editing of video images on a computer is known as nonlinear video. Software packages edit video by creating several-second fragments called **clips.** A clip of video can be combined with sound, previewed, and altered.

Cell animation programs, many of which are vector drawing programs, manipulate discrete objects and create the illusion of motion by showing sequential frames with incremental motion. The cell elements can be independently controlled, allowing the background to remain stationary while objects in the foreground display motion.

Quicktime Movies

Quicktime movies incorporate a series of compression schemes and allow moving images and sound to be created, stored, and viewed. Quicktime movies compensate for the speed of your computer, keeping the sound properly synchronized with the picture.

Three-Dimensional Images

Three-dimensional modeling programs are vector drawing programs that have the capability to render an object and simulate the effects of light. The completed object can be viewed from any angle and direction. Three-dimensional modeling programs are often coupled with an animation component that allows the piece to be presented as a movie.

Interactive Artists' Books

Artists' books allow a maker to conduct an extended dialogue with a viewer. The digital artists' book takes that dialogue one

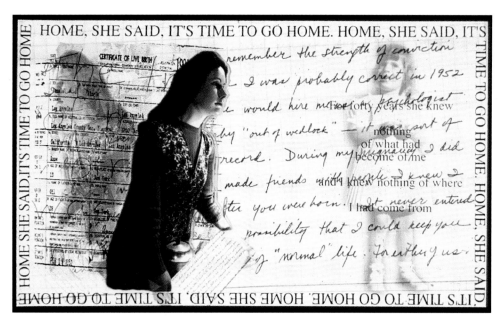

Ruíz's work seeks to question issues of restructured reality by monumentalizing the invisible or visually insignificant. For this piece the object was scanned and retouched in Adobe PhotoShop software. The wire-frame structure was created in Super 3D (a rendering program) and imported into Adobe PhotoShop. Concerning her use of color Ruíz says: "I work digitally and have access to millions of colors. Because they are there, at the ready, does not mean one should use them all at once. Because my work is concerned with internal, conceptual structures, I choose to work in limited color."

© Kathleen H, Ruíz. *Virtual Structure, Study 3*, 1991. 23 × 15 inches. Iris ink jet print.

Flax states that upon being introduced to the computer, it became clear that she could bring information examining the roles of parents and children into her work. Woven throughout the examination of family and society is the ever-present knowledge that these new technologies have an awesome potential to change the way we communicate and understand the world. Flax says: "I try to maintain an awareness of their power, never simply thinking of them as painting tools, but always as communication devices." Working with this technology has caused Flax to rethink the confines of two-dimensional picture space and to produce work that appears as an artists' book on paper, CD-ROM, and on the Internet. This image is part of a series of four Iris prints and also a plate in an artists' book by the same title.

© Carol Flax. *Some (M)other Stories: A Parent(hetic)al Tale, Page 2*, 1994. 26 × 34 inches. Iris ink jet print.

step further by including elements of performance through video, and sound. Interactive programs, embedded in a CD-ROM or other storage device, may require the viewer to make choices that determine content or outcome of a work and are modified with each viewing.

Use an interactive program to manipulate video, text, images, and sound to create a digital artists' book in which the viewer controls the outcome. What are the similarities and differences between the digital and the traditional book? What are the effects of this blending of media? Is it an indistinct hybrid or something new?

The Internet

The Internet is a series of networks used by academic and private research labs to share information. Those not connected to these institutions can gain access through pay-for-use services and private bulletin boards that provide electronic mail (e-mail) and software libraries.

In recent years people have been sharing images on the Internet. Some exist as files that can be downloaded, such as software applications; others can be viewed as images in virtual galleries. As more serious imagemakers access the Internet, the selection and quality of images should expand and evolve.

With the use of a modem a computer user can send digital data via the Internet or can directly send data to any other user who has a modem. On-line services allow the user to download an image file and electronically mail it to a particular user. The advantages to this method are that both users can receive and send material, even if the other person's computer is turned off. The downside to using the Internet is the time involved in transmitting data. Even the fastet modems are slow in computer terms. On-line services may only be a local call, but many charge a fee for every minute you are on-line.

The Virtual Gallery/WWW

The World Wide Web (WWW) and other virtual spaces offer a unique environment for sharing information, images, and other media. A recent Internet trend for presenting images is the digital gallery. Many of these virtual spaces mimic the conventions of the traditional gallery by creating virtual frames and walls. Viewing images in a gallery setting is a separate experience from looking at images on a computer monitor or in a book. A 4-×-5-foot image carries a distinctly different message from one that is 8 × 10 inches. All of these circumstances are changed by the computer screen. All images are (roughly) the same size. The aura of a gallery setting is replaced by the aura of the desktop.

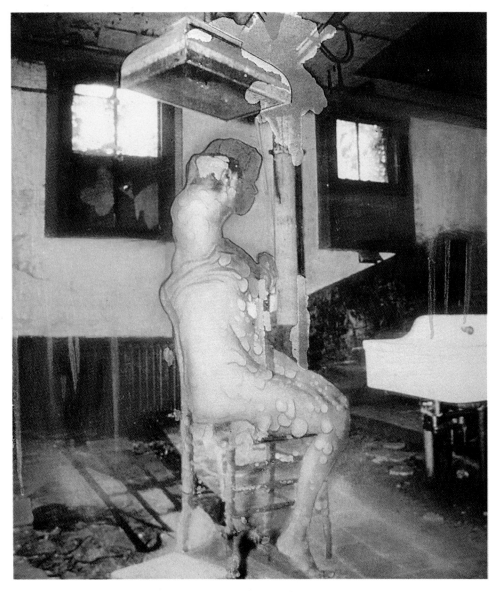

Reuter discusses why he works digitally: "My approach is to use photography's perceived reality in the creation of a mythological one. . . . I find it useful in bringing together disparate realities in the hope that the new combination of images creates something more powerful and captivating. Computer collaging has allowed me the spontaneity I experienced with my SX-70 work . . . with many ideas covered in a very short period of time. Digital manipulation has given me that same fluid methodology with freedoms and possibilities I never dreamed of in 1974." *The Infirmary* combines dissimilar images from the Ellis Island contagious disease ward morgue and an androgynous figure Reuter created in 1985.

© John Reuter. *The Infirmary*, 1995. 24 × 20 inches. Diffusion image transfer with dry pigment and pastel.

The End of the Wet Darkroom?

The reasons for working with any process should be imbedded in the context of the imagery. Any method, including silver-based photography, will continue to be used as long as imagemakers find meaning in the process.

In the future, economic and environmental pressures could make traditional silver-based film hard to find, but by that time the technology and the audience will have also changed. The quality and variety of digital images will also continue to increase and as this occurs the digital image will in all likelihood become imbedded in our daily lives.

References

DiNucci, Darcy, et al. *The Macintosh Bible,* 5th ed. Berkeley, CA: Peachpit Press, 1994.

Grotta, Daniel, and Weiner, Sally. *Digital Imaging for Visual Artists.* New York: Windcrest/McGraw Hill, 1994.

Mitchell, William J. *The Reconfigured Eye: Visual Truth in the Post-Photographic Era.* Cambridge, MA, and London: MIT Press, 1992.

Ritchin, Fred. *In Our Own Image: The Coming Revolution in Photography.* New York: Aperture Foundation, 1990.

Magazines/Journals

Numerous magazines covering technology and digital images have come and gone. A good newsstand or bookstore will carry a selection of journals and magazines that offer information on new products, tips on imaging, and critical analysis of digital media.

Organizations

The Maine Photographic Workshops
Rockport, ME 04856
(207) 236–8581

Special Interest Group-Graphics (SIGGRAPH) of the Association for Computing Machinery (ACM)
11 West 42nd Street
New York, NY 10036

Software

Adobe Systems
1585 Charleston Rd.
P.O. Box 7900
Mountain View, CA 94039
(800) 833–6687

Deneba Software
7400 SW 87th Ave.
Miami, FL 33173
(305) 596–5644

Macromedia
600 Townsend St.
San Francisco, CA 94103
(800) 945–4061

On-line Services

America Online
8619 Westwood Ctr. Dr.
Vienna, VA 22182–2285
(800) 827–6364

Compuserve
P.O. Box 20212
Columbus, OH
(800) 848–8199

FOURTEEN

Zone System for Color

© Eliot Porter.
Reuss Arch and Amphitheater, Davis Gulch, Escalante Basin, Utah, 1965.
Dye transfer print. n/s.
Courtesy of Eliot Porter Archives Amon Carter Museum, Fort Worth, TX.

What Is the Zone System?

In the late 1930s Ansel Adams and Fred Archer devised the Zone System as a method of explaining exposure and development control to students in black-and-white photography. It is based on the old photo adage: "Expose for the shadows and develop for the highlights." Since then, it has been constantly refined and expanded. Through Adams's books and workshops, the Zone System has gained a wide following and can be found, in one form or another, in most photography programs today. According to Adams its purpose was "to provide a bridge between sensitometry—and practical creative work by offering step-by-step working methods that do not require extensive training or equipment."

What Is a Zone?

A "zone" is not a place but a concept. It is the relationship between a subject's brightness and the density it is represented by in the negative and the corresponding tone in the final print. The gray scale of a full-range print has tones that have been divided into eleven zones (Zone 0–Zone X) and are identified with roman numerals to avoid confusing them with all the other numerical combinations used in photography. Each zone is equivalent to a one f-stop difference in subject brightness and negative exposure (see table 14.5 for a list of the basic zones and their physical equivalents).

Previsualization

The photographer measures the brightness range of the subject and "previsualizes" the print tonal range that is wanted to represent the subject and then picks a combination of exposure and development procedures to make this happen. Previsualization is a mental act in which the photographer imagines how the final print will look before the camera exposure is made. It involves combining technique and vision to realize the photographer's subjective response to the subject. The term can be found in the writings and

The Zone System teaches the photographer the importance of learning how materials work and how to control them. In this experiment, Patton shot ISO 100 color negative film at ISO 12 and developed it in EP-2 color print chemistry (pre-RA-4 process) at normal dilution. Variable development times between 6 and 12 minutes at 68°F (20°C) allowed some contrast control (N + 1 and N − 1). Black-and-white stop bath was used for 1 minute and then bleach/fix for 10 minutes. This series challenges the normal expectations of definition, detail, and space. The extreme out-of-focus foreground is so blurred that some objects can be seen through it. The image confronts the accepted notions of traditional landscape depiction and shows that photographers need not place limitations on themselves when rendering a scene.

© Tom Patton. *Gallesteo, NM.* 1982. 12 × 18 inches. Chromogenic color print.

work of Edward Weston and Ansel Adams and has become the keystone of the modernist, realistic approach to photography.

In order to get the maximum effect and the most control, a photographer needs to make equipment and material tests to determine the "true" speed of the film and to learn precisely what alterations in the development process are needed to contract an extremely long tonal range so it will fit on a piece of paper or film or to expand a limited brightness range subject to normal. Once this is done it is possible, based on the exposure given to the subject, to determine what changes in development are necessary to obtain the desired visual outcome.

The Zone System and Color

Using the Zone System for color photography is about the same as for black-and-white. The photographer has to learn the zones, be able to previsualize the scene, and place the exposures. The big difference is that there is less flexibility in processing color because it is necessary to maintain the color balance between all the layers of the emulsion to avoid color shifts and crossovers. Another difference is that contrast is determined not only by light reflectance but by the colors themselves.

Film-Speed Testing

The film-speed test is at the heart of the Zone System. It provides one more option that gives you control over your camera and chemical processes. It can help to achieve the results that you are after and put you in the driver's seat. Do not be a passenger who is merely along for the ride; be the one who determines the ultimate destination of your work. Increase your learning and you will increase your expression.

The Zone System and Transparency Materials

Exposure is everything with transparencies, since the film is the final product. If a mistake is made, such as overexposure or underexposure of the film, it cannot be readily corrected in the secondary process of printing. What is true for negatives is the opposite for positives (transparencies). The areas of greatest critical interest for judging proper exposure are those of minimal density. With negative material these are the shadow areas. With transparencies it is the highlight areas. When using the Zone System method of exposure control, meter off of the important previsualized highlight and then open up the lens to the required number of stops for proper zone placement. All other tones will then fall relative to the placed zone. The darker values will show up as long as the highlight is metered and placed correctly.

Finding Your Correct Film Speed with Transparencies

You will discover your personal film speed upon a correct rendering of the highlights. The zone used for this test is Zone VII. The characteristics of Zone VII (the lightest textured highlight) include blonde hair, cloudy bright skies, very light skin, white-painted textured wood, average snow, light gray concrete, and white or very bright clothes.

Zone VIII actually has less density, but it is so close to clear film that it can be difficult to visually distinguish it as a separate tone. It is the last zone with any detail in it. Zone VIII subjects include smooth white-painted wood, a piece of white paper, a white sheet in sunlight, and snow entirely in shade or under overcast skies. Zone VIII contains extremely delicate values. It is easy to lose the sense of space and volume in very light objects. When seen beside Zone II or III it may seem to feel and be sensed as a pure white without texture.

Test Procedures

For this test, use a standard Zone VII value like a white-painted brick wall, a textured white fence, or a textured white sweater. Make the test with your most commonly used camera body and lens, and set the meter to the manufacturer's suggested film speed. Take the meter reading only from the critical part of the subject and place it in Zone VII. This is done by opening up two f-stops or their shutter speed equivalents. Remember the meter is programmed to read at Zone V (18 percent reflectance value as with the gray card in the back of this book). "Correct" exposure is one that renders Zone V as Zone V (or any single-toned subject as Zone V, if the meter is working correctly). Then make a series of exposures, bracketing in 1/2 f-stops, three stops more and three stops less than the starting film speed. Next, develop the film following normal procedures. Mount and label all thirteen exposures, and then project them in the slide projector that you most commonly use. Look for the slide that shows the best Zone VII value—one that possesses the right amount of texture with correct color and is not too dark. This exposure indicates your correct film speed.

Transparency Film-Speed Observations

Transparency films generally seem to have a more accurate manufacturer's film-speed rating than do negative films. The slower films are usually very close, and you may even want to test them in 1/3 f-stop intervals, two full f-stops in both directions. Medium-speed transparency films tend to run from right on to 1/3 to 1/2 f-stop too slow. High-speed films can be off by 1/2 to one full f-stop. Usually most photographers raise the transparency film speed from the given speed. This gives a richer and fuller color saturation with a little underexposure. With slide film it is imperative that you meter with the utmost accuracy. When in doubt, give it less exposure rather than more. Do not be afraid to use some film. Bracket and be certain you have what you need and want.

Highlight Previsualization   Once you have determined your proper film speed, correct exposure entails previsualizing the highlights only. Pick out the most important highlight area, meter it, and place it in the previsualized zone in which you want it to appear. You do not have to bother to meter the contrast range between the highlights and shadows. If you are in the same light as the subject being photographed, the correct exposure can be determined by metering off an 18 percent gray card or, if you are Caucasian, simply metering the palm of your hand in the brightest light in the scene and then placing it in Zone VI by opening up one f-stop. The contrast of the image, just as with color negative film, will be largely a matter of the relationship of the colors that are in the scene being photographed.

Customizing Film Speed

The biggest technical obstacle most photographers encounter when working with color film is obtaining the correct exposure. This is more critical than in black-and-white photography because the exposure not only determines the density but also the color saturation. Exposure techniques are basically the same as in black-and-white. It does no good, however, to meter the proper areas and make the right decisions if the film speed does not agree with your working procedures. If you do not have any exposure troubles, leave well enough alone. There is no reason to run a test when you could be out making photographs. If you have had problems with exposure, however, especially underexposed negatives, run a test and establish your personal film speed. If your exposures are still erratic, it indicates either a mechanical problem or the need to review your basic exposure methods (chapter 6).

The speed of the film recommended by the manufacturer is simply a starting point; it is not engraved in stone. It is determined under laboratory conditions and does not take into consideration

The Zone System is the traditional way for a photographer to gain greater mastery of materials. As skills are refined, confidence can be gained, thus reducing the time and energy spent on technique. This can free the imagemaker to devote more personal resources to the creation of new ideas and picture making. Photographed in the late morning, Strembicki says: "I was taken by the odd mix of carnival and religious quality of Mardi Gras parades and in particular the intimidating presence of the masked horseman or veiled prophet which often preceded each parade. I used a fill flash to heighten that sense of drama and effect the subject to pop out of the background on an otherwise flatly lit day. The negative film was intentionally over-processed by 20 percent to increase color saturation."

© Stan Strembicki. *Veiled Prophet, Rex Parade, Mardi Gras, New Orleans, LA, 1990.* 16 × 20 inches. Chromogenic color print.

made this less difficult. Even though it is possible to develop many different types of film in a common process, your results will vary widely. This is because each film has its own personality based on its response to different colors. You will need to try a variety of films and even different types of C-41 processes until you come up with a combination that matches your personal color sensibilities.

Exposing for the Shadows: Zone III

Color negatives, as with black-and-white, are exposed for proper detail in the shadow areas. Adequate detail in a Zone III area is generally considered to indicate proper exposure. Zone III indicates "average dark materials." This includes black clothes and leather. In the print, proper exposure shows adequate detail in the creases and folds of these areas. Form and texture are revealed, and the feeling of darkness is retained.

Film-Speed Tests

A Simple Exposure Test

The simplest exposure test is one in which you find a Zone III value (subject) and then meter and place it using a variety of different film speeds (bracketing). The film is developed and examined with a loupe to determine which exposure gives the proper detail in Zone III. This provides the proper film speed.

A Controlled Test

Here is an easy and controlled method that provides more accurate results. On a clear day in direct sunlight, photograph a color chart and gray card (see back of this book). Make the test with the camera body and

your personal lens, the camera body, exposure techniques, the subject, and the quality of light. You can easily customize the speed of the film to make it perform for your personal style and taste. The film-speed test recommended here is based on the principles of the Zone System, but all your results are determined visually, not through the use of a densitometer.

Working With Negative Film

At this time all the major color negative films can be processed in Kodak's C-41 process. This is not only convenient but also necessary. Attaining the correct balance of color dyes in the negative has not been an easy task. Standardization within the industry has

• TABLE 14.1 •

Film Speed Test Exposures (film speed of 400 with an exposure of F/8 at 1/250 second)

f-stop	Film Speed
f/16	1600
f/11 1/2	1200
f/11	800
f/8 1/2	600
f/8*	**400***
f/5.6 1/2	300
f/5.6	200
f/4 1/2	150
f/4	100

*Starting exposure

lens you use most often. Set the film speed according to the manufacturer's starting point. Take all meter readings off of the gray card only. This way there is no need to change exposure for different zone placements. Make an exposure at this given speed. Then make a series of different exposures by bracketing in 1/2 f-stop increments two full f-stops in both directions.

As an example, say you set your film speed at 400 and determined that your exposure is f/8 at 1/250. You would make your exposure at this setting and then make four exposures in the minus direction and four in the plus direction. Leave your shutter speed at 1/250 for all exposures. Table 14.1 gives you the f-stops you would need to expose at and their corresponding film speed.

Visually Determining the Correct Exposure

After making the exposures, process the film following normal procedures. Next place the film in slide mounts with each frame labeled according to its film speed, and then project them in order beginning with the highest film speed. Pay close attention to the black-and-white density scale on the page photographed. As you look at the negatives,

you should notice more of the steps becoming distinct as the speed of the film drops. Your correct exposure will show visible separation for all the steps in the scale.

What If You Cannot Decide?   What often happens is that you can narrow your choice between two frames but then cannot decide which one is correct. If this occurs, choose the one that has more exposure. Color negatives do not suffer as much from overexposure as black-and-white negatives. Overexposing by even as much as two f-stops will not make a negative unprintable. Because the final print is made up of layers of dyes and not silver particles, slight overexposure does not create additional grain. It builds contrast, but the only protection against loss of detail in the shadow areas is overexposure. Color saturation is controlled directly by exposure. Underexposure causes a loss of saturation that cannot be corrected during printing. Underexposure causes colors to look flat and washed out.

The "No Time" Approach

If you do not have the time to test a new film, the guidelines in table 14.2 are offered as starting film speeds for negative film. Table 14.3 recommends starting speeds for slide film.

When in doubt, give color negative film more exposure. However, give color transparency film *less* exposure.

Contrast Control

With color negative films there are two important considerations that determine the contrast. The first is that contrast is produced from the colors themselves in the original scene. Complementary colors (opposite each other on the color

• TABLE 14.2 •

The "No Time" Modified Film Speed for Negative Materials

Starting Speed	Modified Speed
100	50–80
200	100–125
400	200–300

• TABLE 14.3 •

The "No Time" Modified Film Speed for Slide Materials

Starting Speed	Modified Speed
50	64–80
100	125–150
400	500–600

wheel) produce more contrast than harmonious colors (next to each other on the color wheel). This factor can only be controlled at the time of exposure. The addition of fill light when shooting and masking when printing are other methods to control contrast.

Brightness Range

The second factor in contrast control of color negatives is the overall range of light reflectance between the previsualized shadow and highlight areas. This is the same as with black-and-white. It can be changed by modifying the development time. Unlike black-and-white, the development time cannot be changed as much because it will affect the color balance, which is finalized during development. It is possible to adjust the contrast by one zone of contraction or expansion without serious color shifts or crossovers with most color negative films.

Table 14.4 suggests development times for Kodak's C-41 process in fresh developer for the first roll of film.

The Zone System was designed to help photographers think through and plan how they want the final image to look. This piece from a series called *Nature and the Western Landscape* was made at sunset and involved preplanning the point of view, time of day, and observance of what the clouds were doing. The exposure was made using a spotmeter and placing the highlight of the rock face on Zone VI. It is an example of a situation in which an average reflected light reading would have produced an overexposed image. Dzerigian contends: "The tenous balance between change and stability in nature is a pivotal point in my photographic concern with the landscape. In its depth and complexity, order and chaos, the natural world can resonate in the human being an essential beauty, sense of awe, and harmony."

© Steve Dzerigian. *Spider Rock, Canyon de Chelly, AZ,* 1988. 9 1/2 × 13 inches. Dye-destruction print.

• TABLE 14.4 •

Suggested Starting Development Times in Kodak's C-41 at 100°F

Contrast of Scene	Development Time*
N – 1	2 minutes 40 seconds
Normal	3 minutes 15 seconds
N + 1	4 minutes

*All times based on first roll in fresh developer.

What Is "N"?

For those of you who are not well acquainted with the Zone System, "N" stands for normal developing time. N minus 1 (N − 1) is used when you have a higher-than-normal range of contrast and wish to reduce it. N plus 1 (N + 1) is used when you have a scene with lower-than-normal contrast and want to increase it.

Paper and Contrast Control

Compared to black-and-white, contrast control during color printing is very limited. It is possible to slightly increase the contrast of the final print by using a higher-contrast paper, such as Kodak's Ektacolor Ultra II or Ilford's Ilfocolor Deluxe. By combining the higher-contrast paper with an N + 1 development, you can increase the contrast to a true N + 1 or to an N + 1 1/2 and maybe even an N + 2.

· TABLE 14.5 ·

Zone System Values and Their Physical Equivalents

Low Values

Zone 0: Maximum black. The blackest black that a print can be made to yield. Doorways and windows opening into unlit rooms.

Zone I: The first discernible tone above total black. When seen next to a high key zone it is sensed as total black. Twilight shadows.

Zone II: First discernible evidence of texture; deep tonalities that represent the darkest part of the picture in which a sense of space and volume is needed.

Zone III: Average dark materials and low values showing adequate texture. Black hair, fur, and clothes in which a sense of detail is needed.

Middle Values

Zone IV: Average dark foliage, dark stone, or open shadow in landscape. Normal shadow value for Caucasian skin portraits in sunlight. Also brown hair and new blue jeans.

Zone V: 18 percent gray neutral test card (inside the back cover of this book). Most black skin, dark skin, or sunburnt Caucasian skin, average weathered wood, grass in sunlight, gray stone.

Zone VI: Average Caucasian skin value in sunlight, diffuse skylight, or artificial light. Light stone, shadows on snow in sunlit landscapes.

High Values

Zone VII: Very light skin, light gray objects, average snow with acute side lighting.

Zone VIII: Whites with texture and delicate values, textured snow, highlights on Caucasian skin.

Zone IX: White without texture approaching pure white, similar to Zone I in its slight tonality without a trace of texture.

Zone X: Pure white of the printing paper base, specular glare or light sources in the picture area.

Presentation and Preservation

© *Laurie Simmons.*
Untitled, 1994.
40 × 30 inches. Dye-destruction print.
Courtesy of Metro Pictures, New York, NY.

Spotting

Spotting is usually carried out before the photograph is matted or mounted. Good working techniques should keep spotting to a minimum. Spotting is usually done to correct for dust spots and minor print blemishes, but there are other expressive avenues of manipulation that can be investigated. For instance, a very light area in one corner of the print can have density added to lower its luminance (light reflected from the surface) so it does not draw the viewer's attention away from the subject. In color both the density and color balance of the area that is being spotted must be matched. To make this task as easy as possible, the following materials are needed:

1. Premixed color-spotting dyes are made by a variety of companies. Kodak Liquid Retouching Colors and Retouch Methods liquid colors are recommended for chromogenic prints and ILFOCHROME Classic Retouching Colors for IL-FOCHROME Classic prints. These dyes are designed to go directly into the emulsion, blend to a color similar to it, and leave no residue on the surface. Spotone black-and-white materials can also be useful. People do use watercolors, oils, and other types of dyes. A major problem with these materials is that they fade at a different rate than the dyes that make up the print. Over time the area that has been spotted with nonstandard materials can become distinctly visible from the rest of the photograph.
2. Sable brush with a good point, size number O or smaller.
3. Mixing palette. Enamel or plastic watercolor palettes work well. Some people prefer to mix on a piece of paper, clear acetate, or glass.
4. Container of clean distilled water.
5. A couple sheets of white paper or white processed photographic paper (whatever you use).
6. Paper towels.

Selecting the correct medium is crucial to reaching your audience. In the 1970s Wegman began incorporating his dog, Man Ray, into his real-time videos. In 1978 Wegman started condensing these spare studio video performances onto large-format Polaroid material, resulting in the publication of *Man's Best Friend* (1982). Wegman's switch to a still, reproducible format enabled his work to reach a broader public market.

© William Wegman. *Dusted*, 1982. 20 × 24 inches. Diffusion transfer print. Courtesy of Holly Solomon Gallery, New York, NY.

7. Clean cotton glove.
8. Good light source (5000K lamp, north light, or combination of cool and daylight lamps).

How to Spot Color

Follow these procedures when spotting a color print:

1. Put the print on a smooth, clean, and well-lit surface. Place a clean sheet of white paper over the print, leaving the area to be spotted visible. A window can be cut in the paper to spot through, offering additional protection to the print. Put the cotton glove on the nonspotting hand. This prevents the print from getting fingerprints and hand oil on it. Our bodies also contain and give off sulphur, which can stain the print. The paper provides a neutral viewing surface, which helps act as a visual guide in matching the color balance.
2. Place small amounts of the color dyes that will be used onto the palette.

3. Wet the brush in the water. Draw a line with it on a paper towel to get rid of the excess water and to make a fine point.

4. Dab the brush into the dye. Draw a line on the white processed photographic paper or a separate sheet of white paper to see if the color matches. Compare the line with the area to be spotted. Blend with other colors, including black and white until the color matches.

5. Once the correct color balance has been achieved, horizontally draw a line with the mixed dye on the paper towel to remove any excess dye and water. The brush should appear dry, but inside it will remain wet and hold a small amount of dye. To apply the color to the print, gently touch the tip of the brush with a small stroke to the surface. Practice on the processed white paper before working on final print.

6. For very small spots, create a series of dots. This helps to match the grain structure that forms the image. Do not paint it in, because this will be noticeable since the print is made from points, not lines (figure 15.1). Make one pass using this dot method. There should be some areas of white still visible in between the dots. Let it dry for a minute. Make another pass with the dot technique, filling in some more of the spot. Let it dry and see if it matches. Repeat if necessary, but do not apply too much dye. Different movements will deliver different effects. For small areas and fine white lines, start the tip of the brush at the beginning of the line and make tiny side strokes, which blend the line into the surrounding area much easier. For wider spots, slightly bend the brush. For wide lines or for a dye wash, fan the brush (figure 15.2).

7. When finished spotting, wash the brush with warm water and soap. Rinse completely, and carefully re-point the brush between the thumb and index finger.

A blob, a line, or an area that is too dark draws as much attention to the

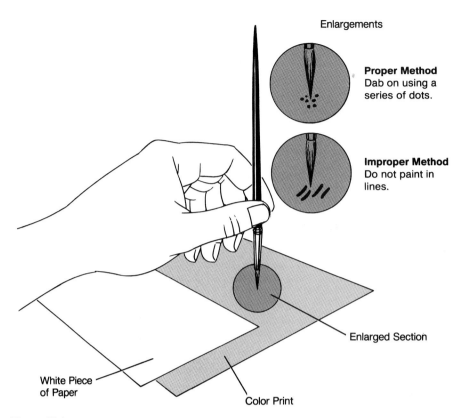

Enlargements

Proper Method
Dab on using a series of dots.

Improper Method
Do not paint in lines.

Enlarged Section

White Piece of Paper

Color Print

Figure 15.1
The method for properly spotting a print: A well-pointed brush containing the properly matched color dye is dabbed onto the print. A white piece of paper reveals the area to be spotted while protecting the remainder of the photograph. It also acts as a visual reference point, letting you see if the spotting dye is making the desired match with the surrounding area.

eye as the spot. Take time and be subtle. Do not overdo it. This is not like painting a brick wall with a roller.

Dealing with Mistakes

If there is too much dye on the print, quickly remove it by letting a piece of paper towel absorb it. Do not rub or smear it.

If the color does not come out correctly or if too much dye is absorbed, attempt to remove the spot with a drop of 5 percent solution of ammonia and water. Apply it with a clean brush. Let it sit on the spot for about 60 seconds, and then absorb it with a piece of paper towel. Let it dry before attempting to start spotting there again. If this does not work, let the spot dry and cover it with white dye and start over.

If you are unhappy with the overall results, wash the print with room temperature water for 5 minutes, dry, and start

over. If the dye does not come out, try putting a tiny amount of ammonia on the print, rub gently, and rewash. Drying can be done with a handheld hair dryer. Excess water can be removed by gently patting the print with a lint-free towel.

Spray Lacquers

After the dyes have dried, there may be a difference in reflectance between the spotted areas and the rest of the print, especially with glossy paper. If this is noticeable, some photographers spray the picture with a print lacquer, which creates even reflectance over the entire photograph. They are available in glossy and mat finishes. There is considerable debate about the long-term stability of prints treated with spray lacquer. There are reports that lacquers can crack, flake off, and discolor the print surface. For these reasons lacquers should not be used on fine art prints or photographs in

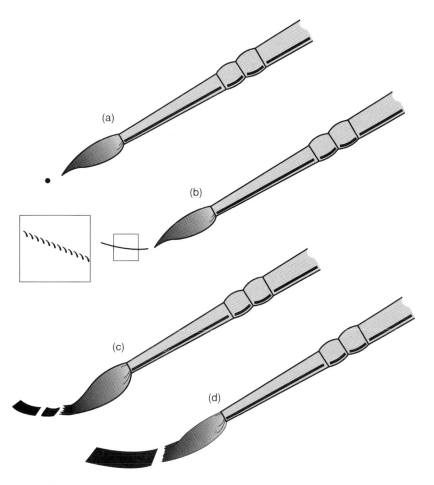

Figure 15.2   Basic brush movements.

Sketch (*a*) For very small spots, just touch the brush to the photograph with a small stroke. Only the tip of the brush should touch the print, releasing the dye onto the emulsion. It is important to work with the tip of the brush in fine or small areas. The dye in the brush flows from the ferrule to the very tip of the brush, which is a single hair. (*b*) For white lines and small spots, prepare the brush with the correct color and make sure you have a good point. Place the very tip of the brush at the beginning of the line and make little side strokes instead of trying to fill it in with a single stroke. The short side strokes will blend the line into the surrounding area more readily than a single stroke. (*c*) To cover a wider spot or to blend, slightly bend the brush. (*d*) To retouch wide lines or to make a dye wash, fan the brush.

correct color can then be applied on the white spot. Large area color reductions, and even total bleaching, can be carried out. Special bleaching agents and solvents can be used to dissolve the cyan, magenta, or yellow emulsion layers. For more information contact Photographers' Formulary, P.O. Box 950, Condon, MT 59826; (800) 922–5255.

For additional information get Ilford's technical information manual, *Retouching Cibachrome* (ILFOCHROME Classic) *Materials*.

Archival Presentation

Every color image has a natural and limited life span. The length of the life span depends on the individual process used and how the image is cared for. The goal of archival presentation is to protect the image from physical harm and to guard against things that accelerate the aging process (see the section on print preservation later in this chapter). This ensures the work lasts as long as it is physically feasible. A capable presentation job can enhance the visual appeal of a work, protect it, and send the message that this work is something worth taking care of.

Choosing Mat Board

To select the proper type of mat board you should become more informed about how various products affect color materials. Consider the following factors:

1. *Composition board* is the most widely available and has the least longevity. Typically, composition board is made up of three layers: a thin top paper sheet, usually colored; a middle core layer, made of chemically processed wood pulp; and a bottom paper backing. The core layer is the troublemaker because it contains a collection of acids and chemical compounds that break down and produce even more acid. These acids are transported in microscopic amounts of airborne water vapor onto the surface of your work.

museum collections. If a lacquer must be used, Lacquer-Mat lacquers and Sureguard McDonald Pro-Tecta-Cote 900-series noncellulose nitrate lacquers are recommended. For best results, read the manufacturers' instructions for proper application and handling of these materials. Work only in well-ventilated areas, and follow all safety guidelines.

Spotting Prints from Slides

When spotting prints from slides, the major difference is that the dust spots appear as black, not white. These black spots have to be covered with white before spotting them. Small black spots can

be removed by etching the surface of the print with a sharp pointed blade, such as a #11 X-Acto, until the speck is gone. This must be done with great care so that the surface of the print does not become too rough and visually objectionable. Color should be applied with an extremely dry brush only. Lacquer spray will probably be needed in both cases to eliminate the differences in reflectance between the spotted and nonspotted areas of the picture.

ILFOCHROME Classic materials often will not respond to conventional retouching methods due to the way the product is manufactured and processed. Special retouching kits can be used to reduce color densities, correct color casts, and bleach colored or black specks. The

Archival presentation is designed to protect the image from substances that will speed up its natural aging process. To achieve that end, it is important the imagemakers understand the interaction that occurs between various mediums. This collage started with a rough pencil sketch on eight-ply museum board. Black-and-white photographs and contact sheets were cut, torn, and glued to the museum board. A layering process began as large areas of gouache were brushed on, photographs were sanded, more drawing occurred, new photographs were glued down, the drawing reworked, and new gouache was introduced as the process was repeated until the picture neared completion. At this point, sheets of gold leaf were glued and burnished to the surface and afterward the entire image was reworked. The motivation for the Angels's collaboration is to "deal with the complexities and many facets of an intimate relationship and in this respect is a self-portrait. We began working jointly and felt confident we could move towards the realization of a shared vision and not sacrifice anything in terms of personal expression."

© Catherine Angel and Dennis Angel. *The Embrace*, 1990. 24 × 32 inches. Gelatin-silver prints with mixed media.

They start attacking the image, often within a year or two, causing discoloration and fading. UV radiation from the sun and/or fluorescent lights can accelerate this chemical reaction.

The same thing can happen when a work is backed with corrugated cardboard or kraft paper. The acids in these materials invade the work from behind, and by the time it makes itself known, irreversible damage has taken place.

2. *Conservation-grade board* consists of thin layers, all of the same color, called plies. One type of board is made from purified wood pulp and is simply known as conservation board. The other type is made from 100 percent cotton fiber and is called rag board. Plain conservation board can be used for most archival operations, since it costs less, has equal longevity, and is easier to cut when making window mats. Most board is available in two, four, six, or eight plies. Four-ply board is good for most presentations.

3. *Acid-free board* is known as the board of choice. Unfortunately, this description has proved to be very misleading. The term "acid free" is no longer considered to be the supreme test of a board's permanence. Some manufacturers have only put a piece of acid-free paper behind the wood pulp of traditional composition board. Others have added regular wood pulp heavily treated with alkaline calcium carbonate. With the passage of time the impurities in the board deteriorate and form acids and peroxides, thus producing or returning to a highly acidic board. When selecting acid-free board, be certain all the materials in the board are 100 percent acid free. Also, as paper ages it tends to shift toward the acid end of the pH scale. This effect can be counteracted by buffering with calcium carbonate (this is added to many conservation-grade boards). The "acid-free" label is still an important criterion, but it is not the only thing you need to consider when making a selection.

4. *Buffered and nonbuffered board* is being debated in the conservation community. Since our physical surroundings are slightly acidic, and because paper tends to become more acidic with age, manufacturers of premium mat board have been adding calcium carbonate to offset this tendency. Current research indicates that color materials may be affected by the presence of this alkali buffer and that for longest life, they should be mounted only on *nonbuffered, acid-free* board. This recommendation applies to all chromogenic prints processed in RA-4, as well as dye-transfer prints. Cyanotype prints are also reported to have discolored in the proximity of buffered materials. At this time, there is no published research indicating a problem with using buffered board with gelatin-silver, black-and-white materials.

The Window Mat

The window mat, now considered the standard enclosure for photographic prints, is made up of two boards, larger in all dimensions than the print. The top board, known as the overmat, has a window with beveled edges cut into it. This is attached, with a tape hinge, along one side of the backing board. The print is positioned and attached to the backing

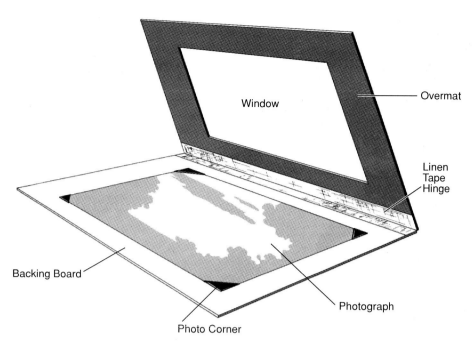

Window

Overmat

Linen
Tape
Hinge

Backing Board

Photograph

Photo Corner

Figure 15.3
The construction of a typical hinged window mat. The use of photo corners facilitates removing the photograph from the mat without harming it.

board so it can be seen through the window (figure 15.3). The mat gives the maximum protection to the print while it is being shown and also when it is stored. It provides a raised border to contain the work and when the work is framed, it keeps the glass from directly touching the print surface. If the window mat is damaged or soiled for any reason, it can always be replaced without damaging the print. A mat can be cut with a hand mat cutter, such as a Dexter or Logan, which requires some practice using. Almost anyone can cut a mat with a machine such as the C & H mat cutter. For those who have but an occasional need of a mat, have a local frame shop make one for you.

Keep in mind the type of light the print will be viewed under when selecting mat board. Daylight tends to have a blue cast, incandescent light is orange, and fluorescent light is generally greenish.

To make a window mat follow these steps:

1. Have clean hands and a clean working surface.
2. Work under light similar to that under which the print will be seen.
3. Protect the cutting surface with an unwanted piece of board that can be disposed of after it gets too many cut marks.
4. Using a good cork-backed steel ruler, measure the picture exactly. Decide on precise cropping. If the picture is not going to be cropped, measure about 1/16 to 1/8 of an inch into the picture area on all sides if you do not want the border to be seen.
5. Decide on the overall mat size. Leave enough space. Do not crowd the print on the board. Give it some neutral room so that the viewer can take it in without feeling cramped. The following is a general guide for the minimum-size board with various standard picture sizes:

Image Size	Mat Board Size
(all dimensions in inches)	
5 × 7	8 × 10
8 × 10	11 × 14
11 × 14	16 × 20
16 × 20	20 × 24

Many photographers try to standardize their sizes. This avoids the common hodgepodge effect that can be created if there are twenty pictures to display and each one is a slightly different size. When the proper size has been decided, cut two boards, one for the overmat and the other for the backing board. Some people cut the backing board slightly smaller (1/8 inch) than the front. This way there is no danger of it sticking out under the overmat.

6. In figuring the window opening it is helpful to make a diagram (figure 15.4) with all the information on it. To calculate the side border measurement, subtract the horizonal image measurement from the horizontal mat dimension, and divide by two. This gives even side borders. To obtain the top and bottom borders, subtract the vertical picture measurement from the vertical mat dimension and divide by two. Then, to prevent the print from visually sinking, subtract about 15 to 20 percent of the top dimension and add it to the bottom figure.

7. Using a hard lead pencil (3H or harder to avoid smearing), carefully transfer the measurements to the back of the mat board. Use a T square to make sure the lines are straight. Check all the figures once the lines have been laid out in pencil.

8. Put a new blade in the mat cutter. The C & H cutter uses a single-edge razor blade with a crimp in the top. Slide the blade into the slot and adjust it so that it extends far enough to cut through the board. Hand tighten only, using the threaded knob at the end of the bolt.

9. Line the markings up with the mat cutter so that it cuts inside the line. Be sure to check that the angle of the blade is cutting at 45 degrees in the "out" direction for all the cuts, in order to avoid having one cut with the bevel going in and the other with it going out. It helps to practice on some scrap board before doing the real thing. When ready, line up the top left corner and make a smooth, nonstop straight cut. Make all the cuts in the same direction. Cut one side of the board and then turn it around and cut

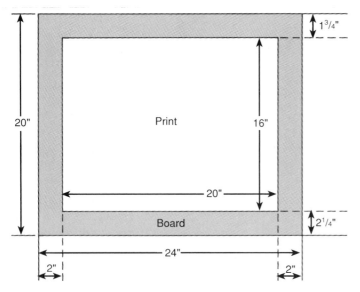

Figure 15.4
The dimensions of a window-type overmat for a 16-×-20-inch print on a 20-×-24-inch board. More space is usually left on the bottom of the mat than at the top to keep the print from appearing to visually sink on the board. The side borders are generally of equal dimensions.

the opposite side until all four cuts are made. With the C & H mat cutter, start the cut a little ahead of where your measurement lines intersect and proceed to cut a little beyond where they end. With some practice, the window will come right out with no ragged edges. If you continue to make overcuts, simply stop short of the corners. Then go back with a single-edge razor blade and finish the cut. Be sure to angle the blade to agree with the angle of the cut. Sand any rough spots with very fine sandpaper. Erase the guidelines with an art gum eraser so that the pencil marks do not get on the print.

10. Hinge the overmat to the backing board with a piece of gummed linen tape (see figure 15.3). The mat will now open and close like a book with the tape acting as a hinge.

11. Place the print on the backing board and adjust it until it appears properly in the window. Hold it in place with print-positioning clips or a clean smooth weight with felt on the bottom.

12. Use photo corners to hold the print to the backing board. They will be hidden by the overmat and make it easy to slip the print in and out of the mat for any reason (see figure 15.4).

Dry Mounting

Dry mounting used to be the most common way to present a finished print for display. It is a fast and neat method to obtain print flatness, which reduces surface reflections and gives the work more apparent depth. There are, however, a number of problems resulting from this method:

1. The possibility of ruining a finished print with dry mounting through accident and equipment or material failure exists.

2. After the print has been dry mounted, changes in heat and humidity, especially if the prints are shipped, can cause the print to wrinkle or come unstuck from the board. This happens because the print and the board do not expand and contract at the same rate. Since they are attached and the board is stronger, the print suffers the consequences.

3. The adhesives in the tissue are not considered to be archival and can have adverse effects on the print, causing it to deteriorate.

4. If the print is dropped face down it is offered no protection and the print surface can be damaged.

5. If the board is damaged in any way

there is a problem. Dry mounting is not water soluble. This means it is almost impossible to get the print released undamaged from the dry mount for any reason. This makes replacement of a damaged board extremely difficult.

6. Many resin-coated (RC) color papers react negatively to heat. High temperatures can produce color shifts and mottling and, with IL-FOCHROME Classic, can cause it to lose some of its glossy finish.

7. Other methods of dry mounting with spray mounts and glues are not recommended because the chemical make-up of these materials has an adverse effect on all color materials over time.

Curators and collectors no longer dry mount work that is received unmounted. It is also not advisable to dry mount unless you made the print yourself or there is a duplicate available. If you still want to dry mount after considering these problems, follow the guidelines in the next section.

The Dry-Mounting Process

Dry-mounting tissue is coated with adhesive that becomes sticky when it is heated. This molten adhesive penetrates into the fibers of the print and mounting board and forms a bond. It is best to use a tacking iron and a dry-mount press to successfully carry out the operation. A home iron is not recommended because it can create a series of unnecessary complications.

When mounting an RC print be certain that the dry-mounting tissue has been designed to be used with RC paper or the print may blister and melt. Use four-ply mounting board so that the print does not bend. Keep the color selection simple. Use an off-white or a very light gray-colored board. The board should not call attention to itself or compete with the picture. To obtain maximum print life, use a nonbuffered, acid-free board. Regular board contains impurities that in time can interact and damage the print.

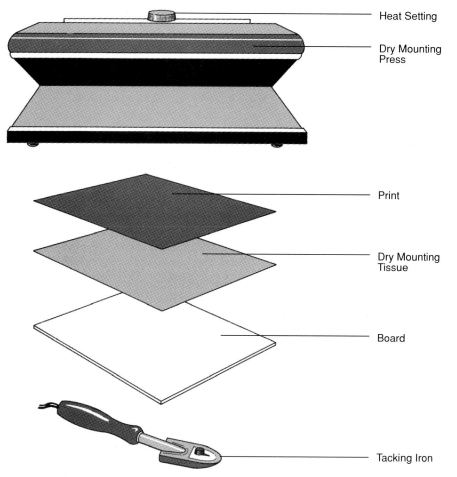

Heat Setting

Dry Mounting
Press

Print

Dry Mounting
Tissue

Board

Tacking Iron

Figure 15.5
The basic materials for dry mounting a photograph. Make certain the temperature setting on the dry-mounting press matches that of the materials being used to avoid damaging the photograph during the dry-mounting process.

Use these steps in the dry-mounting process (necessary materials are shown in figure 15.5):

1. Turn on the tacking iron and dry-mount press. Let them reach operating temperature. Check the dry-mount tissue package for the exact temperature because it varies from product to product. The temperature for RC color material will be lower than that of fiber-based black-and-white paper. Using a temperature that is higher than recommended will damage the resin coating of the print.

2. Make sure all materials and working surfaces are clean and level. Wipe all materials with a smooth cloth. Any dirt will create a raised mark between the print and the board.

3. Predry the board and non-RC prints (do not redry ILFOCHROME Classic prints). Place a clean piece of paper on top of the board (kraft paper is alright but should be replaced after each mounting operation) and the prints to be predried. Place this sandwich in the press for about 30 to 60 seconds (depending on the thickness of the board and the relative humidity). About halfway through this procedure, momentarily open the press to allow water vapor to escape and then close it for the remaining time. This should remove any excess moisture.

4. Place the print face down with a sheet of mounting tissue at least the same size as the print on top of it. Take the preheated tacking iron and touch it against a clean piece of paper that has been placed over the tissue in the center of the print. This one spot should be enough to just keep the print and the tissue together. Do not tack at the corners.

5. Trim the print and tissue together to the desired size. Use a rotary trimmer, a sharp paper cutter, an X-Acto knife, or a mat knife with a cork-backed steel ruler. If you flush mount, the corners and edges of the print are susceptible to damage and it cannot be overmatted unless you crop into the image area.

6. Position the print on the board. The standard print position has equal distance on both sides and about 15 to 20 percent more space on the bottom than at the top. If there is not more space at the bottom, the print appears to visually sink or look bottom heavy when displayed on a wall. Carefully make the measurements using a good metal ruler and mark the board in pencil to get a perfect alignment.

7. Align the print and tissue face up on the board according to the pencil marks. Raise one corner of the print and with the iron, tack that corner of the tissue to the board. Next, tack the opposite corner. Now do the remaining two. The tissue must be flat or it will wrinkle.

8. Put this sandwich of print, tissue, and board with a cover sheet of clean paper on top into the press. Make sure it is at the proper operating temperature for the materials. Use tissue that does not have a release point of more than 205°F (96°C) and watch for any changes in color or on the print surface. Close and lock the press and heat for about 30 to 45 seconds. Check the product for exact times.

9. Remove the sandwich and place it on a level surface under a weight to cool. Seal makes a special metal cooling weight for this purpose.

For specific details on presenting IL-FOCHROME Classic materials see Ilford's technical information manual, *Mounting and Laminating Cibachrome* (ILFOCHROME Classic).

Floating a Print

Some prints do not look good matted or mounted. The board interferes with the workings of the space within the picture. In cases like this, "float" the picture following the guidelines below.

On a clean, level surface, here are the steps to follow to float a print:

1. Decide on the final picture size.
2. Trim the print to these dimensions.
3. Cut a nonbuffered, acid-free backing board or a piece of acid-free Fome-Cor to the same size as the print. Acid-free Fome-Cor will not chemically interact with the picture and is cheaper than archival board.
4. Have a piece of Plexiglas cut to size.
5. Put the sandwich of Plexiglas, print, and board together with a frameless device such as Swiss Corner Clips and it is ready.

Print Preservation

Materials That Damage a Print

There are other methods of displaying finished prints. Whichever method you select, avoid having any of the following materials in contact with the print, because they are harmful to photographs and can cause damage over a period of time: cellophane tape, masking tape, white glues, rubber cement, and adhesive-coated pages and plastic covers in "magnetic" albums. Avoid contact with wood, shellac, varnish, and any material made with PVCs (polyvinyl coatings). Do not write on backs of prints with a ballpoint pen because it can bleed through and stain the print.

Factors Affecting Color Stability

All the widely used color processes are made from dyes. All color dyes are fugitive, meaning they fade over time.

There are three major factors that affect the stability of the dyes. The greatest enemy is known as *light fading* and is produced by all types of ambient light and UV radiation. The duration, intensity, and quality of the light dictate the rate of change. The second is called *dark fading* and it begins as soon as the image is made. It is caused by ambient relative humidity and temperature and would occur even if the image was sealed in a light-tight box. Both these processes affect the cyan, magenta, and yellow dye layers, but not at the same rate, causing the image to change color over time. The last process, called *staining,* is caused by color couplers that remain in the emulsion after processing. It typically produces a yellow stain in the border and highlight areas. The stain forms gradually, and there is no way to remove it. Staining is still a problem with most chromogenic papers, including all current RA-4 papers.

Choosing the correct material for different situations ensures a better outcome. For example, chromogenic papers are not intended to be displayed in direct sunlight in a showroom or studio window. In this case, color display materials should be used. Color stability is a factor photographers need to consider when selecting color materials. However, the combination of film and paper that delivers the color attributes and handling characteristics the imagemaker desires remains the driving force behind most photographers' decisions.

Regardless of which process or material you use, your images can be guaranteed their maximum natural life span if a few precautions are exercised.

Color Material Life Span

In the past color print dyes commonly faded within 10 years. Kodak claims that the images on its latest color paper will still be "acceptable" to most people after more than 100 years in a photo album, without extended exposure to light and more than 60 years under normal ambient light conditions at home.

How long will my color pictures last? is the question many of us ask. The answer is we don't know. There is still not a reliable database to give definite answers. The most current data comes from Henry Wilhelm, an independent researcher in the field of photographic preservation. The following information is based on Wilhelm's published tests (see references at the end of this chapter) and has not been substantiated by other independent research. Clearly more work is needed in this area.

Color Print Materials

The chromogenic papers (RA-4 process) with the longest display life and dark-keeping abilities are Fujicolor Super FA Type 3, Fujicolor SFA3, and Professional Portrait papers. The top-rated EP-2 materials were Konica Color Paper Type SR, Professional Type EX, and Type SR (SG).

In the instant print department, Polaroid Polacolor ER, 64T, 100, and Pro 1000 prints were top-rated but not recommended for any fine art applications and should be displayed with caution.

The most stable of the reversal papers, in both dark- and light-keeping properties, are Ilford ILFOCHROME Classic and Rapid print materials (glossy polyester base). Unlike the chromogenic process, in which the dyes are formed by color couplers during processing, ILFOCHROME (aka Cibachrome) makes use of more stable azo dyes that are manufactured directly into the paper. The longest-lasting R-3 process papers are Fujichrome Type 35, Type 35-H, and Super-Gloss Printing Material.

Of the special and very costly print materials tested, UltraStable Permanent Color Prints, EverColor Pigment Color Prints, Polaroid Permanent-Color Prints, and Fuji-Inax Ceramic Color Photographs (available only in Japan) were by far the most stable of all print processes in both display and dark storage.

Knowing the anticipated life span and compatibility of the materials used in the creation of any picture is vital to the photographer who cares if an image is to survive over a period of time. Chong's recent work has been influenced by religious and spiritual systems of Black African peoples and their descendants in the Caribbean and the Americas. Chong has rephotographed an uncoated (not properly fixed) Polaroid positive (in order to preserve the base image and alter the scale). The deteriorating Polaroid manifests color shifts, especially in the shadow areas, that create hues of polished gold and silver.

© Albert Chong. *The Cowrie Necklace*, 1992–93. 30 × 40 inches. Dye-destruction print.

Color Transparency Materials

The longest-lasting color negative films, rated by ISO, are as follows:

Very Low Speed (ISO 25–50)

Kodak Ektar 25
Kodak Ektar 25 Professional
Konica Color Impresa 50 Professional

Low Speed (ISO 100)

Kodak Ektar 100
3M ScotchColor 100
Fujicolor Super G 100
Fujicolor Reala

Medium Speed (ISO 160–200)

Kodak Vericolor III Professional Type S
Fujicolor 160 Professional Type L
Fujicolor Super G 200
Konica Color Super SR 200 and SR 200 Professional
3M ScotchColor 200
Polaroid OneFilm (made by 3M in Italy)

High Speed (ISO 400)

Kodak Vericolor 400 Professional
Kodak Ektapress Gold 400
Kodak Gold Plus 400
Fujicolor HG 400 Professional
Fujicolor Super G 400
3M ScotchColor 400

Very High Speed (ISO 1000–3200)

Kodak Ektar 1000
Kodak Ektapress Gold 1600
Kodak Gold 1600
Fujicolor HG 1600

Internegative Film

Fujicolor Internegative IT-4

Color negative film should be properly stored in the dark, except when being used to make prints.

The transparency films with the most resistance to light fading (caused during projection) were E-6 films, with Fujichrome Amateur, Professional, Velvia, and Duplicating films receiving the top

Prints made for public exhibition must possess the highest level of overall artisanship in technique and presentation. Sherman's widely shown work has been credited with expressing the postmodernism concerns of the 1980s. The work is ambiguous and self-conscious. It has been called a nonliteral imitation of the world of film and television that surrounds Western culture.

© Cindy Sherman. *Untitled, #119*, 1983. 17 1/2 × 36 inches. Chromogenic color print. Courtesy of Metro Pictures, New York, NY

honors. The least stable were K-14 films, that is, the entire line of all the amateur and professional Kodachromes. However, for dark storage, Kodachrome films are way out in front. If your slides are projected a great deal, as in slide shows, an E-6 film delivers the longest useful life. However, many photographers don't view their slides very often; if this is the case, Kodachrome with its excellent dark-keeping ability is the choice.

The ILFOCHROME Display films offer the longest-lasting translucent and transparent color display materials. Fujirans and Fujiclear SFA3 Display Materials are the longest-lasting RA-4 display materials.

Keeping What You Have

Print Storage Conditions

Ideally, color prints should be stored in a clean, cool (50 to 60°F; 10 to 15°C), dark, dust-free area with a relative humidity of about 25 to 40 percent. Avoid exposure to any ultraviolet source, including sunlight and fluorescent lights because UV rays cause the dyes to fade faster. Archival storage boxes, with a nonbuffered paper interior, offer the best protection for color prints. Use desiccants (a substance that absorbs moisture) if you live in an area of high humidity. Keep photographs away from all types of atmospheric pollutants, adhesives, and paints. Check the storage area periodically to make sure there has been no infestation of bugs or microorganisms. Avoid extended display periods under bright lights. Some people have tried to protect prints with UV-filter glazing on the glass. However, Wilhelm says this will offer little or no additional protection for most types of color prints. Have two prints of important images made on stable material, one for display and the other for dark storage. Make new prints of old images on newer, more archival material. Make copy prints of all one-of-a-kind pictures, including Polaroids. Don't display originals for any length of time.

Film Storage

Keep projection of original slides to a minimum. Duplicate important originals, and project only the dupes. Don't leave slides on light tables or lying about any longer than necessary. Promptly duplicate older slides that show signs of fading. Store slides in archival boxes or in polypropylene pages. Protect negatives in polyester or high-density polyethylene inside conservation paper boxes, metal boxes of baked enamel finished on steel, or safe plastic boxes. See chapter 7 for information on storing unexposed color film.

New electronic image-enhancement systems have the ability to make color corrections to faded negatives and slides at a modest cost.

Cold Storage

Freezing still offers the greatest stability for negatives and prints. Light Impressions (see references) sells cold storage envelopes designed for freezing processed film. With billions of pictures now made every year, photographers should give some thought to what is worth saving.

Copying Work

Making Copy Slides

Making slides of your prints or of pictures in books for a presentation or for appropriation purposes is relatively simple. The pictures to be copied can be positioned vertically on a wall or laid on any convenient flat surface. The camera can be tripod-mounted or handheld, depending on the light source and film sensitivity. Camera movement must be avoided to produce sharp slides. Be sure the camera back is parallel to the print surface and the lighting is uniform. Avoid shadows falling across the picture. A slow film gives the best color rendition and grain structure.

Lens Selection

The choice of lens affects the outcome. Use an apochromatic lens that has been color corrected for three primary spectra colors and that has the flattest field possible along with the best edge-to-edge definition. This will deliver uniform sharpness at the same distance from the center and the edge of the lens. For 35-mm

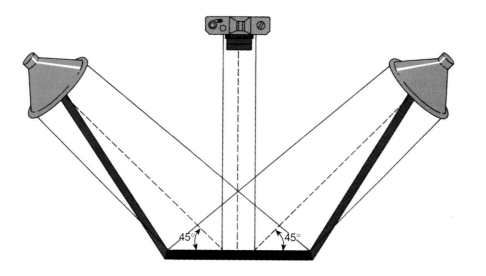

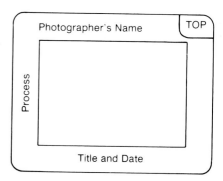

Figure 15.7
Slides must be well presented in order to have a chance of receiving a fair reception. Each slide should be clearly labeled with the photographer's name, the date of the image, and the type of process that was used. The top of the photograph should be identified so that it is obvious how to view the image.

Figure 15.6
When copying work, two lights should be set up at equal distances on each side of the camera at 45-degree angles to the work being copied. Meter from a gray card, not off the surface of the work being copied. Make sure the film and the light sources have the same color temperature. Polarizing filters can be attached to the lights and/or to the camera to allow the photographer to control reflections and to increase color contrast and saturation.

copying a normal-length macro lens, such as the 55-mm Nikkor Macro, is best. Zoom lenses, with a macro mode, tend to produce soft (not sharp) results. Bellows attachments or auxiliary lenses, such as Proxar lens sets of varying degrees of magnification, can convert a normal focal-length lens into a useful copy lens.

With a large-format camera use an apochromatic lens, which is designed for reproduction and often used on a process camera for graphic arts work. It corrects chromatic aberration that produces red-green-blue fringing around the edges of color images and gives maximum sharpness and flatness of field.

Type of Light

Good results can be obtained most easily by using a daylight color slide film and shooting the pictures outside, on a clear day, in direct sunlight, between about the hours of 10 A.M. and 2 P.M., to avoid shadows, which can create an unwanted color cast. Use a UV filter to eliminate unwanted UV radiation.

If copying is done indoors, a tungsten film should be used with artificial lighting. Be certain the film matches the color balance of the lights. Two lights should be placed at equal distances on either side of the tripod-mounted camera at a 45-degree

angle to the picture being copied to produce even, glare-free light (figure 15.6).

Determining Exposure

Indoors or out, take a meter reading from a standard neutral gray card such as the one inside the back cover of this book for the most accurate results. Metering off the picture itself produces inconsistent exposures. Let the gray card fill the frame, but do not focus on it. For close-up work, the exposure should be determined with the gray card at the correct focus distance. Try to let the image fill as much of the frame as possible, without chopping off any of it. If you haven't done much copying or are using a new film, bracket using 1/3 to 1/2 f-stops in the direction of underexposure.

Only those slides that have been accurately exposed should be used. Generally, it is important to choose a group of images that form a cohesive group when viewed together and that reflect the visual concerns of the photographer.

Slide Presentation

Slides must be well presented. This means the photographer's name, the slide title and size (with height before width), the date the image was made, and the type of process should be clearly

printed on each slide mount with the *top* (the correct way to view the slide) of the image indicated (figure 15.7).

Finding the "Top"

A colored dot is often used to indicate the top position. There are two competing schools of thought as to where the colored dot should be placed. The first group puts the dot on the upper right-hand corner of the mount. This way a viewer has no difficulty determining the correct way to view the slide (the top is the top). The second group puts the dot on the lower left-hand corner in order to indicate how the slide should be placed in a carousel tray for projection. In this case, the dot is placed so it is visible on the slide mount when it is in the carousel slot. Many people, not familiar with the image, find this confusing. They are not sure if the dot indicates the true top of the image or its correct position when loaded in a carousel tray. Place the colored dot in the upper right-hand corner of the mount: that way you can be sure the top *is* the top.

If the slides are to be projected, place them, with the dot in the upper right-hand corner, on a light table to sort and position them into the desired order. To place the slide correctly in a carousel tray, position it so the image is how you originally saw it in the camera (dot in upper right-hand corner), turn it upside down (dot now in lower left-hand corner), and drop it into the tray. After all the slides are loaded, project them to make sure they are in the right viewing position. Then make a uniform mark with a felt-tip pen on the upper right-hand edges of the slide mount sitting in the tray. This line provides a visual indicator for the future that the slides are correctly loaded in the carousel but is not noticeable on the front of the mount.

Masking Slides

Mask out any areas of the slides that should not be seen when projected by using black photographic tape, chartpak tape, or special slide masking tape made of aluminum polyester. Wearing a thin cotton glove, remove the slide from its original mount. Put the slide, emulsion side down, on a clean lightbox. Place the tape on the nonemulsion side (shiny side) of the film. Trim the excess with a sharp pair of scissors. Use only one layer of tape or it may get stuck in the projector. Carefully reinsert the masked slide into a new mount.

Avoid a Bad Reception

Slides that are not properly exposed, correctly labeled, numbered, or neatly presented will not receive a favorable welcome at a competition, gallery, school, or job interview. Slides are at best an imperfect way to view anyone's work, therefore give the slides your best effort so they present an accurate approximation of the colors, mood, and tone in your work. Always include a cover letter and appropriate support materials, such as a your resumé, an exhibition list, and a concise statement concerning the work. Be selective, decide what is important, highlight important information, and don't bombard the receiver with too much data.

Shipping Slides

Ship slides in transparent polyethylene pages. Put your name, return address,

The diptych presentation is a key component to understanding Rickard's dualistic message of comparing traditional Native American cultural values to present-day mainline Western European concerns. Rickard's work is about holding onto the power in her culture by making images that speak of her Tuscarora Nation's beliefs.

© Jolene Rickard. *What They Do: What We Do,* 1991. 24 × 36 inches. Chromogenic color prints.

telephone number, and title of the body of work on the slide page. Do not send loose slides. Make sure *each* slide is identified with your name and a number so the person on the receiving end can easily identify which images he or she may be interested in. A separate checklist, referring to the numbered slides, should be included providing each image's title, size, process, and presen-

tation size. Use a stiff backing board in the envelope so that the slides cannot be easily bent. Enclose a properly sized return envelope, with the correct amount of postage and a self-addressed shipping label to help guarantee the return of your materials (SASE stands for: self-addressed, stamped, envelope). Write "Do Not Bend!" on the front and back of the shipping envelope. Valuable and irreplaceable materials should be sent by one of the overnight package services; otherwise send them by first-class mail.

Copyright

According to the U.S. Copyright Office in Washington, DC, it is no longer necessary to place the notice of copyright on works published for the first time on or after March 1, 1989, in order to secure ownership of copyright and the failure to place a notice of copyright on work may no longer result in the loss of copyright. However, the Copyright Office still recommends that owners of copyrights continue to place notice of copyright on their works to secure all their rights. The copyright notice for pictorial works should include three elements: (1) the word "copyright" or the symbol for copyright, which is the letter C enclosed by a circle (©); (2) the year of the first publication of the image; and (3) the name of the copyright owner. For example, © Jane Smith 1996. Copyright notice is not required on unpublished work, but it is advisable to affix notices of copyright to avoid inadvertent publication without notice. It is illegal for photographic labs to duplicate images with a copyright notice on them without written permission from the holder of the copyright. For additional information contact Register of Copyrights, Copyright Office, Library of Congress, Washington, DC 20559.

Where to Send Work

There is fierce competition for exhibitions, gallery representation, and commercial connections. Prepare yourself to be persistent and for rejection. There are a number of publications that identify opportunities, including *Photographer's Market,* published by Writer's Digest Books, 1507 Dana Avenue, Cincinnati, OH 45207 (a new edition is published every year); *Afterimage,* published by the Visual Studies Workshop, 31 Prince Street, Rochester, NY 14607; Art Calendar, Box 1040, Great Falls, VA 22066; and *Art in America/Annual Guide to Museums, Galleries, Artists,* 575 Broadway, New York, NY 10012.

References

American National Standards Institute (ANSI),
  Sales Department
  1430 Broadway
  New York, NY 10018
  (Request a copy of their catalog of photographic standards.)

Clark, Walter. *Caring of Photographs,* vol. 17 of the Life Library of Photography. New York: Time-Life Books, 1972.

Conservation of Photographs, Kodak Publication No. F-40, 1985.

Keefe, Laurence E., and Inch, Dennis. *The Life of a Photograph: Archival Processing, Matting, Framing and Storage,* 2d ed. Stoneham, MA: Focal Press, 1990.

Wilhelm, Henry. Contributing author, Brower, Carol. *The Permanence and Care of Color Photographs: Traditional and Digital Color Prints, Color Negatives, Slides, and Motion Pictures.* Grinnell, IA: Preservation Publishing Company (723 State Street, P.O. Box 775, Grinnell, Iowa 50112), 1993.

Sources of Supplies

In some areas it can be difficult to locate archival materials. The following is a partial list of major suppliers of archival materials mentioned in this chapter:

Conservation Resources International Inc.
8000-H Forbes Place
Springfield, VA 22151

Franklin Distributors Corp.
P.O. Box 320
Denville, NJ 07834

Light Impressions
439 Monroe Avenue
Rochester, NY 14607

TALAS Division, Technical Library Services
213 West 35th Street
New York, NY 10001

20th Century Plastics
3628 Crenshaw Blvd.
Los Angeles, CA 90016.

University Products Inc.
P.O. Box 101,
Holyoke, MA 01041

• S I X T E E N •

Problem Solving

© Gretchen Garner.
A Grove of Birches, 1988.
14 3/4 x 18 3/4 inches.
Chromogenic color prints.

Becoming More Aware/Thinking Independently

Getting ideas to solve problems means becoming more aware and thinking independently. This requires self-discipline and is accomplished by asking questions, acknowledging new facts, reasoning skeptically through your prejudices, and taking on the responsibility of gaining knowledge. It is necessary to believe in your own creativeness. Consider information from all sources. Do not attempt to limit your response to only the rational part of the brain; let your feelings enter into the process. Be prepared to break with habit and take chances. Listen to yourself as well as to others to get satisfaction.

Dealing with Fear

The major block to getting new ideas is fear. Fear takes on endless forms: fear of being wrong, of being foolish, or of changing the way in which something has been done in the past. Fear can be a reluctance to deal with the unknown. It can be brought about by a lack of preparation. Apprehension deters creative development by misdirecting or restraining energy. It is okay to make mistakes; do not insist that everything be absolutely perfect. Beginners are not expected to be experts, so take advantage of this situation. Learning involves doing, therefore make that extra negative; make one more print to see what happens. You are the one who will benefit.

Photography Is a Lot Like Baseball[1]

Photography and baseball both require that participants be skilled in the precise placement of objects and the

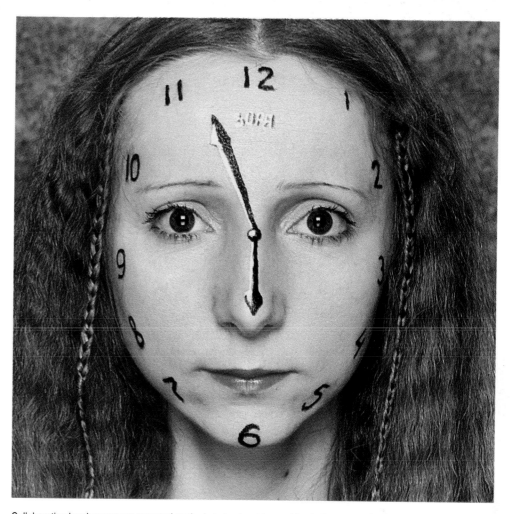

Collaboration has become an accepted method of visual problem solving in the postmodernist era. Teamwork diminishes the importance of the individual creative force. It allows a variety of people to bring their ideas and skills into play. Filmmaking is an example of a major art form of the twentieth century that relies on the collective group consciousness for its success.

© Rimma Geriovine/Mark Berghash/Valery Gerlovin. *A Clock; Time as a Surface of Life*, n/d. 19 × 19 inches. Chromogeni ccolor print.

capture of moments in time and space within fractions of a second. There are periods of thoughtful contemplation, followed by bursts of intense activity, and then a return to quietness. Both activities require patience, practice, and study. Each involves performance and control and the comprehension of a spatial language. But most of all, to be a player one must be there and *play the game*. Warren Spahn, the winningest left-handed pitcher to ever step on the mound said: "Baseball is a game of failure." The big leagues' best hitters fail about 65 percent of the time; the best pitchers can lose twelve games in a season and hundreds over their careers.

Statistics do not always tell the entire story. If a photographer added up the number of frames shot and compared it with the number of satisfying images produced, the typical photographic batting average could be about 1 percent. What is not reflected in an average are all the intangible joys involved within the process of photography that require the integration of abstract ideas and concrete operations. Good photographers overcome their fear and make pictures. Don't be afraid of experience. Go to the plate and swing that bat, even if it means striking out. As Ansel Adams said: "Photography is a way of knowing."

---

[1] During the summer of 1839, Daguerre made public his photographic process and the first modern American baseball game, as devised by Abner Doubleday, was played at Cooperstown, NY.

The Problem-Solving Process

Getting ideas means finding ways to solve problems. The process is a continuous intermingling of events (figure 16.1) that includes acceptance, analysis, definition, idea formation, selection, operation, evaluation, and results. Feel free to skip around or go back and forth between steps. There is no definite order; it is dependent on the pattern of your thinking.

Birth of a Problem

Problems arise from every aspect of life. They can spring from our private world of friends, loved ones, children, or parents. They may come from our work world situations of bosses and co-workers. Others are thrust upon us from the outside world due to educational, economic, political, and even accidental circumstances. We cannot try to solve all the problems we encounter. We must be selective about which problems we decide to take on or be overwhelmed and not able to accomplish anything.

The challenge for Selter in her *Calendar Pictures* was to contrast the violated, dead specimen with the living environment where it once lived. Selter knew that "most hummingbird photographs show the bird hovering while it feeds on nectar from its favored reddish flowers. To help my bird feed again, I made a little harness of orange thread which I could suspend from a pole over the flower in my garden where hummingbirds feed. The most difficult part of making this photograph was eliminating blur as the bird moved through the wind. Because I wanted to use natural light, I solved the problem by using a wide aperture, a fast shutter speed, and worked in the morning when the air is calmest."

© Carol Selter. *December, The Hummingbird*, 1990. 11 × 14 inches. Chromogenic color print.

Acceptance

Acceptance means taking on a problem as a challenge and a responsibility by saying yes to involvement and committing your time and resources to solve the problem. It is like signing a contract that indicates the intention to take charge and see the project through to completion. We can either accept things the way that they are ("I do not know how to do this in color photography") or we can take on the responsibility for change ("I am going to learn how to do this").

Analysis

Analysis involves studying the problem and determining its essential features and feelings. It includes taking the problem

apart, doing research to discover all its ingredients, and working out their relationship to the whole. This is the time to question everything and to generate all the possibilities that are available.

Definition

Definition is getting to the main issues and clarifying the goals to be reached. It entails nonlimiting questioning. Ask yourself, What is the "real" problem? Do not get sidetracked by the symptoms of the problem. We must decide where problems may lie and narrow down the information uncovered. This state defines the direction in which the action will be taken in order to solve the problem.

Figure 16.1

This is one representation of the problem-solving process as a continuous circle of responsible thinking. There is no definite order for thinking. Feel free to devise a method that is suitable to both the problem and problem solver. The steps outlined in this chapter can also be thought of in linear terms, that is, of one step in front of the next until the destination is reached. They may also be considered in a hopscotch manner of skipping around from one step to another, or by crisscrossing the steps. Don't be afraid to switch models.

Idea Formation

Idea formation provides ways of reaching the stated goal. Do not fall in love with one idea or assume the answer is known before this process is started. Go out onto a limb; defer judgment. Try techniques such as attribute listing, which tells all you know about the problem, or morphological synthesis, including the internal structure, patterns, and form of the problem and the breakdown of its individual parts. Attribute listing also involves the search for various signs that occur in the problem and the possible arrangements of those signs. Put together all the solutions that have been considered, and keep an open mind to the alternatives.

Selection

Selection is the process of choosing from all the idea options that have been discovered. Now is the time to decide which way is best to reach the stated destination. Keep a backup idea in case a detour is encountered. Do not be afraid to experiment, to take chances, or to try something that has not been done previously.

Operation

Operation is putting the plan into action. The process of doing is as important as the final product. Do not seek perfection because it is impossible and you will not reach your goal. If the selected idea is not working out, be flexible and attempt something else.

Bring plenty of film. Do not be afraid to shoot. Use the film as an artist would employ a sketchbook. Film is the starting place for your visual ideas. Keep thinking. Do not worry if every picture is not a masterpiece. Do not be concerned about making a mistake; it will be dealt with in the next step of the process. Keep working.

Evaluation

During evaluation the course of action is reviewed. These questions are asked:

What was done? What worked? What didn't work? Why did or didn't it work? What could be done to make the picture stronger? Pinpoint the source of any dissatisfaction. If the result does not meet the goals, it is time to do a "reshoot."

Do not hold onto only one idea. Absolutist beliefs can be crippling to creative problem solving. A large part of learning involves how to deal with failure. We learn more from our failures than from our successes. Picasso said, "Even the great artists have failures."

Results

Good results can render your ideas and intentions visible. A successful solution is one that fits both the problem and the problem solver. To make this happen, you must be prepared to jump in, take the chances, and become a part of the process called photography.

The successful problem solver keeps a record of what has been done and how it was accomplished. This is knowledge—repeatable results gained from experience.

Problem solving means coming to grips with the true nature of the situation. Simplistic solutions to problems offer the wrong answers for the lazy and the unthinking. Be skeptical of anyone who claims to have all the answers. Some people take a course in photography believing that techniques will make them photographers; this is not the case. To be a photographer, you must learn to think a situation through to a satisfying conclusion based on personal experiences and needs that combine the "right" technique for your vision.

The quest for the "absolute" tends to get in the way of good photography. In his book *Perfect Symmetry: The Search for the Beginning of Time,* the physicist Heinz R. Pagels said: "Maybe there is some final truth to the universe I do not know. Yet suspending such beliefs opens us to new ways of exploring. Later we can compare our new knowledge and beliefs with the old ones. Often such comparisons involve contradictions; but these, in turn, generate new creative insights about

the order of reality. The capacity to tolerate complexity and welcome contradiction, not the need for simplicity and certainty, is the attribute of an explorer."[2]

The Role of Photography

Problem solving and technical abilities communicate nothing to others unless attached to convincing personal beliefs. The ultimate question is, What role should photography play in our society? What must be understood is that photography's relationship to reality is paradoxical. Conscientious work can provoke without coercing, while providing pleasure that is mediated by the viewer's judgment. Works by artists such as Robert Mapplethorpe and Andres Serrano have been read as advertisements for unnatural acts because many people see the normal function of photography in our consumer society as promoting products. (See figure 16.2.)

Potent work is often ambiguous and requires interpretation by the viewer. Without being didactic, it can stimulate thinking that leads to an understanding. Such images allow us to be transported to explore other realms while remaining in our habitat, permit us to be transformed, and appeal to our personal freedom and individualism while reminding us of our collective investment in the group.

Images having integrity allow our imagination to enter a dreamlike state where rational thought is suspended, all while retaining our faculty for judgment and reflection. It is possible to return from this journey to reflect on the choices that habitually define and restrain us. In *The Scandal of Pleasure: Art in an Age of Fundamentalism,* Wendy Steiner says: "Experiencing the variety of meanings available in a work of art helps make us tolerant and mentally lithe. Art is a realm of thought experiments that quicken, sharpen and sweeten our being in the world."

[2] Heinz R. Pagels. *Perfect Symmetry: The Search for the Beginning of Time* (New York: Simon and Schuster, 1985), 370.

Figure 16.2
This photograph became a flash point for a conservative crusade to end National Endowment for the Arts (NEA) funding for individual artists and nonmainstream arts and cultural organizations. Why did this piece upset so many people? Is it what you see or what you read? Would anyone have been unnerved had this work been called *Untitled?* Serrano's quandary with his faith has also produced worshipful images, such as *Black Supper* and *Black Mary, Black Jesus*. Serrano refers to himself as "a former Catholic and . . . someone who even today is not opposed to being called a Christian."

© Andres Serrano. *Piss Christ*, 1987. 60 × 40 inches. Dye-destruction print. Courtesy of Paula Cooper Gallery, New York, NY.

Reviewing the Work of Others

Insight into your own working methods and prejudices as well as the varied roles photography may play can be gained by reviewing the work of other artists. Begin by going to the library and browsing through the photography and art sections. If you have access to exhibitions, plan on visiting at least three different ones. Don't go only to see photography; select a variety of mediums, styles, and time periods. Spend some time leisurely studying the work and begin to write down your thoughts in a notebook or on 3-x-5-inch blank cards. Now prepare yourself to write a structured review. Begin by selecting work you find positive, appealing, and involving. State your opinions and observations and back them up with specific facts derived from the work. Pretend you are in a court of law; give evidence, not generalizations. Consider the following:

1. Describe the image, including the subject matter and its form. Form entails how the subject is presented. Refer to chapter 18 on the visual language of design. Can you discover the color and/or composition key? How are figure-ground relationships used?

2. Evaluate the technique. Does it work for you? Why? Discuss exposure, use of light, and printing and presentation methods. What would you do differently? Why?

3. Give your subjective reaction. Listen to yourself. What initially attracted you to this work? Did the attraction last? Did the work deliver what you expected? Would you want to continue to look at this work over a

Baden wanted to represent how television not only mimics our lives and desires but is capable of creating a hierarchy of economic and moral values. "Through a process of dismantling, fragmenting, and re-assembling," Baden reanalyzes and reinterprets television's symbolic language. Baden states: "The prints are made from black-and-white negatives. The color is subjective, not derived from the source images. This is done so that the idea of the color will be psychological rather than literal, the resultant piece being based more on mood or feeling than fact."

© Karl Baden, *Untitled* from Tele-Constructions series, 1986. 20 × 24 inches. Chromogenic color print.

period of time? Is the photographer a visual or haptic (see chapter 4)? Answer each part with a why or why not response.

4. Interpret the work. Ask yourself: Why was it made in this way? What does the work mean? Who made it? What is the point of view of the photographer? What was the photographer trying to say? Does the photographer succeed? Why or why not? Who was it made for? Do the images stand on their own or do they require an accompanying statement or explanation? What is your interpretation of the work? If the work is in a group or series, evaluate how selected images work individually and in terms of the group. Do single images hold their own ground or do they need to be seen in series? Does the imagemaker use any text? If so, how does it alter

your perception of the image's meaning? Present clear and persuasive arguments, citing evidence to back up your thoughts.

5. Incorporate ideas. Define what it is about the work you like/relate to/find moving. Be specific. Then ask yourself how you can integrate these into your own way of working.

6. Go the other way. Go back to the same body of work and pick an image that you do not care for. Repeat the previous steps to figure out what it is you don't like. Identify specific points and ask yourself what you should do to avoid incorporating these unwanted aspects into your work.

7. Ask someone else. Get the opinion of someone else who is knowledgeable and interested in similar work. Present the work to them. Does the other person agree or disagree with your assessment? Conduct a friendly

argument. Do your opinions hold together? Should they be revised? Can you see the other point of view? What new territory did this other person open for you? How will this affect the way you view the work?

References

Barrett, Terry. *Criticizing Photographs: An Introduction To Understanding Images,* 2d ed. Mountain View, CA: Mayfield Publishing, 1995.

Steiner, Wendy. *The Scandal of Pleasure: Art in an Age of Fundamentalism.* Chicago: The University of Chicago Press, 1995.

Turabian, Kate L. *A Manual for Writers of Term Papers, Theses, and Dissertations,* 6th ed. Chicago: The University of Chicago Press, 1995.

SEVENTEEN

The Subject Is Natural Light

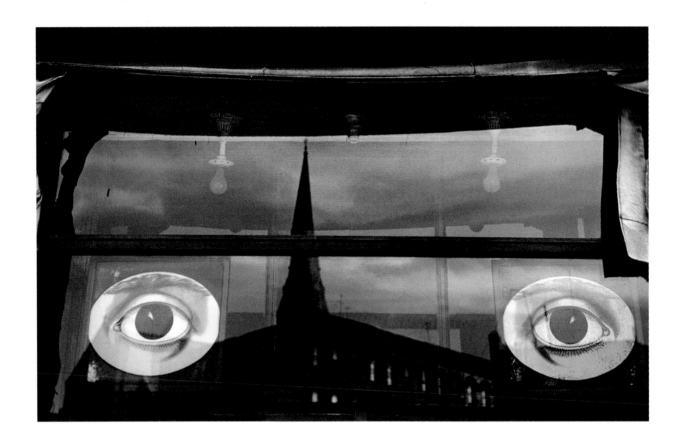

© Leonard Balish.
Window Stare, circa 1990s.
20 × 24 inches. Chromogenic color print.

Williams started this project when her toddler son began his swimming lessons. Williams recalls: "In this small overheated room was a dilapidated pool, made luminous by the natural light which flooded through large south windows. The color of the water seemed to change by the minute." To accomplish a sense of discomfort and distortion, sensations that can accompany learning to swim, Williams used a panorama camera that she "twisted while releasing the shutter." The blurred portions of the image are supposed to reproduce the feeling of actually being in the pool, the natural distortive qualities of water, and the sensation that something is slightly off. "I printed on low contrast paper to adequately and delicately describe the play of light on the water and the many hues of blue, often so integral to the composition of the photograph."

© Jennette Williams. **Emmet Floating**, from **Off the Deep End series,** 1992. 10 1/2 × 24 inches. Chromogenic color print.

Good Light

The definition of "good light" depends solely on the photographer's intent. Have you ever encountered a scene that you knew should make a good photograph, yet the results were disappointing? There is a strong possibility that it was photographed at a time of day that did not let the light reveal the fundamental aspects that were important and attracted you to the scene in the first place. Try photographing the scene again at a different time of day.

What the Camera Does

Your ability to function as a creative photographer depends on your knowledge of how to make your equipment work for you. A camera is merely a recording device, and it will not reproduce a scene or an experience without your guidance at every stage of the process. The camera can isolate a scene; it can reduce it to two dimensions. It freezes a slice of time and sets it into a frame.

It does not record the sequence of events that led up to the moment that the shutter clicked or your private emotional response to what was happening. These are items you must learn to incorporate into your pictures if you expect to make photographs instead of snapshots. The camera does not discriminate in what it sees and records, but you can, and must, discriminate to create successful images.

The Time of Day and Types of Light

Most photographers are familiar with the old Kodak adage, "Take pictures after ten in the morning and before two in the afternoon." This rule had nothing to do with aesthetics. The purpose of this command was to encourage amateur photographers to take pictures when the light was generally the brightest because early roll film was not very sensitive to light. By breaking this canon you can come up with some astonishing results. The day follows a predictable cycle of light that will influence your images.

Light is the key ingredient shared by every photograph. Before anything else, every photograph is about light. Light determines the look of every photograph you make. If the light does not reveal the perceived nature of the subject, the picture will not communicate your ideas to the viewer. Begin to recognize the characteristics and qualities that light possesses throughout the day and learn to incorporate them into the composition for a complete visual statement.

The Cycle of Light and Its Basic Characteristics

Before Sunrise

In the earliest hours of the day, our world is essentially black-and-white. The light exhibits a cool, almost shadowless quality, and colors are muted. Up to the moment of sunrise, colors remain flat and opalescent (figure 17.1). The intensity of the colors grows as the sun rises. Artificial lights can appear as accents and create contrast.

Figure 17.1

Before the sun rises above the horizon, our world is basically black-and-white with colors that tend to be cool, muted, and subdued. This sunrise image was taken from a boat. The photographer used a 200-mm lens with a skylight filter. Dicker comments: "I took a thru-the-lens reading and opened up about one f-stop because experience has taught me the image was lighter than an 18 percent gray card." Recognizing the qualities of light that best reveal the subject, and then correctly interpreting it through exposure helps to ensure a complete visual statement.

© Jean-Jacques Dicker. *Boy on Kasai River, Zaire,* 1977. 24 × 36 cm. Chromogenic color transparency.

Figure 17.2

Meyerowitz uses both the quality of morning light and a high-level camera view to diminish human importance in this scene. A vast sense of space becomes the subject. The angle and color of the beach leads the eye into the water, where the light striking the ripples of the waves takes us to the horizon, where the sea and sky blend into infinity.

© Joel Meyerowitz. *Long Nook Beach,* 1983. n/s. Chromogenic color print.

Morning

As soon as the sun is up, the light changes dramatically. Since the sun is low and must penetrate a great amount of the atmosphere, the light that gets through is much warmer in color than it will be later in the day. The shadows can look blue because they lack high brilliant sunlight, because of the great amount of blue from the overhead sky, and because of simultaneous contrast (see section on color observations in chapter 5). As the sun rises, the color of light becomes warmer (red-orange). By midmorning the light begins to lose its warm color and starts to appear clear and white (figure 17.2).

Midday

The higher the sun climbs in the sky, the greater the contrast between colors. At noon the light is white. Colors stand out strongly, each in its own hue. The shadows are black and deep. Contrast is at its peak. Subjects can appear to look like three-dimensional cutouts. At noon the light may be considered to be harsh, stark, or crisp (figure 17.3).

Late Afternoon

As the sun drops to the horizon, the light begins to warm up again. It is a gradual process and should be observed carefully. On clear evenings objects can take on an unearthly glow. Look for an increase in red. The shadows lengthen and become more blue. Surfaces are strongly textured. An increasing amount of detail is revealed as the sun lowers (figure 17.4).

Twilight/Evening

After sunset there is still a great amount of light in the sky. Notice the tremendous range of light intensity between the eastern and western skies. Often the sunset colors are reflected from the clouds. Just as at dawn, the light is very soft and contrast and shadow are at a minimum. After

Figure 17.3

At midday bright, clear sunlight is its purest white. Colors stand out strongly, contrast is at its peak, and shadows are dark and deep. The visual effect can be that of the "pop-out," heightening the sense of the third dimensionality of the subject.

© David Graham. *Shirley Temple, Mummers Parade, Philadelphia, PA,* 1983. 16 × 20 inches. Chromogenic color print.
Courtesy of Black Star and Laurence Miller Gallery. New York, NY.

Figure 17.4

This image was made with a 1950s Brownie Hawkeye, the camera of Glauber's childhood. "I like the square format and the element of chance inherent in the camera's design." The intense afternoon sunlight evokes a sense of spontaneous childhood summer play. Paralleling snapshots in a family album, Glauber makes "a casual, almost haphazard, sometimes blurred but still informative record of people's lives."

© Carole Glauber. *Portland, OR,* 1990 (Ben with Hose). 14 × 14 inches. Chromogenic color print.

Figure 17.5

In the evening, after sunset, there is still plenty of light in the sky. Its quality is soft, making contrast and shadows minimal. These natural effects can be played off artificial light sources to create contrast and add interest.

© Jan Staller. *Galaxy,* 1985. 15 × 15 inches. Chromogenic color print. Courtesy of Lieberman and Saul Gallery. New York, NY.

sunset and throughout twilight, notice the warm colors in the landscape. This phenomenon, known as "purple light," arises from light from the blue end of the spectrum falling vertically on you from the overhead sky. Observe the glowing pink and violet colors as they gradually disappear and the earth becomes a pattern of blacks and grays (figure 17.5).

At twilight it is possible to observe the earth's shadow (the dark gray-blue band across the eastern horizon just after sunset). It is only visible until it rises to about 6 degrees high; after that, its upper boundary quickly fades. The earth's shadow is immediately visible after sunset because our eastward view is directly along the boundary between the illuminated and nonilluminated portions of the atmosphere. As time passes, we view this boundary with an ever-steepening angle and it shortly disappears. When observing the earth's shadow, notice the red-to-orange-to-yellow development of color just about at its upper edge produced as the sun's ray pass overhead and reflect directly back down to earth. This phenomenon, called "counter-twilight," disappears at about the same time as the earth's shadow.

Night

The world after the sun has set is seen by artificial light and reflected light from the moon. The light is generally harsh, and contrast is extreme. Photographing under these conditions usually requires a tripod, a brace, or a very steady hand. Since an increase in exposure can lead to reciprocity failure and possible color shift, use filters if correction is desired. Combinations of artificial light and long exposure can create a surreal atmosphere (figure 17.6).

Studying the Sky

After looking at a bright portion of the sky, close your eyes for a few moments and allow them to recover from the glare. The color-sensitive area of our vision is easily saturated by intense light and, without short rest periods, our eyes are unable to distinguish subtle color differences. An intriguing way to study specific portions of sky is to use a small mirror held at arm's length. Face away from the area of sky you want to observe and use the mirror to inspect that region. By holding the mirrored image against a neutral background of your choice you can compare the colors of different portions of the sky. The backgrounds can also be of other colors or even different shapes and textures and these combinations can be photographed to alter our traditional way of thinking about the sky.

For more information read *The Nature of Light and Color in the Open Air,* by M. Minnaert, available from Dover Publications, 31 East 2nd Street, Mineola, NY 11501.

The Seasons

The position of the sun varies depending on the time of year. This has a great impact on both the quality and quantity of the light. Learn to recognize these characteristics and look for ways to go with and against the flow of the season to obtain the best possible photograph.

Winter means a diminished number of daylight hours. Bare trees, pale skies, fog, ice, rain, sleet, and snow all produce the type of light that creates muted and subtle colors. Spring brings on an increase in the amount of daylight and the introduction of more colors. Summer light offers the world at its peak of color. Harsh summer light can offer a host of contrast and exposure problems for the photographer to deal with. Fall is a period of transition that provides tremendous opportunities to show the changes that take place in color (figure 17.7).

· A S S I G N M E N T ·

Time of Day/Type of Light
Use any of the standard daylight color slide film (E-6 process) that has a film speed of about 100. Photograph at least two of the following suggestions. Use only available light. It is not enough to show just the differences in the quality of light at the different times of the day. Make a picture that has a strong composition and relates your observations to the viewer.

1. Photograph an object at six different times of the day, in six different locations.
2. Photograph an object at six different times of day in the same location.
3. Make a photograph at a different location at six different times of the day. Do not add anything to the scene. Work with what is given.

Figure 17.6
Working at night, Tulis uses a 4-×5-inch camera to make extended exposures during which he lights up various parts of the composition with a strobe and spotlight using a 12-volt battery. "Sometimes I shift aperture to gain a particular focus. . . . My aim is to make work that is visually pleasurable. [Such an image] is more likely to get the attention of the unlearned in the arts while the learned . . . tend to view art that is "beautiful" as superficial and passe . . . the definition of beauty is now suspect and corrupted. . . . I would be satisfied to get a huzzah from a farmer . . . and consider all the rest casuistry."

© Thomas Tulis. ***Fog,*** from ***Transmission Towers Series,*** 1989. 20 × 24 inches. Dye-destruction print.

Figure 17.7
Ketchum reveals the transitory nature of fall with dramatic side light, delineating the colors, lines, and shapes revealed within the interplay between nature and the human-made world.

© Robert Ketchum. ***Taconic Parkway,*** n.d. 33 × 40 inches. Dye-destruction print.
Courtesy of J. J. Brookings Gallery. San Jose, CA.

Figure 17.8

This picture would not have been possible without "bad" weather. Provided the photographer is prepared and waiting to take advantage of the right moment, storms can provide drama and mystery to the situation. Mosch states: "My work is a personal response to the human gesture within the natural landscape. In this image I used a long exposure time to make visible the interplay between the natural lightning and the artificial lights of the car moving over a bridge."

© Steven P. Mosch. ***Nature/Works Series: Lightning Bolt and Car Headlights, Tybee Island, GA,*** 1990. 11 × 14 inches. Chromogenic color print.

Figure 17.9

Fog and mist diffuse the light and tend to make monochromatic color schemes. The addition of a warm-colored object can break up this two-dimensional effect. In this instance, the red sign was illuminated by flash fill to make its visual impact even stronger.

© Michael Stravato. ***Wrong Way,*** 1987. 11 × 14 inches. Chromogenic color print.

The Weather and Color Materials

There is no such thing as bad weather for making photographs (figure 17.8). Fog gives pearly, opalescent, muted tones. Storms can add drama and mystery. Rain mutes some colors and enriches others while creating glossy surfaces with brilliant reflections. Dust softens and diffuses color and line. Bad weather conditions often provide an excellent opportunity to create pictures full of atmosphere and interest. With a few precautions to yourself and equipment, you need not be just a fair-weather photographer. If the metering looks like it is going to be tough, bring along and use a gray card as a guide.

Fog and Mist

Fog and mist diffuse the light and tend to provide monochromatic compositions (figure 17.9). The light can tend toward the cool side (blue). If this is not acceptable, use an 81A warming filter, or photograph in the early morning or late afternoon, when there is the chance to catch some warm-colored light. If the sun is going in and out of the clouds, wait for a moment when a shaft of light breaks through the clouds. This can create drama and break up the two-dimensional flatness that these cloudy scenes often produce.

Because the light is scattered, both colors and contrasts are made softer and more subtle. If you want a sense of depth in the mist, try not to fill your frame completely with it. Attempt to offset it with a dark area. To capture mist, expose for the highlights or use an incident light meter. Bracketing is crucial.

In fog, take a reading from your hand in light similar to that which is on your subject. Then overexpose by 1/2 to one f-stop depending on how intense the fog happens to be. Film is your cheapest resource; don't be afraid to use it.

Figure 17.10

Made with a Fuji 617 panorama camera, Baylis captured the unworldly stillness of a snowstorm. In this case, the snow has muted the colors and flattened the sense of visual space. Care is required in obtaining a correct light meter reading because the large amount of reflected light often fools the meter into underexposing the film. Keep all battery-powered equipment as warm as possible when not in use to avoid electrical slowdowns or failures.

© Michele Jan Baylis. *Elk in Blizzard, Jackson, WY,* 1990. 20 × 24 inches. Chromogenic color print.

Rain

Rain tends to mute and soften color and contrast, while bringing reflections into play. Include a warm accent if contrast or depth is desired. The shutter speed is important in the rain. The faster the speed, the more distinct the raindrops will appear. At speeds below 1/60 of a second, the drops blur. Long exposures will seem to make them disappear. Experiment with different shutter speeds to see what you can achieve. Keep your camera in a plastic bag with a hole for the lens. Use a UV filter to keep the front of the lens dry. Keep the camera inside your jacket when it is not being used.

Dampness

When working in a situation that is constantly wet, get a waterproof bag to hold your equipment. Inexpensive plastic bag cases are available at camping stores that allow you to photograph in wet conditions without worrying about ruining the camera. Carry a bandanna to wipe off any excess moisture.

Before going out into any unusual weather conditions be certain to check how many frames are remaining on the roll. If there are only a few left, reload while everything is still dry and familiar.

Snow

Snow reflects any predominant color. Blue casts and shadows are the most common in daylight situations. Use a UV filter to help neutralize this effect. If this proves insufficient, try a yellow 81A, 81B, 81C, or even an 81 filter. This technique also works well in higher elevations, where the color temperature of the light is higher (bluer).

Brightly lit snow scenes tend to fool the meter because there is so much reflected light (figure 17.10). The meter thinks there is more light than there actually is and tells you to close the lens down too far, producing underexposed negatives. Avoid this by taking an incident light reading and then overexpose by 1/2 to one f-stop to get shadow detail. If this is not possible, use the palm of your hand. Fill the metering area with it, being careful not to get your shadow in it. Next open the lens up one f-stop from the indicated reading. To bring out the rich texture of snow, photograph when the sun is low on the horizon. Bracket when in doubt and learn which exposure works the best.

Snow Effects

Slow shutter speeds can make snow appear as streaks. Fast speeds arrest the action of the flakes. Flash can also be employed. For falling snow, fire the flash from the center of the camera. The snow will reflect the light back, producing flare and/or spots. The snowflakes can be eliminated by using a synchronization cord and holding the flash at arm's length off to one side of the camera. This stops the snow and provides a scene comparable to the ones produced inside one of those plastic bubbles that are shaken to make the snow fall. Try setting the camera on a tripod, use a lens opening of f/8 or smaller plus a shutter speed of 1/8 of a second or longer, and fire the flash during the exposure. This stops the action of some of the falling snow while letting the rest of it appear blurred. Bracket the exposures until enough experience is obtained to determine what will deliver the type of results you are after.

Dust

Dust can be a bitingly painful experience to the photographer and equipment. Use a UV filter, plastic bag, and lens hood to protect the camera. Use the same shutter speed guide for snow to help determine how the dust will appear. Dust in the sky can produce amazing atmospheric effects. If turbulence is to be shown, expose for the highlights. This causes the shadows to go dark and the clouds will stand out from the sky. A polarizing filter may be used to

Figure 17.11

The bright, harsh desert sun at the Dead Sea, with temperatures exceeding 110°F (43°C), can affect not only the look of the picture but the actual physical condition and color balance of the film itself. Whenever possible, protect all color materials from extreme heat and/or humidity. Exploring her lifetime fascination with water and bathing, Starobin says: "Standing together at the edge of the sea, these two bathers looked statuesque and inanimate. I wanted to capture the stillness and eeriness of their appearance. By overexposing the film, I was able to eliminate any detail in the sky, making a more abstract composition of positive and negative shapes. Because of the overexposure, in the printing process the mud on their bodies translated into a milky brown color, instead of the coal black color it is in reality. The red of their eyes, ears, and mouths then stood out."

© Leslie Starobin. *European Bathers, En Gedi, Dead Sea, Israel*, 1988. 9 × 9 inches. Chromogenic color print.

darken the sky and increase color saturation. If detail is needed in the foreground, meter one-third sky and two-thirds ground with the camera meter and bracket one f-stop in either direction.

Heat

Heat is often accompanied by glare, haze, high contrast, and reflection.

These factors can reduce clarity and color saturation, but if handled properly they can make colors appear to stand out. In extremely bright situations, a neutral density filter may be needed to cut down the amount of light that is striking the film.

Do not point the camera directly into the sun except for brief periods of time. The lens can act as a magnifying glass and ruin the shutter and light meter.

Store the camera and film in a cool place. Heat and humidity can ruin the color balance of the film before it is even processed. Refrigerate the film whenever possible both before and after exposure. Let the film reach room temperature before shooting to avoid condensation and color shift. Avoid carrying unnecessary equipment if you will be doing a good deal of walking in the heat. Do not forget a hat and sunscreen (figure 17.11).

Figure 17.12
Colten was attracted to this scene by the combination of light, atmosphere, and time of day. Working with a Makina 67 Wide camera, she made this exposure on a cold wintry afternoon on Type L film with an 85B filter. The photographer states: "I was struck by the brilliance of the light and the hard coolness that the snow projected. The bright openness of the light contrasts with the feeling of being trapped behind the tree. I had to be careful in exposing the film to ensure the snow, sky, and bark of the trees held detail." When working in cold conditions, carry extra batteries and rewind film carefully to avoid producing static on the film.

© Jennifer Colten. *The Fenway. Boston, MA,* 1988. 20 × 24 inches. Chromogenic color print.

Cold

If you have an electronic camera or flash, check the batteries before going out and carry spares. At temperatures of 20°F (-6.7°C) or less, there is a danger that all battery-powered equipment will become sluggish. Shutters are affected first, with shutter speeds slowing and producing exposure errors. For instance, if a battery-powered shutter is off by 1/1,000 of a second, and if you are attempting to stop the action of a skier speeding downhill at 1/1,000 of a second, then the exposure would be off by one f-stop. This would not present a serious problem unless you are shooting above 1/125 of a second. In cold conditions, make use of the middle and slow ranges of shutter speeds whenever possible to avoid this difficulty (figure 17.12).

Cold Weather Lubrication

Manual shutters also slow down in the cold because the viscosity of the lubricants thicken as the temperature drops. A camera can be relubricated with special cold weather lubricants if you are doing a great deal of work in extremely cold conditions. These lubricants must be replaced when the camera is again used in normal conditions. Most cameras perform well in cold weather as long as they are not kept out in the elements longer than necessary.

Cold Weather Protection

Simplify camera operations as much as possible. Remove any unneeded accessories that cannot be operated with gloves, or add accessories that permit easier operation. If possible, preload cameras or film magazines before going outside. Do not take a camera that has condensation on it out into the cold until the condensation has evaporated because it may freeze. The camera will cease operating, and the inner components will be ruined. Once outside, avoid touching unpainted metal surfaces with ungloved hands, face, or lips because your skin will stick to the metal. Wear thin gloves so that your skin does not come in contact with the cold metal and you can operate the camera with ease. Metal parts can be taped to prevent this from happening. Do not breathe on the lens outside to clean it because your breath might freeze on it.

When bringing a camera in from the cold, let it warm up before using it so condensation does not damage its working gear. Condensation can be avoided by placing the camera in an airtight plastic bag and squeezing out the air. This prevents the camera from being exposed to the warmer temperature. Condensation forms on the outside of the bag instead of on the lens and camera body. After the equipment has reached room temperature, remove it from the bag.

Batteries

Silver-oxide batteries work well if the camera is used often. For the occasional user, lithium batteries have a longer shelf life. Carry a warm, spare set when working in cold weather since all batteries tend to drain rapidly in low temperatures. Keep spare batteries warm by putting them next to your body in an interior pocket. If the batteries appear to have expired, do not dispose of them until they are warmed up and tested again. Lithium batteries seem to work better in the cold.

In cold weather, avoid using power accessories, such as motor winders, to conserve power. Since cold reduces the self-discharge that eventually runs batteries down while they are sitting on the shelf, all types of batteries commonly used in photographic equipment—alkaline, lithium, oxide, silver—will stay active longer if they are stored in airtight bags with silica-gel dryer packets in the refrigerator. Keep them in this wrapper while bringing them up to room temperature—an hour is usually about right. Batteries should *never* be frozen. Freezing can cause leakage or full-scale rupture. It is a good idea to change batteries about once a year so as not to experience a power failure as you are about to make your next masterpiece.

Vintage equipment, such as a Luna-Pro light meter, designed to run on mercury batteries that are no longer made because of environmental concerns, can be powered by less toxic zinc-air cells made specifically for photographic applications. They require special handling to extend their shorter life span and avoid leakage. Read and follow each manufacturer's handling guidelines.

Static

Because static can occur anytime it is cold and dry, it can be the photographer's bane. Rapidly winding or rewinding the film can produce a static charge inside the camera. You will not know this has happened until the film is processed and discover a lightning storm of static across the pictures. Take it easy and go slowly. Do not rewind the film as fast as possible. Do not use the motor drive or auto rewind if possible in these conditions. This helps to prevent those indiscriminate lightning flashes from plaguing you. Keep film warm as long as possible in cold weather since it can become brittle at very low temperatures.

Color and the Visual Language of Design

© Kathleen Campbell.
Angel of Technology, from *Photographs of Widely-Known Non-Exisitent Beings,* 1994.
27 × 40 inches. Gelatin silver print with Marshall's Photo Oils.

Campbell is trying to "touch on our society's simultaneous embrace and rejection of irrational phenomena." Working from Baudelaire's position that "we walk through a forest of symbols," Campbell relies on such emblems in hopes of touching "on the conflicts between the reality of our everyday lives and the universal longing tor transcendence. Heaven is always just outside our reach. We are grounded in a disappointing materialism, forever hoping each illusion will lead us to some spiritual truth."

Seeing Is Thinking

Seeing is thinking. Thinking involves putting together random pieces of our private experience into an orderly manner. The act of seeing becomes an act of construction, making sense out of the world.

We like what is familiar to us and tend to back away from anything unfamiliar. Becoming more visually literate makes us more flexible. Some people think photography is only for recording and categorizing objects. For them the photograph is like a window through which a scene is viewed or a mirror that reflects a material reality. A photograph is nothing more than light-sensitive emulsion on a surface. It is possible that it shows us something recognizable, but maybe it only shows us lines, shapes, and colors. "A work of art encountered as a work of art is an experience, not a statement or an answer to a question. . . . Art is not *about* something; it *is* something. A work of art is a thing *in* the world, not just a text or commentary *on* the world. A work of art makes us see or comprehend something singular.[1]

What Is a Good Photograph?

How do you make a good photograph? This is the question everyone wants answered, but there is no answer. This book offers a number of ideas that may be of help, but they might get in the way. It is a good question, even if we do not have "the" answer. Keep looking. The search will probably reveal there is no single answer but many. Think about what Paul Strand said: "No matter what lens you use, no matter what speed the film, no matter how you develop it, no matter how you print it, you cannot say more than you see."[2]

---

[1] Estelle Jussim, "The Real Thing," in *The Eternal Moment: Essays on the Photographic Image*, by Susan Sontag (New York: Aperature, 1989).

[2] Paul Strand, "Comments on the Snapshot, in Jonathon Green, ed., *The Snapshot, Aperature* 19, no. 1 (1974): 49. Also published as a separate book.

Discovering What You Have to Say

The first and most important step in determining what makes a good photograph is to empty our minds of all images that have bombarded us on television and in magazines, newspapers, movies, videos, or computers. All these images belong to someone else. Throw them away. Next, toss out the idea that we know what a good photograph is. We know what is familiar: that a good photograph is supposed to be centered and focused; that the subject is clearly identifiable and right side up; that it is 8 x 10 inches and has color (unless it is "old," then it is black-and-white); that the people are looking into the camera and smiling; that it was taken at eye level; and that it isn't too cluttered or too sparse. It is just right. And we have seen it a million times before. It is known, safe, and totally boring. Throw all these preconceived ideas into the dumpster, where they belong, and start fresh.

Making a Photograph That Communicates

A photograph is a picture that can communicate your experience to another. A photograph has its own history—past, present, and future—and does not require any outside support; it can stand alone, as a statement. A photograph should be able to state something in a way that would be impossible to do in another medium.

Photography is a matter of order and harmony. The photographer battles the physical laws of universal entropy by attempting to control disorder within the photograph. The arrangement of objects within the pictorial space determines the success of the photograph. Order is good composition, which, as Edward Weston said, "is the strongest way of seeing" the subject. The basis of composition is design.

Design includes all the visual elements that make up a composition. Visual design is the organization of materials and forms in a certain way to fulfill a specific purpose. Design begins with the organization of parts into a coherent whole. A good photograph is an extension of the photographer and creates a response in the viewer. A good photograph possesses the ability to sustain a viewer's attention over an extended period of time. If the intentions are communicated successfully, the design of the photograph must be considered effective.

Putting It All Together

Anything touched by light can be photographed. Since it appears so easy when starting out in photography, many of us try to say too much in a picture. We often overcrowd the confines of the visual space with too much information. This can create a visual chaos in which the idea and motivation behind the pictures becomes lost. Don't assume that anything that happens to you is going to be interesting to someone else. Learn to be selective.

Working Subtractively

When making photographs work simply and subtractively, a painter starts with nothing. Through the process of addition, the picture comes into being. A photographer, on the other hand, begins with everything. The photographic process is one of subtraction. The critical power of the photographer is in the choosing. The photographer must decide what to leave out of the picture. Ray Metzker said: "The camera is nothing but a vacuum cleaner picking up everything within range. There has to be a higher degree of selectivity."

President John F. Kennedy said, "To govern is to choose." So too in the act of photography, *selectivity* is everything. Use *subtractive composing* by going directly for what you want to include in the picture and subtracting all that is not required. This subtractive method of putting the picture together can help you learn the basic visual vocabulary that produces the image. A good photographer is like a magician who knows how to make all the unwanted objects on stage disappear, leaving only the necessary items to create a striking illusion. For this reason it is necessary for the photographer to have a *point of departure*.

Point of Departure

If you pick up a camera and go out to do something deliberate and specific, the possibility of encountering the significant and the useful is greater than if you stand on the corner hoping and waiting for something to occur. Do not be like the photographer described by George Bernard Shaw, who, like a codfish, lays a million eggs in the hope that one might hatch. Have a specific direction, but remain flexible and open to the unexpected. A work that continues to say something visually over a long period of time has what is called *staying power*. It usually takes years to cultivate this ability. It has almost nothing to do with the technical means of producing a photograph, for the truth is found in how we feel about something. When this feeling is found in the picture, something of significance is expressed. The image possesses meaning. For much of what we see, there are no words. As Albert Camus said: "If we understood the enigmas of life, there would be no need for art."

The Photographer's Special License

When you go out with a camera dangling around your neck, society gives you a special license. Learn to use it. If you went to a football game and started crawling around on the ground like a snake, people would at least find you strange. They may even become alarmed. You could be arrested and hauled off in a straight jacket, labeled as an unfit member of the group.

Now imagine the same scene, only this time you have a camera around your neck. People's responses are different when they see the camera. In this

Goin clearly defines the scope of the *Water in the West Project* by stating: "These color photographs represent over 10 years of travel throughout the Great Basin desert, including the Sierra Nevada. They provide evidence of threatened reservoirs, wildlife refuges, and evaporating ponds. Desert lake beds are bleak examples of the increasing crisis of water scarcity, which exists because our culture thinks of water as a commodity, or an abstract legal right rather than the most basic physical source of life. As green lawns and golf courses continue to replace sagebrush and sand dunes, Western civilization continues to improve warnings."

© Peter Goin. *Holding Pond for Project Faultless*, from *Water in the West Project*, 1988. 16 × 20 inches. Chromogenic color print.

Finding a comfortable and suitable working method is essential. Brockmann uses a range of strategies, including text and an abbreviated tonal range that is punctuated by symbolic additions to suggest a narrative that the viewer is invited to enter. The romantic atmosphere is disrupted by the introduction of incongruous elements. Ultimately, there is no *correct* way to work, there is only the way that works for you and your situation.

© Than'l Brockmann. *January 31*, from *iN YeaRS With 12 MoNTHS*, 1995. 12 × 21 inches. Chromogenic color print. Accompanying text reads: "He waits for signs of vanished life while words which once were spoken fall like leaves about his feet."

Figure 18.1

Patton employed the photographer's special license to make this picture happen. He reports: "While kneeling behind the man who is observing the handball action, he kept trying to back up and get out of my way, thinking I was trying to photograph the handball players. I kept walking on my knees behind this man trying to keep him in front of me. Finally I told him that I wanted to show someone as they watched the game, not the game itself. Though somewhat surprised, this man went back to standing where I first encountered him, and stood there until I thanked him and told him it was alright to move. The resulting photograph is the one you see. The spectator acts as both the focal point to the composition and as a metaphor on perception. As viewers, we spectate the spectator spectating."

© Tom Patton. *Culture in Nature: Handball Only, Forest Park,. St. Louis, MO,* 1986. 12 × 18 inches. Chromogenic color print.

case, they identify you by the camera and dismiss your behavior by saying, "Oh, it's that photographer," or "Look at that photographer trying to 'get' a picture." They may even come over and offer suggestions or give technical advice so that your pictures "come out." Since photography has become omnipresent in our society, everyone thinks they are photographers. Use this license to your advantage. It is not an excuse for irresponsible behavior or to harass people as the paparazzi do. Most people will cooperate if you learn how to approach them. You can get people to be in your picture, to get out of your picture, to hold equipment, or to just leave you alone. It all depends on the attitude that you project (figure 18.1).

The Language of Vision

The language and tools of vision make use of light, color, shape, texture, line, pattern, similarity, contrast, and movement. Through these formal visual elements, it is possible to make photographs that alter and enlarge our ideas of what is worth looking at and what we have the right to observe and make pictures of. Photography can transform any object and make it part of our experience by changing it into something that can fit into your hand or onto your computer screen to be studied later at your convenience. Important photographers provide the visual tools that express the ideas and stories of their time. The great photographers push out the

boundaries of the language and invent new tools for the rest of us to use. In 1947, just before Parkinson's disease cut short his photographic career, Edward Weston had this to say concerning his own experiments in color: "The prejudice many photographers have against color photography comes from not thinking of color as form."

In the *Philebus* of Plato, Socrates comments: "I will try to speak of the beauty of shapes, and I do not mean, as most people would suppose, the shapes of living figures, or their imitations in painting, but I mean straight lines and curves and the shapes made from them, by the lathe, ruler or square. They are not beautiful for any particular reason or purpose, as other things are, but are eternally, and by

Figure 18.2
Line generally creates shape and indicates directional movement. Goldberg's vibrant color arrangement provides a strong juxtaposition with the sense of softness associated with lace.

© Gary Goldberg. *Fabric and Lace, Merida, Mexico*, 1985. Dye-destruction print. 16 × 20 inches.

their very nature, beautiful, and give a pleasure of their own quite free from the itch of desire: and in this way colors can give similar pleasure."

These eternally beautiful geometric forms of which Plato speaks can be measured or presented in analytical form. They have proved useful to science and engineering, and since these fields have dominated the intellectual landscape for the past 150 years, they have also had a tremendous influence on imagemaking.

The following categories are offered to provide the basic vocabulary that is needed to communicate in the photographic language.

Line

Line carves out areas of space on either side of it. Any line, except one that is perfectly straight, creates a shape. Closing a line creates a shape. Lines can be majestic, flowing, or undulating. Lines can be used as a symbolic or an abstract concept. They can show you contour, form, pattern, texture, directional movement, and emphasis (figure 18.2).

Line, per se, does not exist in nature. It is a human creation, an abstraction

invented for the simplification of visual statements for the purpose of symbolizing ideas. Nature contains mass (three-dimensional form), which is portrayed in photography by the use of line as contour (a line that creates a boundary and separates an area of space from its background).

Shape

Shape is created by a closed line—an area having a specific character defined

Figure 18.3

Shape is formed by a closed line. Shape is an area having a specific character defined by color value, contrast, outline, or texture with the surrounding area. Epstein relies on shape to create a flowing composition that keeps bringing the viewer back to the beautiful young woman.

© Mitch Epstein. *Carnival Queen*, n/d. 20 × 24 inches. Chromogenic color print.

by an outline, contrast, color value, or texture with the surrounding area (figure 18.3). There are four basic shapes:

1. *Geometric shapes* include the square, triangle, rectangle, and circle.
2. *Natural shapes* imitate things in the natural world: human, animal, and plant.
3. *Abstract shapes* are natural shapes that have been altered in a certain way so that they are reduced to their essence. The source of the shape is recognizable, but it has been transformed into something different. This is usually done by simplification, the omission of all nonessential elements.
4. *Nonobjective shapes* do not relate to anything in the natural world. Usually, we cannot put specific names on them. They are for the eyes, not the intellect. They represent the subjective, not the rational, part of our being.

Space

Space is an area for you to manipulate in order to create form. There are three kinds of space:

1. *Actual space* is the two-dimensional area enclosed by the borders of the camera's viewfinder and the surface on which the image later appears. Three-dimensional spaces are inside and around or within an object.
2. *Pictorial space* is the illusionary sense of depth that we see in two-dimensional work such as photography. It can vary from appearing perfectly flat to receding into infinity (figure 18.4).
3. *Virtual space* exists within the confines of a computer screen or monitor. It may or may not exist in any concrete form.

Texture

Generally, smooth textures tend to create cool sensations and rough textures make for warm sensations. Texture and pattern are intertwined. A pattern on a piece of cloth gives us a visual sense of texture, letting us feel the differences in the surface

Figure 18.4
Conventional perspective tells us that objects always get small as they recede in distance. Pfahl makes use of pictorial space to set up an illusion that does not agree with our assumptions of reality.

© John Pfahl. *Six Oranges*, 1975. n/s. Chromogenic color print.

with our eyes, even though it does not exist to the touch. Texture offers changing sensations either by hand or eye.

Artists have purposefully introduced three-dimensional texture into media that was once considered to be exclusively two-dimensional. In this century, the cubists integrated other materials, such as newspapers and sand, into their paintings. This technique is now known as collage, from the French word *coller,* which means "to glue." Since then other artists have added three-dimensional objects into their work. These works are known as constructions. They are the textural element taken to the limit. The two kinds of texture that we need to be familiar with are tactile texture and light texture.

Tactile is a term that refers to actual changes in a surface that can be felt. They can be rough, smooth, hard, soft, wet, or dry. They possess three-dimensional characteristics.

Variations in light and dark produce visual texture, which is two-dimensional. This illusion is produced by the eye. The relationship of color placement within the composition and the use of depth of field can also determine the sense of visual texture (figure 18.5).

Figure 18.5
Visual texture plays a major compositional role in Hayashi's panoramic collage that speaks of the death of many industries in the Rust Belt section of America. She states: "I use color machine prints, 3 1/2 × 5 inches, to make the composite image. The 35-mm camera is placed on a tripod and pivots around 360 degrees to make the middle row. I angle my camera upward and then pivot around the tripod and then angle the camera downward and pivot around the tripod as I shoot."

© Masumi Hayashi. *Steel Mill, Clay Road*, 1988. 46 × 77 inches. Chromogenic color prints.

Pattern

Pattern is the unifying quality of an object. It is an interplay between shape, color, and space that forms a recognizable, repetitive, and/or identifiable unit. Pattern can unify the composition, establish a balance among diverse elements, or create a sense of rhythm and movement (figure 18.6).

The major difference between texture and pattern is degree. Do not get them confused. Pattern can possess visual texture, but not all texture contains a pattern. A single board has texture, but an entire row of boards creates a pattern. Pattern can be found in the repetition of design. In this case no single feature dominates. Its distinctive look is made possible by its repetitive quality. This form of pattern generally serves well as a background.

Surprises are possible when working with pattern. When elements are placed in repetition with other elements over a large area, they create new elements that may not be foreseen. These are often the result of negative space (the space around the design or playing through it). The shapes created by the interplay of the negative space become interesting themselves. Within the pattern these new shapes become apparent and begin to dominate so that the space or spaces can be the predominating visual factor.

Figure 18.6

Pattern is an interplay between color, shape, and space that forms a recognizable, repetitive, and/or identifiable unit, usually acting as a unifying compositional device. Graham uses the afternoon desert shadows to echo the structural patterning that unifies this scene of roadside vernacular architecture.

© David Graham. *Coffee Shop, South of Phoenix, AZ*, 1993. 24 × 20 inches. Chromogenic color print.

Unity and Variety

A composition devoid of any unifying element usually seems either haphazard or chaotic. A totally unified composition without variety is usually boring. Unity and variety are visual twins. Unity is the control of variety, but variety provides visual interest within unity.

The ideal composition is usually one that has a balance between these two qualities, diverse elements held together by some unifying device.

The repetition of shape, pattern, or size plus the harmony of color and texture are visual ways of creating unity. The more complex the composition, the greater the need for a unifying device. Variety can be introduced through the use of size, color, and texture, but in photography contrast is the major control—light against dark, large against small, smooth against rough, hard against soft. Dramatic lighting emphasizes these contrasts while soft lighting minimizes these differences.

Balance

Balance is the visual equilibrium of the objects in a composition (figure 18.7). Some categories of balance are as follows:

- *Symmetrical, bilateral, or two-sided balance.* If you draw a line through the center of this type of composition, both sides will be an equal mirror image. Symmetrical balance tends to be calm, dignified, and stable.

- *Asymmetrical balance.* Such as a composition that has equal visual weight, but the forms are disposed unevenly. Asymmetrical balance is active, dynamic, and exciting.

- *Radial balance.* This type of balance occurs when a number of elements point outward from a central hub, such as the spokes of a bike wheel. Radial balance can be explosive, imply directional movement, and indicate infinity.

- *Balance through color.* The weight of a color can become the focal point in a picture. Warm colors (red, magenta, yellow) tend to advance and/or have more visual weight than the cool colors (blue, green, cyan). The majority of landscape is composed of cool colors. Warm colors appear mainly as accents (flowers and birds). A small amount of red can be equal to a large area of blue or green. Much of the landscape in the American West is an exception. There are few trees and the predominant colors are the warm earth tones. During daylight hours with fair weather, the amount of cool color can be controlled by the proportion of sky

In this composition the play between color and shape provides a balance between the diverse elements that enables the artist to ask: "Is this cactus really camouflaged against this artificial representation of nature?"

© Biff Henrich. *Untitled,* 1991. 24 × 20 inches. Chromogenic color print.

Figure 18.7

Holt's image is in the tradition of René Magritte, the Belgian surrealist painter, whose misleading realism of common objects provided snapshots of the impossible. Holt relies on the visual weight of the yellow feather to act as a focal point to hold and balance this fantasy composition. This image was created by using a number of partially masked exposures on one sheet of film.

© David Holt. *Derby with Feather,* 1986. 20 × 25 inches. Chromogenic color print.

Figure 18.8

Jude's composition makes use of a series of points of emphasis. He stopped his lens down to f/32 to achieve maximum depth of field, thus creating several "frames" within the frame of the photograph. In the foreground the eye is immediately stopped by the leafy vine on the tree trunk. Next the eye moves into the middle ground, resting on the vine on the tree in the left corner. Now the two trees combine to form a visual arch that frames the background. The light color of the brick is contrasted against the darkness of the trees. These all combine to ensure the viewer will end up peering into the window and see the lamp and television, revealing a common American domestic scene.

© Ron Jude. *Oxford Avenue, Baton Rouge, LA,* 1990. 13 1/2 × 17 inches. Chromogenic color print.

that is included in the frame. The time of day and weather conditions also affect the amount of cool and warm colors, as the color temperature of the light changes.

- *Texture.* An area of texture can balance a large area of smooth surfaces.

Emphasis

Most photographs must have a focal point or points. There must be some element that attracts the eye and acts as a climax for the composition (figure 18.8). Without this, your eye tends to wander and is never satisfied. Focal devices to keep in mind are isolation, light, direction, height and angle, position, color, and size.

Rhythm

Rhythm is the visual flow accomplished by repetition, which can be evenly spaced points of emphasis (figure 18.9). It acts as a unifying device.

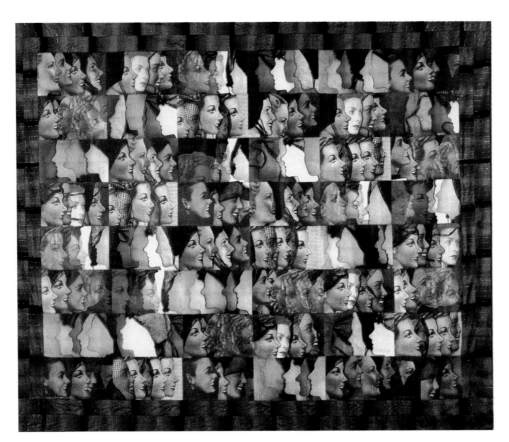

Figure 18.9

Rhythm is created by DeWitt through the repetition of shape and color at regular intervals. Original objects (1940s hairnet display heads) were placed on the platen of a Xerox 6500 color copier and an electrostatic color image was produced onto heat-transfer paper. A dry-mount press was used to transfer the image to 100 percent cotton cloth. Blocks of images were then assembled using a sewing machine. The finished social commentary takes the form of a traditional quilt with cloth border and backing. DeWitt says: "The repetition of the quilt structure is an ideal stage in which to play out a comment on the multitudes of staged smiles which gleam at us from advertising pages and video screens. The fixed grins and gleaming teeth seem to be more visibly transparent when you see many of them, all gazing sightlessly in concert."

© Rita DeWitt. *Too Many Airbrushed Smiles,* 1984. 81 × 96 inches. Electrostatic color transfers on cloth.

Figure 18.10

Mutter makes the viewer do a true double take as he not only plays with our sense of size relationships but also juxtaposes different architectural styles.

© Scott Mutter. *Standard Oil Building with Corinthian Top*, n.d. 12 × 9 inches. Chromogenic color print. Courtesy of J. J. Brooking Gallery. San Jose, CA.

Proportion

Proportion deals with the size relationships within a composition (figure 18.10). Shapes are proportional to the area they occupy within the composition. An example can be seen when making a portrait. If the circle formed by the head is 2 inches in diameter on a 4-inch background, it will be more disproportional than if it were placed on a 10-inch background.

Correct proportion is generally based on what society considers to be real or normal. Just because something is disproportionate does not make it wrong. On the contrary, it is often attention-getting and unique. Because of this, photographers deliberately change the proportions in a composition to create impact. The position of the camera and the distance of the subject from the lens are the easiest ways to distort proportion. Digital

technology makes it easier to make postvisualization modifications such as alterations in proportion and scale.

Scale

Scale indicates size in comparison to a constant standard, the size something "ought to be." By showing objects to be larger or smaller than normal, the viewer is made to see the form in a new way (figure 18.11). This encourages the audience to come to terms with it on a new level. Taking the familiar and making it unfamiliar can allow the viewer to see things that were once not visible.

Symbolism

We communicate through the use of symbols all the time. A symbol is anything that stands for something else. Usually a symbol is a simplified image that, because of certain associations in the viewer's mind, represents a more complex idea or system (figure 18.12).

Lines that form letters, words, or musical notes are symbols. A photograph is a symbol. A photograph of a person is not that person but a representation of the person. It stands for the person, which makes it a symbol.

Symbolism is a great power for the photographer. It permits the communication of enormously complicated, often abstract ideas with just a few lines or shapes. Symbols provide us tools for sorting information and drawing inferences that can aid in more effective communication. Symbols are the shorthand of the artist. Photography is a sign language. Learn to recognize and use the signs to your advantage.

The following categories of symbols are offered to get you thinking about what they can represent. Symbols are *not* absolute terms. They all have multiple readings based on factors such as cultural background, economic status, gender, psychological state, and political, religious, and sexual preference. The subsequent symbols and their conceivable meanings are provided only as a

Figure 18.11

In her series *Premonitions,* Formica makes use of scale as she foresees "an imaginary human extinction. I juxtapose miniature artifacts of Western Society with invertebrates and insects. . . . Due to the distorted scale relationship the opposed becomes the oppressor. The larger than life creatures take on a new significance addressing our perception of nature . . . by visually juxtaposing human artifacts with invertebrates, I hope to build a bridge between the two to show the similarities and complex intricacies of all living organisms."

© Jennifer Formica. *Mealworms with Silverware and Dishes,* 1994. 46 × 36 inches. Chromogenic color print.

Figure 18.12

Nagatani's montages combine powerful symbols of the traditional Hopi Indian culture with those of the contemporary military culture. He manufactures a scene that humorously voices the activities of human beings attempting to ward off their fear of nuclear destruction.

© Patrick Nagatani. *Koschare/Tewa Ritual Clowns. Missile Park, White Sands, NM,* 1989. 17 × 22 inches. Chromogenic color print.

starting point. Symbols are highly complex and each image requires its own reading. Reading and decoding images is a fluid process. Different people give different readings, and your own reading can also be subject to change.

The following are some general symbol categories:

- *Cosmic symbols* such as yin and yang (yin: feminine, dark, cold, wetness; yang: masculine, light, heat, dryness), the zodiac (stands for the forces that are believed to govern the universe), and the four humors within the body that control the personality (blood, phlegm, choler (bile), and melancholy).

- *Magical symbols* such as the Christmas tree, which originated in Rome as a fertility symbol, an emblem of plenty with fruits and nuts decorating it. Cave painting was used to help ensure a successful hunt. Tribal masks were employed for getting the desired results in battle, love, and the search for food. Masks let the wearers both disguise themselves and represent things of importance. This allows people the freedom to act out situations according to the desires of their inner fantasies.

- *Cultural symbols* are mythological or religious concepts that have been changed and incorporated by a culture and become symbolic for a cultural event. St. Nicholas, a tall serious fellow, is now a fat, jolly, and highly commercialized Santa Claus.

- *Religious symbols,* such as the cross, the Star of David, and the Buddha stand for the ideas behind the religion such as faith, generosity, forgiveness, hope, love, virtue, and the quest for enlightenment.

- *Traditional patterns* have been woven into the visual arts for thousands of years. While the pattern remains the same, its context and meaning are altered by the group that makes use of it. The swastika is a good example of how this works. It has been used as an ornament by the American Indians

Neon tubes provide the illumination as Iguchi scrutinizes historic Catholic iconography as it may appear in a contemporary context. Iguchi comments that "assimilating current ideas, materials, and techniques to represent traditional imagery sets up an irony that plays with our conventions and expectations."

© Josh Iguchi. *The Last Supper*, 1995. 45 × 102 inches. Chromogenic color print.

since prehistoric times. It has appeared as a symbol through the old world of China, Crete, Egypt, and Persia. In our time, its meaning was totally perverted, from one of well-being to that of death, when the German Nazi Party adopted it as the official emblem of the Third Reich.

- *Status symbols* indicate exact status or station in life of the owner: wedding rings, military insignia, coats of arms, cars, and clothes.

- *Patriotic and political symbols* in the United States include the Statue of Liberty, the bald eagle, the flag, political parties (elephant and donkey), and Uncle Sam. At a glance they provide a wealth of information and express certain concerns.

- *Commercial symbols* dispense information and/or advertise a service or product to be sold. Examples include three balls symbolizing the pawnbroker, the red-and-white pole signifying the barbershop, international road signs, and logos (Bell Telephone, National Broadcasting Company, Shell Oil, and MTV).

- *Psychological symbols* offer a system for investigating the conscious and

unconscious processes of the human mind. Sigmund Freud's *The Interpretation of Dreams,* and Carl Jung's *Man and His Symbols* are two watershed works that deal with these ideas. Filmmakers such as Ingmar Bergman and Francis Ford Coppola have emphasized the psychological side of human nature in their works.

- *Personal symbols* are symbols the artist creates to meet his or her particular needs. Some photographers whose works reflect these concerns include Man Ray, Lázsló Moholy-Nagy, Barbara Morgan, and Jerry Uelsmann.

Shapes and General Symbolic Associations

Shapes can also have symbolic meaning (figure 18.13). Some possible interpretations follow:

- The circle is associated with heaven, intellect, thought, the sun, unity, perfection, eternity, wholeness, oneness, and the celestial realm.

- The triangle can represent communication between heaven and earth, fire, the number three, the trinity, aspiration, movement, upward, return to origins, sight, and light.

Figure 18.13

Butkus's image relies on shapes to communicate some of his inner concerns. He states he wants to include objects that signify a more remote concept than the original activity. Components such as miniature toys, diagrams, cursive and gestural marks, industrial debris, and photographs themselves all point to a primary source. "Referring to these items in the photograph serves, for me, to create an ambiguity between the replica and its original form. This artificial framework allows me to elaborate and refine my understanding of earlier, more casual photographs (my own) or found objects and materials by juxtaposing and associating them with other strongly connotative elements. Through color, placement, layering, and other devices I hope to create an interpretation which reflects my interest in photographic observation and illusion."

© James M. Butkus. *Untitled 26*, 1986. 18 × 14 inches. Chromogenic color print.

- The square may represent firmness, stability, or the number four.

- The rectangle often denotes the most rational and most secure. It is used in grounding concrete objects.

- The spiral can illustrate the evolution of the universe, orbit, growth, deepening, cosmic motion, the relationship between unity and multiplicity, spirit, water, continuing ascent or descent.

- The maze delineates the endless search or a state of bewilderment or confusion.

Color Associations—Some Traditional Effects and Symbolism

Along with shapes, color has symbolic associations that have come down through ages in Western cultures.

- Red portrays sunrise, birth, blood, fire, emotion, wounds, death, passion, anger, excitement, heat, physical stimulation, and strengthening.

- Orange shows fire, pride, and ambition.

- Yellow indicates the sun, light, intuition, illumination, air, intellect, royalty, and luminosity (figure 18.14).

- Green depicts the earth, fertility, sensation, vegetation, water, nature, sympathy, adaptability, and growth.

- Blue signifies sky, thinking, the day, the sea, height, depth, heaven, innocence, truth, psychic ability, and spirituality.

- Violet marks nostalgia, memory, and advanced spirituality.

Common Symbols and Some Potential Associations

Consider these symbols and how their meanings can be used in your work (figure 18.15).

YELLOW

Figure 18.14

Garner explains: "Yellow is part of a book-length project called *An Art History of Ephemera: Gretchen Garner's Catalog,* a personal taxonomy of visual pleasures in the everyday urban landscape in Chicago. The power of the color is intensified through the collective impact of eight images. The slightly wide-angle lens created additional graphic impact by exaggerating the receding forms in space.

© Gretchen Garner. *An Art History of Ephemera: Yellow,* 1976–78. (Eight) 4 × 4 inches each. Chromogenic color prints.

- Air symbolizes activity, the male principle, creativity, breath, light, freedom, liberty, and movement.

- Fire represents the ability to transform, love, life, health, control, spiritual energy, regeneration, the sun, God, and passion.

- Water denotes feminine qualities, life, and the flow of the cycles of life.

- The earth suggests feminine qualities, receptiveness, solidity, and mother.

- Ascent indicates height, transcendence, inward journeying, and increasing intensity.

- Descent shows unconsciousness, potentialities of being, and animal nature.

- Duality suggests opposites, complements, and pairing.

- Unity signifies spirit, oneness, wholeness, centering, transcendence, harmony, revelation, supreme power, completeness in itself, light, and the divinity.

- Centering depicts thought, unity, timelessness, spacelessness, paradise, the Creator, infinity, and neutralizing opposites.

- The cross portrays the tree of life, axis of the world, ladder, struggle, martyrdom, and orientation in space.

- The dark illustrates the time before existence, chaos, and the shadow world.

- Light stands for the spirit, morality, all, creative force, the direction east, and spiritual thought.

- Mountains demonstrate height, mass, loftiness, the center of the world, ambition, and goals.

- A lake represents mystery, depth, and unconsciousness.

- The moon presents the feminine and fruitfulness.

- An eye illustrates understanding, intelligence, the sacred fire, and creativeness.

- The sun indicates the hero, knowledge, the divine, fire, the creative and life force, brightness, splendor, awakening, healing, and wholeness.

- Food stuffs represent abundance and give thanks to nature for providing what is needed to sustain life.

Figure 18.15

Some imagemakers do not like to make specific statements about their work. They prefer to leave it "open," not directing any particular response from the viewer. Some believe this encourages the audience to become more actively involved, sorting through the symbols in order to think out interpretation. Lesch said: "Artist's statements seem to me a bit like crowing hens; something best kept out of sight. Art, if it reflects life, should have as many interpretations as there are viewers. My opinions could be as likely to limit these interpretations as expand them."

© William Lesch. *Ocotilios and Sunset, Summer Thunderstorm*, 1988. 24 × 30 inches. Dye-destruction print.
Courtesy of Etherton Stern Gallery, Tucson, AZ.

In his *Throne Series,* Chong uses found chairs that are embellished and dedicated to ancestral and other spirit forces. "Offering of food, drink, and objects that are culturally or spiritually infused are offered upon and around the thrones that are meant to attract, appease or seat the deities." Chong uses symbolism to formulate a personalized mystical system that utilizes art as an expressive vehicle.

© Albert Chong. *Throne for Gorilla Spirits,* 1993. 50 × 40 inches. Dye-destruction print with copper frame.

Discover Your Own Interpretation

Now that you have read about symbols and some of their possible meanings, choose one or more of your own pictures and make a list of the symbols you discover in them. Write a description (an artist's statement) that decodes their meaning for others to consider. Remember, the viewer does not have to accept the photographer's meaning, known as *intentionalism.* Although the opinion of the maker can and should help provide clues for understanding the work, the photographer's interpretation should not be the only factor in determining the meaning or set the standard for other interpretations. Think of what Marcel Duchamp, a co-founder of the Dada group said: "It is the spectator who makes the picture."

References

Cirlot, J. E. *A Dictionary of Symbols,* 2d ed. New York: Philosophical Library, 1971.

Dondis, Donis A. *A Primer of Visual Literacy.* Cambridge, MA, and London: The MIT Press, 1973.

Hornung, C. P. *Hornung's Handbook of Design and Devices,* 2d ed. (1946) reprint, New York: Dover.

Jung, C. G. *Man and His Symbols.* Garden City, NY: Doubleday, 1964.

Working Applications with Color

©Erika Leppman.
Although I Am Attractive, 1991.
22 x 28 inches. Chromogenic color print.

Images appropriated from the films *Funny Face, The Eyes of Laura Mars,* and *Blow-Up.* The text reads: "Although I am attractive, I am not at all photogenic. I look terrible in most photographs. My boyfriend, however, loves to take photographs of me. I am continually captured for posterity with my face all screwed up because the sun is shining. If I'm in shadow, my hollow (not at all model-like) cheeks make me appear emaciated. He also has me standing and waiting forever while he sets up the picture. He doesn't warn me when he's ready to snap. By the time he does, my eyes are closed to get relief from the sun's glare, or my mouth is open (about to ask what's taking him so long), or a frown of irritation has appeared. But if I refuse to subject myself to this humiliation, I'm accused of selfishness!" Miss Manners—Judith Martin, *The Boston Globe,* June 15, 1983.

The Angle of View

One of the major tasks of the photographer is to define exactly what the subject *is*. This capacity to compose is what gives clarity and cohesion to the artist's experience. The angle of view, or vantage point, is one of the most important basic compositional devices that any photographer has to work with in determining how the image will be presented. It is such an elementary ingredient that it is often taken for granted and forgotten. The angle of view lets the photographer control balance, content, light, perspective, and scale within the composition. In color photography it also determines the saturation of the hues and whether or not they form color contrast or harmony. This chapter is designed to encourage you to remove some of the self-imposed limits on visualization and to break away from the accepted, standardized conventions, formulas, and procedures of representation.

Breaking the Eye-Level Habit

Many people simply raise the camera to eye level and push the button. A photographer explores the visual possibilities of the scene and attempts to find a way in which to present the subject in accordance with the desired outcome.

Altering the camera position does not cost anything or require any additional equipment, yet it can transform a subject and allow it to be presented in a new and different fashion. It can give the viewer more information or let the subject be seen in a way that was not possible before. It is the difference between seeing and sleepwalking through a scene.

Many times we simply sleepwalk through life because it is so familiar. We walk down a hall without seeing the hall because we have done it a thousand times before. We are merely somnambulists, reorienting ourselves. We know what to expect; everything is in check and in place. There is no opportunity for surprise, no chance for the unexpected to enter.

To see you must be awake, aware, and open. When seeing, you are letting things happen and not relying on past expectations and clichés to get you through the situation.

Seeing is being conscious of color and space. The more you look, the more you can penetrate the subject and then be able to see even more.

Methods of Working

Select a subject and proceed to discover how angle and light affect the final outcome. Here is a suggested method of approach:

1. Begin with a conventional horizontal shot at eye level, metering from the subject. Walk around the subject. Crouch down, lie down, stand on tiptoes, find a point that raises the angle of view above the subject. Notice how the direction of light either hides or reveals aspects of the subject. Move in closer to the subject and then get farther back than the original position. Now make a shot at a lower angle than the original eye-level view. Try getting the camera right on the ground. Look through the camera; move and twist around and see what happens to the subject. When it looks good, make another picture.
2. Think about changing the exposure. What happens if you expose for highlights? What about depth of field? Will a small, medium, or large f-stop help to create visual impact? How is the mood altered? All kinds of questions should be running through the photographer's head at this stage as part of the decision-making process. Answering them requires independent visual thinking. Try not to compete with fellow students. Competition tends to lead to copying of ideas and style. Copying means no longer discovering anything for yourself. Watch out for envy as it can also take away from your own direction. The best pictures tend to be those that are made from the heart as well as the mind.
3. Make a vertical shot. Decide whether to emphasize the foreground or background. How will this decision affect the viewers' relationship with the subject?
4. Get behind the subject and make a picture from that point of view. How is this different from the front view? What is gained and what is lost by presenting this point of view?
5. If possible, make a picture from above the subject. How does this change the sense of space within the composition?
6. Change the lens that you have been using. See what changes occur in the points of emphasis and spatial relationships due to depth of field.
7. Move in close. Henri Matisse, one of the foremost artists of the modern era, said, "It's like when you pass a cake shop, if you see the cakes through the window, they may look very nice. But, if you go inside the shop and get them right under your nose, one by one, *then* you're in business." Look for details that reveal the essence of the entire subject and photograph them. This method of simplification should speak directly and plainly to the viewer.
8. Move back. Make an image that shows the subject in relationship to its environment.
9. Now do something out of the ordinary. Using your instincts, make some pictures of the subject without looking into the camera. This can be a very freeing experience and can present composition arrangements that your conscious mind had been unable to think of using.
10. Do not be shy. If you cannot approach the subject from these diverse points of view, work with an inanimate object or a close friend. Choose a location or time of day when there are not other people around to make you feel overly self-conscious or inhibited.

The camera is society's license to approach the unapproachable in a manner

Most of the work in this series was shot "from the hip." Jude said "this allowed me to work spontaneously on the streets and achieve the radical perspectives that creates the stereotypical sense of looming and foreboding in the business men I was looking at. Because the prints were dark, I mounted them on plexiglas so they could be presented without glass. The overlaminate protects the print surface and is more pleasing to look at than a *naked print.*"

© Ron Jude. *Hand #17, Atlanta, GA* from *Executive Model*, 1992. 38 × 30 inches. Chromogenic color print on plexiglas with satin overlaminate. Courtesy of Jackson Fine Art, Atlanta, GA.

that would not otherwise be deemed acceptable in a normal social situation. Use this license to make the strongest possible statement without being irresponsible or infringing on the rights of others (see the section on the photographer's special license in chapter 18).

Working the Angles

Here are five basic angles and some of their general characteristics to consider:

1. The *bird's-eye view* is photographed from high above the subject and can be very disorientating. We don't normally see life from this perspective, thus the subject or event may initially appear unidentifiable, obscure, or abstract. It enables the viewer to hover over the subject from a God-like perspective (figure 19.1). The subject appears insignificant, reenforcing the idea of fate or destiny—that something the subject can't control is going to happen. Filmmakers such as Martin Scorsese combine overhead views, ambience, and action into a seamless atmosphere of expectation. Shots made from extreme angles are favored by haptic/expressionistic photographers. They confine the audience to a particular point of view, which may be very subjective. Wide-angle lenses are often employed with extreme angles to further exaggerate the sense of space.

2. *High-angle shots,* though less extreme than bird's-eye views, can provide a general overview of the subject. The importance of the surrounding environment is increased. The setting can overwhelm the subject. As the angle increases, the importance of the subject is diminished. It can indicate vulnerability, a reduction in strength, or the harmlessness of the subject. The angle can deliver a condescending view of the subject by making the subject appear helpless, entrapped, or out of control. It reduces the height of objects and the sense of movement is slowed down. It is not good for conveying a sense of motion or speed. It can be effective for showing a situation that is wearisome or oppressive.

3. *Eye-level shots* are more neutral, dispassionate, and less manipulative than high- or low-angle ones. The eye-level shot tends to let viewers make up their own minds about a situation. It presents a more ordinary, normal view of how we see the everyday world. This shot is a favorite style of visual/realistic photographers because it puts the subject on a more equal

footing with the observer. A normal focal length lens is usually used when working in this mode.

4. *Low angles* have the opposite effect of high ones. They increase the height of the subject and convey a sense of verticality. They tend to present an added dimension to the sense of motion. The general environment is diminished in importance; the ceiling or the sky becomes more predominant. The importance or visual weight of the subject is increased. A person becomes more heroic and bigger than life (figure 19.2). A figure can also become more looming, dominating the visual space, thus making the viewer feel insecure. Photographing a person from below can inspire awe, fear, or respect. In a landscape, it can help to create a sense of greater spatial depth by bringing added importance to the foreground.

5. *Oblique angles* occur when the camera is tilted, making for an unstable horizon line. It throws everything out of balance, because the natural horizontal and vertical lines in a scene are forced into unstable diagonal lines. A person photographed at an oblique angle appears to be falling to one side. Oblique angles are disorientating to the viewer. They may suggest anxiety, the imbalance of a situation, impending movement, tension, or transition. It can indicate a precarious situation that is about to change.

Contrast with Color

In black-and-white photography contrast is created by the difference between the darkest and lightest areas of the picture. When working with color materials, the intensity and the relationship of one color to another play a vital role in creating contrast.

Figure 19.1

The photographer's vantage point can add information to the composition and increase the viewer's desire to spend time looking at the work by presenting work in a way that is not familiar. This aerial landscape photograph, made at about 500 feet elevation, is part of a large body of work documenting the factors that influence water quality in the Stillagumish River watershed. Abrahamson adds: "I especially like how the aerial perspective abstracts the landscape, and details the relationships between the watershed's geography and the factors that influence its water quality. I'm not sure if the electromagnetic radiation has deleterious effects on the trees, but it surely can't be beneficial to the people who live or work in close proximity."

© Mark Abrahamson. *Electromagnetic Yule Tree Farm*, 1990. 19 1/2 × 12 3/4 inches. Dye-destruction print.

Figure 19.2
In her exploration of point of view Lang's models are placed on a tall Plexiglas scaffolding and photographed from below. "The studio construction alters the play of gravity on the subject, making the workings of the body visible. The Plexiglas works as a barrier on both a physical and metaphorical level. It shows exactly how far the body can go, makes visible the limitations of the flesh. We, as viewers, stand on the other side of the Plexiglas. We can look in and see people with their families and friends, see traces of their lives, the choices they have made."

© Cay Lang. *American Body Series #26*, 1990. 20 × 24 inches. Chromogenic color print.

Complementary Colors

Complementary colors, opposite each other on the color wheel, make the most contrast (figure 19.3). The subtractive combinations of blue against yellow, green against magenta, and red against cyan form the strongest color contrasts. When looking at the reflected colors of a final print some people prefer to use the pigment primary combinations of red against green, blue against orange, and yellow against purple as the basis of their discussion. This allows the photographic print to be examined with the same language as the other visual arts, such as painting.

It is thought that complementary colors create such contrast because of fatigue in the rods and cones of the retina. This is because each of these wavelengths cannot be accommodated by the human eye at the same time. Think of it as a zoom lens that is going back and forth between its minimum and maximum focal lengths, while attempting to maintain critical focus. This is what the eye tries to do with complementary colors.

Cool and Warm Colors

Cool and warm colors can be used to create contrast. Warm colors tend to advance and are called active colors. The cool colors tend to recede and are generally more passive (figure 19.4). Dark colors against light ones produce contrast, too. Desaturated colors played next to a saturated one make for contrast. Pastel colors can provide contrast if there is enough separation between the colors on the color wheel.

Creating Color Contrast

Color contrast can emphasize the subject if photographed against a complementary background. Areas of contrasting colors can create a visual restlessness that can give a sense of movement within the scene. Active and

Figure 19.3

This series of images was created by painting titanium and niobium metal sheets with electricity. Applying DC current with a paint brush dipped in water and baking soda, the metal oxidizes, creating light interference colors. Specific voltages were selected to create each color, and a grinder is applied for texture. The metal sheet, about 10 × 14 inches, is then photographed with a 4-×-5-inch camera. Dozens of complex, multiple exposures are required to achieve the desired shadow, depth, and highlight.

© Jay S. Dunitz. *Pacific Light #36*, 1986. 40 × 54 inches. Dye-destruction print.
Courtesy of Susan Spiritus Gallery, Costa Mesa, CA and Obscura Gallery, Denver, CO.

Figure 19.4

Warm and cool colors can be used to create contrast in color. Warm colors are active and tend to advance in visual space while cool colors are more passive and tend to recede. Feldstein makes use of this to play the cool colors against the warm colors. This creates more intense color contrast and a vibrant, abstract composition.

© Peter Feldstein. *#03–82*, 1982. 30 × 40 inches. Dye-destruction print.

passive colors can flatten the visual space and bring patterns to the forefront. Warm and cool colors can be used to produce a sense of balance within the picture. Dynamic tension can be built by placing active colors next to each other in the composition.

Make a photograph that incorporates one of the following color contrast effects:

1. *Complementary contrast.* Use colors that are opposite one another on the color wheel, such as a yellow building against a blue sky.
2. *Active and passive contrast.* Use a warm color against a cool one. The proper proportions of each are critical in making this work.
3. *Primary contrast.* The juxtaposition of two primary colors can make for a bright, vibrant, and strong sense of feeling.
4. *Passive contrast.* A quiet, easy, restful mood can be achieved by using a neutral background as a staging area. A simple, dark backdrop can be employed to offset a light area and slow down the visual dynamics of the picture.
5. *Complex contrast.* Complex contrast uses many contrasting primary colors and requires careful handling or the point of emphasis can become confused or lost in an array of colors. With the proper treatment, the multicolored use of contrast can cause tremendous visual excitement and provide a strong interplay of the objects within a composition as well as connecting seemingly diverse elements.

Color Harmony

Harmonic colors are closely grouped together on the color wheel and present a limited group of colors (figure 19.5). Any quarter section of the color wheel is considered to show color harmony. The simplest harmonic compositions contain only two colors that are desaturated in

Figure 19.5
Frazier used drawing, painting, sculpture, and xerography to make an illusory image that has the qualities of the actual site when viewed through the camera. The final construction is photographed, completing the process of deferring the reality presented in the image. The construction is destroyed after this process is completed. Frazier states: "They [the photographs] picture sites which are part of our culture, and extinct at the same time. They document a Grand Tour never taken. These photoworks create a document of society's propensity toward cultural and political obsolescence. The viewer might be reminded of the temporal nature of all civilizations." In terms of photo history, this image parodies the work of Timothy O'Sullivan and Ansel Adams as well as traditional tourist snapshots.

© Bill Frazier. *Simulations—Souvenirs from Extinct Civilizations: Canyon de Chelly*, 1987. 20 × 16 inches. Chromogenic color print.

appearance. The absence of any complementary colors makes it easier to see the subtle differences in these adjacent hues. Evenness in light and tone can help bring out the harmonic color relationship. Saturated colors that may be technically close to each other on the color wheel can still produce much contrast and interfere with the harmony.

Color harmony is found everywhere in nature. Passive colors tend to be peaceful and harmonize more easily than the warm, active hues.

Harmony Is Subjective

Harmony is a subjective matter, and its effectiveness depends on the colors involved, the situation, and the effect that the photographer wants to produce. The actual visual effect depends on the colors themselves. Blue and violet are adjacent to each other on the color wheel, therefore, by literal definition, in harmony, but the effect that is created tends to be visually subdued. Go to the other side of the wheel and take orange and yellow. These two colors harmonize in an animated fashion.

Harmonic effects can be reinforced through the linkage of colors. This is accomplished by repeating and weaving the harmonic colors throughout the composition. This places importance on patterns and shapes within the picture. Soft, unsaturated colors in diffused light have been a traditional way of creating harmonious relationships of colors. Special attention in framing the picture is necessary. Be aware of exactly what is in all corners of the frame. Eliminate any hue that can interfere with the fragile interplay of the closely related colors.

In an urban, human-made environment there is a great possibility of encountering discordant, unharmonious colors. This happens when contrasting colors are placed next to each other in such a way to create a jarring, or even unpleasant, combination to view. Care in the use of light, the angle of view, and the right mixture and proportions of these discordant colors can introduce balance and vitality into a flat or static composition.

Methods to Create Harmony

Basic techniques to orchestrate a mood of unison include using a slight amount of filtration in front of the lens that matches the cast of the color of the light in the scene and desaturating the hues through the use of diffused light or using a soft filter in front of the lens. Differences in diverse colors can be deemphasized by incorporating neutral areas, which provide balance within the picture. Both contrasting and harmonic colors can be linked together by working with the basic design elements such as repeating patterns and shapes. Look for common qualities in balance, rhythm, texture, and tone to unite the colors.

· A S S I G N M E N T ·

Make a harmonic color picture from one of the following areas:

1. Color harmony as found in nature. Pay close attention to the compositional location of the horizon line. Make a landscape that does not follow the traditional compositional rule of thirds. Photograph a scene with little or no sky. Make a skyscape with little or no foreground. Be on the lookout for symmetry in nature. One way to get repetition is to include reflections. This can be especially useful when there is water in the picture. If the harmony produced by cool colors is too uninviting or standoffish, try to add a small area of a muted complementary color. This can draw warmth and interest back into the scene. Look for a detail from the landscape that can provide what you are after in a simplified and condensed manner. Showing less can let the viewer see more.

2. Urban color harmony. Find a place where people have consciously and deliberately made an effort to blend human-made creations into an overall scheme. Flat lighting can be used to play down the differences in the various color combinations within an urban setting. Smooth, early morning light can be employed for the same

effect. Try to avoid the visual hustle and bustle that tend to bring forth visual chaos. Finding scenes of calmness and stillness within a busy cityscape will help to achieve harmony.

3. Still life is a perfect vehicle for creating a working color harmony. The photographer can assume total responsibility for controlling the arrangement of the objects, the background, the quality of light, and the camera position to ensure a harmonic composition. The sparing and subtle use of filters can enhance the mood of harmony.

4. Portraits in harmony can be created by simplifying the background, selecting clothes and props to go with the subject, and using neutral colors and similar shapes. Soft directional lighting can minimize complementary colors. Placing tracing paper in front of any light source is a simple and inexpensive way to diffuse the light and gain control. A bare bulb flash can be valuable in a situation of this nature.

Figure 19.6
Dominant color compositions are established when the colors themselves become the major focus/subject of the composition The color relationships become the prime movers, expressing emotion and mood. There is less emphasis on identifying and relating to subject matter. The viewing experience becomes more subjective. Color is used to express what cannot be said through the conventional use of established forms and symbols. Doherty used fill flash to intensify the luminosity of the red table surrounded by the dark blue canvas walls.

© Dornith Doherty. *Red Table*, 1988. 32 × 40 inches. Chromogenic color print.

Dominant Color

Dominant color occurs when the subject of the picture becomes color itself (figure 19.6). The painter Paul Cézanne observed, "When color is at its richest, form is at its fullest." Painting movements such as abstract expressionism, color-field painting, and op art have explored different visual experiences that are created through the interplay of color. Works that make use of this method tend to use color itself to express emotions or mood. The color relationships can affect all the ingredients that make up a picture. Colors can be used to create calm or tension. They can create the illusion of depth or make things appear flat.

Simplicity

When putting together a composition keep things simple. Beware of incorporating too

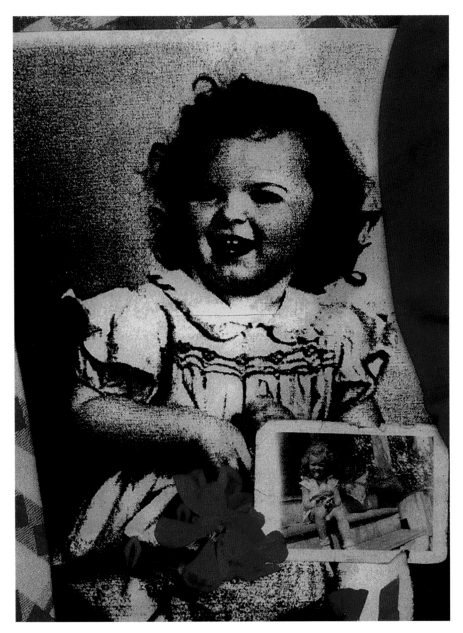

Figure 19.7
Nicholson uses isolated color as a compositional device in her explorations of family emotional issues. Nicholson makes "collages to clarify my own thoughts about aging, illness, and relationships. The work is memorial and uses personal objects, such as handwriting, hair, photos, fabric, and clothing."

© Gail Nicholson. *Posing Eva May,* 1987. 8 1/2 × 11 inches. Electrostatic print.

the subject. Don't let the two clash, or the viewer may have a difficult time determining what the purpose of the picture is. Don't send conflicting or confusing messages to the audience. Be straightforward and provide a well-marked visual path for the eye. Strong colors attract attention. Do something with it once you have it. Shape becomes important. Use tight, controlled framing to make strong graphic effects. Get close and eliminate the nonessentials. A neutral or even black background can make the color stand out.

· ASSIGNMENT ·

Plan and execute a photograph that demonstrates your understanding of dominant color.

Isolated Use of Color

The energy and the visual spark of a hue depends more on its placement within a scene than on the size of the area it occupies. Imagine a scene of cool, harmonious colors that are even, smooth, and unified. Now add a dot of red. Pow! It surprises the eye and instantly becomes the point of emphasis. Its solitariness stands out as a point of beauty. Its individuality introduces needed variety into the picture space.

Most colors have the greatest luminance when they appear against a neutral setting. Warm colors visually step forward, adding depth and sparkle into a picture that was flat. On an overcast or dusty day in which everything looks and feels of the same dimension, add a small amount of a warm hue and contrast, depth, drama, emphasis, and variety appear out of this sameness. Warm colors can also be used as dynamic backgrounds that offset and/or balance monochromatic subject matter. Do not underestimate the power a single individual color can have on the entire composition (figure 19.7).

Advanced Planning

Often getting this single color in the right place at the right time requires

many colors into the picture. This can create visual confusion because the different colors will be in competition to dominate. Let one hue clearly predominate. The proportions of the colors in the scene will determine which is the strongest. A small area of a warm color such as red can balance and dominate a much greater area of cool color such as green.

Dominance may be achieved with a small area of a bright color against a field of flat color. A large area of subdued

color can also be dominant. The value of a hue is a relative quality and changes from situation to situation (see section on color description in chapter 5).

Maintaining a Strong Composition

The dominant color must retain a working arrangement with the main point of interest in the picture. If color is not the subject itself, then it should reinforce and enhance the photographer to be ready in advance. Anticipating the moment greatly increases the likelihood of this happening. Coordinating the light, background, and proportion of the isolated color means the photographer needs to feel confident and comfortable with the equipment and techniques used. Practice and readiness are the prerequisites that let the imagemaker take advantage of chance.

Check the situation out carefully. Ask in advance, Which lens is needed to get the correct proportion of that single color into the composition? Be ready to improvise. If the lens that is needed is not available, will getting closer or farther away make it work? Approach each new situation with openness, which allows adapting and accommodating the subject without becoming static or hackneyed.

Working Plan

Getting the right amount of a unified color background is generally one of the first items necessary to catch this touch of color in the picture. Next comes the actual placement of that hue. Third is being sure of the correct exposure.

For example, a monochromatic sky is the backdrop and the spot of warm color is located on ground level in the shadow area. There are a number of exposure possibilities available depending on the desired outcome. If detail is to be retained in both areas, take a meter reading from the sky and one from the foreground and average them together. If the sky is f/8 and the ground is f/4, the exposure for that situation would be f/5.6. If detail in the foreground area is critical, expose for the key shadow area by getting in close or tilting the camera meter down so the sky is not included. If the light is similar where you are standing, meter off your hand. The sky receives more exposure than necessary. If this is not corrected for during development, the sky can be burned in when the print is created.

Figure 19.8
In a work that directly references process, Henrich printed his black-and-white negative on color paper to produce a monotone effect for what he refers to as his "subjectless" compositions.

© Biff Henrich. *Untitled*, 1993. 20 × 24 inches. Chromogenic color print.

Movement creates visual excitement. It can be produced by placing the camera on a tripod and using a slow shutter speed to introduce a warm object in motion against a static monochrome setting.

· ASSIGNMENT ·

Use one of these suggestions to make a photograph that relies on an isolated color to achieve its effect.

Monochrome

Some people think that a good color photo must include every hue in the spectrum. Often reducing the number of colors in the composition creates more of an effect than assaulting the viewer with the rainbow.

What Is Monochrome?

A narrow definition of a monochromatic photograph would be one that uses only a single hue from any part of the spectrum. In a broader sense it can indicate a photograph that creates the total effect of one color, even though there are other hues present.

When putting together a monochrome picture, the photographer can call into play knowledge, judgments, and understanding of composition that have been developed in black-and-white photography (figure 19.8).

The Subjective Nature of Monochrome

Monochromatic photographs can create powerful moods. Monochrome simplifies the composition so that we tend to react more subjectively and less rationally. The photograph is taken not so much as a document to be read for information but as an event that elicits a sense of time and place. It can alter the normal flow of time and flatten the sense of visual space.

Color Contamination

When dealing with a monochromatic image, beware of what is referred to as environmental color contamination. This occurs when a colored object within the scene reflects its color onto other items within the picture area. Color contamination can occur when a photographer's bright plaid shirt reflects back onto the subject. Often objects within the composition spill their color onto their neighbor. This is most noticeable when working with white items. It is possible for a white object to make another white object appear to be off-white. Careful observation of the scene and the arrangement and selection of objects to be photographed is the best way to deal with this problem.

Exposure

Exposure is critical to maintaining a fragile color and atmosphere. Monochromes need not lack contrast. Subdued colors and harmonious colors can be employed to give monochromatic impressions.

Aerial Perspective

Colors in distant scenes are muted by the atmospheric scattering of light, so tones appear progressively paler as the landscape recedes. This is known as aerial perspective. The blending and softening of colors in this condition can help to create a monotone rendition of a scene. Aerial perspective also makes distant objects more blue.

> **· A S S I G N M E N T ·**

Make a photographic image that uses the monochromatic color concepts to create its visual power. The following situations offer starting places for monochromatic pictures in which both the color and detail are simplified: early morning, late in the day, storms, rain droplets, dust, pollution, smoke, iced or steamed windows, plus scenes that contain diffused light and lower-than-average contrast. Other techniques that can be employed to mute colors include deliberate "defocusing" (putting the entire image out of focus) or selective focusing, moving the camera while the shutter is open, soft focus methods such as a diffusion or soft focus screen, and the use of filters.

Perspective

Perspective allows the artist to give two-dimensional work the illusion of the third dimension and furnishes depth (figure 19.9). Light and shadow begin to provide depth, but the actual illusion that one item in the composition is closer to the front than the other is brought about through the use of perspective.

Basic Types of Perspective Control

The following are eight basic types of perspective control commonly used in photography:

1. *Aerial perspective* is the effect in which colors and tones become blurred, faded, and indistinct with distance due to atmospheric diffusion. The colors in the foreground are brighter, sharper, and warmer and have a darker value than those farther away. There is a proportional decrease in luminance and warmth with distance, which can be reduced with a UV and/or warming filter such as the 81A and 81B.

2. *Diminishing scale* creates depth by using the fact that we assume that the farther an object is from the viewer the smaller it seems. By composing with something large in the foreground and something smaller in the middle or background the photographer can add to the feeling of depth. It is also possible to trick the viewer's sense of depth by reversing this order.

3. *Position* makes the visual assumption that objects, when placed in a higher position within the picture, are farther back in space than those toward the bottom of the frame. The same rules that apply to diminishing scale apply to position.

4. *Linear perspective* happens when parallel lines or planes gradually converge in the distance. As they recede, they seem to meet at a point on the horizon line and disappear. This is called the vanishing point.

5. *Two-point linear perspective* can be achieved by photographing the subject from an oblique angle (an angle that is not a right angle; it is neither parallel nor perpendicular to a given line or plane). This is most easily seen in a subject that has vertical parallel lines such as a building. When viewed from a corner, two walls of the building seem to recede toward two vanishing points rather than one. The closer the corner of the building is to the center of your composition, the more a sense of depth, distance, and space is attained. If the building is placed in one of the corners of the frame it flattens one of the walls while making the other look steep.

6.. *Overlapping perspective* occurs when one shape in the picture is placed in front of another, partially obscuring what is behind it. This is a good compositional device to indicate depth.

7. *Selective focus* is another method open to photographers to create the illusion of depth. To the eye a critically focused object set off by an unsharp object appears to be on a different plane. Employing the maximum lens opening is a way to separate the foreground from the middle ground and background. Since the depth of field is extremely limited, whatever is focused on appears sharp, while the detail in the remainder of the picture is destroyed. Placing a wide-angle lens so near a subject that it can not be sharply focused encourages the viewer to actively search the picture for something sharp. Using a

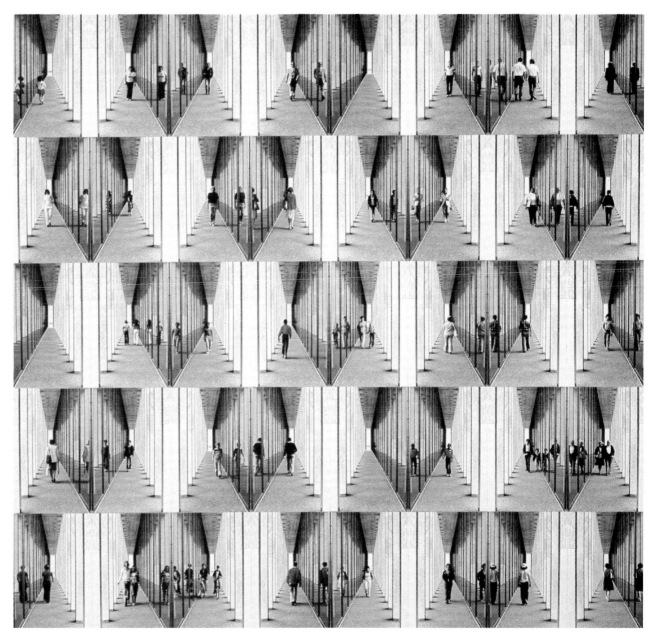

Figure 19.9
Linear perspective is revealed by Crable's use of camera placement plus repetition to create the illusion of depth, distance, and space. The neutral color scheme is broken up with accents of warm colors to create contrast.

© James Crable. *Empire State Plaza, Albany, NY*, 1985. 28 × 28 inches. Chromogenic prints.
Courtesy of J. J. Brookings Gallery, San Jose, CA.

longer-than-normal focal length lens reduces the amount of depth of field at any given f-stop. The longer the focal length of the lens, the less depth of field it will have at any given aperture.

8. *Limiting depth* can be accomplished visually by incorporating a strong sense of pattern into the composition, which tends to flatten the sense of space in the picture.

Converging Lines

A common problem photographers run into when dealing with perspective is converging vertical lines. For example, when trying to make a picture of the entire front of a tall building, it is possible that the camera may have to be slightly tilted to take it all in or that a wide-angle lens is necessary; both of these options cause the vertical lines to converge.

Convergence can be visually pleasing because it emphasizes a sense of height.

If you need to maintain correct perspective and keep the vertical parallel and straight, a perspective-control shift lens is required on a 35-mm camera. On a larger-format camera raising the front or tilting the rear allow for perspective correction. It is possible to minimize this effect by moving farther away from the building and using a longer focal length

Monocular vision, seeing the world from a single, linear viewpoint, is a construct at the heart of classical Aristotelian thinking. This allows Westerners to position themselves at the center of their "uni-verse." Conversely, traditional Native Americans see the world as a "multi-verse" that accepts that there is not one truth, but many. By painting on photographs Odgers hopes "to access a more 'whole world' way of seeing, much like the cubists sought with their simultaneous viewpoints and layered thinking. I am seeking a way of working that not only transcends the usual Western dualistic thinking by unifying what we consider 'opposites'—classical vs. modernist and postmodernist sensibilities, photographic vs. painterly sensibilities, surface vs. implied depth, even work vs. play—but also by thematically unifying the masculine with the feminine, the primal and the classical with the contemporary and the East with the West." As the poet Wallace Stevens observed: "Reality is not what it is. It consists of many realities which it can be made into."

© Jayme Odgers. *Construct #1*, 1991. 60 × 48 inches. Dye-destruction print with mixed media.

Make a photograph that deals with at least one of the uses of perspective covered in this chapter.

Subdued Color

Subdued color photographs tend to possess a uniform tonality and contain unsaturated hues. Soft, flat light mutes colors. Subdued colors can often be found in aged and weathered surfaces. Color can be subdued by adding black, gray, or white through the use of lighting or exposure or by selecting desaturated tones. Low levels of light reduce saturation. Delicate colors can occur in failing evening light with shadows adding gray and black. Any form of light scattering, such as flare or reflection, introduces white, thus desaturating the colors. Choice of backgrounds can make certain colors appear less saturated. A limited or low range of tones mutes color and can be used to induce drama, mystery, sensuality, and the element of the unknown (figure 19.10).

Working Techniques

Some techniques to consider when working with subdued color include the following:

- Use light that will strike the subject at a low angle.

- Expose for the highlights, which lets the shadows be dark and deep. Bracket the exposures until you are able to judge what the final effect will be.

- Minimize background detail by using a higher shutter speed and a larger lens opening.

- Let the subject block out part of the main source of illumination. This produces a rim lighting effect, which also reduces the overall color contrast and tonal range.

- Have a dark, simple, uncluttered background.

lens. This is often not possible in a cramped urban setting. If negative film is being used, there is one course of action still available. In the printing stage, it is possible to tilt the easel upward to correct the converging vertical. If the enlarger permits, tilt the lens stage as well

to maintain image sharpness. Use a steady prop to make sure the easel does not move, focus in the middle of the picture after the easel is in position, and use the smallest lens opening possible to get maximum depth of focus.

Figure 19.10
Harold-Steinhauser made a "reverse" photogram, which she sepia-toned and softly hand-colored with oil, india ink, acrylic, and oil pastels.

© Judith Harold-Steinhauser. *Tulip Tango*, 1984. 14 × 11 inches. Gelatin silver print with mixed media.

Figure 19.11
Haberfeld makes use of tungsten and Roscolux lights to alter the colors in his constructed compositions and thus the viewer's reaction. He says: "I prefer not to discuss content. It is there, but private. The audience supplies their meaning, and hopefully wonders about mine. This may create a little mystery and poetry."

© Aaron C. Haberfeld. *Tablets I*, 1989. 11 × 11 inches. Chromogenic color print.

- Select the major color scheme of dark hues.

- Work with a diffused or weak source of illumination. This often occurs naturally in fog, mist, or storms. This effect also reduces the scene's tonal range.

- Use a diffusion filter. If you do not have one, improvise with a stocking or a piece of cloth.

- Work with a limited color scheme.

· **ASSIGNMENT** ·

Make use of at least one of these ideas to produce a photograph that relies on subdued color for its impact.

Favorite and Unfavorite Colors

Everyone seems to respond positively to certain colors and negatively to others. This also applies to combinations of colors. Think about what colors are most often included in your own work. Do these colors appear regularly in other areas of your life such as in the colors of the clothes you wear or in how you have decorated your living quarters? Which colors do not make many appearances in your work? Are these colors also avoided in other aspects of your life?

Picture Ideas

Possible pictures to shoot with favorite and unfavorite colors including:

- Make one picture that emphasizes your favorite color or combination of colors. What are the qualities of these colors that are appealing to you?

- Make another picture that deals with colors that you have an aversion to. What is it about these colors that puts you off?

- Change the color of a known object through the use of light or paint at the time of exposure or through the use of an unnatural filter pack when printing (figure 19.11).

Overcoming Color Bias

After making these pictures, look at them and see what associations are created for you from these colors. What effect is created by changing the natural color of an object? It is possible, by working with a color that you dislike, to see that something beautiful and meaningful can still be created? This teaches us that our preferences and dislikes in color and in life often result from prejudices, which are a manifestation of fear caused by inexperience, lack of insight, and the failure to think for ourselves. Do you really hate the color orange or was it your mother's least favorite color? Question yourself about these things. Keep your possibilities open so that you can achieve your full potential.

Figure 19.12

In Campus's work, opposites are stated but never reconciled. Nature is removed from its context and superimposed on another computer-based universe. There is a play between the intellectual and the sensuous and the synthetic and the natural. The organic appears arrested and rigid while the inanimate becomes active and transmutable, leaving the viewer to ruminate on their relationship.

© Peter Campus. *as if on wings*, 1994. 25 3/8 × 36 1/16 inches. Iris ink jet print.
Courtesy of Paula Cooper Gallery, New York, NY.

Pairs of Contrast

Use color to make pictures that express pairs of contrast. The object of prime visual importance is not only the actual subject matter in the scene but the colors that make up the scene. It is the colors themselves that should be used to express the ideas of contrast.

Counterpoints

Consider these counterpoints: old and new, happy and sad, old and young, large and small, soft and hard, high and low, bright and dull, fast and slow, evil and good, calm and stormy, peaceful and warlike, hate and love, apathy and decisiveness, individual and group, female and male, intimacy and distance, seduction and horror. Counterpoints can also be purely visual in nature, angular and flowing, or sharp and circular. Counterpoints may also be more conceptual, relying on the play of opposites, such as inner and outer reality or the natural and the fabricated (figure 19.12).

• A S S I G N M E N T •

Make a photograph that deals with the use of pairs or counterpoints (such as those listed in the previous section) as its major theme.

Reaction to Counterpoints

What are your reactions to these pairs of color contrasts? Are they what you expected? When shown to an audience, do the reactions to the color associations seem to be consistent or do they vary widely from person to person? What does this tell you about the nature of color response?

The Interaction of Color, Movement, Space, and Time

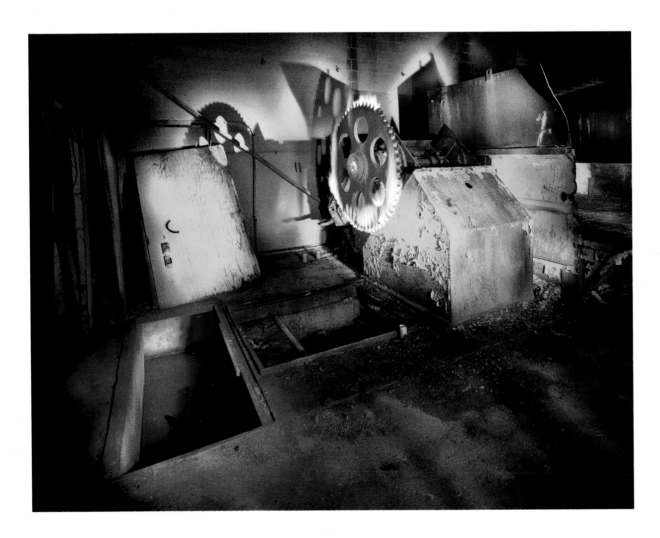

© Patrick T. Darby & Trevor C. Davis.
Hutchinson Island, Savannah, GA, #10, 1995.
16 × 20 inches. Chromogenic color print.

The Search for Time

Most of us, like St. Augustine, think we know what time is until someone asks us to explain it. Even for contemporary scientists the nature of time remains mysterious. In 1905, Albert Einstein's Theory of Relativity revealed that commonly held concepts concerning time were not always true. For instance, Newton's notion that time moved at a constant rate was proved wrong when it was demonstrated that time passes more slowly for rapidly moving objects as compared to slow ones. The conviction that two events separated in space could happen at precisely the same time—simultaneity—was shown to be false. Whether two events appear to happen at the same time depends on the viewer's vantage point, and no one observer has any intrinsic claim to be the authority.

Einstein's work produced even more fantastic conclusions about time. For example, clocks run faster at the top of a building than in the basement. Succinctly, Einstein tells us there is no universal time or no master clock regulating the essence of the cosmos. Time is relative and it depends on motion and gravity. Time and space are not simply "there" as a neutral, unchanging backdrop to nature. They are physical things, malleable and mutable, no less so than matter, and subject to physical law.

The Flow of Time

When most of us think of a photograph, we still tend to think only of a tiny slice of time, removed from the flow of life with a frame around it. Everything is still, nothing moves. That brief instant of time is there for examination. The Western convention of reality, based on Renaissance perspective, has come to dictate that everything be presented like evidence at a trial—clear and sharp. "The more readable the detail, the better the picture," is a photographic maxim that has been the standard of a picture's worth for many people. This has been based on the assumed modeling of the camera, with its lens and film, to that of the human eye, with its lens and retina. A number of critical thinkers in photography have been challenging this concept.

The notion that a photograph shows us what we would have seen had we been there ourselves has to be qualified to the point of absurdity. A photograph shows us "what we would have seen" at a certain moment in time, *from* a certain vantage point *if* we kept our head immobile *and* closed one eye *and if* we saw things in Agfacolor. . . . By the time all the conditions are added up, the original position has been reversed: instead of saying that the camera shows us what our eyes would see, we are now positing the rather unilluminating proposition that, if our vision worked like photography, then we would see things the way a camera does.[1]

This chapter calls into question basic photographic axioms dealing with the representation of space and time. This is not meant to discourage photographers from working in this traditional mode but to encourage growth in unexplored territory.

Controlling Photographic Time Through the Camera

While relativity mathematics shows how the rate of time differs depending on velocity, it does not explain why time seems to pass more slowly, or more rapidly, depending on how boring a given activity is or how eagerly we anticipate a future event. This chapter encourages the photographer to engage great riddles that even stumped Einstein, such as the glaring mismatch between physical time and subjective or psychological time.

Another major ramification of relativity is that time is not a series of moments—some not yet having occurred—but rather a block in which we exist at a specific position, much the way we exist at one point in space. The rest of the universe exists even though we are only in one place at one time; perhaps the remainder of time exists even though we have not visited the future. Since Einstein, physicists have generally rejected the notion that events "happen," as opposed to merely *existing* in the four-dimensional space-time continuum. The discrepancy between the frozen "block time" of physics and the flowing subjective time of the human mind suggests the need to rethink our concepts about time. Most humans find it impossible to relinquish the sensation of flowing time and a moving present moment. It is so basic to our daily experience that we reject the assertion that it is only an illusion or misperception. During the early days of moving pictures the practice of "reversing" (time), running the film backwards, provided a unique photographic experience that altered a basic concept of how we were taught to perceive our world. As many of Aristotle's theories point out, personal experience and/or intuition is by no means a trustworthy guidepost to scientific understanding. By diverting from standard photographic practice, we can begin to incorporate new ways to thinking about and portraying time using photo-based images.

Breaking Away from 1/125

By turning the shutter to a slower speed, that is, increasing the time of exposure, we can increase the amount of time encompassed by the photograph. When the amount of time incorporated into the image is increased, more events become involved in the structure of the composition. This extended play of light on the film can have spectacular results. As light is recorded over a period of time a new fascination with color emerges as the hues swim together and blend into new visual possibilities. A new way of seeing and experiencing is presented to the viewer. Past conditioning has ingrained the concept that the photograph is supposed to be a single frozen moment (the Decisive Moment). Maybe the photograph isn't only a distinct, isolated, moment, but made up of many moments. The simplest way to begin to break away from the standard 1/125 second mentality is by working with the different methods of dealing with motion. The following are offered as starting points.

[1] Joel Snyder and Neil Walsh Allen, "Photography, Vision, and Representation," *Critical Inquiry* 2, no. 1 (Autumn 1975): 163–64.

Stop Action

Stopping the action of an event can be achieved by using a fast shutter speed or flash in conjunction with a high-speed film. Consider freezing motion when it offers the viewer the opportunity to see something that happens too quickly for the eye to fully comprehend. It also offers a way to stop an event at a critical point of the action for further analysis and study, thereby providing the viewer with a new way of visualizing a situation (figure 20.1).

Anticipation and timing are crucial to capture the climax of an event. Whenever possible, watch and study the action before shooting. Become familiar with how the event takes place. When shooting a stop-action photo select the appropriate vantage point and lens, and then preset both the exposure and focus, taking care to use the smallest aperture to attain maximum depth of field. A wide-angle lens allows more room for error because it has more depth of field at any given aperture than a normal or telephoto lens.

The telephoto lens can be used to isolate the action. A minimum depth of field separates the subject from the background. Prefocusing becomes critical, because any inaccuracy results in the subject being out of focus.

The shutter speed needed to stop motion depends on the speed of the subject and its direction and distance from the camera (table 20.1). The nearer the subject or the longer the lens, the higher the shutter speed needs to be. A subject moving across the frame requires a higher shutter speed than one approaching head-on or at the peak of its action.

Dim Light and Flash

In dim light, flash rather than shutter speed can be used to stop action. The ability to stop movement is dependent on the duration of the flash. A normal flash unit usually gives the equivalent speed of between 1/250 to 1/500 second. Fractional power settings can supply much faster times, up to 1/10,000 second.

Figure 20.1

Adams has used stop-action photography to give the viewer the opportunity to analyze a camera-created event on two levels: as the story told in the picture and the story of the making of the picture. Adams has this to say: "I am photographed by an assistant as I move around to various positions within the field of a stationary 4-×-5-inch camera (strobes used for this one), wearing different costumes for each exposure. I enlarge the sections in which I appear within each negative, cut them out, and tape them together to form a collage. The pictures are thus continuous scenes (the space does not appear fractured or distorted), in which I play numerous characters visually interacting with each other."

© Bill Adams. *Untitled,* 1989. 44 × 55 inches. Chromogenic color print.

The Blur and Out-of-Focus Images

The blur and out-of-focus images are as inherent to photographic practice as those that are clear and crisp. The blur interjects the suggestion of movement into the picture. This bends the traditional concept of photographic time, producing a miasma image capable of representing a sense of the past, the present, and the future (figure 20.2). The blur destroys the notion of a discrete parcel of framed time depicting the past. The blur can provide a sense of suspension in the eternal process of becoming by confronting viewers with change itself. The lack of focus frees the images from the confines of photographic exactitude by offering a different representation of reality.

Begin your experiments by determining what shutter speed is needed to stop the subject's movement in relation to the camera position. A slower shutter

• TABLE 20.1 •

Shutter Speed Needed to Stop Action Parallel to the Camera

1/125 second: most everyday human activities, moving streams and rivers, tree in a slight wind.

1/250 second: running animals and people, birds in flight, kids playing, balloons and kites, swimmers, waves.

1/500 second: car at 30 miles per hour, bicyclists, motorcyclists, baseball, football, tennis.

1/1,000 second: car at 70 miles per hour, jet airplanes taking off, skiers, speedboats, high-speed trains.

speed causes more blur and consequently more contrast between the moving and static areas. This can isolate a static subject from its surroundings. Consider which details are crucial and need to be retained. Decide whether it will be more effective to blur the background or the subject.

Figure 20.2
The blur lets the photographer interject the suggestion of movement into the photograph. Roberts's hand coloring sets the mood, eliminates the unnecessary, and supplies additional items in time and space that were not included at the time of exposure.

© Holly Roberts. *Bob Dreaming*, n.d. 16 × 20 inches. Gelatin-silver print with oil paint.

The Pan Shot

The camera can be intentionally moved to create a blur. One of the most effective ways to convey lateral movement, while freezing the subject and blurring the background, is the pan shot (figure 20.3). Range finder cameras are easier to use for this because, unlike a single lens reflex camera (SLR), they contain no moving mirror to black out the viewfinder during exposure. With practice, most any camera can be used with success.

Start out with a subject whose movement and speed are consistent. To accomplish the pan shot, use a slow film, holding the camera comfortably in the horizontal position. Prefocus on the spot that the subject will cross and set the needed shutter speed. For example, 1/15 of a second can be used to pan a vehicle moving at 30 miles per hour and 1/30 of a second for 60 miles per hour. Correlate the aperture with the speed, using the

smallest aperture to get maximum depth of field. Frame the subject as soon as possible. Do not tighten up or hold the camera with a death grip; stay loose. Make the pan clean and smooth by following the subject with your entire body, not just with the camera. Gently release the shutter as the subject fills the frame and continue to follow through with the motion. Generally, take care not to crowd the subject. Leave it some space to keep moving unless containment is the object. After you learn this technique, try incorporating some variations such as panning faster or slower than the object in motion. Further motion effects can be created by using a slow shutter speed and intentionally moving the camera in nonparallel directions from the subject.

Many random elements enter into these situations that involve long exposures. It becomes a deliberate combination of intent and chance. With practice, it is possible to get an idea of what the

final outcome will look like. The unpredictability of these situations adds to their fascination.

Moving the Film

Film movement can achieve the effect of blending colors in motion. Put the camera on a tripod and hand crank the film past the shutter during exposure using a speed of 1/8 of a second or slower (figure 20.4).

Equipment Movement

Equipment-induced movement can provide an exaggerated sense of motion. Consider the following ideas:

- Use a *wide-angle lens* (24 mm or wider). This produces dramatic feelings of motion when employed to photograph movement at close range and at a low angle. The exaggerated sense of perspective created by this lens produces distortion and causes background detail to appear smaller than normal, thereby losing visual importance. Conversely, foreground objects seem larger and more prominent.

- A *multi-image prism* that fits in front of the lens is another possibility. Its use requires care because it has been overused. All these ideas can be abused by the unthinking. When a piece of equipment is used in place of an idea, the result is a gimmick. When a photographer has to resort to gimmicks, control of the situation has been lost. Whenever equipment is used to strengthen and support an idea, the imagemaker is working with a technique.

- The *zoom lens* is one of the most popular pieces of equipment available to photographers today. It falls into the same danger category as the prism. When used as a tool, the zoom lens can extend the range of photographic vision. Most commonly used is the zoom during exposure to create the illusion of motion. In this method blurred streaks of color come out of

Figure 20.3
Panning furthers the sense of movement in the composition. It concentrates the viewer's attention on the subject while deemphasizing the background. In this case, flash was used in conjunction with a long handheld exposure. The mixture of artificial and natural light sources allowed the photographer to capture moving subjects in a poorly lit environment. It also provides a sense of place for the subject as well as creating a visually engaging ambiguity of space in the three-dimensional setting.

© Ron Giebert. *Ballroom Dance Competition, Okayama, Japan,* 1987. 7 1/4 × 11 inches. Chromogenic color print.

Figure 20.4
Jurus's strip photograph blends the subject and colors, achieving the effect of motion in a method that relies on a unique aspect of camera vision. Jurus built his own linear strip camera with a slit shutter to make this image. The film was exposed by cranking it past the slit. In this case the exposure time was about 5 seconds.

© Richard E. Jurus II. *Zing TA TA,* 1987. 3 1/4 × 10 inches. Chromogenic color print.

the camera until the operation becomes second nature. Once you learn the basic method, it can be combined with other techniques.

- The *pan zoom* technique requires the photographer to pan with the subject while zooming and releasing the shutter. The camera needs to be on a tripod with a pan head. One hand is used to zoom while the other works the panning handle and shutter. A cable release is helpful, as is an assistant to fire the shutter at your instruction.

- The *tilt zoom* technique needs a tripod with a head that can both pan and tilt. Follow the same basic zoom procedure, but use longer exposure times (start at 1 second). Try tilting the camera during the zoom while the exposure is being made, and then try working the pan into this array of moves. The long exposures give the photographer the opportunity to concentrate on this variety of camera moves.

Free-Form Camera Movement

Colored sources of illumination at dusk and after dark give the photographer the chance to weave line and pattern into a still composition. With a stationary light source, try using slow shutter speeds (starting at 1/8 second) while moving the camera in your hand. Start by making simple geometric movements with the camera while visualizing the effect of the blending and overlapping of color and line. If the camera being used is an SLR, try to sight above the viewfinder or to not look at all, going by feel and instinct. Using a wide-angle lens should make this easier. If the camera is jerked and waved about too much the resulting color patterns and lines may become confusing.

Moving lights can put color and motion into a static environment. With the camera on a tripod using small apertures, make exposures at 10, 20, 30, or more seconds. Try not to include bright, nonmoving lights because they will become extremely overexposed and appear as areas with no discernible detail.

the center of the picture. It is a way to give a stationary subject the feeling of momentum. Put the camera on a tripod, set the lens to its longest focal length, and focus on the critical area of the subject. Start at 1/15 second and then make a series of exposures using even longer times. Be sure to change the aperture to compensate for changes in speed. Zoom back to the

shortest focal length as the shutter is tripped. Be prepared to make a number of attempts. Write down the exposure information so that you know which combination produced each picture. Do not depend on your memory. Part of any learning experience is the ability to use the acquired skill in future applications. It helps to practice the zooming technique with no film in

Figure 20.5
A small, on-camera flash was used, and the camera was moved across the subject during a 1/4-second exposure. A separate meter reading was used to determine the exposure for the ambient light, and the aperture was set to allow for the fill-flash effect. In this instance, a visual play is set up in which the background appears to have a fluid sense of movement while the subject remains frozen in contradiction to the apparent movement going on behind it.

© Stephen Petergorsky. *Untitled,* 1985. 17 1/2 × 12 inches. Chromogenic color print.

Flash and Slow Shutter Speed

The combination of flash with a slow shutter speed permits the incorporation of stillness and movement within the same scene. It is an impressionistic way of increasing ambiguity and mystery. The effects can be varied depending on the amount of flash to ambient light and by the amount of movement of the camera (if it is handheld) or the subject or both.

Using a color negative film, begin work in the early morning, evening, or on a cloudy day when the ambient light level is low. A neutral density filter is needed when shooting in brighter light. A basic working technique is to cut the ISO rating of the film by one-half and use this new rating to take a normal exposure reading of the scene (ambient light). Set your flash with the same modified ISO rating. Determine the flash exposure based on the distance of the key object(s) in the composition. If the ratio of flash to ambient light is the same, the color palette will be soft. As the ratio of flash to ambient light is increased, the color palette tends to become more saturated. Use an exposure speed of 1/4 second or longer. The flash exposure freezes the subject and the length of exposure time determines the amount of movement that is apparent in the image (figure 20.5). Bracketing your exposures and movement is a good idea until you gain a sense of how this interplay works.

Extended Time Exposures

Long exposures can be made over a period of time with the camera attached to a tripod and the lens set to a small aperture. A slow film can be used to make the exposure longer. To make an even longer exposure, use neutral density filters in front of the lens. Avoid bright static sources of light. Events like wind and passing lights introduce motion. Reciprocity law failure causes a shift in the color balance (figure 20.6).

Rephotography

Rephotography is when a photographer returns to a subject that had been previously photographed and attempts to make the exact picture again to show how time has altered the original scene. Precise records are maintained so the returning photographer can more easily duplicate the original scene. The original photograph and the new one are usually displayed next to each other to make comparison easy.

In another form of rephotography, the photographer returns to the same subject over a period of time (figure 20.7). Examples of this would range from making a picture of yourself every day for a week to Alfred Stieglitz's photographs of Georgia O'Keeffe that span decades. The relationship of the photographer and the subject is pursued over a period of time. The results should represent the wide range of visual possibilities that can be produced from this combination due to changes in feeling, light, and mood.

Figure 20.6
The color shifts that occur in long exposures are produced by the reciprocity failure of the film. Filters and additional exposure are needed for correction, but the unusual color balance can provide a starting visual impact.

© Arthur Ollman. *Untitled*, 1980. n/s. Chromogenic color print.

Multiple Exposure

Making more than one exposure on a single frame of film offers another avenue of exploration (figure 20.8). Try it out in a controlled situation with a black background. Light the setup, mount the camera on a tripod, and prefocus and calculate the exposure based on the number of exposures planned. A good starting point is to divide the exposure by the number of planned exposures. For example, if the normal exposure is f/11 at 1/4 second, two exposures would be f/11 at 1/8 second each. A camera with automatic exposure control can do the same thing by multiplying the speed of the film by the number of exposures and then resetting the meter to that new speed.

Try varying the amount of exposure time. This can give both blurred and sharp images as well as images of different intensity within one picture. Repeated firing of a flash provides multiple exposures when the camera shutter is left open on the T or B setting. Move the subject or the camera to avoid getting an image buildup at one place on the film.

Sandwiching Transparencies

A simple way to work with more than one image is to sandwich transparency film into a single slide mount. Transparent color tints can be added to modify the atmosphere. Tints can be made from any transparent medium or by photographing discrete portions of a subject, such as the sky or a wall. Bracketing provides a range of color choices from supersaturated to high-key. An internegative can be made of the final result and used to make regular chromogenic color prints.

Figure 20.7

Daily Portrait began in 1978 with photographs that formed a dialog between Jeffrey Fuller, Madigan, and a beech tree on the shore of Lake Michigan and has been in continuous progress. With the birth of their children, *Daily Portrait* has shifted to include their developing relationships. Madigan says: "Every day, a snapshot portrait is made of each child, and I often photograph them together. Every season marks a shift in *Daily Portrait*. From March 21 to June 21 during the years 1982 to 1988, I photographed my children in front of this magnificent azalea bush. *Daily Portrait* makes a cyclic journey tangible through the photographs as evidence. It is an attempt to touch the absolute through constant change." "What is eternal is circular and what is circular is eternal," said Aristotle.

Figure 20.8

Bernstein created this image by making four separate exposures. Bernstein explains: "Using a copystand, all the pieces are placed on black and photographed on one piece of film. I draw a simple acetate mask and place it in the viewfinder of my Hasselblad for placement. Extension tubes and Proxar filters allow me to work close-up. I used a photograph of Alois Brunner (Nazi war criminal) to create an image of a serial killer stalking female victims. Secrecy is maintained as sins are committed."

© Audrey Bernstein. *The Sin*, 1993. 30 × 30 inches. Dye-destruction print.

To create this image, Balish sandwiched two transparencies, made 10 years apart, together. A custom lab made a 4-×-5-inch internegative, and then a trial print, which Balish examines and corrects before the final print is produced.

© Leonard Balish. *Facades*, circa 1990s. 16 × 20 inches. Chromogenic color print.

Expose the Same Roll Twice

Another multiple exposure idea is to run the film through the camera twice (figure 20.9). Cut the ISO rating of the film being used by one-half. Try photographing the same subject, from a different point of view, at a different time of day, closer up, or farther away or photograph an entirely different subject. If you want the frames to line up, mark or cut a small V-shaped notch on the edge of the film. Make a pencil mark inside the camera body, below the film plane, which will serve as a guide to realign the film. Make a contact sheet of the roll and examine it carefully. What new ways of seeing and composing has chance provided? How can this new knowledge be applied to other, maybe more controlled shooting situations to expand your visual limits?

Painting with Light

Using light as a paintbrush requires setting the camera on a tripod with a medium to small lens aperture. Start with a subject against a simple backdrop in a darkroom. Prefocus the camera, and then use a small pocket flashlight with a blind to control the amount and direction of the light. Leave the lens open (use the T setting or the B setting with a locking cable release). By wearing dark clothes, the photographer can quickly walk around within the picture and draw with the light without being recorded by the film. Imagine how the light is being recorded. Since the final effect is difficult to anticipate, be prepared to make a series of exposures. Vary the hand gestures used with the light source to see what effect will be created. Colored gels can be applied to any light source in order to alter its color output. The gels can be varied to introduce a variety of hues into the scene. As experience is gained, more powerful light sources, such as strobes and floods, can be used to cover larger areas, including outdoor scenes (figure 20.10).

Figure 20.9

The first exposure for this photograph was made of a mural by O'Gorman in Mexico City. The second exposure was made in a market in San Cristobal to fashion a cinematic narrative of time and culture. This multiple exposure process involved exposing portions of a roll on fragments of murals, making notes, rewinding the film, and later reexposing it in a random frame overlay. The uncut roll is edited to slightly less than two frames to make the final image. Full color saturation is achieved by exposing Kodachrome 64 at ISO 125 and reexposing it at ISO 185. The layering of colors, masses, and spaces forms its own contrast mask, thus cutting the inherent contrast in both the Kodachrome film and the lifochrome Classic printing process.

© Lorne Greenberg. *Victims of the Colonial Regime*, 1988. 5 1/2 × 14 inches. Dye-destruction print.

Slide Projection

A slide projector with a zoom lens can also be used to paint a scene with light (by placing a colored gel or gels over the lens) or to project an image onto a scene to create a visual layering effect (figure 20.11). Try using old slides, making new slides of the same subject, using black-and-white slides, appropriating images or text from other sources, projecting more than one image, projecting different images into different parts of the composition, or using the zoom lens to vary the size of the projection. For a naturalistic color balance, make certain the type of film used matches the color of the light source. Filters in front of the camera lens may be necessary to make color corrections.

Figure 20.10

With a large-format camera mounted on a tripod, an initial daylight exposure was made on the film, the shutter was closed, and the camera and film left in position until after dark. Then the shutter was opened and another series of exposures, using a small battery-powered light with colored gels, was made on the same piece of film.

© William Lesch. *Heart of Saguaro/Blue*, 1990. 16 × 20 inches through 30 × 40 inches. Dye-destruction print.
Courtesy of Etherton Stern Gallery, Tucson, AZ.

Figure 20.11

Walking the streets of Berlin, Attie kept asking himself, "Where are all the missing people? What has become of the Jewish culture and community which had once been at home here? . . . I wanted to give this invisible past a voice." Attie projected prewar photographs of Jewish street life in Berlin onto the same location today in order to introduce fragments of the past into the present. Using photography as an archaeological tool Attie explores the presence of absence. "By attempting to renegotiate the relationship between past and present events, the aim of the project was to interrupt the collective process of denial and forgetting."

© Shimon Attie. *Almstadstrasse/Corner Schendelgasse, Berlin: Slide projection of former Jewish religious book salesman (1930),* 1992. (On-location installation). 20 × 24 inches. Chromogenic color print. Courtesy of Nicole Klagsburn Gallery, New York, NY.

Postvisualization

The darkroom offers the photographer a postexposure opportunity to expand and induce movement and time into a still scene. Application of these postvisualization methods can break the photographic idea that time is a mirror rendering the appearance of nature into the hands of humans. These methods let the photographer increase the possible modes of interaction with the work. These techniques include the interaction between positive and negative space, and interaction between different aspects of the same event, the interaction between static structure and movement, and interaction between the viewer and the object being viewed. Be ready to experiment and rely on intuition.

Moving the Easel

When moving the easel, prepare to print in the normal fashion. Calculate the proper exposure, giving the print 75 percent of that figure. Make a second exposure of the remaining 25 percent and move the easel during this time. This ratio may be altered to achieve different results. The easel may be tilted during the exposure or the paper can be curled and waved outside of the easel for additional effects. The easel can be placed on a device such as a "lazy Susan" and spun to create circular motion.

Moving the Fine Focus

Moving the fine focus control on the enlarger is a method of expanding the picture. Give the print two-thirds of its required normal exposure time. For the remaining one-third exposure time, move the fine focus adjustment on the enlarger. To give yourself more time to manipulate the fine focus control stop the lens down and increase the exposure time. The outcome will be determined by how fast the fine focus control is moved, how long it is left at any one point, and the proportion of normal exposure to moving exposure (figure 20.12).

Painting the Print with Light

Painting the print with light can be accomplished with a small penlight fitted with a handmade opaque blinder. The blinder acts as an aperture to control the amount of light (figure 20.12). If this is done during the development stage of the print it produces a partial Sabattier effect (see chapter 22). Different transparent filters can be placed in front of the flashlight to alter the color effects. This technique can often be effective when combined with other methods, including the masking of specific portions of the image.

Multiple Exposure Using One Negative

Exposing one negative a number of separate times onto a single piece of printing paper can vastly alter the perception of time within the picture. Many variations are conceivable.

- Reduce the size of the picture and print it a number of times on a single piece of paper. Let parts of each picture overlap to form new images.

- Vary the size of the picture as it is printed on the paper.

- Change the exposure times in order to create a variety of densities.

- Print the full frame on part of the paper and then print different parts from the negative onto the paper.

Combination Printing

Printing more than one negative on a single piece of paper jettisons the traditional picture vision and embraces a far more complex image of reality (figure 20.13). This is commonly done by switching negatives in the enlarger or by moving the paper to another enlarger and easel that has a different negative set up for projection. Opaque printing masks are used to block out different parts of the paper in order to control the areas of exposure.

Combination printing can also involve combining a negative with a photogram or varying the exposure time of different parts of the print. Determine the proper exposure and give a percentage of it to the paper, and then mask certain areas and give the remainder of the exposure.

Multiple Filter Packs

Making use of more than one filter pack can transform the picture's sense of time. Start with a negative that contains a basically monochromatic color scheme and simple linear composition. Print one area of the picture with the normal filter pack while holding back the exposure on another part of the print. Now change the filter pack.

Consider working with complementary colors. Print in the area that was dodged out during the first exposure while holding back that part of the print that was already exposed.

The Cinematic Mode

The cinematic mode of picture making, in which each new frame implies a new episode or another step, modifies the way photographic time is perceived. It is concerned with the interaction among the objects of the composition. The space between objects can become part of the same structure as the objects. Forms actually reverse themselves.

Figure 20.12

The negative was etched using a knife, the fine focus control on the enlarger was moved during exposure, and the resulting print was painted with light during the exposure phase of processing. A red filter and masking were used to control the areas that were struck by light. Synthetic color was added later with an airbrush.

© Robert Hirsch. *David*, 1984. 16 × 20 inches. Gelatin-silver print with enamel paint.

Figure 20.13

Davis tells us: "Using a hand-held 4-×-5-inch Speed Graphic allowed me both spontaneity and superior image quality. Pairing two images side by side further added to a greater complexity in visual structure. The double exposure was, in fact, an accident common with using sheet film. This *mistake* yielded an effect consistent with my goals, both in regards to formal structure and in the desire to rework the sequence of time."

© Steve Davis. *Tourism in the Spirit World*, 1986. 20 × 32 inches. Chromogenic color print.

Figure 20.14

Using a stereo camera Heller makes sequences to extend and elaborate on a theme. "These strips have several different entry points for the viewer; they need not be read from left to right. When most successful, they should return the viewer to the entry point and thus serve as its own punctuation point for the sequence."

© Steven A. Heller. *Dishes & Things: NY*, 1993. 15 × 40 inches. Chromogenic color print.

Cinematic Sequence

The vitality of movement can be conveyed through the use of traditional still pictures linked together to form a cinematic sequence of events. This group of pictures is designed to function not individually but as a group (figure 20.14). The sequence must be able to provide information that a single image would be incapable of doing. A sequence can tell a story, present new information over an extended period of time, or supply a different point of view.

The Matrix-Grid

The grid can be used as a device to lead the viewer through the details and visual relationships of a scene (figure 20.15). Get a few packs of Polaroid film. Photograph a person or object so that the pictures have to be combined to make a complete statement. The pictures do not have to be made from one frozen vantage point but rather from a general point of view. It is possible to incorporate a number of variations of the subject into one single statement.

This type of picture invites the audience to spend time looking at it because the sense of time is fluid; it cannot be taken in all at once. The viewer must take many separate glimpses and build them up into a continuous experience, much as we see the actual world around us.

Figure 20.15

Crane's Polachrome transparencies were printed onto Polaroid Type 668 and transferred onto Arches watercolor paper with colored pencils used to enhance selective areas. The grid offers the audience infinite ways to construct their own viewing patterns and hence meaning of the piece.

© Barbara Crane. *Visions of Enarc #3*, 1990. 57 × 48 inches. Diffusion-transfer image transfers.
Courtesy of Ezell Gallery, Chicago, IL.

Figure 20.16

An incredible painterly sense of time, space, and place is woven by Hockney's masterful application of the "many make one" method. Exposing 650 rolls over a 9-day period, Hockney used about one thousand single images to create a new photo-based interpretation of the originally seen landscape.

© David Hockney. *Pearblossom Hwy.* 11–18th April 1986 (2nd version). 78 × 111 inches. Chromogenic color prints.

Many Make One

"Many make one" describes the visual process of photographing a scene in numerous individual parts and then fitting these single pieces of time together to create one image (figure 20.16). The single pictures of the original scene are not made from a specific vantage point but a general one. This encompasses different points of view over an extended period of time.

The focus may also be shifted to emphasize important elements of each single frame. Have the film processed and printed. Take all the prints and spread them out on a big piece of mat board. Begin to build an entire image out of the many components. It is okay to overlap pictures, discard others, and

have open spaces and unusual angles. Try not to crop the single pictures because a standard size seems to act as a unifying device. When the arrangement is satisfactory, attach the prints to the board. They do not have to be flush.

This method of picture making can expand the sense of space and time that is often lost in an ordinary photograph. It breaks down the edges of a regular photograph. It expands the frame beyond the conventional four perpendicular edges and can bring the viewer right into the picture.

Contact Sheet Sequence

The contact sheet sequence is a modified technique of using many single contact-

size images to make a statement. Pick a scene and imagine an invisible grid pattern in front of it. Photograph that scene using this invisible pattern as a guide. Process the film, then arrange the negatives into the desired order based on your grid pattern, and contact print them to form a complete image.

Joiners

Joiners are created when a number of separate images of a scene are combined to make a whole. The subject can be divided into separate visual components and photographed individually (figure 20.17). Each part provides information about the subject that could not have

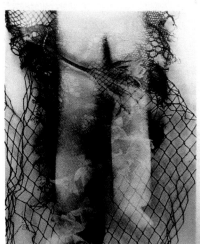

been included if the subject was shot in a single frame. These additional exposures should alter how the subject is perceived. This includes its relative position in time and space, changes in vantage point and angle, and variations in subject-to-camera distance. Single prints are made, laid out on a mat board, arranged, fitted, or trimmed, and then attached into place.

Slices of Time

Slices of time occur when a single scene is photographed a number of separate times to show the visual changes that can occur over a period of time

Figure 20.17
Working from her Mexican American culture, Vargas makes double exposures to represent the duality of time: life and death presented at once. "Death is simply a part of the cycle of living. I depict the starkness of death within the complement of beauty. People look at the soft colors and find there's a little death waiting inside; or they look at the harshness of death and find life waiting for them in the seduction of the colors."

© Kathy Vargas. *Missing #1 (left panels)*, 1992. 48 × 20 inches. Gelatin-silver print with mixed media.

(figure 20.18). Intentional alterations in light and placement of objects can be made each time the scene is photographed. Prints can be butted together, overlapped, or cut into slices and pieced together.

With practice the pieces may be cut into a variety of different sizes and shapes. Keep each cut picture separate. Select one of the pictures to be the base print. Arrange it on a mat board and begin to combine the slices from the other prints into the single base print. When complete, attach the slices to the board.

Composite Pictures

Composite photographs occur when visual elements from various sources and mediums are intertwined and then cut out or pasted on a common support material and rephotographed to obtain the final image. If it is not rephotographed, it is considered to be a montage (figure 20.19). Pictures of astonishing paradox can be produced using this method.

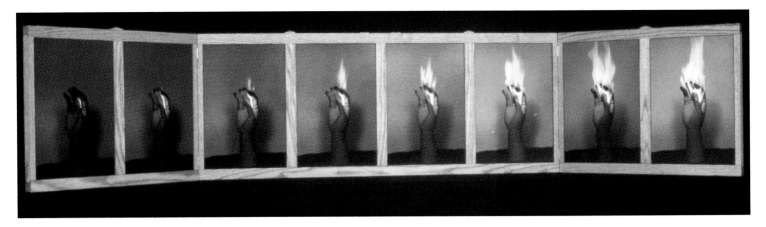

Figure 20.18
This work can be summarized by Helen A. Harrison's 1987 review of "About Time" in the *New York Times*. "The photography of sequential motion, pioneered by Eadweard Muybridge and the basic technique of movie making, is represented by Norman Colp, who uses both observed and staged incidents to compose narrative documentaries, often with a touch of ironic humor."

© Norman B. Colp. *Right Makes Light*, 1990. 21 1/2 × 108 inches. Chromogenic color prints with hinged wooden frames.

Figure 20.19

Farber thinks "of these pictures as a kind of X-ray, revealing the passage of time, history, memory, memories pushing toward consciousness, internal feeling or presences, the psyche. Photographs of what the camera cannot literally see. I'm interested in photography having assumed the burden of memory, and I certainly trade on the photograph's privileged connection to reality and the formation of belief. The process of rephotographing an original collage references the passage of time and layering that memory consists of and replaces the materiality of the collage surface with the photographic surface, in this case one with a very painterly look."

© Dennis Farber. *Flyboy*, 1993. 24 × 20 inches. Diffusion transfer print.

Photographic Collage

A photographic collage is made when cut or torn pieces from one or more photographs are pasted together, often with three-dimensional objects, to produce the final picture (figure 20.20). It is not rephotographed. In this technique no attempt is made to hide the fact that it is an assemblage.

Three-Dimensional Photographs

Three-dimensional photographs can be made by emphasizing one attribute of a subject—color, pattern, shape, or texture—and having it physically come off the flat picture surface (figure 20.21). This exaggeration in time and space calls attention to that aspect of the subject while deemphasizing its other qualities.

Photo-Based Installations

Photo-based installations comprise an entire arrangement of objects, not just a group of discrete images/objects to be viewed as individual works, presented as a single work. Installations provide viewers with the experience of being in and/or surrounded by the work, often for the purpose of creating a more intense sensory

Figure 20.20

Deschamps cut and scored prints and other materials and attached them to an old foldout postcard folio to make a unique three-dimensional pop-out.

© F. Deschamps. *Four Seasons*, 1982. 30 × 14 inches. Chromogenic color prints with mixed media on printed postcards.

Figure 20.21

Byrd's work is autobiographical, but "rather than documenting my daily experience, I have chosen to use photography to create visual metaphors for what happens to me. Since my work stems from the relationship between reality and fantasy I use applied colors (toners, pastels, and paint) on black-and-white photographs." The repetition of hanging three hundred gold-leafed razor blades with red thread relates to the performance aspect of Byrd's work. "The blades would move with each gentle breeze as people walked by. They looked surprisingly like butterflies fluttering above the body. I only cut myself three times."

© Jeffery Byrd. *Untitled*, 1993. 75 × 36 × 24 inches. Gelatin-silver print with mixed media.

Kumao's "cinema machines" utilize nineteenth-century cinematographic technology to project sequences of photographic imagery and probe the psychological aspects of repetitive behavior. Kumao "glues down twelve transparencies in an order which animates a certain gesture or creates a certain rhythm of body movement." The animation is created through the principle of the "persistence of vision." A light goes through the image, is reflected onto the mirror, and is focused by the lens onto an external surface. The illusion of movement is created by the mirrors acting as shutters. Each single still image is registered on the eye's retina, but the continual overlapping of sequential images in the retina creates the illusion of seamless motion.

© Heidi Kumao. *Adore*, 1995. 48 × 48 × 120 inches. Mixed media.

realization. Precedents for installations can be found in the Pop Art era of the late 1950s and 1960s, such as Allan Kaprow's "sets" for *Happenings* or Red Groom's theatrical environments such as *Ruckus Manhattan*. Most installations are unsalable and generally are exhibited and dismantled, leaving only photographic documentation of their existence.

Penetrating the Photographic Mirror

Being able to understand this type of nontraditional photographic time means continuing to penetrate the mirror of reality. Whenever traveling into the un-

known we can hope to be rewarded with understanding. Ironically, the information that is brought with you may prove to be invalid in new circumstances. Be prepared to expand your previous concepts of how reality is composed.

Many times the most important aspects of a scene are hidden because of their familiarity and simplicity and our own lack of knowledge. When an urban dweller drives by a field with cattle in it, the urban person sees a field with cattle in it. When a farmer drives by the same field the farmer sees something entirely different. The farmer can identify the types of cows and knows what kind of condition they are in, what is planted in the field, and how the crop is growing. Both are viewing the same scene, but the farmer's broader knowledge and understanding of what is there allows the farmer to read more of the visual clues that are in the scene. This provides the farmer with a richer and more accurate account of the scene.

By expanding our picture-making endeavors we create new ways to look at the world and enlarge our understanding of its complex system of interaction.

References

Detailed information about many of the processes discussed in this chapter is available in Hirsch, Robert. *Photographic Possibilities*. Stoneham, MA: Focal Press, 1991.

For information concerning time and space see:

Hawking, Stephen W. *A Brief History of Time: From the Big Bang to Black Holes*. New York: Bantam, 1988.

Morris, Richard. *Time's Arrow: Scientific Attitudes Toward Time*. New York: Simon and Schuster, 1985.

Russell, Bertrand. *The ABC of Relativity,* 4th ed. New York: New American Library, 1985.

Sheldon, James L., and Reynolds, Jock. *Motion and Document Sequence and Time: Eadweard Muybridge and Contemporary American Photography*. Andover, MA: Addison Gallery of American Art, Phillips Academy, 1991.

TWENTY-ONE

Thinking About Color and Photography

© Dinh Q. Lê.
Self Portrait After Bosch, The Haywain, 1991.
40 x 57 inches. Chromogenic color prints and tape.

Self-Portraits

Since the time of German artist Albrecht Dürer (1471–1528), artists have expressed many inner concerns through self-portraits. They have shown awareness of their own appearance and traits, producing evidence, which will probably outlive them, of the great complexity of their lives. Their portraits continue to gaze back at the viewer in another time. Self-portraits can show you as you are or may reveal an ambition of yours to be something other than your ordinary self. These pictures often reveal the secret self. Recently, some artists have been using the self-portrait as a means of assuming historical guises to confront and challenge archetypes and stereotypes that have been formulated about the roles men and women play within society (figure 21.1).

Making a Self-Portrait

With these ideas in mind, make a self-portrait. The photograph should express a self-awareness and reveal something that is important for the viewer to know about you. A good way to reacquaint yourself with yourself is to sit down in front of a mirror, alone, without any outside distractions. After studying your image in the mirror, get a pencil and paper and make a series of contour drawings. To make a contour drawing look into the mirror and draw what you see and feel without looking at the paper until you are finished. Based on what you learned from making the contour drawing, make a photographic portrait of yourself.

Figure 21.1

Sherman's use of self-portraits reveals her secret ambitions, dreams, fantasies, and hopes within the framework of a media-image-saturated society. This work also shows the fun of dressing up and playacting before the camera.

© Cindy Sherman. *Untitled #131*, 1983. 34 1/3 × 16 1/2 inches.
Chromogenic color print.
Courtesy of Metro Pictures, New York, NY.

Figure 21.2

Pinney remarks: "My engagement with contemporary cultural issues lies in examining ways that women construct their chosen identities. I am drawn to the intense self-involvement and camaraderie that constitute the communal work of women 'getting ready' to present themselves. Familiar yet unnamed rituals performed by women while dressing or at the beauty salon make visible the ways we have been taught to build and exhibit feminine identity. This series focuses on women's dialogue with the feminine self: who we are and how we measure up to the current ideal displayed virtually everywhere we look."

© Melissa Ann Pinney. *Feminine Identity Series: The Aveda Girl*, 1988. 16 × 20 inches. Chromogenic color print.

Portrait of Another Person

Next, make a photographic portrait of someone you know following these same guidelines. This photograph should present information to the viewer that shows something important about this person's character (figure 21.2). Try photographing yourself and another person in the same surroundings. Compare the resulting differences and similarities.

Environmental Portrait

Make a portrait that shows the viewer how the individual interacts with his or her environment (figure 21.3). Consider showing only one part of the sitter's surroundings to not diminish the importance of the person.

Portrait of an Object

Compose a photographic portrait of an object that tells your audience something about your feelings and relationship toward it (figure 21.4).

Here are technical considerations that will guide you through this process:

Figure 21.3

Devlin explains: "This image is part of a series titled *Habitats* which explores artificial environments created for captive animals. I am particularly interested in the intended interaction (be it passive) between humans and this exhibit via the various visual media involved. This image combines three light sources and required an exposure of 15 seconds."

© Lucinda Devlin. *Penguin Encounter, San Diego Sea World*, 1987. 15 1/2 × 15 1/2 inches. Chromogenic color print.

- *Camera.* Any.

- *Lens.* What will best fit the situation.

- *Film.* Daylight balanced color film.

- *Image size.* Print the full frame of your negative; don't force it to fit the standard 5-×-7-inch or 8-×-10-inch sizes. Make the size of your print fit the concerns of the subject. Don't try to fit them into an arbitrary size.

- *Point of view.* At least this one time, break with tradition and make some photographs that are not at eye level.

- *Light.* Make all your pictures using daylight as your only source of illumination. Do not use any artificial light, including flash.

Ideas Make Photographs

Think before starting to make this series of images. Develop an idea and let it lead you through the process. Edmund Carpenter said, "Technique cannot conceal that meaningless quality everywhere characteristic of art without belief." Techniques well learned can help us to speak, but some of the greatest thoughts have been expressed by the simplest means. Ideas, not equipment, create powerful photographs.

View From Within/Portrait as Social Identity

There has been much interest in using photography to represent groups that in the past had their visual identity created from outside rather than from within their own social group. Historically, photography has played a major role in shaping how different groups of people are perceived. Beginning with nineteenth-century ethnological studies, such as John Thompson's *The Antiquities of Cambodia* (1867) and *Illustrations of China and Its People* (1873–74), outside observers have brought back exotic images that reconfirmed the preexisting attitudes, prejudices, and stereotypes of those in power. Thompson made pictures for people who were part of the capitalist system that considered "the other" to be primitive and inferior. His work reflected the values of the British colonial system, which believed it had the right and the duty to govern other lands and enlighten the natives to Christianity and the Queen. Such practices helped to objectify and exploit the native populations, which had no control over how they were pictured or the context in which their pictures were deployed within the society at large.

Your assignment is to examine how the practice of photography can become part of the process of dismantling preconstructed notions and shape a new portrait that more closely reveals how a group currently would like to represent itself. Make images of members of your specific cultural subgroup(s) or of those with whom you have shared similar circumstances. The purpose is to provide a contextualized reading from the point of view of that private experience within your particular subculture. Discover

Figure 21.4

Kline relates: "By including a few specific objects in a very specific light I hope to stimulate a resonant synergy between the viewer and the environments beheld. In order to successfully communicate the emotional essence of these solitary places, it becomes crucially important to control the Kelvin temperature relationship of the scene's varying light sources. The color of light, the feel of a room, the sense of time, and the season outdoors all combine to provoke the many buried memories we all carry. Much of my approach has been affected by the contemporary American short story writers such as Raymond Craver, Grace Paley, and Gordon Lish."

© Jon Kline. *Attic Train,* 1989. 30 × 40 inches. Chromogenic color print.

Lê's work is about "trying to establish my identity in relation to the culture I have entered. As a Vietnamese living in a Western society, educated in Western institutions and surrounded by Western popular culture, I am a product of both East and West. Through my work, I explore the exchange and interweaving of cultures and identities from a bicultural perspective."

© Dinh Q. Lê. *Looking Within*, 1994. 65 x 30 inches. Chromogenic color prints with tape.

ways to express an understanding of the social rituals of your group that allows you to deliver intimate, firsthand accounts of the group's values. This offers a view from within rather than a gaze from without. There should be a sense of comfort, ease, and openness between the subject and the photographer. These pictures will be a result of the photographer's bond to the group, which provides an innate sense of trust with the subjects. Through such work it is possible for

groups to begin to reclaim control over their own image by modifying misrepresentations that have been previously placed in circulation.

Representing Rituals

Try concentrating on specific rituals that provide your group with a common, cohesive experience. Ritual is an act of bonding. It provides a way for us to

forge a loyalty that transcends our individuality. It is a uniting force that allows us to blend into a community that shares common ambitions, despairs, dreams, passions, and values. It reveals how the act of photography can supply the power of ownership over how our visual image is defined.

Make photographs that question historical depictions and in turn realize and discover your group's own stories. Rejected being embarrassed by cultural features that do not fit into mainline esteem. Examine a heritage that may have been intentionally concealed out of shame and ridicule. Ask the question: What does it mean to be a member of this specific circle?

The results are often private stories, based on personal involvement within a specific community, that have the capacity to expand outward, encompassing the universal in a narrative tradition that embraces the collective of human nature. Such work can function as an act of reclamation and provide a new telling by recognizing that the earlier legends were incomplete. It also infers that community is an ongoing process that requires the participation of each new generation to keep the story alive and relevant. The picturing and preserving of rituals extends the time that the participants can spend celebrating and contemplating their own values. Your images can proclaim that what is of worth is of our own creation, thus recognizing differences through the process of deconstructing myths. This picturing of core experiences can provide an infrastructure of social events that becomes part of the group's consciousness. This alteration in self-perception can help provide the strength and confidence necessary to reformulate a community's social identity.

Truth and Illusion: What Is a Hot Dog?

It is estimated that Americans consume an average of eighty hot dogs per person per year. It is clearly a national passion.

Pretend our government has been contacted by aliens from another planet. They communicate only through pictures. They have no spoken or written language. They want to know only one thing: What is a hot dog? The president does not know if the aliens' intentions are peaceful or warlike. The president calls on you to solve the dilemma.

· A S S I G N M E N T ·

Your job is to make two pictures for astronauts to take with them to the aliens. The first one must convey everything that is known about the hot dog (figure 21.5). Make a list of everything that enters your mind when you think of hot dogs (taste, texture, color, mustard, bun, baseball, beer, or phallic object).

The other picture must not reveal anything about the true nature of the hot dog. It must be shown, but its true identity has to be hidden, disguised, or camouflaged (figure 21.6).

Depending on how the astronauts view these aliens, they will determine which picture will be delivered. The fate of humankind on the planet earth now hinges on your ability to show and hide and to tell the truth or lie.

Photographic Reality

The photograph has become a major part of our decision-making process. Its inherent ability to transcribe external reality enables it to present what appears to be an accurate and unbiased validation of a scene. While photography is expert at expressing events, it also subtly interprets events by constantly interacting and integrating with the current values of the society at large. In reality, the so-called impartial lens allows every conceivable distortion of reality to take place (figure 21.7). Yet people continue to believe in the authority of the photograph. We know a painter may insert or leave out objects not in the original scene to depict a scene from the imagination. This is a profound psychological difference between photography and painting as we continue to bestow on the photograph the power of

Figure 21.5
Neal has visually conveyed the attributes of eating a hot dog in a warm, funny manner.

© Ellen Neal. *Untitled*, 1985. 8 × 10 inches. Chromogenic color print.

Figure 21.6
Here the hot dog is disguised by altering its traditional context. Bosworth comments on his approach: "A photographer's stockpile of props often becomes a large portion of their visual vocabulary. The more formally pleasing, easily manipulated, or recognizably symbolic objects become the most common part of that vocabulary. As I have never stopped playing with toys, they are still a part of my environment. When I interact with toys, I tell myself things that I did not know. Although they are a vocabulary which I use for myself, I would like to widen this conversation to include others."

© Michael Bosworth. *Untitled*, 1991. 24 x 36 cm. Chromogenic color transparency.

Figure 21.7
Photographic reality permits the photographer to interact with the subject and interject into it, thereby changing and interpreting reality. Hirsch demonstrates how the process of photography allows all sorts of distortions of outer reality to take place.

© Robert Hirsch. *New World*, 1991. 16 x 20 inches. Gelatin-silver print with paint and mixed media.

authenticity. We want to believe it can recreate the original scene with absolute fidelity because this makes us feel better. It rescues and saves the past, often lending it dignity and romance, and makes us feel a little less mortal.

The hot dog assignment points out how the camera can not only capture infinitesimal detail and accepted propor-

tion but also how these same features can be employed to "lie" or distort what is before the camera. What questions does this raise in your mind about the role of the photographer, the use of the picture, and the subjective nature of the medium? What impact has digital imaging had on the believability of the photo-based image?

What Is Important? Internal Color Events

Photography in Everyday Life

Photography has become the most important medium to tell people about their world. It has replaced painting as the

Figure 21.8

Grant conveys: "My work consists of previsualized imagery created from my journal that contains writings and sketches synthesized from confronting personal issues, relationships, dreams, and inner preoccupations." Some of the issues raised in this piece include tensions between longing and being repulsed, wanting acceptance but not seeking it, father and daughter difficulties, older man and young women, the strain between male/female relationships. The work in this series was created by dissecting 4-x-5-inch color negatives and enlarging them into nine segments. The segments are each 20 x 24 inches, some of the panels are printed backwards, some are placed out of order, and some are enlarged more than others. The images are then reassembled to make up a whole image.

© Susan Kae Grant. *Accept*, 1989. 5 × 6 feet. Chromogenic color prints mounted on aluminum.

prime communicator of human emotion. Photography is with us in our daily lives through television, magazines, newspapers, movies, videos, and computers. It reaches out in all directions, even encompassing those who do not want to be touched. Many people still seem to only think of photography for its documentary abilities. For this project use the camera to probe the inner realities of your mind rather than the outer reality of the street.

· A S S I G N M E N T ·

Make a photograph that uses the power of color to deal with each of the following themes:

1. Produce a *picture of something that bothers you or that you find disturbing* (figure 21.8). Use your fears or neuroses for a chance at development and growth. Consider these possibilities: Can your pictures be used to confront something that makes you unhappy? Is it possible for the act of photography to lead to a new understanding of this situation? Can a picture increase your knowledge of the world? Does picture making cause you to change your attitudes about something? Do not be like the dog that runs in circles chasing its own tail. Use the picture-making experience to break out of your habits and routines and *see*.

2. Construct a *photo of an inner fantasy* (figure 21.9). Let your creative energy spring from yourself. Your own ideas and experiences communicated directly to another are always more important, instructive, and powerful than the secondhand imitation of someone else's style. Let it out in your imagemaking. Keeping all this inside can make you aggressive, crabby, irritable, or depressed. People can become intolerable when they cannot be creative. Bring forth yourself.

3. *Construct a photograph or a series of photographs that recall an important aspect of a memorable dream* (figure 21.10). It is okay to set things up to be photographed. You are the director. Do not take what is given if it is not what you want. Take charge. Do it your way and do it right.

4. *Use photography to politicize a social issue that you feel strongly about* (figure 21.11). Such topics can deal with women's issues, people of color, or AIDS. Address issues with which you have direct personal experience. Ask yourself if these images are being made solely to express your own feeling or do you want other people to seriously consider adopting your position? Approaches can be varied to meet the needs of specific viewing groups. Think about the type of response and reaction you want the viewer to have. This may be new material or something the audience does not completely or deeply understand. If you want them to be sympathetic, figure out a way not to alienate your audience. If this is of no consequence, then fire away.

5. *Make use of photographic means to portray a psychological drama* (figure 21.12). What is it you want to suggest? Do you need a literate, explicit narrative or can your concepts be implied? Are you raising questions or seeking answers? What do you want your audience to realize?

Figure 21.9

Some things that concern photographers do not visually coexist in the natural world. Skoglund constructs fantasy installations for the purpose of being photographed. She uses color contrast as a method of portraying adult anxieties in a childlike context. In discussing her working method Skoglund says: "I find photography to be convenient as a unifying device for a variety of disparate mediums. It is, in a sense, a container to put many meanings in, with its own shape and rules and behavior."

© Sandy Skoglund. *Revenge of the Goldfish*, 1981. 30 × 40 inches. n/p.
Courtesy of Castelli Graphics, New York, NY.

Fabrication

This section raises an important issue confronting the contemporary worker. In the past, the majority of photographers went out and "found" things to photograph in the natural world. Today a segment of the photographic community has rejected this notion that the only photograph is a found one. In order to achieve and show their concerns many people create and stage productions whose sole purpose is to be photographed (figure 21.13). People, animals, and objects are collected and arranged, sets may be painted, lighting can be altered and/or controlled, the photographs are made, and the stage is struck leaving no evidence, except the photograph, that the event ever occurred. The final result may not be a traditional two-dimensional representation but a three-dimensional installation.

· A S S I G N M E N T ·

Fabricate your own environment. Arrange the existing objects, rooms, space, and light to create an environment for the sole purpose of photographing the manipulated event.

For more information see Hoy, Anne H. *Fabrications: Staged, Altered, and Appropriated Photographs.* New York: Abbeville Press, 1987.

Figure 21.10

Goodine expresses: "I sometimes dream the structure of work and then choose a cast of characters to play out the particular scene. It resembles living out a myth: we all carry out personal myths with only brief glimpses of recognition and in that split second of perception a spark flies up and with it a complete history of emotion. Yes, it is a stage. Yes, it is a symbol. Yes, it is real."

© Linda Adele Goodine. *Infant Joy*, 1987. 4 × 5 feet. Dye-destruction print.

Figure 21.11

As part of a series that addresses some of the social, political, and cultural issues of contemporary life, Kaida declares: "This staged tableau is ideologically feminist. It's postmodern in that it attempts to deconstruct the female as object, the nude as female centerfold (here replaced by a male nude) in high art and popular pornographic sources." Some feminist theorists have argued that traditional visual and verbal representations of women do not represent a biologically given "feminine nature." Instead, women have to adapt and take on the roles that these societal representations portray. Hence, deconstruction (tearing down) of these models becomes important.

© Tamarra Kaida. *Centerfold*, 1988. 24 × 30 inches. Chromogenic color print.

Words and Photographs

In Western culture we are surrounded by words. More and more through the media we find the combination of pictures and text to create and play off two effects at the same time. With two separate sets of symbols the brain is forced to deal with two competing sets of messages. This juxtaposition can be effectively used to convey additional straightforward information, humor, irony, and surreal spatial arrangements or to create conditions of fantasy impossible with only one set of symbols. The combinations give the artist more power to delve into psychological relationships, while also showing the major characteristic of photography, its adaptability in a multitude of situations (figure 21.14). Notice how dependant the meaning of the image is on its accompanying text. Wright Morris, who has spent more than 50 years investigating the wily synergy between words and photographs said: "The mind is its own place, the visible world is another, and visual and verbal images sustain the dialogue between them."

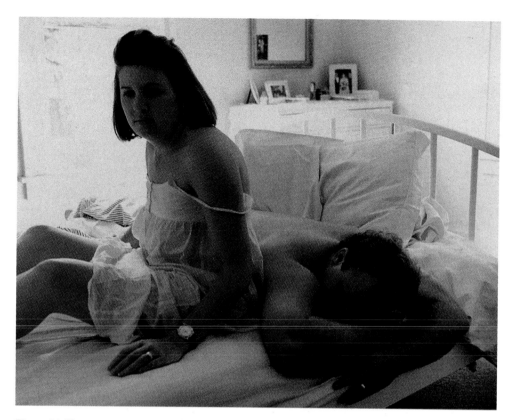

Figure 21.12

Letinsky is concerned with the way single moments can suggest psychological dramas. "I am striving to depict emotionally more uncomfortable, sometimes explicit situations between heterosexual couples. My photographs show couples in the midst of realizing their seductions, for better or for worse. . . . My intention is to picture what sexual intimacy can look like between adults. . . . I address questions concerning identity and representation, foregrounding women as protagonists, I have drawn upon feminist theory to examine gender roles, power relationships, and the gaze who activates it and who receives it."

© Laura Letinsky. *Untitled*, 1992. 35 1/2 × 28 3/4 inches. Chromogenic color print.

Figure 21.13

The fabrication of an environment in order to photograph it allowed Nagatani and Tracey to densely pack recognizable symbols from our society into a controlled situation that permits elaborate commentary from the artists.

© Patrick Nagatani and Andrée Tracey. *34th & Chambers*, 1985. 24 × 60 inches. Diffusion-transfer prints (triptych).
Courtesy of Jayne H. Baum Gallery, New York, NY.

Figure 21.14
Kruger says: "I work with pictures and words because they have the ability to determine who we are, what we want to be, and what we become." Her work asks: Who speaks? Who is silent? Who is seen? Kruger also recognizes the changing usage and reality of the photographic message and designs work to function in numerous environments, including book form, gallery wall, installation, and billboard.

© Barbara Kruger. *Installation*, 1991.
Courtesy of Mary Boone Gallery, New York, NY.

The combining of images and text can be an attempt to get past the barrier between image and spoken language. We tend to think in pictures but in order to communicate we generally have to transform these images into thoughts and the thoughts into language. During this process the flexibility, plasticity, and texture of the image is often a casualty. This process is further complicated as viewers translate this collection back in their minds. Translation errors and personal bias make it unlikely the received message will exactly match what was sent. Marcel Proust believed we pack the physical outline of what we see with our own previously formed ideas so what we essentially recognize (or don't) is ourselves, and this is also why we fall in love with our own creations.

Think of some situations where text can be used with a photograph. A good way to practice and gain experience with this is by doing collages and appropriating (using) found images and text. After completing this exercise, contemplate making your own image(s) and text combinations. Consider some of these ways to use pictures and text:

1. Include words within the original camera image,
2. Cut text from newspapers and magazines or generate on a computer and glue it on the photo,
3. Add text with press-on letters,
4. Use a rubber stamp set,
5. Write directly on the photo,
6. Incorporate other photographic or computer methods for the addition of text,
7. Set the text separately from the image in the form of a caption or box of text.
8. Use text to expand the original meaning of the image.
9. Use text to drastically alter the original intent of the image.

What do you notice happening when you combine pictures and text? Does one overwhelm the other? Do you want to strike a balance between the two? Is there a blending or a duality of the two media? Should you give more weight to one than the other? How does the addition of text affect the direction in which you read the work? Which do you read first? In a literate culture which has more importance? How can you effectively play one off of the other? If you want to ensure the supremacy of the photograph, use your words as a support and not as a crutch to hold up a weak photograph. Let them supply information that enhances your imagery. If this is not a concern, create arrangements that challenge the traditional relationships between pictures and words. How does the meaning of an image change when text is added or the original text altered?

Camera Formats

The camera is the key component that makes up photographic vision. The job of the camera has been to make an "acceptable" and recognizable depiction, based on accepted visual conventions, of what was seen. In the Renaissance, the early camera, called the camera obscura, was designed to imitate the visual ideas of perspective and scale that were formulated during this period (see chapter 22). Even today, the combination of camera and lens determines many of the basic characteristics of the final photographic image, including field of view, depth of field, sharpness, tonal range, and graininess. A knowledgeable viewer can often identify the type of camera used to make an individual image. Because the camera plays such a vital role in the formation of the final picture, the photographer must be sure the type of camera used supports his or her personal aesthetic goals. No single camera can produce acceptable results in every situation. This is because the standard of what is acceptable changes depending on a variety of factors, including the subject being photographed, the audience, the purpose for which the picture is being made, and the desires of the photographer. Photographers should learn about the differences in cameras, their strengths, and their drawbacks so they are able to make intelligent choices to achieve the desired outcome. "A photograph can only look like how the camera saw what was photographed. Or, how the camera saw the piece of time and space is responsible for how the photograph looks. Therefore, a photograph can look any way. Or, there's no way a photograph has to look (beyond being an illusion of a literal description)."[1]

Special Cameras

Besides the familiar SLR, range finder, and twin-lens cameras, there are a number of cameras to work with, including the following:

1. Medium formats, such as the 6-x-4.5-centimeter, 6-x-6-centimeter, 6-x-7-centimeter and 6-x-9-centimeter, which provide a larger image while still retaining the convenience and versatility of a handheld camera.
2. View cameras, such as the 4-x-5-inch, 5-x-7-inch, and 8-x-10-inch, which offer the largest film area and the greatest amount of perspective control, but do require the use of a tripod (figure 21.15).
3. Toy cameras, such as the Diana and its many imitations, which challenge the accepted standards of image quality and encourage playfulness and simplicity.
4. Disposable cameras, which provide an inexpensive way to experiment with different imagemaking devices including waterproof, underwater, and panorama machines.
5. Homemade cameras, such as the pinhole camera (covered in chapter 22), which you can construct to suit your own way of seeing.
6. Panoramic cameras, which are used to expand the ordinary photographic viewpoint.

Figure 21.15
Formica's choice of camera format reveals the relationship between theory and practice. "My concept was to create an imaginary world where bugs and slugs take over a posthuman world. The dollhouse objects needed to become life-size to create this illusion while the invertebrates would become larger than life. The 4-x-5 camera was crucial to this project because the prints are 46 x 36 inches. The quality of the resolution after enlarging is impeccable, a quality you would not be able to get with a 35-mm negative. Though the 4-x-5 camera carries burdens due to it's size and cost, it made me bring subject matter to the camera rather than bringing my camera to the subject. Within this restriction my interests became more apparent and I became more self-aware of what I was shooting."

© Jennifer Formica. *Lady Bugs with Wheels*, 1995. 46 × 36 inches. Chromogenic color print.

7. Sequence cameras, which make a series of exposures over a specific amount of time, on either one piece of film or on consecutive frames.
8. Stereo cameras, which allow the imagemaker to work with the illusion of depth.
9. Underwater cameras, which allow the camera to be used in wet conditions or submerged in water.
10. Photomicrographs, which can be made by means of a special apparatus that permits a camera to be attached to a microscope.
11. Electronic cameras, such as still and moving video, which enable an image to be recorded electronically on a disk or tape without the need of a darkroom. The captured image can be immediately played back on a television or introduced and manipulated in a computer.

Whenever the opportunity presents itself, try to work with a camera format different from the one you normally use. Compare the results. Notice how the camera itself affects what you look for and how you see.

[1] Garry Winogrand, "Understanding Still Photography," in *Garry Winogrand* (portfolio) (New York: Double Elephant Press, 1974).

For more information on cameras see Adams, Ansel. *The Camera.* Boston, MA: Little Brown, 1983 and Hirsch, Robert. *Photographic Possibilities.* Stoneham, MA: Focal Press, 1991.

What Is the Landscape?

The term *landscape* originates from the Dutch word *landschap,* meaning "land-ship." It represented a segment of nature that could be taken in at a glance, from a single point of view, and encompassed the land as well as animals, buildings, and people. In *Discovering the Vernacular Landscape,* John Brinckerhoff Jackson defines the landscape as an artificial collection of man-made spaces on the earth's surface that have been devised to meet the human need of organizing time and space. Since the nineteenth century there has been an aesthetic movement to separate nature from humanity. The images from publications such as the Sierra Club, glorifying pristine, unpeopled nature, have come to be the publicly accepted definition of the landscape. John Szarkowski, former Curator of Photography at the Museum of Modern Art in New York, said that people are thankful to Ansel Adams because his pictures stirred our collective memory of what it was like to be alone in an untouched world. This may be, but it leaves out the way the majority of people see the landscape.

Traditional Viewing Concepts

Many people still see the landscape through the English-gentleman concepts of the *sublime,* the *beautiful,* and the *picturesque* as presented by Edmund Burke and John Ruskin. Briefly, some major aspects of the sublime include astonishment, confusion, darkness, infinity, monsters, obscurity, silence, solitude, terror, and vastness, with its major colors being blacks, browns, and deep purples. The quality of light can be intense and directional with great play between the shadows and highlights. The beautiful was less strong, being rounded, smooth, and well-proportioned without surprise or terror. It was admirable but was not as capable of arousing such great passion. The colors of beauty tended towards the warm hues and favored a softer, more diffused light. The picturesque was a series of motifs that were used by artists wishing to elicit known responses from the audience. The picturesque provided a structure for seeing what in nature would make a good picture. Far less threatening than the sublime, it provided a more complex view of nature based on the then-popular ruin of the world theory. Typical picturesque subject matter featured shattered trees, rotten stumps, overgrown foliage, rushing brooks, and tumbled-down structures. Detail and texture were of paramount concern when used within the confines of academically approved compositions (the rules of painting).

For over a hundred years, Gustave Courbet's so-called realistic landscapes, emphasizing subjects of immediate, preordained appeal, served the public as the exemplifier of many of these notions including the one that nature had to be improved upon in the interest of the ideal. Although Courbet stated that "painting is an art of sight and should therefore concern itself with things seen (Show me an angel and I will paint one)," it was nevertheless vulgar to portray what one saw. In *Landscape Into Art,* Kenneth Noland cuts through the numerous falsehoods surrounding Courbet's concentration on the tangible reality of things with his observation that Courbet "cheerfully substituted a false sensation for a real one, and the remarkable thing is that his false sensations are exactly those which have satisfied the popular eye ever since." Such academic guidelines of "good taste" continue to influence us today with models and expectations of how photography should be judged.

Photography and the American West

Beginning with Solomon N. Carvalho's daguerreotypes (now lost), made on the 1853 Frémont expedition, photography has been the instrument that awakened America to the sublime and mysterious landscape of the "West." Throughout the twentieth century photography has been the keeper of the flame, shaping the ideas and perceptions of the Great American West. The major religions of the Western world were all born in the desert. In *Satanic Verses,* Salman Rushdie says: "God is in the desert." So too in America, God must be in the West. The American West has become a visual concept for a spacious, waterless, wonderland of repeating geometric shapes, dominated by a horizon line where the earth meets the sky. It is a place of personal freedom that is also cruel, harsh, bright, clean, sharp, and completely unforgiving; one wrong move and you could be in serious danger. This wild and tough image dominates the American psyche and character has been generated by photography and has become one of our major cultural exports.

The Landscape Today

Contemporary landscape has broader parameters than in the past. The successful landscape can convey a sense of time, place, and human experience. Some pay homage to the beauty and grandeur of nature by making views that give the audience a sense of actually looking at the scene without any political message. Today many photographers specialize in recording how the landscape is shaped by human presence (the *social landscape*), combining ethics and aesthetics. More and more the landscape becomes a site to express the personality, ideas, and social/economic/political concerns of the photographer. Here the quest becomes making the unsavory truth, the thing we would like to ignore, into something that challenges the viewer and provokes thought within the landscape tradition (figure 21.16). In his book *Why People Photograph,* Robert Adams comments:

If the state of our geography appears to be newly chaotic because of heedlessness, the problem that this presents to the spirit is, it seems to me, an old one that art has long addressed. As defined by hundreds of years of practice—I think history is vitally important—art is a discovery of harmony, a vision of

Figure 21.16

Goin's *Nuclear Landscapes* represent the artifacts and sites that encompass the myth and political ritual surrounding the nuclear age. The title of this piece is branded on the image to reflect a nuclear impact. "This allows the photographs to maintain their context while in a viewing circumstance whereby the full sequence and narrative [from the book] is absent. Given that these landscapes are also branded, it made aesthetic sense to present this disharmonic element. No one need judge these scenes as celebratory!"

© Peter Goin. *Orchard Site*, from *Nuclear Landscapes*, 1991. 11 × 14 inches. Chromogenic color print. Accompanying caption in *Nuclear Landscapes* reads: "Abandoned and scarred peach or apricot orchard from the Hanford farming area.

disparities reconciled, of shape beneath confusion. Art does not deny that evil is real, but it places evil in a context that implies an affirmation; the structure of the Creation, suggests that evil is not final.[2]

These are all legitimate means in which to consider the landscape. Regardless of which approach you take, there are a number of common basic considerations to think about.

[2] Robert Adams, *Why People Photograph* (New York, NY: Aperture, 1994), 181.

· ASSIGNMENT ·

Basic Working Considerations

Decide what your landscape subject is, and then spend time looking at the subject and determine the essential qualities you want to convey. Now consider these points:

- What type of light and which film will best realize your ideas? Would low, directional light, revealing pattern and/or texture, be effective or would a clear, hard, contrasty midday light show the qualities you find essential?

- Identify the key colors and decide the most effective method to convey them.

- Would a wide-angle lens, emphasizing a great deal of depth with an exaggerated foreground, be effective or would a telephoto lens, concentrating on detail, compressing and foreshortening the space, do the job? Would a detail shot or a panorama better express your idea?

- Should the point of view be horizontal, vertical, or oblique?

- Using your camera position, how should you compositionally control the spatial relationship of the foreground, midground, and sky? Should the sky or the ground dominate? Do you want a dramatic or naturalistic point of view?

- How can perspective be used to draw the viewer into the scene?

- How does setting up spatial relationships affect the psychology of the picture?

- Which key elements will be used to determine how to control the exposure? Will a filter, such as a polarizer, add strength to the image?

- How will you convey a sense of scale? Do you want to use a human figure as a contrast to the size of natural forms? Or would it be better to play natural shapes off one and another? Remember the human figure is visually very powerful, and it immediately attracts the viewer's eye.

- What type of focusing techniques will be employed? Will you go for maximum depth of field or make use of selective focusing to direct the interest of the viewer? Is it necessary to clearly separate the subject from busy or confusing surroundings?

- How should the print be made? What would happen by increasing or decreasing the exposure time? What about burning, or dodging, including edge burning?

- Is one image enough or would a group or collage/montage be more effective?

- How will presentation affect the viewer's response?

Follow up: Make and carry out all your initial decisions. Then return to the same subject and begin to reconsider your first thoughts. For instance, how would changing the angle of view or extending the exposure time affect the outcome? Make a new group of pictures based on your second group of thoughts. Compare the two. Are your first ideas always the best? What did you learn from the second effort? What would you do differently if you photographed the scene a third time? Keep asking questions and trying new ideas until the results are satisfying. When we think of making landscape photographs, we think about traveling somewhere, taking a voyage. The curiosity of exploration has been responsible for many of the concepts we hold about the landscape. But what do such images reveal about the inner journey of the photographer? Do we go out in an attempt to discover what is within?

For additional sources of information see Jussim, Estelle, with Elizabeth Lindquist-Cock. *Landcape as Photograph.* New Haven, CT: Yale University Press, 1985, Clark, Kenneth. *Landscape Into Art,* new edition. New York: Harper & Row, 1976, Jackson, John Brinckerhoff. *Discovering the Vernacular Landscape,* New Haven, CT: Yale University Press, 1984, and Schama, Simon. *Landscape and Memory,* New York: Alfred A. Knopf, 1995.

In *The Drive-In Theater Series*, Nakagawa uses the idea of a frame within a frame. "I digitally paste images I have photographed, representing some aspect of American culture, onto abandoned and decaying drive-in screens. The nostalgic mythology of the drive-in theater is juxtaposed with explicitly public and political messages. Similarly, the commercial nature of the billboard is subverted. The series proposes a critical inspection of Western society from my viewpoint which is Eastern in origin and Western by immersion."

© Osamu James Nakagawa. *K.K.K.*, from *The Drive-In Theater Series*, 1992. 26 1/2 × 40 inches. Chromogenic color print.

The Power of Nature: Visceral versus Theoretical

Most photo-based imagemakers do not spend much of their time discussing Hegel, Descartes, or Derrida. What they do discuss is what work gets shown in the major venues and what work is ignored. During the past 15 years photography's critical dialogue has been dominated by European academic theoreticians whose philosophies appear to maintain that there is greater value in the role of the interpreter than that of the maker. Intolerant of nonpolitical interpretations and any nonmaterial focus, the deconstructionists disallow any firsthand experience of aesthetic pleasure. Their theories are a continuation of the mechanical philosophy of the sixteenth and seventeenth centuries in which people are viewed as isolated (alienated) observers and not as active participants in the cosmos. Their coolly academic approach brings a foreign sensibility and

class consciousness that deconstructs American mythology but replaces it with nothing; leaving a void without a sense of community or hope.

The shift to the radical right in American culture and politics makes it vital for artists not to throw up their hands and say they have no answers, for to do so is to cede the issues of humanity and spiritually to only the political conservatives. Under such circumstances, it is imperative for artists to offer countermeasures that deploy our fundamental American strengths and engage the belief in the power of nature as an effective weapon against blaming, stereotyping, and pretentious standards.

· ASSIGNMENT ·

Launch a cognitive and holistic investigation that stresses a full participatory relationship with your subject as a way of knowing. Concentrate on a visceral rather than a theoretical approach to the work. Engage your body as well as your mind and celebrate the intimate connections between humans and nature. Search

for methods that blend the emotional, intuitive, sensual, spiritual, and intellectual. Strive to represent the great metaphysical struggle of our culture: reconciling what we know in our heads with what we know in our hearts.

Now turn it around and represent the same subject emphasizing the theoretical point of view. Which approach works better for you? How does the audience response differ? Under what conditions does one approach work better than the other?

Still Life

A photographer can undertake exciting explorations without traveling to exotic, far-off places. The studio can provide a setting for contemplating visual problems. The tradition of still life was established in the beginning of photography by Daguerre and can be traced back to fifteenth-century painting. Today still life is pursued in both the artistic and commercial photographic communities and has laid the infrastructure for advertising and product illustration photography.

Figure 21.17

Under the guise of the traditional still-life genre, Whaley manufacturers a composition that alludes to the richness and bounty of the natural world. But that's where the affinity with the historical still life ends. The conflict between science/technology and the natural world is addressed through the use of nonsensical devices; pointing out there is something wrong with a system that in its quest for knowledge often destroys that which it is examining.

© Jo Whaley. *Analytical Behavior*, 1994. 16 × 20 inches. Chromogenic color print.

The challenge is to build an image, from the camera's point of view, that delivers a distinct outcome (figure 21.17).

Thinking About Still Life

Visit the library and look at work done for commercial and artistic purposes by photographers and artists using other media, especially painting. Analyze what you are attracted to and repelled by in these images. Consider taking a simply done advertisement and duplicating it to learn some of the basic problems in doing still life. Now formulate your own still-life vision. Picking a theme can provide structure for the entire operation.

Still-Life Considerations

Still life affords the opportunity to control all the elements within the composition. You can work entirely alone, setting your own pace, without the distractions and problems characterized by working with live models. Working with still life can provide a sense of privacy and meditation that permits a great deal of concentration.

Consider using a view camera because the adjustments it offers (swings, tilts, and rising front) can increase the control over the final image (especially depth of field). Polaroid materials can be used with the view camera to make test shots. Collect and organize your objects and props. Select a location. It can be the corner of a room or a larger studio space. It can be beneficial if you have a spot where the setup can be left undisturbed. This allows you the time to study, linger, and interact with your construct before shooting. It also lets you go back and make adjustments after the first round of photographing has been completed. Pick the background setting. It may be a seamless paper or a personal construct. Play with the objects. Stay loose and try different compositional arrangements. Look for combinations of colors, shapes, and textures that promote the theme. Once the composition is set, decide what are the prime factors to be revealed. Is precise detail important? Which film's grain structure and color characteristics best suit the needs of this still life?

What type of lighting is required to accomplish your goal? Should you use natural, artificial, or a combination of both types of light? Will more than one light be needed? Start with only one main light. What direction should it come from—front, side, top, or bottom? Are reflectors or diffusers required? Use a second light only to bring out the background or reduce shadows. Watch out for double shadows when working with two lights, because overlapping tends to make visual confusion. What about filters or colored gels? What type of psychological atmosphere do you want to create? Where and how should your exposure reading be determined?

The direction and quality of light is determined by numerous considerations such as the mood, the message, and personal aesthetic tastes. The challenge in lighting is to reveal the natural properties of what is being photographed. Opaque, translucent, and transparent objects each require special considerations. How the combination of these properties is handled determines whether the composition seems to glow with a lifelike aura or whether it remains flat and lifeless.

How will the final piece be presented? Will postvisualization techniques help to strengthen the message?

The Macro Lens

Beginners often attempt to make still-life photographs using a 35-mm camera with a macro lens. This can prove unsatisfactory because of its lack of depth of field. The macro lens is excellent for doing flat field work, such as copying and making slides of original prints, but even stopped down to f/32 it may lack the depth of field often critical for a successful still life. The shorter focal length macro lenses (in the 50-mm range) provide more depth of field at any given aperture than their longer focal length (100-mm range) counterparts. The same depth of field problem will also be encountered when using an add-on close-up lens, reversing ring, or extension bellows. If this is not acceptable, you should consider using a view camera.

The macro lens can also serve as a postmodern tool, capturing images that will be given new meaning by altering their original context (figure 21.18). These images can be digitized and manipulated on a computer.

The Human Form

The human body has proved to be a challenging and controversial subject since the beginnings of photography. Some of the interest in the human body has been solely prurient, as in the making of pornography. But the nude has long been a venerable subject for artists. The vitality of the genre can be seen in the diverse ways that the human form has been portrayed (figure 21.19): beautiful, delicate, soft, whole, inviting, sculptural, hard, unavailable, horrific, broken, fractured, faceless—the list goes on.

In the early nineteenth century, the traditional male nude became a taboo subject. Photographers, like other artists, began to concentrate on the female form. It was also considered to be objectionable to show pubic hair. This convention is still enforced in many areas.

Figure 21.18

Henry uses a macro lens to make slides of her collected materials, such as dolls, toys, and beads, to construct what she calls "lariats." "I use color Xeroxes made from slides of the aforementioned which I stuff with poly-fil, shredded money, excelsior or whatever seems appropriate. They are then sewn up in clear vinyl and hung from binder rings, chains, braided waxed nylon or telephone wiring. I call them lariats because they are so malleable—they take on a new shape every time they're handled. Each lariat has a narrative. Some of the written passages accompany the work the way an exhibition label would, others are sewn, stuffed, and interwoven with the piece."

© Janet Henry. *Barbara Prysock #2, Mrs WPM*, (detail), 1994. 66 x 17 inches. Mixed media.

Figure 21.19
Hafkenscheid's work was inspired by glimpses into other people's homes. "At night when the curtains are open, living rooms often resemble a small theatre. This theatre aspect is emphasized by the quality of light [a combination of ambient and flash]. . . . These images are intended to be voyeuristic and seductive and to provide windows into private moments in the subject's home environment."

© Toni Hafkenscheid. *Greg and Gordon*, 1992. 30 x 30 inches. Chromogenic color print.

Only recently has the male form been reintroduced into the public arena, often with a great deal of public outcry as witnessed in the work of gay photographers such as Robert Mapplethorpe.

Decide what is important to reveal and how you can go about it. Do you want to show the entire figure or part of it? Is it going to be realistic or abstract? Should the color scheme be cool or warm, high key or low key? Is the sense of texture important? Will soft, indirect light, good for revealing subtleties of form through tonal graduations, be effective? Or would stronger, directional light, creating more contrast, darker shadows, and a bolder more graphic mood, meet your intentions? What mood do you want: innocent, dramatic, sensual, romantic, erotic, secretive, provocative, vulnerable, loving? How can choice

of camera lens and position be employed to create this psychological effect? Should focus be sharp or diffused? What type of background will work? Will you need props? Pick a human form that personifies your idea. Establish a good working rapport with the model(s). Explain to the model what you are looking for. Offer direction without being a bully. Be willing to take suggestions. Leave any hidden agendas or expectations somewhere else, and concentrate on making photographs.

For more information on the human form see Ewing, William, ed. *The Body: Photographs of the Human Form*. San Francisco: Chronicle Books, 1994 and Gill, Michael. *Image of the Body:Aspects of the Nude*. New York: Doubleday 1989.

Pictures from a Screen

Making pictures from a television screen or monitor offers the photographer the opportunity to become an active participant in the television medium instead of being a passive spectator. The camera can be used to stop the action on the screen or extend the sense of time by allowing the images to blend and interact with one another. The literalness of photographing directly from the screen is both its strength and weakness.

To make pictures from a television or monitor screen try following these steps:

1. Make certain the screen is clean.
2. Place the camera on a tripod. A macro or telephoto lens can be used to fill the entire frame or to work with a small area of the screen and minimize the distortion produced by a curved screen.
3. Turn off the room lights and cover windows to avoid getting reflections on the screen. A black card put in front of the camera, with a hole cut in it for the lens, helps to eliminate camera and other reflections. If available, use a "hood" device (designed to capture images directly from a computer screen) with a camera attachment to cover the screen area and block out ambient light.
4. Adjust the picture contrast to slightly darker (flatter) than normal for an accurate, straightforward rendition.
5. Adjust the color to meet your personal considerations.
6. Most monitors generate a new frame every 1/30 of a second. If the shutter speed is higher than 1/30 of a second, the leading edge of the scanning beam will appear on the picture as a dark, slightly curved line. If you do not want this line, a shutter speed of 1/30 of a second or slower should be used. Experiments should be carried out with shutter speeds of 1/15 and 1/8 of a second since the shutter speeds of some cameras may be faster than indicated. If the image being photographed is static or can be "frozen" on the screen, try using the slower speeds to ensure the

A macro lens was held at an extreme angle to the surface of the television to inject the image distortion. The unnatural color is achieved by adjusting the color, contrast, and tint controls of the television set. The print is mounted on a Voice Print frame, a device capable of recording and playing back a 10-second sound bite. The sound is recorded from a prerecorded video segment. The satirical photograph becomes an interactive piece; viewers can repeatedly hear the sound segment by pushing a small "play" button on the frame.

© Diane Bush and Steven Baskin. *Jesus Removes All Human Ingenuity*, from the *Televangelist Series* 1995. 5 × 7 inches (image), 11 x 14 inches (framed). Chromogenic color print with Voice Print frame. The sound bite says: "Jesus removes all human ingenuity, all human "intuity." He removes all innovations from man."

- Make a series of multiple exposures from the screen onto one frame.

- Put a transparent overlay of an image or color in front of the screen. Make your own using litho film.

- Another possibility for incorporating images into a picture is to project a slide or slides onto a scene, rather than onto a screen, and then rephotograph the entire situation. A zoom lens on the slide projector can be useful in controlling the image size.

- Movie theater screens, including drive-ins, can also provide the photographer with a rich source of imagery to call upon.

- Create images using computer graphics programs.

- Incorporate the screen image with its surroundings or other events.

- Fabricate a situation to be photographed that includes a screen image.

frame line is not visible. Cameras with a leaf-type shutter may synchronize better with the monitor's raster lines.

Once the correct shutter speed is determined, make all exposure adjusts by using the lens aperture.

With daylight balanced color film, the resulting image will probably have a blue-green cast. This may be partially corrected by using a CC30R, CC40R, or 85B filter, with appropriate exposure compensation, at the time of initial exposure.

Different films deliver a variety in color renditions due to the film's spectral sensitivity and dye-image formation system. If color film is used to photograph a black-and-white monitor, the resulting image may have a blue cast.

If no screen lines are wanted, the image will have to be captured by using a film recorder that makes its image based on electronic signals rather than from a screen.

A videocassette recorder (VCR) gives the photographer the chance to be selective about the images on the screen and also provides the ability to repeat the image on the screen until it can be photographed in

the manner that is desired. The VCR can be an effective visual arts teaching tool as demonstrated by Quentin Tarantino, director and screenwriter of *Reservoir Dogs* and *Pulp Fiction*. Tarantino used it as a poor person's film school to instruct himself about filmmaking while working in a video rental store.

Alternative Modes of Working

Nonstraightforward representations from the screen are possible using the following methods:

- Vary the shutter speed from the standard 1/30 of a second.

- Adjusting the color balance of the screen from its normal position.

- Vary the horizontal and vertical hold positions from their standard adjustment.

- Use a magnet to distort the television picture. Be aware that this could put the television out of adjustment, requiring a repairperson to correct it. Try this on an old set that you no longer care to use.

Postcards

The postcard format, about 3 1/4 x 5 1/2 inches, first appeared in Europe in 1869. In America at the turn of this century free rural delivery; reduced rates for cards; small, folding, handheld cameras; and the new postcard-size printing papers contributed to making the postcard immensely popular. Before the rise in technology led to telephones and mass-circulation picture magazines, postcards were a fun and inexpensive way for people to keep in touch.

Folk Art Communicates

The postcard's form and style are in the folk art genre and throw to the winds all the sacred rules of picture making. Many cards possess an amazing sense of irreverent good humor in how the subject is depicted. Originally the postcard was of a highly personal nature. People went to the local photographer's studio and had their own cards made that dealt with subjects of current importance in their lives. Portraits

TWO BLOCKS FROM FALL.

Close Cover Before Striking

327 Footfall   J. Mead '92

Working in the postcard format, Mead used numerous depictions of Niagara Falls including postcards, a matchbook cover, a chromolithograph, and a color Instamatic print he made of the falls as a teenager. "The inclusion of shredded U.S. currency and bar coding refers to the commercialization of the Niagara Falls area. The title is derived from the fact that the average heights of the American and Canadian Falls is 327 feet. The choice of scale is very deliberate. It invites close inspection and encourages a greater level of intimacy with the work."

© Gerald C. Mead, Jr. *327 Footfall,* 1992. 3 1/2 × 5 1/2 inches. Mixed media.

were popular and included all members of the family from the new baby to the dog. These were then sent to friends and relatives. At present most postcards are commercially printed and mass circulated. They serve primarily as documentation, offering evidence that you were in a certain place, at a certain time, and this is what you saw. Being able to write a message on the back makes it more personal. It is a form of simple communication that is quick, cheap, educational, and often entertaining. Commercially printed postcards are used by the travel industry to provide pictorial stereotypes. They have become part of the tourist experience. People tend to value the kind of scenery that has been aesthetically validated in travel brochures, advertisements, and other mass media visuals. Often, when tourists encounter the original scene they want to confirm its "picturesque" value by making a snapshot or purchasing a postcard. Today postcards are often used by photographers to announce the opening of an exhibition of their work.

· ASSIGNMENT ·

Making Your Own Postcards

Look at the Griffin & Sabine series of books by Nick Bantock for some beginning ideas. Know what it is you want to communicate with your finished work then create your own postcards following these instructions:

1. Start with the 3 1/2-x-5 1/2-inch size (larger-size cards require regular first-class postage). Cards can be different sizes and do not have to be rectangular, but unusually shaped pieces risk being damaged in the mail.
2. Print on one side, leaving the other side blank.
3. On the nonpicture side, divide the space in half vertically with the word *postcard.*
4. To the right of the word *postcard,* address the card to the receiver and put on the correct postage.
5. On the left-hand side of the word *postcard,* in the upper left-hand corner, write a title or description to go with the photograph.

6. Below this write a message for the receiver.
7. Beneath the message, give the photo credit: the copyright symbol, the year, and the name of the photographer.
8. Mail the completed card.

Kodak Kodabromide black-and-white paper, which can be easily hand-colored, is available in 3 1/2 x 5 7/16 inches, in 100-sheet boxes, with a standard postcard layout printed on the back.

Self-sticking backing material cut to postcard sizes (3 1/2 x 5 and 4 x 6 inches) is available from Porter's Camera Store, Box 628, Cedar Falls, IA, (800) 682-4862.

Milk Carton

Photographs have become an automatic, unthinking part of our normal daily lives. They are simply there, inescapable, delivering messages in the most unlikely places, influencing our thinking. This in turn affects our decision-making process, which shapes the world. The once-innocent milk carton has now become a minibillboard sitting intimately with us at the kitchen table.

Confronting New Information

As we start each day, we are confronted with written and visual symbols on every available space of the milk carton. As we sit with our breakfast, we unconsciously look at it. What do we see? One side proclaims the brand and type of milk while another delivers its nutritional information and a third side announces some kind of mail-away product offer. All this seems rather straightforward and believable, until we encounters the fourth side. Here we might see a barely recognizable picture of a child. The text tells us that this child has "disappeared," sometimes years ago, without a trace. The inference is that this child has been kidnapped. Reading on through this "wanted" poster, we may discover that the child was a teenager when the disappearance happened. Ask yourself, has this person been

Steele's milk carton pokes fun at the now discontinued toy Diana camera. This inexpensive plastic camera achieved a cult following and was used by serious photographers to purposely produce soft-focus images.

© Tom Steele. *The Missing Diana*, 1987. 9 1/2 × 2 1/2 × 2 1/2 inches. Mixed media.

What Does It Really Say?

When encountering new information, be prepared to get beyond the surface and discover what is actually taking place. Do not be fooled by appearances and symptoms. In this instance, the message is being delivered in three different modes: photographs, words, and the interaction between the two media. Each has its own private, independent meaning, but the juxtaposition creates an entirely new and different result. Be aware of how an anonymous voice of power is being used in both an economic and social framework to manipulate the viewer.

· ASSIGNMENT ·

What is something that you feel strongly enough about that you would like to express it to millions of people in the privacy of their kitchen on a milk carton? Create such an image and attach it to a carton of milk. You may use text. Fill the carton with milk and keep it in your refrigerator. Use it in your normal household eating activities. See what reactions are generated by it during the course of a week.

Stereo Cards

Sir Charles Wheatstone discovered the stereoscopic effect in binocular vision (using both eyes at once). In the 1830s he invented both the reflecting (mirror) and refracting (lens) stereoscopes for use with hand-drawn designs. Photography provided answers to many of the difficulties of these hand-drawn designs. Stereo pictures were tremendously popular from about 1854 to 1880 and again from about 1890 to 1919, with millions of cards and viewers sold.

How the Stereo Effect Is Achieved

Stereo cards create a three-dimensional effect by taking separate photographs of a subject from two lateral viewpoints 2 1/2 inches apart, which is the average distance between the human eyes. This is accomplished with a twin-lens camera

kidnapped or has this person run away from a situation that was intolerable? What should we believe? A 1988 Justice Department study reports an estimated 3,200 to 4,600 children (anyone under the age of eighteen) were abducted in the United States by nonfamily members; more than 350,000 were abducted by family members and almost 450,000 were listed as runaways.[3]

This is not meant to trivialize the issue of lost children. However, we are confronted with conflicting information that in turn puts the validity of all the messages on the carton in doubt. Does this milk really contain the stated amount of vitamin D or was the amount of vitamin D determined in the same manner in which it was decided that the person was kidnapped? What should we think? Is the kitchen table the place for such a confrontation? What is public information and what is private? When should the line be crossed? What is the role of photography in all of this? What is the real issue being raised here? Could the truth be that a family conflict that has not been resolved in one house has, through the use of photographic methods, spilled over into someone else's house?

[3] Patricia Davis, *"The Milk-Carton Kids," Washington Post National Weekly* 7, no. 28, May 14–20, 1990.

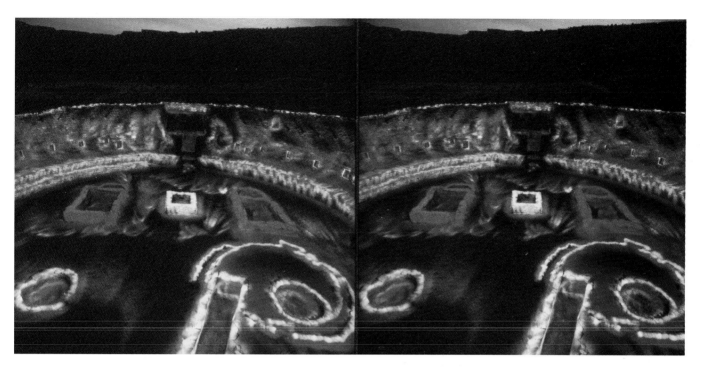

Meares informs us: "Stereo light-painting has enabled me to 'see' a world that does not exist in perceptual time or space. Stereoscopic photography further helps defy the eye/mind limitations that we place on reality. Images in the 3-D format have the power to become a kinetic interpretation. Making the picture involves lengthy time-exposures at night; this allows me to walk about unseen in front of the camera while selectively illuminating with a flashlight or other continuous light source all that is aesthetically desirable. The exposure is a collective of the entire lighting sequence; gels are selected and placed in front of the flashlight."

© Lorran Meares. *Casa Rinconada, Chaco Canyon, NM,* 1988. 3 1/2 × 7 stereo card. Dye-destruction prints.

that has an interlocked double shutter that makes two images of the subject at the same time, side-by-side on the film. Stereo cameras can also produce a three-dimensional effect by interlacing the images with one another through the use of a lenticular screen.

It is also possible to produce stereo pictures of subjects that contain no movement with a regular camera. This is done by making the first exposure of the subject and then shifting the camera exactly 2 1/2 inches and making the second exposure. It may be moved to either the right or the left, but be certain to move it in the same direction every time. If this is not done, it gets confusing which is the right-eye view and the left-eye view. If they are mixed up the stereo effect will not work. There are also stereo devices that can be attached to the front of the camera lens and permit simultaneous exposures with a conventional camera.

It is also possible to produce stereo images on the computer that can be viewed with red and blue 3-D glasses. These can be made at home with medium-density red and blue cellophane (red lens over left eye and blue over the right). The results can be printed using low-cost tools and techniques.

The Effect of Distance

The normal stereo effect starts at about 5 feet from the camera and is exaggerated at closer distances. Stereo infinity is the distance that the stereo effect ceases. This can range from 200 to 1,500 feet and is dependent on the number and variety of visual depth clues that are included in the view. The hyperstereo effect, in which the depth and size of the objects are exaggerated, occurs when there is too great a separation between the picture-taking viewpoints. It is generally noticeable in the foreground of the picture. Improper separation of the images on the viewing card can also produce this effect. Pictures up to 2 1/2 inches wide can be mounted in a simple viewer with the proper distance between their centers. Larger images, having more than 2 1/2 inches between their centers, need to be viewed in a stereoscopic viewer with a lens or prism to compensate for this distance, which is greater than that between human eyes.

Standard Stereo Card Size

Following the model card in figure 21.20, make a standard 3 1/2-x-7-inch stereo card that is designed to be viewed in the basic refracting stereoscope. This style was devised by Sir David Brewster in 1849 and was improved into its current form by Oliver Wendell Holmes in 1861. It consists of a T-bar with a handle beneath the stereoscope body. A hood at one end of the bar contains two short-focus spectacle or prism lenses; a crossbar at the other end holds wire clips in which the card with the stereo photographs is inserted. The crosspiece can be moved back and forth along the bar for focusing. An opaque divider extends part way along the T-bar between the lenses, preventing each eye from seeing the opposite image. The stereo effect can be seen without a viewer. A simple opaque divider can be placed between the two images, maintaining the focus of the left eye on the left image and the right on the right image. Inexpensive twin plastic lenses, held up to your eyes, are also marketed.

Guidelines for successfully making a stereo card include the following:

1. Think in three dimensions. Consider how the objects in the foreground, middle ground, and background will affect the final visual illusion. Provide the necessary visual depth clues to make the picture function in three dimensions. Use the depth of field to expand or contract the depth of the camera's vision.
2. Shift the camera exactly 2 1/2 inches for the second exposure.
3. Match the print density of both images.
4. Use a 3 1/2-x-7-inch support board on which to attach the images. Check to make sure the right image is on the right side before attaching the views to the card.

Artists' Books and Albums

The idea of illustrating books with photographs appeared shortly after the invention of photography. Anna Atkins's *Photographs of British Algae: Cyanotype Impressions* (1843–53) and William Henry Fox Talbot's *The Pencil of Nature* (1844–46) are examples of paper prints being hand pasted into books. The images had to be added by hand since there was no perfected method for direct reproduction of photographs until the halftone process of the 1880s.

The carte-de-visite, French for visiting card, was a 2 1/4-x-3 1/2-inch photograph, usually a full-length portrait, mounted on a 2 1/2-x-4-inch card. It was introduced in the early 1850s and became a fad during the 1860s in America and Europe. Millions of

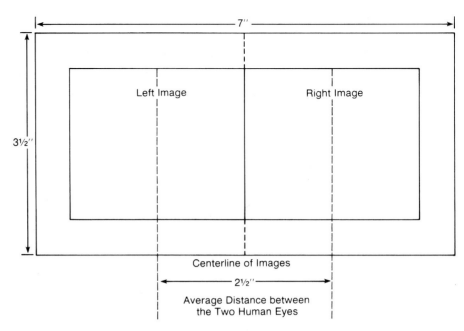

Figure 21.20
A model for making a stereo card that can be viewed in any standard refracting stereoscope. Both the left and right images must be of equal size. The left and right images are positioned so the distance between the center of each image is about 2 1/2 inches. The distances to the top, side, and bottom borders surrounding the images need to be equal.

Sligh works with various photographically based prints, artists' books, video, audio, sculpture, and writing to explore the intersection of memory and history, reality and myth. "I am interested in the visual tensions which result from the integration of machine generated and hand-made image and text." Her starting points can be anything, a found photograph, a memory, a word, an interaction, a place, almost anything that resonates with her. From there she does research in libraries and archives. "This leads me to shoot more photographs and conduct interviews." Sligh uses copiers, computers, drawing, and writing to combine repetitious elements of marks, words, and photographs into one frame. Successive and simultaneous time elements are brought into the present in one frame, one place, or one event.

© Clarissa Sligh. *What's Happening with Momma?* (interior view), 1987. 11 × 36 inches. Van Dyke brown prints.

"cartes" were made of individuals, celebrities, and tourist attractions. People did not use them when they called but exchanged and collected the cards, keeping them in albums with special cutout pages for easy viewing. The birth of the photo album can be traced back to this custom.

The mixed media work of Lady Filmer, who cut and pasted cards into designs that were interlaced with watercolor and text, is an early prototype of an artist-made book (circa 1864).

The artist-made book can bring together a play between photographs, text, drawings, marks, and appropriated

Golding's self-project was influenced by the film *Shoah* and the photographs of Roman Vishniac. The series conveys a sense of traveling to a place where life is askew. The visual references to ancient Egypt speak to their reverence for building cities for the dead. This work began as black-and-white photomontages. Color was applied with oils, dyes, and an airbrush. The result is rephotographed and printed. This process allows Golding the freedom to abstract his reactions to social and political issues. Golding says: "These highly manipulated images derive their visual impact in part due to the preconceived notion that a photograph is inherently a truthful statement."

© Stephen Golding. *The Series: Road to Necropolis*, 1990. 16 × 20 inches. Chromogenic color print.

materials into a variety of formats. Since the late 1960s, photographers have been rediscovering the idea of the book as a way of working. They have dealt with themes of a narrative and diaristic nature as well as those of sequential time, dreams, friendship, and social and political issues. Many photographers who were denied access to the traditional outlets, such as museums and galleries, began to cut and paste and make use of quick-copy centers, rubber stamps, and old, unwanted printing equipment. The handmade book has provided an inexpensive alternative, artist-controlled, method of getting the work out to a larger audience. There are workshops, classes, conferences, printers, distributors, and book shops that specialize in artists' books. Digital imaging methods are providing access to previously inaccessible imaging and printing techniques.

Create your own book or album. Begin by selecting a theme. If this is your first book, keep it simple, work with the familiar, and give yourself a time frame. For instance, decide to keep a diary of a trip. Get yourself a bound, unruled artist's sketch book and a nonbleeding, permanent marker pen or soft-leaded pencil. Include a map of your route, a written account of a conversation, or anything that grabs your interest. Leave space to include pictures. Photograph the people you are traveling with and those whom you meet. Collect local newspaper articles, business cards, menus, postcards, and tourist pamphlets. Use your photos or make drawings to help convey your impressions. Break with the single image concept. Shoot the foreground, middle ground, and background and combine them on the page. It's okay to cut and paste. Make a panorama and tape it into the book. Make a series and stack them up on top of each other to make a flip book. Include signs; show exteriors and interiors.

Be spontaneous. As experience is gained, consider tackling other themes and altering the format presentation. Select your own paper size and color, and bind them to make your own book. Artist Norman Colp suggests this simple binding method: Take a handheld hole punch and measure three or four equally spaced holes (on the left side or top) and punch. Using the first as a guide, punch the remaining pages in the same manner. Use small metal key rings as binders or heavy thread. Visit stationery stores for other possibilities.

For more information on artists' books see Lyons, Joan, ed. *Artists' Books: A Critical Anthology and Sourcebook.* Rochester, NY: Visual Studies Workshop Press, 1985 and Smith, Keith. *Structure of the Visual Book, Text in the Book Format,* and *Non-Adhesive Binding: Book Without Paste or Glue.* These titles are available directly from the author, 22 Cayaga Street, Rochester, NY 14620-2153 or Visual Studies Workshop. Also see Druker, Johanna. *The Century of Artist's Books,* 1995. (Available from D.A.P.)

Write and Evaluate Your Own Assignment

This is the opportunity to make that picture you have been dreaming about and then measure the plan against what was accomplished.

Guide to Evaluation—Before Photographing

Before you go out to make any pictures, consider the following:

1. Write a clear, concise statement of the exact goals you intend to accomplish.
2. Describe and list your objectives, both objective and subjective, and how you plan to reach them.
3. What problems do you anticipate encountering? How do you propose to deal with them?

Guide to Evaluation—After Photographing

After making your pictures, answer these remaining questions:

1. *Achievement*: How many of the stated objectives were obtained? How well was it done? Are you satisfied? What benefits have been gained? Has new knowledge been acquired? Have new skills been developed? Have any attitudes been either changed or reinforced? Has the way in which you see things been altered?
2. *The unexpected*: What were the unforeseen benefits and problems that were encountered? Did anything happen to alter or change the original plan? How do you think you did with the unplanned events? Was there anything that you should have done to make a better picture that you did not do? How will this help you in the future to be a better imagemaker?
3. *Goals compared to achievement*: Compare the final results with the original list of goals. What did you do right? What did you do wrong? What are the reasons? What would you do differently next time? Were the problems encountered of an aesthetic or technical nature? Which were more difficult to deal with? What has been learned? How has it affected your working methods? Make yourself the teacher and measure how well the objectives of the assignment were met. What grade would you give a student on this project if you were the teacher? Why? Be specific.

Sources of Photographic and Artists' Books

Aperture
20 East 23rd Street
New York, NY 10010

A.R.T. Press
5820 Wilshire Blvd., Suite 402
Los Angles, CA 90036

Center for Book Arts
626 Broadway, 5th Floor
New York, NY 10012

Center for Exploratory & Perceptual Art
(CEPA Gallery)
700 Main Street, 4th Floor
Buffalo, NY 14202

D.A.P.
636 Broadway 12th Floor
New York, NY 10012

Hacker Art Books, Inc.
45 West 57th Street
New York, NY 10019

Hoffman's Bookshop
211 East Arcadia Avenue
Columbus, OH 43202 (used books).

Light Impressions
439 Monroe Avenue
Rochester, NY 14607-3717

Nexus Press
535 Means St.
Atlanta, GA 30318

A Photographer's Place
P.O. Box 274
Prince Street Station
New York, NY 10012

Photo-Eye Books
376 Garcia Street
Santa Fe, NM 87501

Printed Matter Bookstore at Dia
77 Wooster Street
New York, NY 10012

University of New Mexico Press
1720 Lomas Boulevard, N.E.
Albuquerque, NM 87131

Visual Studies Workshop
31 Prince Street
Rochester, NY 14607

TWENTY-TWO

Color Operations into Practice

© Jo Babcock.
Intersection Rocks, 1993.
40 × 65 inches. Chromogenic color print.

Babcock, who likes to build cameras, has converted a VW van and an Airstream motorhome into giant cameras. The exposures are made on color mural paper (which could be used as a negative), but Babcock prefers the negative image because it "represents the photographic process" and delivers an "expressively convincing post-nuclear frame-of-mind."

Color Pinhole Photographs

Go into a dark room and make a small round hole in the window shade that looks out onto a bright outside scene. Hold a piece of translucent paper 6 to 12 inches from the hole and you will see what is outside. This optical phenomenon, which dates back to the ancient Greeks, provides the basis for making pinhole photographs. Note: The image will be upside down, the same as in our eyes. Our brain turns it right side up.

Birth of the Camera

The *camera obscura* (Latin for "dark room") is a drawing device used to project an image onto a flat surface where it can be traced. It is based on the same principle underlying pinhole photography. By the sixteenth century the camera obscura was in common use by artists, such as Leonardo da Vinci. In 1658 Daniello Barbaro placed a lens on the camera obscura. It was this device that helped to work out the understandings and uses of perspective, which had been baffling artists, scientists, and scholars for centuries. Daguerre's camera was a simple camera obscura with a lens.

How Does the Camera Work?

An optical image is made up by what is known as tiny circles of confusion. Technically, the circle of confusion is the size of the largest circle with an open center, which the eye cannot distinguish from a dot, a circle with a filled-in center. It is the major factor that determines the sharpness of an image and the limiting factor of depth of field. When these circles are small enough to form an image they are called "points" and the image is considered to be in focus. The pinhole camera has infinite depth of field, because it creates circles of confusion that are about the same size as the pinhole all over the inside of the camera. This means that these tiny circles of confusion

Wright's direct exposure of reversal material, such as ILFOCHROME, produces a one-of-a-kind pinhole photograph. Filters are placed over the pinhole to make color corrections. Exposure times can run from 3 to 6 minutes.

© Willie Anne Wright. *Our Lady of the Nectarines for San Francisco*, n/d. 16 × 20 inches. Dye-destruction print.

are small enough to be considered points of focus with enough resolution to become a coherent image. If you add a lens, it makes smaller points of focus and the image is sharper and more coherent.

Materials to Build a Pinhole Camera

These items are needed to make a pinhole camera:

1. A sheet of stiff mat board or illustration board at least 1/16 inch thick. One side of the board should be black. This will be the inside of the camera. The black helps to reduce internal reflection.
2. A sharp X-Acto (number 11 blade is good) or mat knife.
3. A 2-×-2-inch piece of brass shim or aluminum. An offset plate, obtained from a printer, is ideal. You can also use an aluminum pie pan or TV dinner tray.
4. Glue. Any household white or clear glue is fine.
5. A steel-edged or plain straight-edged ruler will deliver a far more accurate and close cut than a cheap wooden or plastic ruler.
6. A number 10 or number 12 sewing needle.
7. A small fine file or number 0000 sandpaper.
8. A ballpoint pen.
9. Black photographic pressure tape or black electrician's tape.
10. A changing bag (optional).
11. A piece of black-and-white, single-weight, fiber-based enlarging paper.
12. Polaroid Time-Zero film and SX-70 camera for color pictures.
13. The blueprint of an adjustable focal-length pinhole camera provided in figure 22.1.
14. A 35-mm camera can be converted into a pinhole camera. Cover a UV filter with black (opaque) construction paper with a good pinhole in the center. Place it on a 35-mm camera and it becomes a pinhole camera. A body cap, with a pinhole constructed in its center, can also be used.

Variable Focal-Length Pinhole

The focal length of a pinhole camera is determined by the distance of the pinhole from the light-sensitive material. Building a camera with a variable focal length gives you the flexibility similar to that of having a zoom lens. The adjustable focal-length camera should be built to the dimensions given in the blueprint in figure 22.1 if you plan to shoot any Polaroid film. You can use the film pack as a movable focal plane or make one out of cardboard. If you make one, be sure to glue on an upside-down set of cardboard steps to hold the paper flat during exposure. Save the used film packs because they make an excellent ready-made holder for any other materials you want to expose. They are structural and can be easily moved forward or backward inside the camera to vary the focal length. As the focal plane is moved closer to the pinhole, the angle of view becomes wider and the exposure time drops as needed.

Pinhole Camera Construction

Following the blueprint in figure 22.1, lay out the dimensions on the board. Carefully cut out all the pieces using a sharp knife and a straightedge. Sand any rough areas. Now proceed to the next two sections, making the pinhole and the shutter. After this is done, glue all the pieces together. Do not rush; allow the glue to dry. Finally, use the black tape to make all the seams lighttight. Mark both the right and left sides of your camera clearly in the number of inches the focal point is from the pinhole. This is to give you more accurate and repeatable results. The closer to the pinhole, the wider the angle of view and the shorter the exposure will be.

Making the Pinhole

Do not stab a hole in the metal; gently drill it with the needle on one side and then the other. Sand or file. Repeat until the hole is as perfectly round and as free from defects as possible. With aluminum you can increase image sharpness by thinning the metal around the pinhole. This can be done by placing the metal on a book and punching it lightly in the center with a ballpoint pen and then smoothing the back with a file. Then make the hole with the needle.

Now find the center of the front end of the camera. Cut a square opening equal to half the diameter of the metal pinhole material and glue or tape it into place.

The Shutter

You can create a simple shutter by making a sliding door in front of the pinhole with some thin board, or save the piece you cut out of the center of the camera front for the pinhole. Darken the sides with a marker and use a piece of tape to build thickness and to act as a handle. This creates a trapdoor-type shutter. Another option is to simply use the black plastic top from a film container and hold it in place with your hand or tape. Aluminum foil and tape also work.

Exposure

If you know the needle number you can figure out what the f-stop will be, based on the focal length. A light meter can be used to give a ballpark exposure figure provided you know the speed of the light-sensitive material being exposed.

The Aperture Formula

The f-stop is a simple ratio expressing the relation of the size of the opening that emits light, the pinhole, to the distance from the opening to film plane (table 22.1). Therefore, a 1-inch opening and a 7-inch focal length gives a ratio of 1:7, or an f-stop of f/7. A number 10 needle makes a pinhole diameter of .018 inches with a 5-inch focal length and would make an f-stop of f/277, which can be rounded off to f/280 (.018 divided into 5 is 277.777).

Starting Exposure Times. Outdoor exposure times run between 1 and 15 seconds, depending on quality of light and the focal length. Trial and error will provide a starting point for acceptable exposure.

Getting the Hang of It. If you have never worked with a pinhole camera, begin by exposing black-and-white photographic paper. Process the paper following standard black-and-white procedures. If it is too light, give it more exposure; if it is too dark, give it less exposure. When you get a good negative, dry it and make a contact print. After experience is gained it is possible to expose any type of photographic material in the pinhole camera.

· A S S I G N M E N T ·

Make the following pinhole pictures:

1. *A portrait of one person that makes a statement about that person.* Go beyond a pinhole mug shot.
2. *A group portrait of two or more people.* This compounds the problems of composition and technical limitations.
3. *An architectural study (portrait of a building).* Show how this building is unique and what made you stop and photograph it.
4. *An object from nature.* Show the life force at work.
5. *A human-made object.* Show why it is important to you.
6. *A self-portrait.* Tell something about yourself.

In the course of creating these six pinhole pictures, change the focal length. Have a minimum of one wide-angle view, one normal view, and one telephoto view. List the focal length and other exposure information on the back of every print.

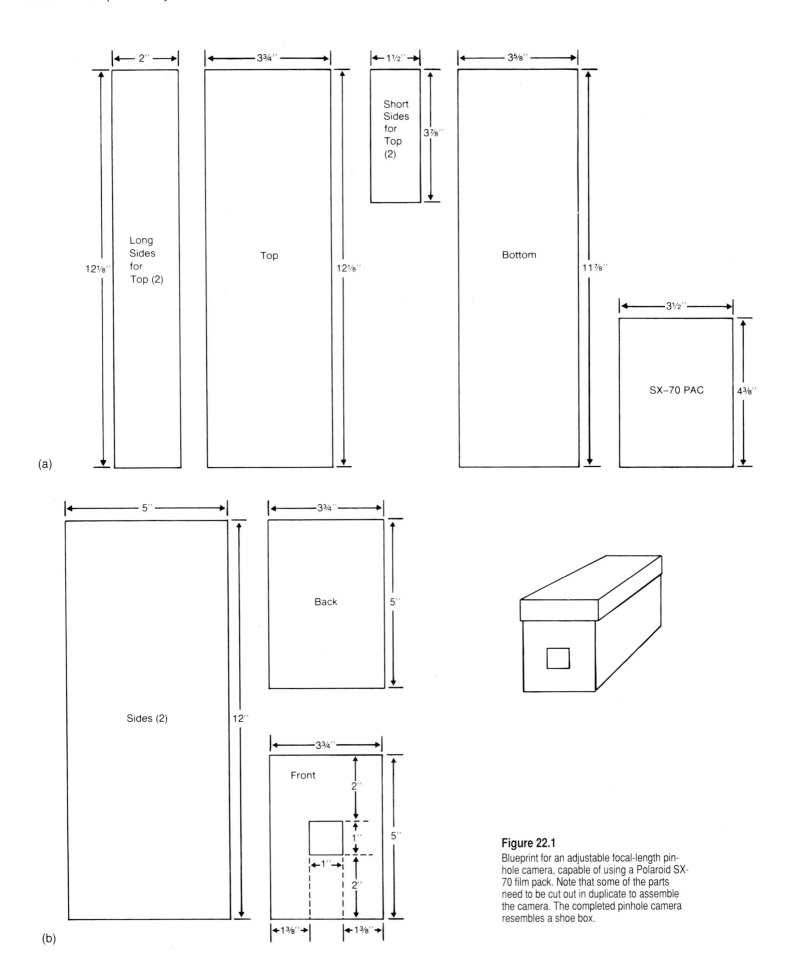

Figure 22.1

Blueprint for an adjustable focal-length pin-hole camera, capable of using a Polaroid SX-70 film pack. Note that some of the parts need to be cut out in duplicate to assemble the camera. The completed pinhole camera resembles a shoe box.

· **TABLE 22.1** ·

Standard Needle Sizes and Their Diameters

Needle Number	Diameter
4	.036 inches
5	.031 inches
6	.029 inches
7	.026 inches
8	.023 inches
9	.020 inches
10	.018 inches
12	.016 inches
13	.013 inches

SX-70 Film Exposure

After learning the basics of the pinhole camera, you will be ready to start with color materials. SX-70 Time-Zero film offers a quick entrance with color. SX-70 follows the same basic rules as color slide film. If the print is too light, it means it has been given too much light, so cut back on the exposure. Should it be too dark, this indicates it was not given enough light. To correct this, increase the exposure time.

SX-70 Filtration

With the SX-70 film, prints are often too "cool" looking. They have either a blue or cyan cast. This can be corrected by using the Kodak plastic color-compensating filters. To make the print warmer, use yellow or magenta plus yellow filters to correct. Twenty points of filtration is a good starting place. Use yellow to reduce blue and magenta plus yellow to reduce cyan.

You can also use the color filters to experiment in purposely altering the color to change the mood or feeling of a scene. Filters create added density, and you may have to increase the exposure time.

What next? Go on and expose color negative material or ILFOCHROME Classic paper, or even modify the camera to take a Polaroid 4-×-5-inch back.

For more detailed information read Shull, Jim. *The Hole Thing—A Manual*

Using a pinhole camera with an extremely short focal length, Ess exposed 4-×-5-inch Polaroid positive negative film. Ess uses filters to produce "psychological colors" suitable for her image content. To create these two monochrome colors Ess "blocked out the top part of the image with a customized dodging tool. I then exposed the bottom part of the paper using filtration to create the greenish, yellowish grey of the bottom. I changed filtration and then blocked out the bottom and exposed the top to get the purplish blue. The theme of my work is the subjective relationship of the self to the phenomenal world and the fact that our memories, emotions, and thoughts determine how and what we see."

© Barbara Ess. *Untitled*, 1993. 39 1/2 × 27 1/4 inches. Chromogenic color print.
Courtesy of Curt Marcus Gallery, New York, NY.

To get the feel and look of a frantic shopping spree Burchfield rehearsed and directed live models and various objects on eight pieces of dye-destruction paper. The photogram was created as Burchfield walked into and around the picture space exposing the paper with a penlite flashlight and colored gels for about 20 minutes.

© Jerry Burchfield. *Art and Commerce*, 1986. 8 × 16 feet. Dye-destruction print.

of Pinhole Photography. Hastings-on-Hudson, NY: Morgan & Morgan, 1974; Renner, Eric. *Pinhole Photography: Rediscovering a Historic Technique,* Boston: Focal Press, 1995; *How to Make and Use a Pinhole Camera,* Eastman Kodak Publication AA-5, 1973; or Zakia, Richard D., and Todd, Hollis N. *101 Experiments in Photography.* Hastings-on-Hudson, NY: Morgan & Morgan, 1969; or contact Eric Renner at the Pinhole Resource Center, Star Route 15, Box 1655, San Lorenzo, NM 88057.

Photograms

A photogram is a cameraless image created by placing a two- or three-dimensional object on top of light-sensitive material, and then exposing the entire setup to light. After development the image reveals no exposure effects where an opaque object was in touch with the emulsion. Instead, it produces an outline of the object.

A wide variety of tones and colors are produced where translucent objects were placed on the emulsion and where partial shadowing occurred under opaque objects that were not totally in contact with the emulsion. Areas that were left uncovered receive the maximum exposure and do not record any detail.

A Concise History

The early explorers for a workable photographic process, Johann Schuluze in 1725 and Thomas Wedgwood and Humphry Davy in 1799, all began their experiments with cameraless images. The technique remained dominant until 1918, when Christian Schad, a dadaist painter, used this method to make abstract images known as schadographs. Man Ray followed with his rayographs and then László Moholy-Nagy with what we now call photograms.

Color Photograms

Color offers expanded possibilities for the creation of photograms. Photograms can be made on any light-sensitive

material. Color paper offers a starting place for beginning experimentation. Paper is easy to work with and it can be handled under a safelight, which enables you to see where to place the objects. It can be processed quickly so the results are immediately known.

The choice of objects to use in photograms is endless. Give it some serious thought and don't just use what happens to be in your pocket. There are natural objects such as plants, leaves, flowers, feathers, grass, sand, and rocks. Consider using artificial objects such as colored glass, or make your own materials. These can include cut paper in a variety of colors and shapes. They may be either translucent or opaque. Here are some additional ideas:

- Liquid-colored inks, such as Dr. Martin's, can be put on a piece of thin glass and exposed through onto the paper. The thickness of the glass affects the outcome. Both inks and objects can be combined.

- Different-colored light sources can be used to make various color effects.

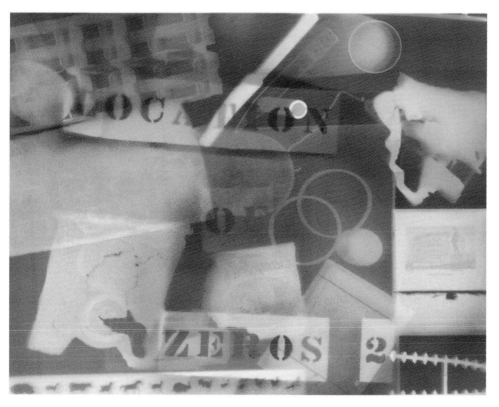

The photogram is used here by Barrow as a vehicle of inquiry into the nature of photography itself. The spray-painted colors on the image call attention to the fact that photography is not a depiction of reality but an extension of our own private experiences and perceptions.

© Thomas Barrow. *Location of Zeroes 2*, 1981. 16 × 20 inches. Gelatin-silver print with enamel spray paint. Courtesy of J. J. Brookings Gallery, San Jose, CA.

- The color enlarger can be used as the source of exposure. Try changing the filter pack to produce a range of colors. Another effect is created when you expose an area with one filter pack and another area with a different filter pack. Also, try using an electronic flash, filters, or transparent plastic to color the light. Another technique is to employ a penlight as the source of exposure. It can also be used to draw with and to emphasize certain areas. Attach it to a string and swing it above the paper to make an unusual exposure effect. Filters can be placed in front of it to color the light, too.

- To maintain a naturalistic color balance when printing on negative paper (RA-4), put a clear, processed piece of negative film in the enlarger to make use of its orange mask.

- Combine a negative that has been made with a camera with one or more of the cameraless techniques.

- Rephotograph the photogram and incorporate it with another camera or cameraless image.

- Remember, all the regular guidelines for printing apply. This means areas may be burned and dodged during exposure.

- Do not just plop some junk down on a piece of paper, turn on the light, and expect it to look good. Feel free to explore as many arrangements and uses of the materials as possible.

Chemograms

A variation of the photogram is the chemogram, which involves applying photographic chemicals to a camera or cameraless image with a brush or by dribbling (figure 22.2). Begin with a photogram on black-and-white paper. Selectively paint the developer on the paper with a brush. By permitting time to elapse between exposure, painting, and fixing, limited color effects (yellow and reddish tones) can be produced as the photochemicals and the components of the emulsion oxidize. Another option is to use a strong reducing agent such as thiourea and a base such as sodium carbonate as a painting medium before the image is fixed. Mixing these two chemicals produces a silver sulfide stain. This can create unusual juxtapositions in image makeup, contrast, and spatial relationships. Normal fixing and washing should render the image and colors permanent. Further effects can be achieved by toning.

Cliché-Verre

Cliché-verre combines the handwork of drawing with the action of the light-sensitive materials of the photographic process to make a picture. Shortly after Henry Fox Talbot made public his photogenic drawing, three English artists and engravers, John and William Havell and J. T. Wilmore, devised this method of working. In their technique a piece of glass was covered with a dark varnish and allowed to dry. A needle was then employed to etch through the varnish to the glass. The glass was used as a negative and contact-printed onto photographic paper. They exhibited prints from their process in March 1839, making it one of the first spin-off methods to come from the invention of the photographic process.

In France the process was "reinvented" in 1851 when Adalbert Cuvelier used the glass collodion plate method. He introduced it to Jean-Baptiste-Camille Corot, who made it popular. It was employed by many other artists of the Barbizon school and proved to be an accurate, easy, and inexpensive way to make monochrome prints.

The process was revived again in the United States in the late 1960s and early 1970s. At this time there was renewed interest in nontraditional approaches to the photographic medium, which got a boost in part from the effects of the counterculture and its interest in alternative modes of expression.

Figure 22.2
An offshoot of the photogram, chemogram, juxtaposes a camera-made image and painting with chemicals. A print was made from two negatives. As it developed, it was worked with a brush very close to the safelight to produce the Sabattier effect. Next it was painted with stop bath in some areas. The lights were turned on and thiourea and sodium hydroxide were introduced. After the print was fixed, hypo cleared, and washed, it was soaked in a gold protective solution (GP-1) for 8 hours, and then rewashed and dried.

© Nolan Preece. *Au Descends on Ag,* 1989. 16 × 20 inches. Gelatin-silver print with applied chemicals.

Working Procedures for Making a Cliché-Verre

Begin making a cliché-verre by getting a piece of glass and covering it with an opaque paint or varnish. Black spray paint works well. The glass can be smoked instead of painted to make a different type of visual effect by creating uneven densities. One method to smoke the glass is to hold it over the chimney of a lighted kerosene lamp. A sheet of film that has been exposed to white light and developed to maximum density can be used instead of glass. Scratching on a photographic emulsion generally produces a more ragged-edged line than that obtained with a coated piece of glass.

Once the glass is dry, a drawing is made with a stylus (needle, X-Acto knife, razor blade, piece of bone, or whatever you can imagine) by scratching through the coating to the glass. The glass can now be used as a negative to make a contact print or enlargement on a piece of photographic paper.

Traditionally only black-and-white prints were made with this technique, but by using color photographic paper and dialing in different filter pack combinations it is possible to achieve a wide range of colors (figure 22.3). Color can be used in a variety of ways for different effects:

- Use colored inks to opaque the glass. Applying a series of different colored inks and not scratching down all the way to the glass can provide a multi-level color effect.

- Apply translucent colored inks to the glass or plastic negative as a way to introduce different colors into the final print.

- Combine the cliché-verre method with a camera-made negative. Scratch directly onto the camera-made negative and then make the print.

- Combine the use of colored inks and scratching onto a camera-made negative.

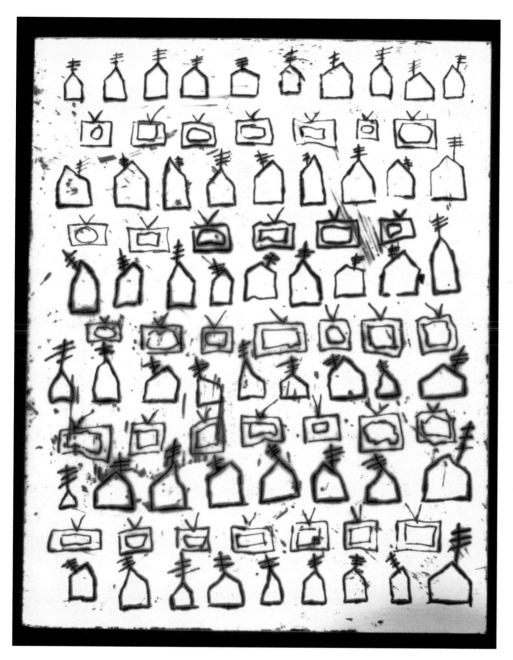

Figure 22.3

According to a recent A. C. Nielsen survey, American households annually watch a total of 224,372,599,000 hours of television. The cliché-verre technique is applied here to lampoon the influence that television has come to have in our society.

© Robert Hirsch. *Television Land*, 1986. 20 × 16 inches. Chromogenic color print.

to have a preference for the "two penny coloured" pictures as opposed to the "penny plain." The hand coloring of black-and-white photographs continued to be widely practiced by commercial photographers for over the next 100 years.

Why Hand Alter the Work?

At present hand altering the negative or print allows you to circumvent and explore ideas that would not normally find their way into current photographic processes. It lets you introduce nonrepresentational colors, lines, patterns, and shapes into the photograph. It pushes the boundaries and limits of photography, enabling you to achieve a unification of materials, practice, and vision that is not possible to achieve in standard practices. It also alters the sense of time, because hand alterations expand and prolong the interaction of the imagemaker within the process.

Methods to Consider

Some of the methods of modification of the negative and/or print include scraping or scratching with a stylus (figure 22.4) and drawing or painting directly onto the image surface. This can be done with a brush, spray paint, an airbrush (see next section), cotton balls, or other means of application. Colors can be either transparent or opaque. The medium can be acrylics, food coloring, dyes, ink, oil paint, or watercolors (figure 22.5). Heat can be selectively applied to distort or destroy part of the image. Chemicals or chemical processes can be used to physically alter the appearance of the image (figure 22.6). Optical distortion materials can be placed in front of lenses or light sources to dramatically change the image. Electronic signals can be employed to create a pattern on a screen that is photographed or used to directly expose the film or the paper. The photobased image can be combined with other media such as engraving, lithography, silkscreening, or one of the many forms of printmaking (figure 22.7).

Hand-Altered Negatives and Prints

The first color photographs made their appearance in the form of hand-colored daguerreotypes. This was done to correct for the fact that all the early photographic processes lacked the ability to record color. The demand for color was greatest in portrait work. Miniature painters, who found themselves instantly unemployed by Daguerre's process, met the need by tinting daguerreotypes and painting over calotypes (the first photographic negative/positive process done on paper). In England the public seemed

Figure 22.4

An in-camera double exposure was made by first covering the left side of the lens and then making the second exposure covering the right side. Casey "decided to 'draw' on these prints with a small X-Acto knife blade [in order] to penetrate through to the space behind the picture frame."

© Casey Williams. *Studies and Models: Untitled #12,* 1988-90. 3 1/2 × 5 inches. Chromogenic color print.

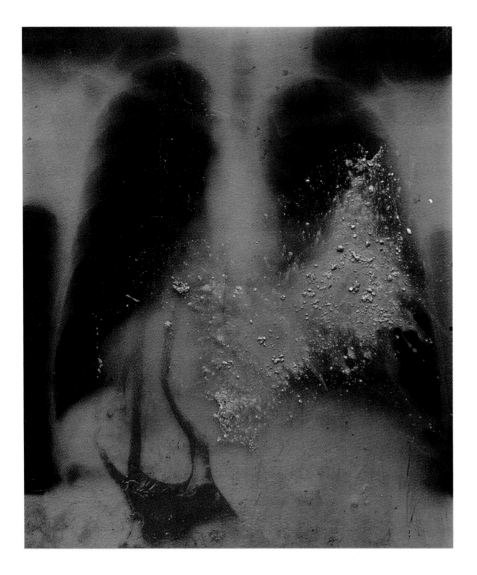

Figure 22.5

Cohen states: "The conventional purpose of the X-ray is the investigation of ill health and disease. I have chosen to hand-alter the X-ray with color in order to expose and undermine this purported neutrality of use. The mediums I employ react chemically and physically with the film, producing changes in color and consistency, making the unseen visible. Decomposing the X-ray, these actions parallel the decay and evaporation of the body [this X-ray is of a person with AIDS]. They also invoke an empathic response to its transience. The colors become metaphors for the non-corporal, the immaterial, those aspects of the person the X-ray as a diagnostic device circumvented. The X-ray's power to make the internal visible is not neutral; it invokes terror. I do not allow the scientific/diagnostic to abolish the possibility of ecstasy which is on the other side of terror."

© Cora Cohen. *R8,* 1993. 17 × 14 inches. Exposed roentgenograph film with mixed media.

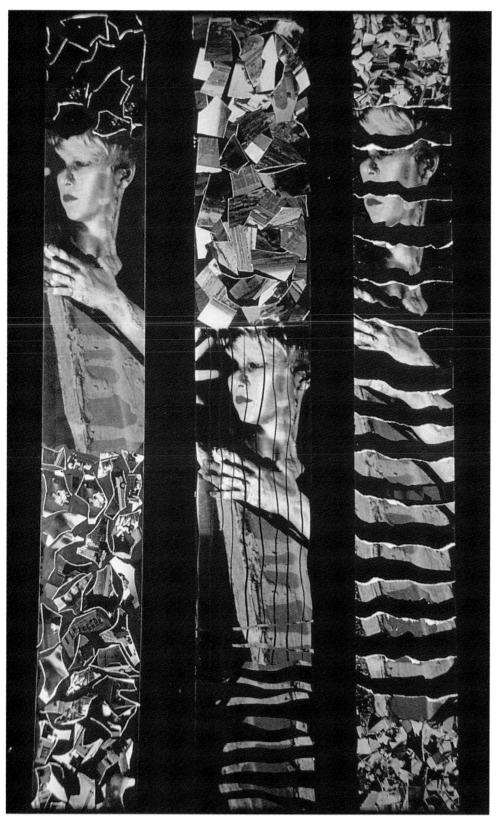

Figure 22.6

A slide-projected image was directed onto the model and photographed. Prints were made from slide film that was processed in C-41 chemicals. These were collaged onto clear acrylic with a mat gel. A sharp object was used to scratch patterns directly into the emulsion of the prints.

© Joyce Roetter. *Split Triptych,* 1990. Each 1 × 8 feet. Chromogenic color prints on acrylic.

Airbrushing

The airbrush, invented in 1882, is a small handheld spray gun able to transmit a precise mixture of fluid (dye, ink, or paint) and air to a specific surface location. A dual-action, internal mix brush with a fine head assembly is a good choice for most photographic applications. It permits the operator to do detailed work and alter the width of the line and the value or opaqueness of the fluid without having to stop and make adjustments. The use of an optional bottle container is recommended to extend the normal spraying range without having to stop and refill. The airbrush is powered through a flexible hose by pressurized canned air, such as Badger Propel, or by a compressor with an air pressure regulator. Being able to adjust the air pressure from 10 to 100 pounds per square inch (PSI) gives extra control over the line quality and intensity. Start at about 20 PSI and add pressure at the rate of about 5 PSI to see how it affects the character of the spray line.

The fluid medium needs to be thin. Typical starting places are one part water to one part nonclogging ink or watercolor, seven parts water to one part acrylic, or one part enamel to one part enamel thinner. Spraying requires a constant steady motion to avoid dips, runs, and sags. Work rapidly to avoid having the head clog. After each operation, spray clean water or solvent through the airbrush until all the color is out. Most technical difficulties, that is, equipment failures, are due to improper cleaning. Follow the manufacturer's cleaning and maintenance instructions. Airbrushing must be done, following all safety guidelines, in a well-ventilated area with an exhaust fan and with the operator wearing a double-cartridge respirator.

For additional detailed information on many hand-altered methods see Hirsch, Robert. *Photographic Possibilities.* Stoneham, MA: Focal Press, 1991.

Figure 22.7

As a printmaker and painter, Henderson uses photo-based techniques whenever it is necessary to serve a particular image. In this piece the background was created with ink brayers, the red "lifesaver" was painted in oils, and the drawings were appropriated from eighteenth-century medical texts with the aid of a copy machine. Copiers can be used to create an image that will accept ink and can then be printed to any absorbent or semiabsorbent surface. For Henderson, "The process becomes a mode of inquiry, an open ended dialectic that bears directly on the formal content. A discourse is formed between the handmade and the reproduced, the pictorial sources and their signifiers, and between the tradition of painterly expressiveness and postmodern strategies of appropriation and representation."

© Adele Henderson. *Ontogeny No. 5*, 1995. 40 × 30 inches. Acrylic, oil, litho ink transfers from electrostatic prints on gesso panel.

Making Black-and-White Prints from Color Negatives

The time will come when you need to make a black-and-white print from one of your color negatives. Maybe one of your pictures is going to be reproduced in the local newspaper, or a client may want a black-and-white print from a job that you did in color. You may make a photograph in which the composition appears strong but the colors do not work well together. It could be that the picture may work better in black-and-white, rather than in color. In certain situations, shades of gray communicate better than colors.

Basic Problems

There are some basic problems that need to be overcome to make a good black-and-white print from a color negative. If you simply attempt to print a color negative on regular black-and-white (blue-sensitive) paper, there will be a loss of contrast. The colors from the negative will not be reproduced in the correct shades of gray. Most commonly, reds print too dark, which is noticeable in the skin tones of the print, and the blues appear too light, revealed in the tonality of the sky. Such a print will not look natural. Also, regular black-and-white paper produces a much grainier image because it only responds to the cyan dye layer of the color negative. This creates gaps in the grain pattern because the paper cannot record the dye image from the magenta and yellow layers of the negative. As a result the grain has a very coarse appearance. It should be noted that imagemakers have made use of these characteristics to produce unusual effects.

Black-and-White Prints from Color Paper/Ektamax RA Paper

There are a number of ways to overcome these problems. You could make a color-corrected black-and-white negative on panchromatic film, but this is a difficult

A black-and-white print was made from a negative etched with a knife. Acrylic paint, ink, and Gesso were applied with a Badger dual-action airbrush and a handbrush. Selected areas were colored with Prismacolor pencils. Materials, appropriated from magazines, were glued onto the print with TALAS archival white glue. This composite, layering approach allows nonlinear thinking and feeling to influence events in time and space.

© Robert Hirsch. *Remembering and Forgetting: A New Way of Seeing*, 1991. 16 × 20 inches. Gelatin-silver print with paint, colored pencil, and collage materials.

and time-consuming process. The simplest solution is to use a color paper, such as Kodak's Ektamax RA Professional, that allows the direct production of neutral-tone black-and-white prints from color negatives in the normal RA-4 color process.

Ektamax RA is a resin-coated paper that is similar to panchromatic paper, such as Kodak Panalure Select RC Paper, grade M. The paper is available in two contrast grades: L for low-contrast applications such as portraiture and M for medium-contrast commercial applications. The starting filter pack remains the same as used for printing color negatives (or use 45M and 45Y as a starting place). Limited contrast control can be obtained by altering the filter pack. To lower contrast, subtract 20M and 20Y. To increase contrast, add magenta and yellow. Adding more than twenty units of magenta or yellow can affect the red color lightness reproduction. The presence of any color

cast in the image may indicate that your process has a developer or bleach-fix problem. Ektamax is good for quick and general work, but panchromatic paper continues to offer more versatility and contrast control over the final image.

Black-and-white negatives can be printed onto this paper at normal filtration by sandwiching a clear piece of processed C-41 film to provide the missing orange mask. Without this mask you run the risk of having the neutral tones show a distinct color cast (this can be used as a method to introduce monochromatic color into a black-and-white print). Without the mask, use a filter pack of 80M and 110Y as a starting place.

Panchromatic Paper/Panalure

Panchromatic enlarging paper, such as Kodak's Panalure, is sensitive to green and red as well as to blue light. There are

other materials available, such as Seagull RP Panchromatic paper, but it is not safelight safe and must be handled in total darkness.

Panalure Select RC is a warm black tone, medium-weight, developer-in-emulsion, resin-coated paper, available in a glossy (F) surface. It comes in three contrast grades: The L (low) grade for printing negatives having high contrast, the M (medium) grade for negatives of average contrast, and the H (hard) grade for printing negatives of low contrast. It is designed for machine development in an activator-stabilization processor, but it may be tray processed.

Safelight Conditions

Since Panalure paper is panchromatic (sensitive to all the colors of the visible spectrum), it should *not* be handled under a standard black-and-white safelight. The regular #13 color safelight is recommended. Keep safelight exposure to a minimum. If you do not have a #13 safelight, simply do not use a safelight.

Development

Panalure can be developed in a normal black-and-white developer such as one part Dektol to two parts water (1:2) or one part Selectol to one part water (1:1). Normal development temperature is 68°F (20°C). Standard development time for Dektol is 1 1/2 minutes. Selectol's development time is 2 minutes. Both have a useful range of 1 to 3 minutes in the developer. All the tones produced will be warm blacks. All processing procedures are the same as for any regular black-and-white paper. Contrast can be further modified by choice of developer and how it is mixed. To increase the print contrast, use Dektol mixed equally with water (1:1) or even use Dektol straight and print using a condenser-type enlarger. To decrease print contrast, use one part Dektol to three (1:3) or four parts water (1:4). If this does not do it, switch to one part Selectol or Selectol Soft to one or two parts water (1:2) and print using a diffusion or cold-light-type enlarger.

Panalure paper can be toned with warm toners such as Kodak's Sepia and Brown toner.

Use of Filters

Normally exposures are made using only white light. On a color enlarger start out with all the filters set on zero. You can use dichroic or CC filters during exposure of the Panalure paper to change the gray tonal values in the final print. The filters work in the same manner as if they were used on a camera with black-and-white film. If you want to make a gray tone lighter, use a filter of the same color as the photographed object. For example, if you made a picture of a yellow flower and wanted the gray tonal value of the yellow to be lighter in the final print, you would add yellow filtration. If you would like to make a gray tonal value darker, use the filter of the complementary color of the subject photographed. To make the yellow flower darker, add blue filtration.

Black-and-White Prints from Regular Color Paper

What if there is no panchromatic paper available to make a black-and-white print? The standard color negative papers are panchromatic. It is possible, by altering the development process, to make a black-and-white print on color paper. There will be a loss of image contrast and quality when compared with Panalure paper.

What to Do

Expose the color paper normally, as if making a regular color print. Instead of processing it in the color process, process it in a standard black-and-white process. Use fresh, undiluted Dektol because the prints made in this manner tend to be flat. No color developer is used. Dektol processes the metallic silver and the fixer removes the unexposed and undeveloped silver halides. Do not use a color bleach-fix because it removes all the silver. This procedure exhausts the

chemicals rapidly, and they should be replaced often.

For this project, make the following prints from a single negative:

1. Perfect color print (figure 22.8).
2. Panchromatic print; use filters if necessary (figure 22.9).
3. Print on regular black-and-white paper (figure 22.10).
4. Color paper processed in black-and-white chemistry (figure 22.11).
5. Ektamax print (not shown as the subtle differences are lost in the reproduction process involved in making this book).

When you have completed all the prints, compare all the black-and-white prints to the original color print and see which one works best. Pay close attention to the red and blue colors to see which offers the best translation. Learn all you can about the different ways that the photographic processes can be put to work for your picture ideas. There is no telling when you might need one or where it might lead you.

Toning for Color

Toning is a method of adding or altering the color of a black-and-white photograph. The following are commercially available ways of affecting the color of a print.

Development

The combination of paper developer and printing paper offers the most subtle way to control color through chemical manipulation of the emulsion. The age, dilution, temperature, time, and type of paper developer all affect the final tone of the print. Silver bromide papers usually produce a cool neutral to green color while silver chloride emulsions make warmer tones. The combination of both the type of developer and kind of paper also has an effect on the tones produced

if any other method of toning is employed later.

Replacement

Process the print with a nonhardening fixer, such as Kodak Rapid Fix, without adding Solution B. Now the silver compounds in the emulsions can be converted with inorganic compounds—that is, gold, iron, selenium, and sulfur—to produce a wide range of muted and subtle colors. Factors influencing the color are the metallic compound used, the degree of toner dilution, the type of paper and developer, the temperature of the solution, and the length of toning (figure 22.12).

Dye Toning

Dye toning produces the most vivid and widest range of colors. The dye base is usually attached to the silver in the emulsion through the action of a mordanting chemical. Mordants such as potassium ferrocyanide act as a catalyst and combine with the dye to fix it in place. This prevents it from bleeding or migrating within the dyed area. The print is placed in the dye solution. The dye is deposited in the emulsion in direct proportion to the density of the ferrocyanide image.

A variety of colors can be achieved by mixing dyes, immersing the image in consecutive baths of different dye, and selectively masking parts of the print with a frisketlike rubber cement. There are also straight dye applications in which the silver is not converted, but the toner simply dyes all parts of the image equally. Dyes often lack long-term stability and fade when exposed to any type of UV light. Dyes often leave residues that can be seen in the base of the paper even after complete washing.

Safety

Many of the toning compounds are extremely toxic. Before using any toner read the directions and follow the safety procedures outlined by the manufacturer and in the chapter on safety. Always

Figure 22.8
A normal well-crafted color print. Compare it with figures 22.9 to 22.11 to see how it translates into a black-and-white image.

© Paul Marlin. *The Bagheads*, 1987. 8 × 10 inches. Chromogenic color print.

Figure 22.9
This figure offers an excellent translation of the color print. This print was made on Panalure paper, a panchromatic paper sensitive to green and red light in addition to blue light. This provides an accurate tonal rendition of all colors into shades of gray.

© Paul Marlin. *The Bagheads #2,* 1987. 8 × 10 inches. Gelatin-silver print.

Figure 22.10
This print was made on a normal fiber black-and-white paper that is sensitive to blue light. There is a reduction in the tonal range and the colors are not reproduced in the correct shades of gray. Notice how the outline around the sign letters comes up looking white.

© Paul Marlin. *The Bagheads #3*, 1987. 8 × 10 inches. Gelatin-silver print.

Figure 22.11
This photograph was made on color paper that was processed in a normal black-and-white process. There is a noticeable loss of image quality and contrast when compared with the Panalure print. It will do in an emergency and produce an acceptable halftone for reproduction purposes.

© Paul Marlin. *The Bagheads #4*, 1987. 8 × 10 inches. Chromogenic color print.

Figure 22.12
This solar photogram was made with two different exposures, the figure in the late afternoon and the leaves in the midmorning, directly onto printing-out paper. After fixing, the image was placed in a gold toning solution. Madigan gives this summary: "This series of photograms is about the very fragile relationship between the human being and the natural world. The process engages life through the use of constantly changing foliage. Not only is the image a drawing with light, but also an expression of energy. . . . In a time of great social and political turmoil, my work attempts to respond to the essential joy within the human spirit."

© Martha Madigan. *Leaf Drawings: Earth, Air, Fire, Water,* 1989.
72 × 40 inches. Printing-out paper with gold toner.

wear rubber gloves and work in a well-ventilated space.

Further information is available from Kodak, Edwal Imaging (Falcon Safety Products) 25 Chubb Way, Somerville, NJ 08876–1299 and Berg Color Tone, 72 Ward Road, Lancaster, NY 14086–9779. Also see Davidson, Jerry. *From Black & White to Creative Color: How to Tone, Tint, and Retouch Photographs,* also available from Berg and Hirsch, Robert. *Photographic Possibilities.* Stoneham, MA: Focal Press, 1991. *Darkroom Dynamics,* edited by Jim Stone (Stoneham, MA: Focal Press, 1979), and *Alternative Photographic Processes,* by Kent E. Wade (Dobbs Ferry, NY: Morgan & Morgan, 1978), both offer sections on toning. If you are interested in making your own toners contact Photographers Formulary, P.O. Box 950, Condon, MT, 59826, (800)922–5255. They offer a complete range of materials for the photographic chemist.

Cross-Processing/Slides as Negatives—E-6 at 1,200

Astonishing visual events can occur by taking color slide film and processing it to produce negatives. It is possible to push the film up to a speed of 10,000, dramatically increasing the color saturation, raise the level of contrast, and create a pointillistic grain structure à la the French neo-impressionistic painter George Seurat.

What to Do

Get a thirty-six-exposure roll of Kodak Ektachrome 200 Professional film. Set the film speed at 1,200. Bracket your exposures 1/2 f-stop and one full f-stop in both directions. If you push the film higher, be extremely careful in your exposures to retain acceptable shadow detail. You will be able to shoot in very low levels of light or use very high shutter speeds to stop action.

Look for Dramatic Changes

Contrast will be greatly increased, as in all push processes. A scene of low contrast will come out to be one of at least average contrast. A scene of high contrast will come out looking like it was shot on litho film.

There will be a noticeable increase in color saturation. Colors can begin to vibrate, look very intense, take on a "Day-Glo" appearance, and become deeper and more brilliant. The grain will appear quite oversized. You can literally pick out the different points of color.

Overall, the composition will tend to become more abstract, bold, impressionistic, and striking. The process is great for creating a mood. It is not suited for a situation that requires clarity and sharp detail. It should offer the opportunity to see things in a different manner. Predawn, after sunset, and night now become times that are accessible for you to photograph. This is not the time to go and shoot by the beach at noon. With these posterlike colors, the images tend to cry out to be printed bigger than normal. Consider getting some larger paper to print on if you find these images successful.

Development Procedures

After exposing the roll, the film will be developed *twice*, once in a special black-and-white process and then a second

• TABLE 22.2 •

Development Procedures for Processing Transparency Film as Negative Film

First Development Process Black-and-White Development Chart
After black-and-white development is completed, the same roll of film must be developed for a second time following regular C-41 procedures.

Solution	Time/Temperature		Agitation
1. Acufine (1,200)	12 min	75° F	30 sec*
Acufine (10,000)	25 min	75° F	30 sec
2. Water stop	30 sec	75° F	Continuous
3. Color film fixer or black-and-white fix without hardener	5 min	75° F	1 min†
Remaining steps can be carried out under normal room lights.			
4. Wash	15 min	75° F	
5. Bleach (C-41)	15 min	75° F	1 min
6. Wash	30 min	75° F‡	
7. Dry	Room temperature§		

Second Development Process

C-41 Color Development
Follow all steps as listed in table 8.1 on p. 71.

* Agitate continuously for first 30 seconds and then for 5 seconds every 30 seconds.
† Agitate continuously for first 15 seconds and then for 5 seconds every 10 seconds.
‡ Water must be constantly flowing. If the wash is not complete it is possible to contaminate the color chemistry.
§ At the end of this process your negatives will appear extremely thin with a light creamy pink color cast. This is normal.

time in the normal C-41 color process (table 22.2). After completing the black-and-white process you can either dry the film and carry out the C-41 process at a later time or continue on and complete both processes in succession. Be certain not to use any type of wetting solution like Photo-Flo if the film is dried before doing the C-41 process. At this point, watermarks do not matter because the film will be developed again and the wetting agent can cause difficulties in the color development.

Color Development

After completing the special black-and-white process develop the film again in the regular C-41 process, following normal C-41 procedures. The C-41 color developing process adds the color couplers and the density and color saturation will appear more normal. The entire C-41 process may be carried out under normal room lights. Be certain to maintain accurate temperatures.

Evaluation

After the film has dried inspect it. It appears pink because the slide film does not contain the orange mask as do regular color negatives. Make a contact sheet to see exactly what you have to work with. The highlights should be fairly dense and bold and the shadow detail will look thin. The colors should be intense with the grain quite visible. Negatives with good detail in the shadow area and with highlights that are not blocked indicate proper exposure. You should have exposures at 600, 800, 1,200, 1,800, and 2,400. Check to see which film speed worked best.

Printing

Because there is no orange mask you will probably have to add about 20 to 30 units of yellow to your regular starting filter pack (or sandwich a clear piece of processed C-41 film over your film). A low-contrast scene should print like a normal negative. A

Karady makes use of the changes in contrast, grain structure, and increased color saturation achieved by processing slide film in C-41 chemistry to play with photographic representation's relationship to reality and truth. In her *Surgically Altered Fruit* series, Karady fabricated fruits and photographed them in an attempt to emphasize the artifice inherent in photographic practice: "In context with our current technological society this work evokes genetic engineering, plastic surgery, and computer manipulated photographs, all of which have shaken our notions of truth. Metaphorically they evoke the body and the experience of clothing or reinventing one's self through the recreation of one's exterior appearance. Just as the skins mimic the idea of shape of the fruit inside, we desire to take attributes of the other through similar mimicry and masquerade."

© Jennifer Karady. *Banana Honeydew*, 1995. 4 1/2 × 5 1/2 inches (image size), 6 × 7 inches with frame. Chromogenic color print with polyester resin and fruit frame.

one f-stop (set ISO at 50) and then process the exposed transparency film in the C-41 process.

Color Infrared Film

Kodak Ektachrome Infrared film is a false-color reversal film that originally was designed for camouflage detection by aerial photography. We are interested in how the unusual color effects of this material can find an application in artistic, fashion, illustration, or pictorial photography.

Infrared waves are electromagnetic radiation waves that are below the visible spectrum and are made of wavelengths that are longer than those for red. The infrared range extends into the wavelengths that we associate with heat. Infrared film actually allows us to see things that are not visible to the human eye.

Characteristics of Infrared Film

Infrared color reversal film is made up of three layers of emulsion that are sensitive to red, green, and infrared instead of the standard sensitivity to blue, green, and red. When this film is processed the green layer responds to form yellow, the red produces magenta, and the infrared makes cyan. All three layers are sensitive to blue, producing a magenta cast unless a yellow filter is used.

Infrared film can be used in daylight, artificial light, and even in total darkness to record the invisible infrared waves. Infrared waves cut through haze and mist, making the use of this film effective to photograph scenes that encompass great distances.

Since this film is sensitive to waves we cannot see, it is a good idea to load and unload the camera in total darkness. Refrigerate this film before and after exposure, but let it reach room temperature before exposing or processing it. After rewinding the completed roll, return it to its container and process as soon as possible.

contrasty scene may require exposure times of over a minute. Although the colors will be much more saturated and the grain very noticeable, the overall color balance of the scene should remain the same as you saw it. This process does not create false colors as with infrared, but it enhances what is already there.

Use this process to step into some new areas that you had felt were off-limits with your conventional use of materials. Normally you would use color materials to depict a scene. Now is your chance to open up and express your feelings and mood about a subject.

Another Cross-Processing Method

E-6 film can be processed in C-41 chemistry to achieve an artificial, hyperenhanced color scheme with intense contrast. Take a 100 ISO daylight transparency film and overexpose it by

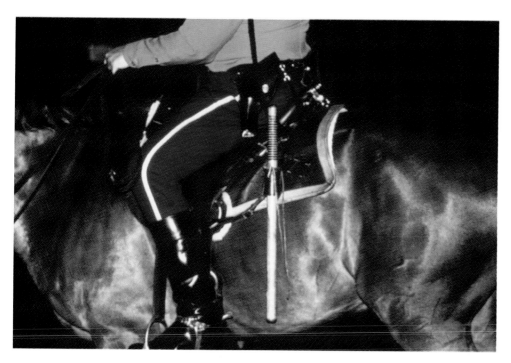

With Kodak Ektachrome Infrared film, an orange filter in front of the camera lens, and some flash fill, Bessoir made this image at dusk. The mounted policeman was wearing the standard matching dark blue shirt and pants, which the infrared film recorded as different shades of pink and red due to the amount of infrared light they reflected. Infrared light is rendered as red by the film.

© Tom Bessoir. *Mounted Policeman, New York City*, 1982. 24 × 36 cm. Chromogenic color slide.

Filtration and Color Balance

With color infrared film, a Wratten filter No. 12 (deep yellow) is recommended in daylight at all times. Without it the slides will look magenta. You can use other yellow filters to achieve different effects, but a deep yellow works best. The addition of a polarizing filter to the yellow filter can give foliage a deeper red or darken the sky dramatically. When working with tungsten light sources of 3200 K or 3400 K a CC20 cyan and a Corning Glass Filter CS No. 3966 plus the yellow filter is the suggested starting place. For pictorial pictures CC50 cyan and the yellow filter are recommended.

Try these suggestions to change the color balance of infrared film: To increase magenta or decrease green add a cyan filter; to increase red or decrease cyan add a blue filter; to increase yellow or decrease blue add a magenta filter.

When high levels of infrared are present, as with chlorophyll-rich plant life, what appears to be green to the eye records in the infrared color (red) instead.

Exposure

Because this film is sensitive to infrared, a regular film-speed rating cannot be applied. Most meters will not even measure infrared. A preliminary daylight starting point is a film speed of about ISO 100 with a Wratten filter No. 12 and ISO 50 under tungsten light with CC20 cyan. Due to the uncertainty of actual infrared conditions, bracketing is a good practice in 1/2 f-stop increments. At shutter speeds of 1/10 second or longer reciprocity failure can happen. To correct for this, increase the exposure about one full f-stop and add a CC20 blue filter.

Focusing

Infrared film does not focus at the same point as regular film. Most lenses have an infrared focus mark on their barrel, the most common being a red dot or a red "r." If the focus of the subject is 10 feet, move the 10-foot spot on the lens barrel from its regular position over to the infrared one. Now the 10-foot mark is next to the infrared one rather than its normal place of focus. By using a wider-than-normal lens and stopping down the aperture to f/8 or f/11 you can generally compensate for this if you do not have the time or forget to refocus the camera to the infrared mark.

Chance

As you can tell, this process is not exactly precise. There are quite a few variables. Chance certainly enters into your calculations. Experimentation is in order. To begin to obtain repeatable results it is necessary to keep a written record of your exposure and filtration for each picture. Do make some pictures that include foliage, sky, human skin, and water. See the effects this film produces on these subjects.

Processing

Infrared film processing is generally carried out with the E-4 process. Kodak no longer offers this service or makes packaged chemicals for E-4. Kodak will supply formulas for mixing your own E-4 chemicals and a list of labs that do the processing (800–242–2424). Some people have obtained good results by processing with some of the chemicals in the Kodak E-6 Hobby Pac. Although Kodak does not recommend this method, it is being presented here to increase user access to this material (table 22.3). In most pictorial applications, small differences in false color renderings will be acceptable. Consider this method to be experimental, and do not hesitate to make changes. No safelights or inspection equipment can be used. Beware that some plastic developing tanks can be penetrated by infrared waves; stainless steel tanks continue to deliver the best results.

Criterion Photoworks, 119 East 4th Street, Minden, NE 68959 presently sells an infrared film that it processes as a negative. For more detailed information about this film, obtain the Kodak publications M-28, *Applied Infrared Photography,* and N-17, *Kodak Infrared Films.*

• TABLE 22.3 •

**Processing Kodak Ektachrome Infrared in a
Modified Kodak E-6 Hobby Pac Kit.***

Step	Time†	Temperature‡
First developer	4 min	110° F
Wash	30 sec	110° F
Color developer	3 min	110° F
Wash	30 sec	110° F
Bleach-fix	6.5 min	100° F
Wash	1 min	100° F
Stabilizer	30 sec	Ambient

* Not all the solutions included in the Hobby Pac are needed in this process.

† Includes drain time.

‡ High processing temperatures mean timing and agitation are critical. In first developer, agitate constantly for first 30 seconds and then 5 seconds for each 15 seconds thereafter. In color developer, agitate constantly for first minute and 5 seconds for each additional 15 seconds. In bleach-fix, agitate constantly for first 30 seconds and 5 seconds for each remaining 30-second cycle. Washing times are the suggested minimum (four complete rinses) and may be extended. Use a water bath, as mentioned in chapter 7, to maintain temperature.

Color from Black-and-White: Litho Film

Litho films offer photographers a wide array of possibilities in altering and enhancing their vision. Here are some of the basic methods that can be applied in the making of color photographs.

Bas-Relief

Bas-relief is a technique that creates the illusion of the third dimension in a two-dimensional photograph by emphasizing the shadow areas of the picture. The effect is achieved by placing a normal continuous-tone negative in contact with, but slightly out of register with, a high-contrast positive of the same negative. Variation in the registration method alters the intensity of the effect. The negative and positive are then placed into the enlarger together and printed with a single exposure onto a piece of color paper.

The tonal range can be sharply reduced to produce extremes in the highlight and shadow areas. The final print will be a simplified version of the original scene; there will be no subtle details. The image will be graphic. Line and shape become the key compositional elements. Colors appear bold, bright, and striking. Be visually dynamic in the selection of the composition.

Litho films can be employed in many operations involving color imagery. Seeley summarizes his method: "Bits of ribbon, florist wires, cut paper, and other objects or drawings are arranged on a light box and photographed using a 4-×-5-inch enlarger as if it were a copy camera. The unexposed 4-×-5-inch litho film goes into the carrier, and the light box is switched on to initiate a series of silhouette exposures. The litho negatives are then tray processed. These negatives are enlarged onto 16-×-20-inch litho film. Three to five copies of this master positive are modified by the addition or elimination of specific areas so that they may serve as separations for the addition of color in the final printing process. Each color separation is then conventionally screen-printed on paper. The final prints are the result of three to five layers of color ink, normally printed on black paper."

© J. Seeley. *Flatware, Red State*, 1985. 16 × 20 inches. Photo screen print on paper.

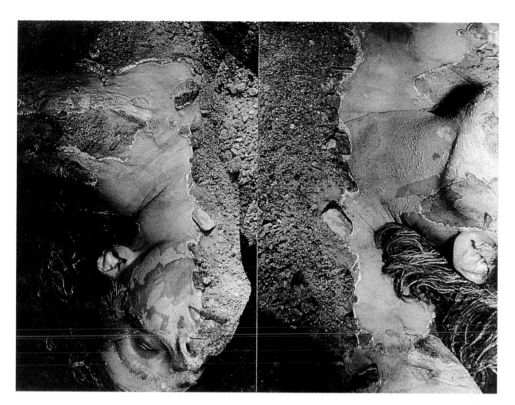

Notari finds another way to sandwich black-and-white and color negative films. She declares: "I combine a black-and-white negative of my figure (covered in a layer of clay slip) with a color negative of a textured ground to create a color image which transforms into an abstract or imagined experience and space. By sandwiching the negatives, each image transmutes into a symbolic vision beyond what an individual image can offer."

© Carrie Notari. *The Eternal Return: The Myth of Persephone*, 1989. 9 × 14 inches. Chromogenic color print.

Litho Production Materials

The production of both positive and negative lithos from the original through the use of both contact printing and projection printing is done to make the final pictures. It is possible to work from either a negative or a slide. You will need the following materials: An original continuous-tone color negative, two clean pieces of 11-×-14-inch glass, color paper, litho film such as Kodak's Kodalith film, litho developer such as Kodak's Kodalith Developer A & B, and a red ortho safelight filter (1A).

All darkroom procedures with litho film must be carried out under a red 1A filter. With the exception of the developing and washing of the film, the darkroom procedures are the same as regular black-and-white printing. Mix all chemicals beforehand and allow them to reach an operating temperature of between 68° and 72° F (20° and 22° C). Process in trays that are a little larger than the size of the film used.

Chemicals

Start readying the chemicals by preparing a working solution of litho developer by following the manufacturer's mixing directions. Make sure that there is enough solution to cover the film completely. Next, make up a tray of stop bath, and then prepare a tray of paper-strength fixer. Have a deep tray for washing. Finally, mix a tray of wetting agent, such as Kodak's Photo-Flo, with distilled water.

Making the Contact Positive

When the chemicals are prepared and at operating temperature set the enlarger to 8-×-10-inch print height, and then over a clean opaque surface, place the clean negative on top of an unexposed piece of litho film, emulsion to emulsion. The lighter-colored side of the litho film is the emulsion side. The dull side of the negative is its emulsion side. Put a clean piece of glass over this entire sandwich. Dust creates pinholes that have to be retouched.

Set the enlarger lens to f/11 and make a test strip. The exposure time should be similar to the time used for making an 8-×-10-inch proof sheet. White light, without any filters, is used to expose the litho film.

Develop the litho film by sliding it into the developer emulsion-side up. Agitate the tray by lifting one corner and setting it back down. Lift another corner and repeat. Complete development takes 2 minutes and 45 seconds. The dark areas should be totally opaque. Develop by visual inspection under the safelight and pull the film when the density appears correct. Do not develop for too short a time because streaks and pinholes may appear in the opaque areas. If the image comes up too rapidly reduce the exposure time and try again. If the density is too light after 2 minutes and 30 seconds, increase the exposure time.

When the development is complete lift the film out by one corner and slip it into the tray containing a working solution of stop bath. Agitate the film gently for about 10 to 15 seconds in the stop bath. Lift the film out, drain it, and put it into the tray of fixer.

In the fixer, agitate the film constantly and gently. In about 60 seconds the image will start to clear. Note how long it takes for this to occur. The total fixing time will be about twice the clearing time.

Rinse the film off, and then inspect it in white light for proper exposure and processing. Do not attempt to judge it under the red safelight, because it will appear darker in the developer than in white light. If everything looks good continue to the next step. If not, decide what the trouble is and redo the process.

Wash the film for at least 5 minutes. To preserve the film for a longer time, use a hypo eliminator and then wash the film again for at least 10 minutes. Handle wet film with care to avoid scratching it.

After washing prepare a wetting agent mixed with distilled water and apply for at least 30 seconds.

Hang the film by one corner in a dust-free place to dry. Excess water can be removed with a Photo-Wipe on the

Tharp has found yet another method to incorporate black-and-white film into her color imagemaking. She tells us: "I borrowed my parents wedding album and rephotographed it with black-and-white negative film and color slides. I then took the slides and projected them onto myself creating a tatoo-like image on my skin (and made photographs of this set-up on black-and-white negative film). This was processed and printed onto color paper. I get great tonal ranges and have the capability to make a print slightly sepia or bluish in coloration."

© Deborah Tharp. *Self-Portrait with Mother*, 1988. 24 × 20 inches. Chromogenic color print.

nonemulsion side. This helps to get rid of processing debris, streaks, and watermarks and speeds up the drying time.

After the film is dry, make a contact positive based on test information. Burning and dodging can be employed.

Retouching

Opaque can be applied with a spotting brush to retouch litho film. Any place

that opaque is applied the light will be blocked. The opaque eliminates dust spots, pinholes, scratches, and any unwanted details by simply painting over them. Work on the base side of the film. Opaque is water soluble and can be removed with a damp Photo-Wipe if a mistake is made. Litho film is versatile and can also be collaged, drawn on, scraped, and scratched to make an image.

Making a Litho Projection Positive

While the litho contact positive is drying, make an 8-×-10-inch positive from the same original negative using the following procedure: Place a clean negative in the carrier and put it into the enlarger, which should already be set to the 8-×-10-inch format. Then focus and set the enlarger lens to f/11 and make a test strip. The exposure time should be close to the time used to make the positive litho contact. Repeat the processing procedures and evaluate.

Now proceed to make an 8-×-10-inch projection positive based on the test information.

Making Litho Contact Negatives

To make a litho contact negative take the dried litho positive contact and place it, emulsion to emulsion, with an unexposed piece of litho film on a clean opaque surface and cover with glass. Repeat the processing steps.

Take the dried 8-×-10-inch litho positive and repeat the previous steps.

At this point you will have an original color negative, a contact litho positive, a contact litho negative, an 8-×-10-inch litho projection positive, and an 8-×-10-inch litho negative.

· ASSIGNMENT ·

This series of lithos can now be used to change the original image in various ways. Make the following color prints using a combination of the negatives and positives you have made:

1. *A straight print from the original continuous-tone color negative.* This acts as the standard of comparison for the rest of the prints that will be made using the lithos.

2. *A bas-relief print.* On a light table place the litho contact positive with the original negative. Carefully arrange the two just slightly out of register, so they do not exactly coincide. When a pleasing registration is obtained, tape the two pieces of film

together. Put this sandwich into the negative carrier and place it into the enlarger. Make a color print following normal working steps.

3. *A high-contrast bas-relief print.* Arrange the 8-×-10-inch litho negative and positive slightly out of register and tape them together. On a clean opaque surface, lay the film sandwich on top of an unexposed sheet of color paper. Make a test print to determine the correct exposure, and then make the final print.

4. *A high-contrast black-and-white negative or positive.* Make a contact print using the 8-×-10-inch litho negative. Adjust the filter pack to make three prints that have entirely different color balances. Record the filter pack information so that you will know how to alter colors with black-and-white film. Some typical filter packs and the colors that they will produce include:

$$150Y = \text{purple}$$
$$150M = \text{yellow-green}$$
$$150C = \text{sepia}$$
$$150C + 60Y = \text{red}$$
$$150C + 60Y = \text{yellow-brown}$$

5. *A high-contrast black-and-white positive.* Follow the same procedure as for print number 4.

6. *Carbo print hues (optional process).* To produce colors that have a flat tonal range, such as a copy of an old Fortune magazine, make two black-and-white positives from the negative. Sandwich all three together and make a print.

7. *An offshoot of this process is to make a color print from a regular continuous-tone black-and-white negative.* The color filter pack information gained from the litho film should apply.

8. What other ways can litho film be incorporated into color photography?

Litho Paper and Color

Special litho papers, such as Sterling Premium Lith, deliver a noticeably gritty grain structure and brown tones that can be controlled by varying the

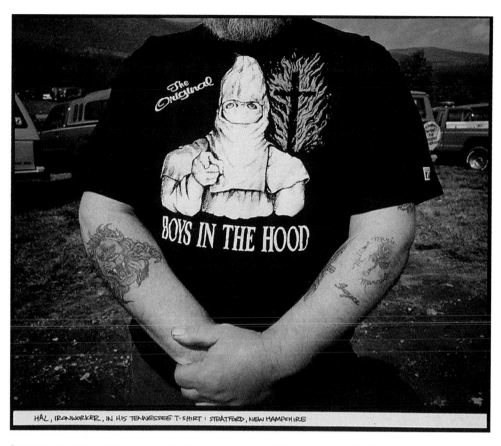

Stone's text supplies additional context for the viewer to interpret his headless portrait. Litho film was used to produce the black border and title bar, which were overprinted with a second enlarger.

© Jim Stone. *Hal, Ironworker, in his Tennessee T-shirt: Stratford, NH*, 1994. 16 × 20 inches. Chromogenic color print.

The figure was intentionally grossly overexposed with an electronic flash. The gritty grain, extreme contrast, and brown tones were produced by varying the exposure and development times of the litho paper in Super Kodalith developer.

© Robert Hirsch. *Demon-Dream*, 1973. 16 × 20 inches. Gelatin silver print.

concentration of the litho developer (the effect is similar to Kodak's discontinued Kodalith paper). The gritty grain effect is enhanced by overexposing the paper by about two f-stops and using a diluted developer for an extended time (roughly, doubling the dilution rate doubles the development time). The paper can also be processed in a standard black-and-white developer for a greater continuous-tone effect. Litho paper should be handled under a red safelight. For details about this product and processing contact Sterling Imaging Inc., 123 West Service Road, Champlain, NY 12919, (800) 295-3740.

• A S S I G N M E N T •

Print the same negative on a regular black-and-white paper and then on litho paper. Experiment with different developers, dilutions, development times, and temperatures. Compare the results. What changes and what remains is the same? What can be communicated with the litho paper that cannot be expressed in a normal black-and-white print?

The Sabattier Effect

The Sabattier effect, often referred to by the misnomer of solarization, is the partial reversal of an image caused by exposing it to light during development. The result contains both negative and positive colors and tonalities.

This effect was first observed in the making of daguerreotypes in the 1840s. Armand Sabattier, a French scientist, discovered what caused this phenomenon in 1862. The process is one that is still not completely understood by scientists today.

The results of this effect are never the same. Many photographers have been attracted to this process because of the expressive uniqueness of each image, the influence that chance plays in the creation of the picture, and the mysteries that continue to surround, defy, and frustrate rational scientific explanation.

The Sabattier effect can be carried out on either negatives or prints. This section deals only with prints since this process does not put the original negative at risk and offers many picture possibilities for someone attempting the method for the first time. Negatives that have been sabattiered do tend to produce more dramatic results than those made directly on a print from an unaltered negative. In order to preserve the original negative, those wishing to sabattier the negative often make copy negatives from the original. The copy negatives are sabattiered at various times and distances in order to produce a wide variety of effects.

How the Effect Happens

The Sabattier effect occurs when a burst of light strikes the paper or film during the development cycle. This fogs the paper or film and reverses the colors and tones. By controlling the duration and intensity of the burst of light, it is possible to control the extent of the effect. Too much exposure produces black by converting all the silver halides to silver. Too little exposure does not change enough of the silver halides to produce the desired results.

Mackie Lines

A definite demarcation, known as a mackie line, is produced at the boundary between the reversed and unreversed areas. If it were not for these lines, the print would appear to be a positive version of a very dense and fogged negative.

What to Look for

Scenes that contain higher-than-normal contrast and possess a wide range of tonal differentiation are good candidates with which to begin experimentation.

Images that have a strong sense of pattern or have distinct shapes will show noticeable changes. This will also make up for the loss of detail and subtlety of tone that accompanies this process. Since light-colored subjects contain more unconverted silver halides than darker ones, they generally respond more strongly to reexposure. When this technique is successfully carried out, the image can appear more graphic with light glowing areas competing against dark mysterious spaces that contain a surreal sense of place, space, and time.

Sabattier Procedure

The Sabattier effect can be produced without any special chemicals or equipment. The print should be developed in a tray because it offers the greatest control, but a drum can also be used. Make the print on the highest-contrast paper obtainable. Mix chemicals to regular strengths, but add a tray of water between the developer and the bleach-fix. Expose the print normally. Develop it for about one-half to three-fourths of the normal time. The print should contain essential shadow detail without full development of the highlights or midtone areas. At this point, remove the print from the developer and place it in a tray of water for up to 30 seconds with agitation. This dilutes the developer tremendously, but it does not completely stop the action of the developer. Next, take the print out of the water bath, drain it, and place it on a clean sheet of Plexiglas, glass, or an unribbed darkroom tray. Squeegee the excess water from the print and put it and the backing under a light source for reexposure.

Sources of Reexposure

A variety of light sources can be used for reexposure. Plug the light into a timer for accurate reexposure control. A small light, such as an architect's lamp with a 15-watt bulb, placed about 4 feet above the print works well. The enlarger can also be used as an accurate, controllable, and repeatable source of reexposure. It also presents the opportunity to easily work with either white light or, by dialing in filters, colored light. Coloring the light source increases the range of effects that it is possible to achieve. Place a towel on the baseboard of the enlarger to catch any dripping water. Remove the negative from the carrier before reexposure. Refocus the enlarger if the negative is returned to make another print. An electronic flash with a diffuser may also be used as a light source.

Degree of Effect. The degree to which the Sabattier effect takes place is determined by when the reexposure takes place and its duration. The earlier the picture is reexposed and/or the longer or brighter the light, the more intense the reversal becomes in the final print. Reexposure time is a matter of seconds or a couple of bursts from the flash. A digital timer allows exposures to be made in fractions of a second, providing even greater control.

Procedure after Reexposure

After reexposure, the image can sit for up to 30 seconds. This can serve to improve the overall contrast and enhance the edge effects that are created along the borders of the different densities.

Now place the picture back into the developer and continue to process normally. The results cannot be judged until the entire process has been completed.

Trial and error is the rule. Nothing is predictable. Not all pictures are suited for this technique. Do not force the method onto a picture. Wait for a situation in which this technique can be used to enhance the statement. Some control can be gained by using a constant light-to-image distance from a timed light source, but careful record keeping of exact working procedures, experience, and experimentation provide the main guideposts.

Tuckey discusses his use of the Sabattier effect: "I took this shot of native Indian men who were inducted into the Guatemalan military, where an effort is made to separate the people from their cultural roots. By solarizing this print, I hoped to evoke some of the emotion I felt while observing this scene. While processing, I flashed the print with a small pocket penlight for an instant (1/2 second) at 1 minute into its development. I was using a Jobo tube and simply removed the lid (in the dark) and shined the penlight in, producing an uneven Sabattier effect. Fortunately, the most dramatic color shifts took place in the highlights—the white uniforms of the conscripts."

© John Tuckey. *Two Faces of Guatemala*, 1991. 8 × 13 inches. Chromogenic color print.

Nonsilver Approaches

The majority of the material covered thus far, with the exception of digital imaging, has its foundation in silver-based photographic methods. In these methods, silver is used as the prime light-sensitive material in the chemical formation of the photographic image. There are other ways in which a photographic image can be formed. This section provides an introductory overview of a few of the major methods. There are older, commercially obsolete processes such as blue printing and gum printing.

Others, such as the UltraStable and Ever-Color processes, combine new and old technologies. These techniques permit the exploration and extension of the demarcation between the photographer, the subject, and the process of photography. The ensuing images can expand the scope of photographic vision by opening new pathways in both ideas and working methods. Before working with any new process, read and follow all safety recommendations supplied by the manufacturer as well as those in the safety chapter. Processes that make use of potassium ferricyanide, ferric ammonium citrate, or ammonium and potassium dichromates can be disposed of by pouring them into a plastic bag filled with kitty litter. This bag can then be sealed and placed in a protected outside trash container.

Cyanotypes, or Blueprints

If you consider blue a color then the cyanotype (aka the blueprint) certainly qualifies as a color process. The cyanotype offers the photographer certain advantages over conventional image processes. Prints can be made without a darkroom, an enlarger, or special developing chemicals. Images can be put on all types of material. The final picture is quite permanent and it is fun to do.

Blueprinting is one of the easiest and most versatile of the nonsilver approaches to working with color and a photographic process, but there are other processes, including Carbon, Gum, Kwik, and Vandyke printing. It is possible to combine different nonsilver methods, creating a new personal blending of the processes tailored to suit your own vision.

History of Blueprints

The process known as cyanotype was invented in 1842 by the distinguished English astronomer and scientist Sir John Herschel (1792–1871) as a way to make fast copies of his notes and sketches.

Herschel made a number of important contributions to photography, including the

Zinn began working with cyanotypes after a move left her without access to models, studio, or darkroom. Negatives were made from hand-drawn images (stencils) on glass. After processing, the surface of the dried paper was worked to make the thin white lines. Zinn explains: "I enjoyed the opportunity of digging into the heavy (rag) paper with nails, needles, and thumbtacks to create a tactile surface." The addition of texture and hand-applied color helped to "direct the feeling of the images."

© Zelda Zinn. *Impasse*, 1990. 11 × 14 inches. Cyanotype with pencil, gouache, watercolor, and oil pastel on paper.

discovery that sodium thiosulfate would act as a fixing agent for silver-based photographs and the first photograph on a glass plate. He introduced the terms "photography," "negative," "positive," and "snapshot" into our vocabulary. It was not until the 1880s that the cyanotype process caught on. It was at this time that precoated cyanotype paper became available for use by architects and shipbuilders, who nicknamed the process "blueprinting."

How It Works

The cyanotype does not rely on silver salts but on ferric salts to form an image. A salt is the result of the mutual action of an acid with a base. Some salts of iron are reduced to ferrous salts when exposed to light in the presence of organic matter. These ferrous salts act as powerful reducers of other metallic salts that are not affected by the ferrous salts. Ferric ammonium citrate

gets broken down by the action of light to a ferrous salt. The ferrous salts react as reducers on the potassium ferricyanide. The areas not exposed to light remain in their ferric state and are washed away during development.

Paper

Cyanotypes can be made on a variety of paper surfaces and cloth. The Rives BFK paper is a good one to start with for general applications. Arches's watercolor 130-lb. paper gives a more textured image with a loss of detail. Any type of paper from a grocery bag to typing paper offers possibilities. Improper paper selection results in discouragement due to failure to produce good image quality.

Sizing

Sizing is not critical but some sizing is needed for this process. It supplies the organic material that is needed for the reduction of the ferric salts to ferrous salts, and it helps to keep the image on the top of the paper, which prevents it from appearing flat. Many papers such as Rives BFK have enough sizing, but others may require additional sizing to produce a good print. Sizing can be applied and allowed to dry before the paper is coated. It is available in liquid form and can be brushed on. It is available at a grocery store (see section on gum bichromate printing later in this chapter).

Sensitizing Solution

The sensitizing solution is made from two chemicals. Ferric ammonium citrate (the green granular form is the most sensitive and stable) is mixed 50 grams (1.76 oz) to 250 milliliters (8.45 oz) of distilled water. In a separate container mix potassium ferricyanide, 35 grams (1.23 oz) with 250 milliliters (8.45 oz) of distilled water. Be sure the potassium ferricyanide crystals appear bright orange before use. If they look rusty red they will not be effective. Mix only enough solution for your immediate needs. Store each separately in a dark brown plastic container with the air squeezed out. Combine the two solutions right before you are ready to coat the paper. Discard the solutions by pouring them into kitty litter, placed inside a plastic bag. Seal the bag and put it into an outside trash container. Coated paper can be stored like regular photographic paper, but it is most sensitive right after it has been coated.

The Coating Process

The entire coating process should be carried out in a safelight darkroom if possible. It can be done in a dimly lit room, but some sensitivity will be lost. When you are ready to sensitize the paper, mix the two solutions together. There are two methods for accomplishing this.

In the first method, the paper is floated in a tray of solution for about 3 minutes. Tap the paper with a print tong very gently to dispel any air bubbles. Also use the tong to agitate the paper in the solution, taking care not to get any of the solution on the back of the paper. Use the print tong to carefully remove the paper, letting the excess drip into the tray, and hang the paper to dry with newspaper underneath to avoid staining the floor. Use a hair dryer on the low setting to speed the drying.

In the second method, the chemicals are applied to the paper with use of a polyfoam brush. Dip the brush into a tray of emulsion, press the brush onto the side of the tray to get rid of the excess, and apply it to the paper being careful to get an even coat.

Blueprint paper can also be purchased precoated from various sources. It is often called by a different name such as solar paper or sun paper. The quality and sensitivity vary greatly; check them out carefully before purchasing any large amounts of paper.

What to Shoot. When selecting subjects for this process remember the final image will be cool and that midtonal range details will tend to get lost. Simple, strong graphic images with a minimum of clutter work well.

Printing

Take the dry paper and place your negative over it (emulsion to emulsion) in a contact printing frame or cover with a piece of clean glass and a backing board. Take this sandwich outside and expose to bright sunlight. This nonsilver printing-out process is fairly fast, but exposure times vary greatly depending on how the material was coated, the time of day, the time of year, and the location. Exposure times can vary from as short as 3 minutes to as long as 8 hours. Test strips can be made to determine exposure, but visual inspection is reliable and faster. The print is properly exposed when it appears about 20 percent darker than the final image is intended to be. The highlights will look glazed and possess a metallic sheen. The paper will change color from a yellow-green to a blue-gray as the image appears. Typical sunlight exposures are between 3 and 15 minutes.

If artificial light is used for exposure, be certain it is an ultraviolet source such as carbon arc lamps, mercury vapor lamps, or sunlamps. The exposure times are usually longer than with sunlight. Start at 15 minutes with the lamp about 24 inches from the print frame.

After properly exposing the print, remove it in dim light and wash in running water until the highlights clear (look white) and then dry.

Handle the paper from the back or the corners. You will leave fingerprints if you touch the surface.

Spotting and Storage

Cyanotypes can be spotted with watercolor, Prussian blue, or Marshall's photo pencils.

Cyanotypes are a very stable process. For maximum life, they should be treated following the suggestions for color materials in the preservation section of chapter 15. Nonbuffered board is recommended for matting cyanotypes.

Troubleshooting

If you get muddy blues or cloudy whites, try blueprint intensification. After the picture is processed, soak it in a 4 percent solution of fresh hydrogen peroxide and distilled water. Mix 1 ounce (29 ml) of hydrogen peroxide to 25 ounces (740 ml) of distilled water. Soaking time is determined by visual inspection, but it is generally brief. This should intensify the blue and make it richer and at the same time clean up the white highlight areas. When it looks good, rewash for at least 5 minutes.

The Gum Bichromate Process

Gum bichromate printing is a simple process that uses a pigment (water colors or tempera), a liquid gum to carry the pigment, and a light-sensitive chemical (ammonium dichromate or potassium dichromate) to produce a nonnaturalistic color image from a contact negative. The softening of the photographic image and the subjective use of color allow the photographer a great amount of freedom in the creation of the print.

The first workable gum process was developed by an Englishman, John Pouncy, in 1856. It was made popular in the 1890s by Robert Demachy and Alfred Maskell, who renamed the process photo aquint.

There are many different recipes for making gum prints. This simple recipe is presented as a starting place and to show how the basic process works. Feel free to make adjustments and personalize the process. Much of what is discussed in the blueprint section can be applied to the making of gum prints, including the safety rules.

Paper Selection, Presoaking, and Sizing

Pick a high-quality etching or watercolor paper since it must be able to withstand being soaked and dried many times. Rives BFK and Arches's watercolor paper offer good starting points and are widely available. The more texture the paper possesses, the less detail there will be in the final image.

The selected paper should be presoaked in hot water (100°F, 38°C) for 15 minutes and hung up to dry. Without a presoak, the paper will shrink after the first time it is processed, making accurate registration of all the following exposures impossible.

Next, the presoaked paper must be sized to seal the pores of the paper. This step may be skipped if the paper has been presized by the manufacturer. Some printmakers carry out this step even if the paper has been presized in order to maintain better control over the pigment in the highlight areas. Sizing is accomplished by soaking the paper in a solution of gelatin to minimize pigment staining in the highlight areas.

Knox gelatin, available in most grocery stores, works well. Stir one packet

As the keeper of her family album, Sligh began examining the differences between the projected impressions of the family snapshots and her memories of the secrets hidden behind the public posturing. The combination of these visual memories with handwritten text becomes a way for Sligh to bridge that gap to examine the forces that shaped her identity. The obscuring of information demonstrates how we often must grapple to get the correct information. The process becomes one of empowerment, allowing the artist to push beyond the restraints of an identity given to her and African Americans by society.

© Clarissa Sligh. *She Sucked Her Thumb*, 1989. 14 × 11 inches. Cyanotype with mixed media.

into a quart of hot water (100°F) until it is dissolved and then pour it into a tray. Put the paper into the tray of dissolved gelatin for 2 minutes. Squeegee the paper and hang it up to dry. Some people give the paper a second coat of sizing after the first one has dried.

Preparing the Sensitizer, Gum, and Pigment

Mix 1 ounce (29 ml) of ammonium dichromate, which is twice as sensitive to light as potassium dichromate, to 10 ounces (296 ml) of water and set it aside.

Koenig, author of *Gumoil Photographic Printing,* has related the gum process to the nineteenth-century "oil" or bromoil printing process. This gum/oil/bleach process achieves the buildup of color through successive cycles of oiling, bleaching (etching) of the remaining gum, washing, and drying, not with successive layers and exposures of differently pigmented gum coats. Multicolored works can be achieved without concern for registration, shrinkage, or sizing. This image began as a 6-×-6-centimeter black-and-white negative from which an enlarged positive transparency was made. This was contact-printed on a bichromated gum surface without pigmentation (no color added) and then developed. On the dried print surface, oil color (black) was then worked into the paper surface, portions of the remaining gum were bleached away, and further oil (crimson) was worked in before final bleaching to remove all gum traces.

© Karl Koenig. *Newcastle Upon Tyne,* 1980/90. 9 × 9 inches. Gum, oil, bleach print on paper.

the liquid gum. Tube watercolors are easy to begin with. Put the lid on and shake until the solution is completely mixed. The amount of pigment used varies with the brand and color. Experience will guide you with future mixing. Now combine 1 ounce of the liquid dichromate to make a working solution. The gum and dichromate are generally mixed together in equal amounts.

Preparing the Paper for Printing

Tape or pin the prepared paper by its corners to a flat board. Brush the working solution, as quickly as possible, onto the paper in long, smooth, horizontal strokes and then with vertical ones, slightly overlapping the previous stroke. Make a complete stroke without redipping the brush in the emulsion. Disposable polyfoam brushes work well. Do not oversoak the paper or let the solution puddle. Coat an area larger than the negative that will be used to make the contact print. Let the paper dry in a darkened room. It is not sensitive to light until it is dried. Drying time can be reduced by using a hair dryer on a low heat setting. Expose the paper as soon as it is dry, because it will not keep for more than about 24 hours.

Registration and Making the Print

One approach to making gum prints is by printing the negative a number of times using different colors. To ensure each exposure lines up with the previous one, a system of registration is helpful. This can be done visually or by gently outlining all four corners of the negative on the paper with a soft-leaded pencil before the first printing. If critical registration is a must, a punch and registration buttons (available at graphic arts suppliers) should be used.

After the registration method has been selected and carried out, put the negative onto the dry-coated paper and cover with a clean piece of glass or place

The dichromate and dry gum can be purchased at a chemical supply company.

The gum is available in premixed lithographer's gum or dry powder acacia gum. The lithographer's gum can be obtained at a graphic arts or printing supplier. It lasts a long time provided it has

an antibacterial agent. The dry gum solution is made by mixing 2 ounces (57 g) of dry gum to 4 ounces (118 ml) of water. Stir it until it is dissolved, and set it aside.

Next, place about a 1/2-inch (1.3-cm) ribbon of pigment into a baby food jar and mix it together with 1 ounce of in a printing frame. When sunlight is not abundant and consistent, a daylight photoflood or a sunlamp can be used to make the exposure. With the light source at a distance of 24 inches (61 cm) from the paper starting exposure time should be about 10 minutes. Different-colored pigments require different exposure times. Most of the exposures should be in the range of 5 to 20 minutes.

A blowing fan will lengthen the life of the light source and keep the print from getting too hot. Too much heat can produce a pigment stain on the print.

Developing the Print

After the exposure is made there should be a distinct image where the light has darkened the gum bichromate on the paper. Remove the negative and store it safely. Place the paper face down in a tray of water that is between 70° and 80° F (21° and 26° C). Let it soak for a minute or two. Turn the paper face up and gently wash the loosened solution away. Hang the paper up to dry.

Multiple Printing

After the paper has dried, additional colors and coats of emulsion may be applied and the paper reprocessed. This can create depth, increase color saturation, extend the overall tonal range, and produce a sense of the surreal. One negative can be used for many different exposures. A wider variety of results can be produced by making negatives that possess different densities (such as those used in making posterization prints) or by using entirely different negatives.

For more information on nonsilver processes read Crawford, William. *The Keepers of Light.* Dobbs Ferry, NY: Morgan & Morgan, 1979; Reeve, Catherine, and Sward, Marilyn. *The New Photography.* Englewood Cliffs, NJ: Prentice-Hall, 1984; Nettles, Bea. *Breaking The Rules,* 2d ed. Urbana, IL: Inky Press Productions, 1987; Scopick, David. *The*

Kenny works with the gum bichromate process because it allows her "the greatest latitude in hand manipulation of the photographic image, use of color, with a minimum of expensive materials and equipment. *Dog Tales* is a narrative of single images that reflects the anthropomorphic roles pets play in our lives. This narrative work concerns itself with the human condition and relies upon the animals as stand-ins."

© Kay Kenny. *"Dog Tales #22, Could the animus in Picasso's painting survive dogs and demoiselles?,* 1989. 15 × 22 inches. Gum bichromate with mixed media on paper.

Gum Bichromate Book. Rochester, NY: Light Impressions, 1978; Blacklow, Laura. *New Dimensions in Photo Imaging.* Stoneham, MA: Focal Press, 1989; Koening, Karl P. *Gumoil Photographic Printing.* Stoneham, MA: Focal Press, 1994; and Hirsch, Robert. *Photographic Possibilities.* Stoneham, MA: Focal Press, 1991.

For premodern supplies contact Photographers' Formulary, P.O. Box 950, Condon, MT 59826 (800)922–5255; for papers and brushes contact Daniel Smith, 4130 First Ave. S., Seattle, WA 98134–2302, (800)426–6740.

The Dye-Transfer Process

The invention of films such as Kodachrome, Agfacolor, and Ektachrome provided solutions for an accurate, easy-to-use, nonscreen, and integral method for making color transparencies. A problem that all these processes shared was a way to make prints from slides.

Prints had to be made by a commercial lab that used the carbro process, an improved version of Thomas Manly's 1899 Ozotype and his 1905 Ozobrome processes.

The carbro process used carbon tissue in conjunction with a bromide print, not silver, to make an image of permanent pigment. In the carbo process black-and-white prints were made from each of the three separation negatives made from the original transparency through red, green, and blue filters. The gelatin emulsions were stripped from each of the prints after development and dyed cyan, magenta, and yellow. They were then superimposed on a new paper base. The carbro process offered excellent control in the making of the print but was complex, costly, and not suitable for assembly line production of photographs. The dye-transfer process grew out of these techniques.

The dye-transfer process was originally introduced in 1935 as the Eastman Wash-off Relief process. It was replaced by the improved Kodak Dye Transfer process in 1946 and discontinued in 1993. Dye transfer materials, which operate very similarly to the discontinued Kodak process, are now available from Dye Transfer Corporation, 3935 Westheimer Rd., Suite 306, Houston, TX 77027.

In the dye-transfer process, separation negatives were made by photographing the original transparency or print on black-and-white film through red, green, and blue filters. If archivally processed, these negatives could be used to make new prints at a future date, long after the original color image disappeared. These negatives were used to expose special matrix films that would in turn transfer the dyes in printing.

Dyes of any color could be employed, but the subtractive system (magenta, yellow, and cyan) was used when a normal full-color print was required. The matrix made from the blue separation was dyed yellow, the matrix from the green separation was dyed magenta, and the matrix from the red separation was dyed cyan. The print was made on a special receiving paper, which was attached face up on a smooth surface. Each of the matrices was squeegeed face down against it and allowed to remain until the dye was absorbed. The dyes were transferred in the order of cyan,

North has modified the standard dye-transfer process to achieve her own visual ends. A 35-mm black-and-white negative was enlarged onto Kodak Matrix film and processed to make a positive relief. This was hand-colored using the regular Kodak Dye Transfer Dyes. North discusses her method: "When you handcolor a dye transfer print the dyes carry the detail of the image, unlike coloring the darkened silver of a black-and-white print. The luminosity and pastel palette of these prints emphasize my interests in light and development of a personalized color. I was playing off the image of women presented by the media, the implicit sensuality of the figure when placed in an improbable environment." Prints made from this method are unique.

© Kenda North. *Trish with Cholla*, 1980. 16 × 20 inches. Dye-transfer print.

magenta, and yellow. Accurate registration was necessary to avoid blurred outlines and color fringing.

A subjective variation of this process entails making a single black-and-white matrix from a black-and-white negative and then selectively hand coloring the matrix with colors mixed from the subtractive dyes. It was a technically demanding process that required careful attention to detail. It provided the photographer with extra control over color, contrast, and density while making the print in full room light. The dyes used in this process were more stable than those in the conventional chromogenic processes, giving the print a longer life.

Until the 1980s, most color work was rejected as vulgar, gaudy, or too technically unstable for serious noncommercial work. The use of the dye-transfer process by such photographers as Eliot Porter has helped to legitimize the use of color in all areas of photography.

The Fresson Process

The Fresson process, invented by Theodore-Henri Fresson at the turn of the century, uses a "secret" carbon printing technique to create a pointillistic print from colored pigments. The Fresson Studio, which is in France, currently produces only about two thousand color prints each year. It requires about 6 hours to make each print. The Fresson process offers its own unique color look and excellent image control, and it is said to be one of the most archival of any of the commercial procedures in use today.

To make a Fresson print, four color separations are made from an original color transparency. A separate exposure is then made for the cyan, magenta, yellow, and black separations, using a carbon arc light source, onto the special

Friedman's *12 Nazi Concentration Camps* confront the viewer not with atrocities but the banal normality of everyday life as these former death camps become tourist attractions. Friedman used the 8-x-10 inch camera to juxtapose a beautiful summer afternoon with kids riding their bikes with our collective memories of the black-and-white photographs of the obscenities committed earlier at these same sites. Jonathan Green wrote: "It is precisely the distance between historical memory and contemporary reality that makes Friedman's photographs so disturbing and painful. . . . Friedman's images become both heroic and ironic commentaries on the capacity of society and the human imagination to memorialize and to forget."

© James Friedman. *Survivor of Three Nazi Concentration Camps, Survivors Reunion, Majdanek Concentration Camp, Poland,* 1983. 16 × 20 inches. Dye-transfer print. Courtesy of the Visual Studies Workshop Gallery, Rochester, NY.

Keats's interest in atmosphere, light, and texture are revealed by the Fresson process's painterly, pointillistic, and tactile look.

© Doug Keats. *Ranchos de Taos Church,* 1984. Fresson print. Courtesy of The Albuquerque Museum, Albuquerque, NM.

Fresson paper, which is made up of pigments similar to those used in oil painting. The paper has to be coated, exposed, developed, and dried four consecutive times, once for each of the separations.

The Sawdust Developer

During the exposure, the pigment is hardened in proportion to the amount of light it has received. Now the print is "developed" using a solution of water and sawdust. During the development process, the pigment that has not been hardened by the action of light is softened by the water and removed by the sawdust, which acts as a mild abrasive. What remains after this operation makes up the final color image. This unusual developer permits local control of the image by pouring varying amounts of sawdust onto the print. It is possible to use this sawdust developer anytime in the future, after the initial image has been created, to make alterations to the print.

UltraStable Color Process

The UltraStable system, a modern version of Ducos du Huron's tricolor carbon process, claims to produce photographic prints that are unaffected by exposure to light and thus are truly permanent. According to Charles Berger, who codeveloped this method with Richard Kauffman, "Independently conducted accelerated light-fading tests conducted by Henry Wilhelm have concluded that UltraStable prints may be displayed under normal viewing conditions for more than 500 years without fading, staining or any other changes in the color image."[1]

In this process four color-pigmented, gelatin relief films (cyan, magenta, yellow, and black) are used to

[1] From a letter to the author from Charles Berger, June 18, 1990, and confirmed by phone conversation with Henry Wilhelm.

Figure 22.13
This is how the UltraStable image appears after the black pigment was transferred to the white receiving sheet.

© Charles Berger. *Bottle Brushes*, 1991. 6 × 8 inches. (1 color) Carbon print.

Figure 22.14
This is how the UltraStable image looked after the yellow pigment was transferred on top of the black pigment.

© Charles Berger. *Bottle Brushes*, 1991. 6 × 8 inches. (2 color) Carbon print.

Figure 22.15
This is how the UltraStable image evolved after the magenta pigment was added to the black and yellow pigments already on the receiving base.

© Charles Berger. *Bottle Brushes*, 1991. 6 × 8 inches. (3 color) Carbon print.

Figure 22.16
The cyan pigment was applied last to create a four-color-pigment UltraStable image.

© Charles Berger. *Bottle Brushes*, 1991. 6 × 8 inches. (All four). Carbon print.

make continuous-tone color images. Figures 22.13 to 22.16 show how a print is assembled using this process. Pigment images are much less fugitive than dyed ones and thus provide an unusual degree of permanence. The presensitized, non-silver pigment films (using a diazo-type sensitizer) and opaque white bases (smooth and glossy) can be handled under normal incandescent light. Exposure is by conventional, high UV graphic arts light sources. Precise, pin-registered prints can be tray processed in about 20 minutes. The manufacturer says the process is nontoxic, environmentally safe, and produces no hazardous waste or pollution.

For additional information about the process, materials, and color printing services contact UltraStable Color Systems, 69 Brackney Road, Ben Lomond, CA 95005.

EverColor/Digital Meets Carbon-Pigment

EverColor is the latest archival refinement of the carbon-pigment process to enter the market. An EverColor Pigment Transfer print starts as a color scan from a negative, transparency, reflective piece, or digitized file. From the electronic file CMYK (cyan, magenta, yellow, and black) color separation negatives are outputted. The digitized information allows the color balance, contrast, sharpness, tonal scale, and retouching to be edited electronically. The four continuous tone resolution black-and-white negatives are contact exposed on separate CMYK silver (not Azo dye) pigment sheets. Each pigment sheet is pin registered and separately wet laminated to a dimensionally and chemically stable polyester-base material, which is then exposed to a high-intensity ultraviolet light and processed. The procedure is done four times, once for each color separation. Since the colors are stacked on top of the support, rather than developed within the emulsion, the final print has a sharpness and three-dimensional quality that is unique to the EverColor technology and cannot be seen in regular four-color reproduction such as this book uses. EverColor is a high-end commercial process and not intended for home use.

For additional information about EverColor digital imaging services contact EverColor, 5145 Golden Foothill Parkway, Suite 140, El Dorado Hills, CA 95762, (800)533–5050.

Color Electrostatic Processes

Using a color electrostatic photocopier such as a Canon, 3M, Sharp, or Xerox lets the photographer investigate a combination of manual, mechanical, and electric processes for imagemaking with instant feedback.

Archival standards for the collectability of color photography is an important issue for professionals such as Wolcott, who make their living through print sales. Wolcott poses the question: "How can a collector justify spending money on prints that might not last more than 20 years?" Wolcott has worked with EverColor because he believes "that unless color prints have the longevity of black-and-white, they will never become truly collectable and accepted as a true art form. EverColor can offer a print life of 500 years on display, allowing collectors to rest assured that the value of their pieces is protected."

© Timothy Wolcott. *Mono Lake Sunrise*, 1986. 4 × 5 inches. Pigment transfer print.

The Xerox System

The Xerox system, whose use is widespread, works on a subtractive method. Magenta, yellow, and cyan pigments, similar to those found in acrylic paints, are coupled with a polymer resin in the toner. This makes a filmy layer of color that is electronically fused onto the paper, thereby producing a permanent image. The lens on the copier acts like a simple camera without a bellows so there is only one focal range possible, providing a limited depth of field (1/4 to 1/2 inch above the copier glass). This type of system offers the creative user great flexibility and many possibilities in the making of a print.

Options available on a machine of this type include duplication with accuracy; quick print production; conversion of three-dimensional objects into a rapid printout; transformation of a 35-mm slide into a hard copy; printing on all types of supports, including artist's papers and acetate; stability and permanency of the pigments; production of an image on silicon transfer material, enabling the picture to be moved onto other surfaces such as fabric or glass; multiple exposure capability; image enlargements and reductions; color adjustment that allows the operator to balance the colors in any direction including color from black-and-white; one- or two-color prints; and high contrast or normal full-color reproduction.

The Canon Laser Copier

The Canon Laser Copier CLC 500 is a new generation of copier that forms its

There is a wide range of color copiers an artist can now choose from to work with. Casey used a Sharp CX5000S digital copier that uses a "film" (looks like plastic wrap), rather than a powdered toner, on which cyan, yellow, magenta, and black are fixed. The collected materials were arranged on the copier glass and printed at a 30 percent reduction. The copy machine lid was left open during exposure with a black background in place. The changes in color cast around the objects are the visual product of the Sharp's recognition of three-dimensional space. The images are intended to speak to the fragility of our environment, as well as to our disregard for a symbiotic lifestyle. The title symbolically alludes to Eadweard Muybridge's name and locomotion studies (included in the image) plus the possessive pronouns: my, your, and our.

© Sigrid Erica Casey. *M/y/ourflight Transfixed*, 1988. 8 1/2 × 11 1/2 inches. Electrostatic print.

images by scanning the original and encoding the pictorial information into a binary code of digital data. The system's path from original to copy is not jeopardized by dirty, scratched glass or dusty mirrors. The machine has a menu-driven, touch-activated control panel with commands, prompts, questions, and options. It can reproduce up to 256 gradations of each color. The Canon also uses a fourth black toner so blacks are true black and not a combination of cyan, magenta, and yellow. In addition, the particle size of the dry toner has been decreased in size by about one-third, thus reducing apparent granularity and increasing perceived sharpness.

The Canon Laser Copier has all the features of a regular color copier plus extensive special effects such as stretching an image along the x- or y-axis to make a panorama; adding texture by memorizing a textured surface placed on the copier and adding it to the print; posterizations, by changing more than one color with no density graduation; inserting a small image within the larger one; mosaics, by breaking the image into small rectangular chips; contour drawing, by outlining the subject; custom cropping to any geometric or free-form shape; and an accessory digital scanner for negatives and slides.

Another Rapid Print System

Need a color print in a hurry? Machines such as Kodak's kiosk-based Creation Station incorporate digital technology, which allows consumers to make and enhance prints and enlargements from negatives, prints, transparencies, or photo CDs. The consumer places the image into the Creation Station scanner, which processes the image and displays it on a color monitor. A simple push-button program allows the client to perform a variety of computer image editing functions, including zooming in and out and adding text, backgrounds, and other graphic elements. When the operator is satisfied, a thermal dye-transfer printer is used to output an 8-×-10-inch digital color print.

Experiments to Consider

Consider using a color photocopying machine to make these pictures:

- Have an enlarged Xerox color print made from a slide. This is performed by the copy machine with a special attachment for making prints from a slide.

- Make a color copy of one of your regular color prints.

- Now perform at least one of the following methods. Compare the results with the original and note what changes have taken place.

- Have a print made on a good-quality drawing paper. Hand color all or part of it with colored pencils, inks, or watercolor paints.

- Cut out a series of images, arrange them on the copier glass, and make a print. Try combining both two-dimensional and three-dimensional objects.

- Explore a theme such as food. Collect various items that are central to the theme—beans, bread, fruit, grains, leaves, nuts, pastas, seeds, and spices. They may be whole, broken, or cut up. Compose them on the copier glass and explore their color and spatial and textural relationships.

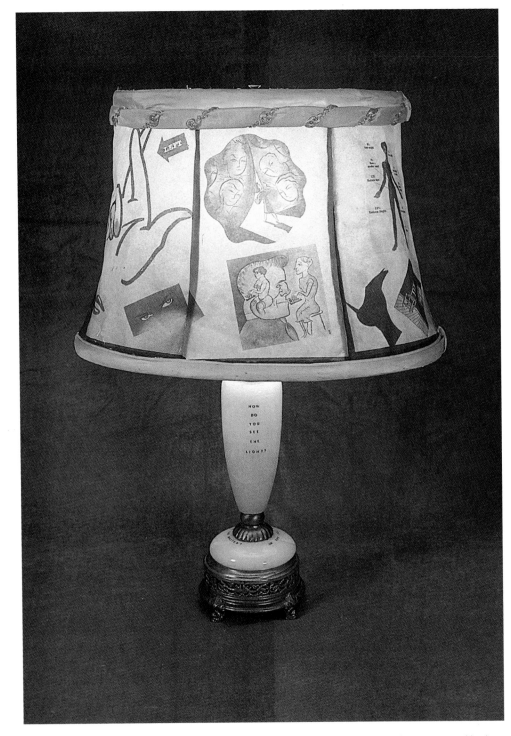

Tani painted Vandyke brown emulsion onto vellum and exposed the negatives she fabricated on a copy machine in sunlight. Tani says: "The images and text of this photosculpture convey the conflicts and changes which have occurred in the women's movement since the 1970s. The small illustrations encourage the viewer to consider the complexity of sexual harassment, their role in the family, physical appearance, self-image, social influences, and the direction of women as a group towards the future. The lamp represents a domestic element, yet in its altered state implies a restructuring and a revision of the expected form which can be carried over to how we define our notions about women."

© Sharon Tani. *Now do you see the light? Or are you making light of the matter?*, 1992. 21 × 16 × 9 inches. Electrostatic transfers with Vandyke brown.

- Combine a series of electrostatic prints to form larger images. Start with a group of four prints that visually connect and expand it into a mural.

- Place a live model on the copy glass. Pose the model so that the changes in the model's position on the copy glass can be combined to form a whole image. Sequence the prints as you proceed to ensure that the visual mosaic being produced is coming together in the desired manner. Redo any prints that are not properly positioned. Try incorporating colored acetate and/or cloth into blank areas for added color, depth, and textural variation.

Holograms

Holography, from the Greek meaning "entire message," is a process for generating three-dimensional photographic images. It differs from traditional stereoscopic photography because it presents a virtual image of the subject in three dimensions that changes in parallax and perspective as the viewing angle is changed. This means that objects visually cover and uncover one another as the angle of view shifts, just as it would when we stroll by the actual object. Also, the distances between objects change as we move toward or away from the hologram. Holograms are made by using a coherent light source such as a laser. The laser produces light in which all the waves are precisely in phase (vibrating in unison), are of the same amplitude (size), and are traveling in the same direction. Regular photographs are made with incoherent light, a mixture of wavelengths with random phase relationships. Research is continuing to find practical and less-expensive ways of using lasers to make color holograms.

Future Developments

In the future, students of photography will probably concentrate less on learning its current chemical foundations. Energy will be devoted to learning more about digital imaging, the elements of composition, and the interaction of color. Technical advances are hollow unless they are intelligently applied to the creation of meaningful photographs.

During its brief history photography has subverted the hypothesis that art was fundamentally immersed with the imitation of appearances. Photography has disrupted the single, ordered, consistent style of traditional classicism. By familiarizing us with a worldwide range of art and culture, photography has enlarged our realm of aesthetic experiences beyond those directly observed in nature.

As the technical barriers continue to fall away, photography can make the most of its democratic tradition. People with a variety of voices will be able to interact more easily with the medium, enhancing its aesthetic concerns and growth. Photographers should be open to saying yes to a multitude of working practices. The underpinnings of photography's future potency lie in our willingness to tolerate the messiness of diversity.

Index

HISTORICAL EVENTS IN THE DEVELOPMENT OF COLOR PHOTOGRAPHY

1925 Jos-Pé Company introduces a dye-imbibition process whose images are assembled by a transfer process, forming the basis for the Technicolor, Wash-off Relief, and Dye Transfer processes. Oskar Barnack markets first Leica camera. Anatol Josepho patents first photo booth.

1926 First underwater Autochromes made.

1928 Kodacolor lenticular film introduced for movies. Leitz markets 35-mm filmstrip projector for lenticular color films.

1929 Finlay Colour plate process introduced.

1930 Mannes and Godowsky join Kodak Research Lab.

1932 Technicolor produces the first three-color film, the Disney cartoon *The Flowers and the Trees*. Agfa introduces 35-mm lenticular film. Lumière Autochrome glass plates are replaced by Filmcolor.

1933 Gasparcolor process, first commercial dye-destruction process, launched.

1934 Technicolor produces first "live" three-color film, *La Cucaracha.*

1935 16-mm Kodachrome movie film, first successful monopack, subtractive color reversal process, introduced. Eastman Wash-Off Relief process marketed.

1936 8-mm, 35-mm, and 828 Kodachrome roll film introduced. Agfacolor Neu, integral tripack film unveiled in 16-mm movie and 35-mm still formats. Henry Luce begins publishing *Life* magazine.

1938 Ready-mounting service for Kodachrome started.

1939 Agfacolor provides a monopack color negative and paper for negative/positive printing.

1940 Sakura Natural Color film made in Japan. Museum of Modern Art in New York opens its Department of Photography.

1942 Kodacolor films and papers unveiled.

1945 Kodak's Dye Transfer process replaces Wash-off Relief.

1946 Ektachrome color sheet film, processable by the photographer, introduced.

1947 Polaroid camera, producing a sepia print in 60 seconds, is invented by Dr. Edwin Land.

1948 Nikon 35-mm camera introduced.

1950 Xerox copying machine produced. Kodak introduces Eastman Color negative/positive process for motion pictures.

1953 *Playboy* magazine debuts with Marilyn Monroe as its full-color pinup.

1954 Eastman Kodak signs consent decree after anti-trust action by U.S. government, ending monopoly on photofinishing.

HISTORICAL EVENTS

1920 League of Nations forms without the United States. Nineteenth Amendment gives American women right to vote.

1921 KDKA in Pittsburgh begins first transmissions of regular radio programs in the United States.

1925 John Logie Baird transmits recognizable human features via television. Heisenberg, Bohr, and Jordan develop quantum mechanics theory. John T. Scopes goes on trial for teaching evolution.

1927 *The Jazz Singer,* first full-length commercial "talkie," released.

1929 New York stock market crashes. Museum of Modern Art opens in New York.

1930 Worldwide economic depression begins.

1931 Empire State Building opens.

1933 Adolf Hitler appointed German chancellor. Boycott of Jews begins. First concentration camps erected by Nazis. All modern and Jewish art suppressed in Germany; about sixty thousand artists emigrate. Nazis win 92 percent of German vote. Franklin Roosevelt inaugurated as President of the United States. James Joyce's *Ulysses* is ruled not obscene by the U.S. Supreme Court.

1934 Stalin begins major purge of Communist party.

1936 Mussolini and Hitler proclaim Rome-Berlin Axis, sign Anti-Comintern pact with Japan. Hitler receives 99 percent of the vote in German general elections. BBC London begins television service.

1937 Basque town of Guernica is destroyed by German bombers. Japan invades China. Amelia Earhart is lost on Pacific flight.

1939 World War II starts. Computer experiments begin at Harvard. RCA introduces television at the World's Fair in New York.

1941 Japan attacks Pearl Harbor, United States enters World War II.

1942 Enrico Fermi splits the atom.

1945 World War II ends. United States drops atomic bombs on Hiroshima and Nagasaki. Thirty-five million war dead, plus 10 million in Nazi concentration camps.

1946 United Nations formed. Nuremberg war trials begin.

1947 Bell Labs invents the transistor. Jackie Robinson becomes the first black baseball player in the major leagues with the Brooklyn Dodgers.

1948 Gandhi assassinated. The State of Israel is proclaimed by the United Nations. Peter Goldmark invents the long-playing record.

1949 Communists under Mao Tse-tung take control of China. South Africa establishes apartheid program.